Motives of Woe

Motives of Woe

Shakespeare and 'Female Complaint'

A Critical Anthology

EDITED BY

JOHN KERRIGAN

CLARENDON PRESS · OXFORD

1991

Oxford University Press, Walton Street, Oxford OX2 6DP
Oxford New York Toronto
Delhi Bombay Calcutta Madras Karachi
Petaling Jaya Singapore Hong Kong Tokyo
Nairobi Dar es Salaam Cape Town
Melbourne Auckland
and associated companies in
Berlin Ibadan

Oxford is a trade mark of Oxford University Press

Published in the United States
by Oxford University Press, New York

British Library Cataloguing in Publication Data
(data available)

Library of Congress Cataloging in Publication Data
Motives of woe: Shakespeare and 'female complaint': a critical
anthology/edited by John Kerrigan.
Includes bibliographical references and index.
1. Women—Poetry.   2. Complaint poetry, English.   3. English
poetry—Early modern, 1500–1700.   4. Shakespeare, William,
1564–1616. Lover's complaint.   I. Kerrigan, John.
PR1195.W6M68   1991
821.008′0352042—dc20   90-26025
ISBN 0-19-811770-1

Typeset by Wyvern Typesetting Ltd, Bristol
Printed and bound in
Great Britain by Biddles Ltd,
Guildford and King's Lynn

Preface

THIS book began as an essay on Shakespeare's *A Louers Complaint*. It expanded when it became clear that a proper evaluation of that neglected poem would only be possible if the literature of 'female complaint' known to its early readers was recovered. The result is a collection, even larger in scope, which keeps *A Louers Complaint* at its centre (giving sources and analogues which should have been assembled long ago), but which also prints a range of texts of great potential interest. During the period covered by this anthology—*c.*1300 to 1729—thousands of complaints involving 'male' figures were written, and the kinds of loss and frustration which they record are various. Fewer plaints featuring 'female' characters survive, but they form a definite corpus not least because so many of them focus on the erotic and maternal experiences which, throughout the Middle Ages and early modern period, made up (especially as far as men were concerned) the core of women's lives. There is such a wealth of lively and absorbing material in the subgenre that selection has led to the exclusion of texts of substantial merit. Those who regret omissions ought not to assume that their favourites have been set aside without qualms. The Introduction is designed in part to help readers unfamiliar with medieval and Renaissance writing decide which works not included here would reward further attention. It has, above all, been difficult to choose between texts which illustrate recurrent properties of 'female complaint' and those which claim a place on their own terms. In the end quality of writing has been the decisive criterion, and only one poem—Matthew Stevenson's 'Sapho to Phaon'—is included on account of its revealing incompetence.

It is not possible in the Introduction to an anthology to give a fully contextual and theoretical account of 'female complaint'. My chief aim has been the modest one of showing how far the texts selected are representative of, or stand out from, currents of literature little explored since the eighteenth century. It might seem an obvious and straightforward task to list the characteristics of 'female complaint' and explain how the subgenre varied through time. The danger lies in misrepresenting the way generic factors bear upon composition, and in obscuring the ability of literary kinds to discover and realize their potential as they evolve. Genres do not spring fully armed into the world, and, in most writing of permanent value, generic features are not so much reproduced as rediscovered, from new angles, out of need. The Introduction therefore uses particular texts, within a broadly chronological account, to suggest how guiding features of 'female complaint' emerged. There are pauses in the exposition for analysis of recurrent thematic and formal traits, and passages which loop back or look forward to point up consistencies within the kind. The development of 'female complaint' is entangled with that of the masculine strain in the genre. It is also shaped by the pressures of social and intellectual history. Limited space means that only the most significant relations between feminine and masculine plaint are noticed here. While the effects on complaint of post-Reformation attitudes to confession are briefly explored (in sections 3 and 5), less influential, though still significant, historical contexts—such as the anxieties about urban wealth and power registered within the corpus (p. 14) and its interaction with fears about growing female literacy in the seventeenth century (pp. 72–3)—can be no more than mentioned in passing.

The Introduction is meant to be read as a whole. Section 1 discusses the medieval formation of 'female complaint'. It touches on the influence of Ovid and begins to think about differences between masculine and feminine personae. Section 2 moves into the Tudor period. Continuing from the previous section an analysis of 'framing' devices, it uses both medieval and Renaissance texts to characterize the musicality of lament. In 'Complaint Reformed' the effects of sixteenth-century revisions in penitential doctrine are considered, and some attention is given to the value of plaint as a vehicle for exploring the past—as a branch of historical writing. Section 4 considers how feminine figures are 'seen' in complaint. Section 5, based on *A Louers Complaint*, shifts attention to what is 'heard'. 'Complaint Enlarged' examines the diffusion of plaintful writing through such Elizabethan and seventeenth-century genres as tragedy, prose romance, petitionary grievance, and song. Section 7, 'Wit and Distress', discusses the comic potential of 'female complaint', harnessed by poets from the Middle Ages through Shakespeare, but most subtly exploited by such writers as Marvell, Gay, and Henry Carey. In section 8 Ovid returns as the inspiration behind epistolary plaint, the most vital element in the subgenre during the seventeenth century. Finally, section 9, 'In the "concaue wombe" ', considers the role of women writers in this late phase of generic history, and, after a brief account of Pope's *Eloisa to Abelard*, sketches the decline of 'female complaint'.

The title *Motives of Woe* is taken from *A Louers Complaint*, 63, where, as often in medieval and early modern English, 'motives' describes not only those causal promptings which the typical feminine plainant discloses behind her distress, but the surges of emotion which 'motivate' her words and which lead her to use received 'motifs' within those 'moving' discourses which were themselves known, during the period of this anthology, as 'motives'. The title therefore stands as much for the emotional immediacy of what appears spoken or written in 'female complaint' as for the corollary that what is felt has an inward order which amounts to a rhetoric of passion. Inverted commas set off 'Female Complaint' in my subtitle because, as a glance at the Contents shows, most of the works collected here were written by men. This reflects a general pattern of composition for texts in the kind. Women did write plaints centred on feminine figures. Some of these works are immensely accomplished, and all (by virtue of the congruence of author and persona) are of interest. But one of the questions raised by this anthology—paradoxical though it may sound—is whether the conventions of 'female complaint' did more to frustrate than enable women writers in the subgenre. Mixed authorship makes clear terminology hard to achieve and sustain. So does the conflicting use of 'masculine' and 'feminine': words which in everyday language tend to be loosely managed and highly associative but which can also, as in this volume, more restrictedly denote represented gender. At every point, 'female complaint' describes a class of writing composed by women (it is female-authored) as well as men, which centres on feminine personae who might encounter masculine interlocutors or framing reporters. Some texts, being epistolary, claim to have been written by 'female' characters; others posit speakers and maintain the fiction of being 'female'-voiced. These formulations, which are not rigorously symmetrical and exclusive, are sometimes modified in practice, but the immediate context of any description should remove all ambiguities except those which chronically and aptly disable attempts to discriminate too neatly between the realms of gender.

It is less than a joke to say that, without my parents, this anthology would not exist. Thanks are due to Sylvia Adamson, Marie Axton, Jonathan Bate, Julia Boffey, Germaine Greer, Guy Lee, Ruth Luborsky, Richard Luckett, and Tom Morris for words of encouragement and advice. At OUP Kim Scott Walwyn was exemplary in her assistance. Frances Whistler was an acute and supportive editor. John Waś prepared the typescript for printing with formidable scholarly attentiveness, and improved the commentary at a number of points. At various stages A. S. G. Edwards, Peter Holland, and Jill Mann generously read material. Richard Beadle—best of colleagues— advised on medieval matters. Despite the pressures of a busy Easter term, Jeremy Maule examined the entire typescript and prompted some second thoughts. Alison Hennegan interrupted her work for The Women's Press Bookclub to scrutinize the Introduction. Peter Kerrigan, my brother, judiciously helped with proofs. The remaining errors are my own responsibility. Tarlton, who oversaw the production of various drafts, cannot be forgotten. My greatest debt is to Anne Barton, who supported the research and (as importantly) insisted that it should stop.

J. F. K.

Contents

Illustrations

Figs. 1, 2, and 3 are reproduced, with permission, from holdings in The Bodleian Library, Oxford: the manuscript miniature, usually said to be by William Abell, can be found on fo. 14ᵛ of the Fairfax manuscript; Rome (in the woodcut derived from an engraving by Marcus Gheeraerts the Elder or, more probably, Lucas de Heere of Ghent) is opposite fo. 14 of Douce N.36; and Hannay's music appears on an extra bifolium in Malone 462. Figs. 4 and 6 appear through the kindness of the Syndics of Cambridge University Library: Samuel Gribelin's engraving of Louis Chéron's Eloisa comes from 7720.d.1575, that in *The Shepherd's Week* (by Louis de Guernier) from Williams. 568, C2ᵛ. Fig. 5 is reproduced from a ballad in the Pepys Collection, for which thanks are due to the Master and Fellows of Magdalene College, Cambridge.

Editorial Procedures

ALL the texts in this anthology have been edited afresh from early manuscript or printed sources. This means that readings sometimes differ from those in other modern editions. For several reasons it has not been possible to apply editorial principles with complete consistency. English changed so much between *c.*1300 and 1729 that the problems involved in reproducing 'Als i me rode ...' are not the same as those raised by 'A Sorrowful Lamentation for the Loss of a Man and No Man'. Editorial intervention must be flexible when some texts aspire to the high polish of Ovidian epistle, while others are lyrics for singing, or have the provisionality of a play-text. Given that scribes and compositors work (and corrupt) in different ways, the conventions brought to bear on manuscript cannot be identical with those applied to printed texts. Overall my policy has been to edit as conservatively as seemed compatible with making material accessible to non-specialist readers. No attempt has been made to deal with press variants or issues within first editions. Upper-case and italic are standardized in titles. Abbreviations, including 'yt' and '&', have been expanded, and long 's' removed. Word-division and punctuation have been silently modified in the medieval lyrics. Elsewhere, no pattern of punctuation has been imposed. Disruptive errors are corrected, but refinements are only made when demanding syntax or semantic complexity combine with accidentals likely to obstruct the general reader. Initial capital letters are rationalized at the start of verse-lines. Insubstantive irregularities caused by badly-inked letters, reversed brackets, or false spacing between words have not been recorded in the textual notes.

The poems have been grouped and printed in more or less chronological order. Only the dates of long works are given in the Contents; further indications of chronology are provided in the headnotes. Approximate dates for poems in manuscript, and dates of publication for material taken from printed sources, are summarized in the textual notes. The commentary has no philological pretensions. Only words and spelling variants which might mislead a general reader are glossed, while detailed analysis is avoided. Recurrent items are not always explicated after their first appearance; glosses vary according to context. While these notes often differ from those in previous editions, there are also debts and agreements. Without the labours of F. N. Robinson, Vincent J. DiMarco, Hyder E. Rollins, W. R. Renwick, Richard Schell, Arthur Colby Sprague, Josephine A. Roberts, and others the difficulties would have been overwhelming. Everywhere in the volume biblical quotations follow the Authorized Version. The Yale Elizabethan Club facsimile (New Haven, 1964) is used for Shakespeare's poems, except *A Louers Complaint*. The Norton facsimile of the first Folio, ed. Charlton Hinman (New York, 1968), is cited for the plays, with conventional act and scene references added to its continuous line-numbering.

Introduction

1. Towards Shakespeare

Set before a cave mouth, or in the hollow of a vale, a 'female' figure laments. Individualized yet impersonal, at the abandoned limits of society, she utters her loss through a landscape that yields nothing but that voice. Hence the ellipsis and redundancy, as sorrow for a lover's absence reverberates into clamour. And hence, more psychologically, distress's closed reciprocation: rapt auditor of herself, recoiling into solipsism, the persona images the other in something like her likeness. Anger against the vow-breaking lover lends this text an edge, making a grievance of complaint. Regret modifies the plainant's case, rendering her sorrow confessional. Either way the lines are pitched to be heard yet involve towards opacity. Intent on unpacking her heart with words, the speaker appears indifferent to her audience. Less theatrical than self-absorbed, her verse is too formulaic to be taken as dramatic monologue, too entangled with the grammar of repentance to be merely an expression of love-longing. Despair is the ostinato that runs beneath its argument. Opened out to hopelessness, constrained by images of closure, the poem cannot make an end of its ending in woe and desire.

The work just generally characterized is not, as it happens, the text on which this anthology centres, Shakespeare's *A Louers Complaint*—or at least not only that—but fifty-three lines in the Exeter Book (*c.*970) known as *The Wife's Lament*. That terms used of an Old English poem can be applied to one by Shakespeare helps give the lie to those accounts of the latter which judge it a sport or exercise, the product of 'a vogue of complaint poems about women in the 1590's'.[1] There was undoubtedly a resurgence of 'female'-voiced plaint in the sixteenth century. But, as this collection shows, it is difficult to determine how long that 'vogue' lasted and still harder to judge where it began. Shakespeare and his contemporaries were familiar, not only with forms of chronicle-complaint leading back through *A Myrroure for Magistrates* to Boccaccio, and with pastoral, epic, and epistolary laments stemming from Theocritus, Virgil, and Ovid, but with ballads and courtly lyrics which carried into the Renaissance motifs from the early Middle Ages. The presses of early modern England poured out political laments, petitionary grievances, complaints of religious abuses, and, increasingly through the seventeenth century, works drawing on the comic potential of distress. This ample, generically complicated literature, now

[1] Hallett Smith, 'A Lover's Complaint', in *The Riverside Shakespeare*, gen. ed. G. Blakemore Evans (Boston, 1974), 1781.

known to most readers through only a handful of texts, flourished well into the eighteenth century. Overall it is interesting because it includes so many works about women from phases of history not rich in such representations. But complaint makes broader claims, offers varied pleasures: crossing lyric with narrative, the dramatic with the epistolary, it absorbs styles and subjects not synthesized by other kinds. Complaint admits poems of spiritual intensity but also social anger, mixes love lament with burlesque, borders into elegy. Rhetorically it tends to an elaboration which can seem, initially, alienating. Once attuned the reader becomes aware of discourses capable of finely calibrated shifts of feeling and an impressive enlargement of effect.

It is important to emphasize at once that, while 'female complaints' have been written by women, most are the work of men. Inciting prosopopoeia in general, complaint fosters impersonation of the feminine in ways which raise interesting questions about gender, but which also, more frustratingly, make it difficult to judge the authorship and tone (since views about one affect perceptions of the other) of anonymous texts. This problem reaches back to the origins of the kind. It used to be argued that vernacular lyric as a whole emerged from women's dance and carolling.[2] Few would now claim as much, yet the range of early medieval writing is being reconstructed in ways which make it impossible to regard it as a male preserve. A famous capitulary of Charlemagne forbids nuns to compose love poetry; objections to the 'lewd songs of dancing women' are recorded from as early as the sixth century.[3] Several sources, including the *Carmina Burana*, speak of dance and song as female activities. The *cantigas de amigo* of Spain and Portugal, performed by women known as *jograresas*, were doubtless on occasion composed by their singers.[4] In German and French (notably *refrains* of the twelfth and thirteenth centuries), and in such collections as the *Cambridge Songs*, poems imagined from a female point of view can be found. Some two dozen lyrics by women troubadours survive, and several of these are plaintful. A useful list of 'female'-voiced *planctus* (most of them probably male-authored) drawn up by Peter Dronke adds poems from Norse and Icelandic, Mozarabic *kharjas*, texts in Irish and Welsh, medieval Latin—and, of course, Old English.[5] For *The Wife's Lament* belongs to an extended Anglo-Saxon family, including some of the most intense passages of epic.[6] Its closest affinities are with *Wulf and Eadwacer*, that poignant lament uttered by

[2] See e.g. Theodor Frings, *Minnesinger und Troubadour* (Berlin, 1949).
[3] John F. Plummer (ed.), *Vox Feminae: Studies in Medieval Women's Songs* (Kalamazoo, 1981), 6.
[4] Peter Dronke, *Women Writers of the Middle Ages: A Critical Study of Texts from Perpetua (†203) to Marguerite Porete (†1310)* (Cambridge, 1984), 98.
[5] *Poetic Individuality in the Middle Ages* (Oxford, 1970), 27–8.
[6] See e.g. Alan Renoir, 'A Reading Context for *The Wife's Lament*', in Lewis E. Nicholson and Dolores Warwick Frese (eds.), *Anglo-Saxon Poetry: Essays in Appreciation* (Notre Dame, 1975), 224–41.

a 'female' figure forced to live in the protection of one man while yearning for another.

Even so approximate a description is rash. Expressively understated and associated in manuscript with the Old English Riddles, both *Wulf and Eadwacer* and *The Wife's Lament* resist elucidation. From its vernacular beginnings, 'female complaint' has at times devolved—through a reticence grounded on the weakness of its personae—towards obscurity. With her emotional appeal to 'Wulf, min Wulf' and allusion to her offspring as a 'hwelp',[7] the speaker of *Wulf and Eadwacer* has been judged 'a female dog of romantic temperament' howling for her wolvish mate.[8] The text has been read as a charm against wens, a puzzle with the answer 'millstone', even a grumble about scribal error. Because *The Wife's Lament* is fuller and more circumstantial, speculation about it has enjoyed less latitude. Nevertheless, scholars have provided a range of roles for its narrator, from ill-treated wife to witch-like accuser. Gender has been wrested to make the poem a thane's lament for his lord, while, more plausibly, some have wondered whether the speaker in her gloomy vale ('in þam eorðscræfe') or earth-hall ('eorþsele') might be one of the ancient pagans haunting a burial-mound. Certainly she carries hints of the *revenant*, is at least figuratively a ghost returning to justify herself and condemn her enemies—much as the spirit of Rosamond haunts Samuel Daniel (in the plaint reproduced here), and as Shakespeare's speaker carries into *A Louers Complaint* the pathos and death-chill ('a fickle maid *full pale*') of earlier ghostly plainants. Partly because of the abjection of its speakers, love plaint is well-adapted to explore spiritual issues. Given the genre's later history, it comes as no surprise that the first lines of *The Wife's Lament* resemble those of the Old English Psalms. Indeed the text interacts with another book of the Old Testament, present in the liturgy for Holy Week 'interspersed with verses including: "My friend betrayed me by the token of a kiss" ':[9] the Lamentations of Jeremiah. There are links between sacred and profane love here, between erotic loss and the penitent soul's desire for God, which will exert pressure on complaint as far as the high Renaissance.

Already apparent in this poem are traits that become standard in 'female complaints' centred on speaking subjects. But a second tradition is relevant. For *The Wife's Lament* seems to be the earliest English poem influenced by Ovid's *Heroides*.[10] Verbal debts are difficult to trace from Latin to Old

[7] Quoted, like *The Wife's Lament*, from *The Exeter Book*, ed. George Philip Krapp and Elliott van Kirk Dobbie (London, 1936).

[8] W. J. Sedgefield, 'Old English Notes (1 *Wulf and Eadwacer*)', *Modern Language Review*, 26 (1931), 74–5, at p. 74.

[9] *Anglo-Saxon Poetry: An Anthology of Old English Poems in Prose Translation*, ed. S. A. J. Bradley (London, 1982), 383.

[10] Cf. Helga Reuschel, 'Ovid und die Ags. Elegien', *Beiträge zur Geschichte der deutschen Sprache und Literatur*, 62 (1938), 132–42.

English, and similarities of contour between the lament and some of Ovid's feminine epistles could owe more to recurrent patterns of experience than literary imitation. Yet the *Heroides* were copied and circulated in early medieval Europe, and would be widely read by the twelfth century.[11] The fourteen or (if 'Sappho to Phaon' is authentic) fifteen epistles which Ovid produced early in his career elicited masculine 'answers' from the poet's friend Aulus Sabinus. These replies prompted Ovid to pair Helen, Hero, and Cydippe in *Heroides*, 16–21, as correspondents with Paris, Leander, and Acontius. Some think *The Husband's Message*, later in the Exeter Book, a similar companion piece to *The Wife's Lament*. An extended claim for Ovidianism, across both texts, seems unconvincing. Yet the fact that *The Wife's Lament* lacks the trappings of a letter, and cannot, like the *Message*, be taken as the utterance of a rune-stick,[12] does not damage its own case for indebtedness. It is part of the experience of reading *Heroides* that the letter-writing occasion should merge (however provisionally) into a flow of eloquence. Ovid in his epistles is aware of and responds to the intonations of such vocal laments as those of Penelope and Briseis in Homer, Sophocles' Deianira, Euripides' Medea and Phaedra, Catullus' Ariadne. Reversible relations between voice and script will remain a feature of complaint. Some texts shaped by *Heroides* (such as Dido's tale and lament in Chaucer's *The House of Fame*) escape the formality of letter-writing into spoken immediacy. At least as often, woeful speeches gravitate to epistolary form, as when Drayton (in a poem reproduced here) reconceives Daniel's Rosamond as the author of a verse letter. Even within texts plaint cultivates shifts of this kind, starting from the voice and advancing to testaments and bills of grievance (the trajectory of Chaucer's 'Complaint unto Pity'), or, as in *A Louers Complaint*, presenting 'letters', 'sonnets', and 'schedulls' displaced by impassioned utterance.

Rhetorically the *Heroides* owe much to Roman school exercises known as *suasoriae*, and they would in turn contribute to medieval and Renaissance classrooms. Yet pedagogic utility does not explain their literary impact, clear in the impression left upon such early women's compositions as the letters of the nun Constance (corresponding with Baudri of Bourgueil in the eleventh century) and Héloïse writing to Abelard. One source of the epistles' appeal is that, compared with the woes of Virgil's Dido or, for the most part, Ovid's own in *Tristia*, they are rich in plunderable fables and figures. Though plaintful passages called *questus* and *querelae* (successors of

[11] R. J. Tarrant, '*Heroides*', in L. D. Reynolds (ed.), *Texts and Transmission: A Survey of the Latin Classics* (Oxford, 1983), 268–73; Ralph J. Hexter, *Ovid and Medieval Schooling: Studies in Medieval School Commentaries on Ovid's 'Ars Amatoria', 'Epistulae ex Ponto', and 'Epistulae Heroidum'* (Munich, 1986), Introduction.

[12] For this claim see e.g. F. A. Blackburn, '*The Husband's Message* and the Accompanying Riddles of *The Exeter Book*', *Journal of English and Germanic Philology*, 3 (1901), 1–13.

the Greek σχετλιασμοί) are not rare in Latin poetry, they nowhere congregate with such stylish fertility as in the *Heroides*. The effect of so many related texts, read together, can be hypnotic. Yet Ovid's heroines, starting from unlike predicaments, write in subtly diversified tones: Phyllis' moody changes, the level naïvety of Canace, Helen rebuking Paris. The centrality of *dolor ira mixtus* permits rapid deflections of idiom, *miseratio* competing with *indignatio* in a verse which flashes with unpredictable facetious mirth. What this anthology shows at large—complaint steadily reinventing itself, rather than boldly innovating—is writ small within the letters, where Ovid repeats with glancing difference such topics as the 'tear-stained . . . letter', 'the inauspicious "wedding"-night'.[13]

Though *The Wife's Lament* displays some of the classic features of complaint, it is arguably pre-generic. Not until the fourteenth century do English writers use 'complaint' to classify and affiliate laments. Chaucer is the first major poet freely to employ the term. As it happens, the poem of his printed here, *Of Quene Annelida and False Arcite*, also exemplifies the narrative simplicity which underlies and secures much of the kind's elaboration. Annelida, visitor to Thebes, falls for Arcite in the glamorous aftermath of war; at first responsive, he betrays her for a mistress who holds him with seductive aloofness; the rejected queen writes him a letter of rebuke. Summary belies the emotional intricacy of this work, dependent (as often in Chaucer) on the reader's being prompted to compensate for sympathies in the narrator which still determine the climate of the poem. Between inflected telling and our uncertainties about Arcite the verse becomes elusive. Terraced levels of authority further complicate the text. Chaucer's claim to have drawn his tale from 'Corinne' (21) suggests that he is following the ancient poetess Corinna. To imply that you are, though male, working from female sources is a recurrent means by which plaintful ventriloquism claims authenticity. Yet 'Corinne' is also calculated to remind us of those texts of the *Amores* named after Ovid's mistress. Certainly Ovid contributes to the lithe and pointed verse of *Annelida*—as when the queen (with an echo of *Heroides*, 7) compares herself to a dying swan (342–8). Even more clearly than *The Wife's Lament*, this is Ovid with a Christian accent: unlike the classical swan, Chaucer's sings a 'penance' (347). More curiously 'Heroidean' are Annelida's swooning, her cramped limbs and 'asshen' pallor (e.g. 169–75). Throughout the period of this anthology, the misunderstood roots of the word 'heroine' contributed to complaint. When Chaucer describes the 'loveris maladye | Of Hereos' which seizes Arcite in *The Knight's Tale* (1373–4), *eros* merges with *herus*, 'lord, knight', and *heros* ('man of courage'). For medieval and later writers, complaint would explore the effects of a love 'malaise' on the spiritually if not socially 'gentle' and lofty-hearted.

[13] See Howard Jacobson, *Ovid's 'Heroides'* (Princeton, 1974), ch. 21.

The complexities of *Annelida* are textual as well as tonal. Canonically the poem consists of 210 lines of narrative followed by the queen's epistle, plus a dubious stanza which promises more of the tale. This format might be Chaucer's: *The Complaint of Mars* has a similar shape, as does *The Squire's Tale*, while the Ovidian tales of *The Legend of Good Women* (which would do much to bring 'female complaint' to later readers) finally gesture towards the letters of Dido, Medea, and Ariadne in *Heroides*.[14] Yet few early manuscripts give *Annelida* in the compound form handed down to editors, and it is possible that the work read today was produced by scribal amalgamation.[15] Because it at least implicitly presents the outcome of events, most plaint can separate into, or combine from, story and lament. This makes it narratively unstable, liable (in religious as well as secular writing)[16] to embed itself in larger works. *The Complaint of Mars* is found in manuscript paired with and run into a text now called *The Complaint of Venus*. When the latter was translated by Chaucer from three ballades by Oton de Grandson he changed the 'male' persona of his originals, creating a feminine plainant. But there is nothing mythological in the French or English texts, and only the ingenuity of scribes, associating the poem with *Mars*, would seem responsible for the title it now goes under. When linked in this way, *Venus* resembles the interpolated laments which, common in French and Chaucerian narrative, were prone to move from one text to another. Readers as well as copyists noticed such passages and interpreted them as distinct entities.[17] Pleasure lay in the separableness which allowed intercalated plaints to be transcribed and read as 'pseudo-documents'.[18]

Yet the medieval reader who marks material of a plaintful character need not be acting from generic conviction. Chaucer, who took 'complaint' from French as a literary term, applied it 'loosely to a variety of forms, from Ovid's *Heroides* to relatively brief lyrics'.[19] His flexibility can only have been encouraged by continental practice. For Deschamps, ' "complainte" seems to have referred to content, not form', yet Machaut 'cited it, with *rondeaux*,

---

[14] Cf. W. A. Davenport, *Chaucer: Complaint and Narrative* (Woodbridge, 1988), chs. 2 and 3.

[15] A. S. G. Edwards, 'The Unity and Authenticity of *Anelida and Arcite*: The Evidence of the Manuscripts', *Studies in Bibliography*, 41 (1988), 177–88.

[16] See e.g. C. W. Marx on the *Complaint of Our Lady* entangled with the Middle English *Gospel of Nicodemus*: 'Beginnings and Endings: Narrative-Linking in Five Manuscripts from the Fourteenth and Fifteenth Centuries and the problem of Textual "Integrity" ', in Derek Pearsall (ed.), *Manuscripts and Readers in Fifteenth-Century England: The Literary Implications of Manuscript Study* (Woodbridge, 1983), 70–81.

[17] See e.g. Ardis Butterfield, 'Interpolated Lyric in Medieval Narrative Poetry' (diss. Cambridge, 1987), 174–8, on *Troilus and Criseyde* scribes; Julia Boffey, *Manuscripts of English Courtly Love Lyrics in the Later Middle Ages* (Woodbridge, 1985), 56–8, esp. p. 57, on 'cantus' and 'litera' in the margins of *The Legend of Good Women* in Bodleian MS Tanner 346.

[18] The term is Boffey's, *Manuscripts of English Courtly Love Lyrics*, 91.

[19] Laila Z. Gross, 'The Short Poems', in *The Riverside Chaucer*, gen. ed. Larry D. Benson, 3rd edn. (Boston, 1987), 631–7, at p. 632.

virelais, and *ballades*, as a member of the lyric category'.[20] The word itself,
an intensification of older 'plaint', has its roots in Latin *plangere*, 'to beat the
breast, lament', ultimately from πλαγ- ('to strike, noisily thump').
Etymology draws helpful attention to the self-inflicted element of anguish
cultivated by some plainants, but it cannot rationalize the word's uses in the
fourteenth century. With strong legal connotations, since it described the
kind of 'bill' submitted by a 'plaintiff' (a written plea typically uttered and
ornamented in court by the lawyer as plaintful *conteur*),[21] 'complaint' was
applied to many sorts of articulate dissatisfaction. On the other hand,
entries in the *Middle English Dictionary* do suggest an emphasis on grievance
for wrongs done. From the outset, it would seem, 'compleint' (a common
spelling) had retrospective implications. This is tonally significant because
relations with the past do much to determine the atmosphere of most
plaints. Complicating, however, is 'Complaint against the Times', a strain of
social, at times quasi-scriptural, writing which could use a feminine persona
and (as in Alan of Lille's *De planctu naturae*) rise to heights of philosophic
complexity, or interact with elegy and genealogy (as much later in Spenser's
Ruines of Time), but which most often generated short bitter lyrics or merged
with petitionary literature.[22] Some poems now placed in this class—largely
the creation of modern scholarship—share with *The Wife's Lament* and *Of
Quene Annelida* an emphasis on loss, on virtues out of use, but most shun the
resonance of *ubi sunt* (the 'where are they now?' of elegiac irrecoverable-
ness) to attend directly to 'Evils of the Time'. These texts have traits in
common with complaint as Chaucer understood it, but, given their attention
to 'the Time', show this in the idioms of grievance they employ (including a
trend to rhyme royal) rather than in structure or overall tone.

If the criterion of retrospective distress is borne in upon Chaucer,
another distinction emerges—one more extensively clarifying, since it
relates to gender. In a text like 'Complaint to his Lady' the poet sues for love
and laments 'This hevy lif I lede, lo, for your sake' (52). His rhetoric is
anguished and relentless, broken by cries of grief. But how far does it recall
Heroides or *The Wife's Lament*? As against *Annelida* it resembles social plaint
because it speaks of a wrong that should be put right rather than recalling
the past. Compared with lyrics on 'Evils of the Time', it is more like the
queen's lament in that the poet's desire for 'My dere herte and best beloved
fo' (58)—for an object almost organically inward yet (the verse keeps

---

[20] Nancy Dean, 'Chaucer's *Complaint*: A Genre Descended From the *Heroides*', *Chaucer Review*,
19 (1967), 1–27, at p. 2.
[21] See M. T. Clanchy, *From Memory to Written Record: England 1066–1307* (London, 1979),
221–3.
[22] See e.g. John Peter, *Complaint and Satire in Early English Literature* (Oxford, 1956), chs. 3 and
4; Siegfried Wenzel, *Preachers, Poets, and the Early English Lyric* (Princeton, 1986), ch. 6.

realizing) not possessed—makes its yearnings intimate with loss. An important consideration emerges: plaint which is uttered without hope of recovering loss slips beyond its genre into elegy, yet the kind is most cogently extreme when dealing with betrayal rather than unfulfilled desire because the hope implicit in wooing gives less licence to distress than the juxtaposition of past pleasures with a destitute present and unpromising future. Gender comes into question since, for long-sustained and socially ingrained reasons, 'female'-voiced poems that woo are rare, though common for masculine personae, while abandonment leaves (fictive and actual) women in a more grievously trapped circumstance than is true of their masculine equivalents. While poems in which masculine figures sue for grace are more abundant than those lamenting female infidelity, there is an even greater disproportion in 'female'-voiced poems between those which long for love and the many which regret its loss. Significantly, examples of the former kind of 'female complaint', such as Lydgate's 'Balade, Sayde by a Gentilwomman . . .' (printed here), tend to incorporate elements which align them with the latter. This creates a situation in which the rhetoric of abandonment seems feminine, while wooing belongs to men. Lyrics of lost love, such as 'The man that I loued Al-ther-best', might shift in manuscript between genders,[23] but there is a bias working to naturalize such plaint as feminine. Chaucer followed more than whim when revising Grandson's pronouns in his *Complaint of Venus*.

One looks in vain for an English Héloïse or woman troubadour. Find a 'female'-voiced text like *The Lay of Sorrow*, paired in manuscript with an awkwardly high-flown *Lufaris Complaynt*,[24] and the prospect of female authorship is dimmed by a final stanza which firmly distinguishes the poet's voice from that of the 'lay'. The plaints of Venus and Mars, as yoked and handsomely illustrated in Bodleian Library Fairfax MS 16, begin to seem iconic. An ostensible balance between 'male' and 'female' gives way to asymmetry, visually enforced (Fig. 1) by the armoured strength of Mars and vulnerability of the smaller, naked goddess. Holding sway is a bearded patriarch, Jupiter—notorious for infidelities and rapes. What appeared 'female' in this male-depicted scene (work of the 'lymnour' William Abell)[25] then dissolves under scrutiny. A scribal gloss on a male translator's version of a male poet's impersonation, Venus is one of many speakers in complaint drawn into a pairing which cannot conceal the genre's repeatedly male structuring of the feminine. Yet the gendered patterns of the kind are not,

---

[23] Interlined variants in Cambridge University Library Add. MS 5943, fo. 178ᵛ, recorded by R. H. Robbins in *Secular Lyrics of the XIVth and XVth Centuries*, 2nd edn. (Oxford, 1955), 16–17.

[24] Ed. and discussed together by Kenneth G. Wilson, *Speculum*, 29 (1954), 708–26.

[25] See Jonathan Alexander, 'William Abell "Lymnour" and 15th Century English Illumination', in Artur Rosenauer and Gerold Weber (eds.), *Kunsthistorische Forschungen Otto Pächt zu seinem 70. Geburtstag* (Salzburg, 1972), 166–72, at p. 168.

1. Venus, Mars, and Jupiter, from Bodleian MS Fairfax 16 (*c.* 1450–60)

even in the highly stylized idiom of medieval lyric, unshakeable. In a miscellany such as the Findern Manuscript (in which women's names are suggestively inscribed) one finds plaints which, in their poised questioning of male poetry, are consistent with female authorship.[26] Two of the most impressive are printed in this anthology. 'What so men seyn' recommends female 'New fangellnys' with a wit which, far from damning the speaker, highlights the 'dowbilnys' (usually imputed to women) of men. Drily complaining about 'male' complaint, the poem has a rhythmic deftness which makes its voice one to be listened to rather than just heard:

> What so men seyn
> Loue is no peyn
> To them, serteyn,
>   Butt varians.
> For they constreyn
> Ther hertis to feyn,
> Ther mowthis to pleyn
>   Ther displesauns.

The second Findern poem, written in the same hand, is more expansively emotional. Yet it does not drop its guard. Love, in 'My woofull hert . . .', is raised to a pitch which would tempt the male author of such a poem into flattering masculine complacency: 'He is my comfort in all payn; | I loue hym and no moo.' But the sentiments of this speaker are braced by a formality which metrically subdues large gestures to 'plainness', and subordinates them (with a hint of the marriage service) to overarching values: 'To hym I woll be trywe and playn . . . Tyll deth departe us to.' An impression of creative control is confirmed by the manuscript's showing that 'I loue hym and no moo' was not the writer's first thought but was arrived at by the deletion of a routinely grandiose 'My Joy ffor well or w[oo]'.

This is not the kind of change that scribes make when copying. It is, to say the least, consistent with female composition of both poems. But how many anonymous plaints were written by Lydgate's sister? One class of work can safely be denied female authorship: those satirical pieces, catalogued by F. E. Utley,[27] in which plaining maids and widows are condemned out of their own mouths for pride and fecklessness. In works like *A Louers Complaint* complex syntax and diction dissuade the reader from construing the speaker through the folk linguistics which expect women's

---

[26] See e.g. Elizabeth Hanson-Smith, 'A Woman's View of Courtly Love: The Findern Anthology, Cambridge University Library MS. Ff.1.6', *Journal of Women's Studies in Literature*, 1 (1979), 179–94; but note Julia Boffey's scepticism, 'Women Authors and Women's Literacy in Fourteenth- and Fifteenth-Century England', in Carol Meale (ed.), *Women and Literature in Britain c.1150–1500* (Cambridge, forthcoming).

[27] *The Crooked Rib: An Analytical Index to the Argument about Women in English and Scots Literature to the End of the Year 1586* (Columbus, 1944).

speech to be limited by parataxis and restricted vocabulary.[28] Satirical
plaints, by contrast, harness the energies of the genre to reinforce commonly held fallacies[29] about uninterruptable female garrulity. Lyrics in the
style of 'Þis enþer day I mete a clerke' (reproduced here) gleefully contrast
the chatty physicality of undone maidens ('Now wyll not my gyrdyll met— |
A, dere god, qwat xal I sayn?') with the sexual skill of men, phallic guile
inseparable from their access to clerkly knowledge: 'he was wylly in hys
werke . . . I trow he cowd of gramery'. In some ways these poems are the
obverse of *planctus* written for the Virgin, the most abundant variety of
'female'-voiced lyric in the medieval period. Where the two sorts of poem
coincide is in their simplicity of speech. Yet, while the naïvety of the
abandoned maid in a lyric such as 'Y louede a child . . .' (collected here)
bolsters the male reader's ego and makes pity gratifying to extend, the
Virgin's directness humbles. In more ambitious lyrics her clarity, inter-
woven with scriptural material, achieves a haunting resonance. The Marian
poem printed here, for instance, embeds a refrain from the Song of
Solomon to memorably poignant effect:

> In a tabernacle of a toure,
> As I stode musyng on the mone,
> A crouned quene most of honoure
> Apered in gostly syght ful sone.
> She made compleynt thus by hyr one,
> For mannes soule was wrapped in wo,
> 'I may nat leue mankynde allone,
> *Quia amore langueo.*'

More than biblical overtones modify these lines. Unlike the other medieval works discussed so far, *Canticus Amoris* has a narrator. As the poem
unfolds and 'mankynde' is implored, the 'I' bulks less in our reading. But
his presence casts an aura of 'musyng' and a changed heart over the whole
lament. Increasingly from about 1300 'female'-voiced lyrics recede into
frames of this kind: dream visions, overheard monologues, the venturesome
encounters which make up *chansons d'aventure*. When these settings are
employed, a potentially infinite complication, by virtue of the speaker's
ambiguous and the narrator's reporting stance, ensues. The plaintful subject becomes an object, the narrator's 'I' a refracting medium. Significantly,
letter plaints which could be called framed are almost impossible to find. It
is the pregnant difference between reported voice and the script that conveys it (through a narrator) to the world which underpins contrasts between
lamenter figures and the 'I's who describe them. This difference is often

[28] See e.g. Jennifer Coates, *Women, Men and Language: A Sociolinguistic Account of Sex Differences in Language* (London, 1986), 18, 25–6.   [29] Ibid. 31–4, 99–101.

developed, however, in ways which depend integrally on gender. A framing 'I' is hardly ever feminine in medieval poetry. The weight of cultural authority lay so much with men that texts inevitably recommended what they enclosed with the sanction of 'male' narration. Poems could powerfully dramatize the unlikeness of framing 'I' and subject/object by setting the authority of 'male' narrators against naïve (or dishonoured) speakers characterized as plaintful women. This paradigm was not just effective because it reinforced gender stereotypes. The feminine subject, reduced to an object, could dramatically re-emerge as the primary agent of a poem by overwhelming her frame with a flood of eloquence. Then again, as Marian lament reminds us, the subject might seize moral ground from the narrator, undercutting his 'authority'. And how could a framing 'I' mediate without gender-derived distortion? Built into the criteria of difference were reasons for doubting that the masculine 'I' could communicate what female grief might be.

The compulsive dialectic of framed plaint, oppressing the plainant while subverting the narrator, can be found in the earliest Middle English examples. The first lyric of this anthology, for instance, describes a maiden overheard 'Als i me rode'. The 'i' tells us that he 'rode' for amusement, 'pleyinge'. Evidently the pleasurable occasion was not one which would lead him to hijack the maid's grief as his own (some *chansons* motivate the narrator's wanderings by having him unhappily in love). Yet other distortions are possible. Though the maid reportedly vents grief and defiance of her faithless lover ('Þe clot him clingge . . . it shal him rewe'), the 'i' blithely assimilates her song to the day's amusements:

> Son icche herde þat mirie note,
>   Þider i drogh;
> I fonde hire in an herber swot
>   Vnder a bogh
>   With ioie inogh.

The poem is often, and rightly, celebrated for its mingled tones. But the frames of plaint have the effect of making a reader familiar with the genre wonder what the source of such buoyancy is: how far the 'mirie note' and 'ioie' are imposed by the narrator. As in many texts, the language of grievance is neither quite that of the speaker nor the 'i', but is a continual index of the larger ambiguities which structure the scene. The sense of distortion oscillates between registering the force of the narrator's imposition and the not completely censorable vehemence of the speaker's efforts to assert her position as subject. 'Female complaints' in this mode are provocative not just because of the anguish dealt with, but because they are miniature devices for generating interpretative instability.

Beside a stream or at the edge of woodland, under a tree and almost invariably alone, the 'heroines' of *chansons d'aventure* are found. In early French versions they inhabit a scene which is standardized but vivid. The narrator skirts a flowery meadow, a *jardin* or *boschel*, or he passes 'entre un bois et un pre'. Hearing a *dame* or shepherdess sing, he pauses to listen, and might announce himself and ask what grieves the speaker. Such an encounter can lead into seductive *pastourelle*, with the narrator becoming the subject's lover—as in the French analogue of 'Als i me rode . . .'. More often the *je* remains hidden, or asks a few questions to elicit lament, and a feminine voice fills out the poem. In these *chansons dramatiques*, though love is typically unsatisfied, the tone is not invariably plangent. Anger, jealousy, and reproachful judgement strike through, and poems can be explicit in their account of betrayal. English texts take these conventions for granted to the extent, by and large, of under-articulating the circumstances of the 'I' and the landscape he surveys. The compacted first stanzas of *A Louers Complaint* can be seen as the outcome of a process of foreshortening which begins in the fourteenth century. Moreover, 'the English poet   manifestly prefers forms in which he is not an active participant'.[30] Here again the 'I' of Shakespeare's poem, conspicuously placed but deliberately invisible, an interested but cautious eavesdropper ('From off a hill . . . downe I *laid* . . . Ere long *espied*'), carries to an extreme traits apparent in the 1300s. As though to compensate for the 'I' 's detachment, Shakespeare puts a frame inside his frame, introducing the 'reuerend man' as the maiden's interlocutor. His double *chanson* conflates alternatives and recalls (much as 'downe I laid' suggests dream vision) the phases through which complaint had developed. For the 'I' of English *chanson d'aventure* passed from lovers' into priestly hands before returning to the secular figure of the poet: 'clerks, in fact, hold the monopoly in these woodland adventures until Tudor times, when they make way for worldly poets who listen in the wilderness to the laments of love-lorn Besse or of a lady fallen from royal grace.'[31] When *A Louers Complaint* was first published it followed Shakespeare's Sonnets in quarto. Its 'I' might begin like the betrayed lover of the later fourteen-line poems—low 'spirrits', 'accorded' with the maid's plaint (3), prompting him to range the fields. But the text develops him, rather, as a worldly poet who stumbles upon an old-fashioned *chanson* (that encounter of maid and 'reuerend man'), which he observes with the involved disengagement of the on-stage audience at a play within a play.

[30] Helen Estabrook Sandison, *The 'Chanson d'Aventure' in Middle English* (Bryn Mawr, 1913), 41.
[31] Ibid. 1–2.

2. 'Sad Tun'd Tales'

Continuity between medieval and early modern complaint is nowhere more apparent than in the broadside ballads which circulated so widely during Shakespeare's lifetime. In these (often *chanson d'aventure*) poems heart-sick and abandoned women, some left with child or driven mad by grief, are plentiful.[1] More dolorous than vehement,[2] such texts can be in two parts, featuring a lover's reply or the narrator's amorous advances.[3] Sometimes a woeful swain is doubled on the broadsheet with an ill-used maid; 'male' and 'female' discourses are folded together,[4] as in *A Louers Complaint*. Many contrast court or city values with those of the virtuous countryside—plaint transposing, and providing an outlet for, widespread anxieties about decadence in high places and socially threatening urban wealth. This scheme, impressively developed by Daniel's *Complaint of Rosamond*, is given a fresh twist by Shakespeare, who makes his auditor feature in the contrast: now a swain, the 'reuerend man' was 'Sometime a blusterer that the ruffle knew | Of Court, of Cittie' (58–9). Later ballads enliven the polarity by satirizing London fashions. In *The Countrey Lasse* (*c.*1628), for instance, the singer compares her lot favourably with that of masked city wives: 'A homely Hat is all I aske, | which well my face protecteth.' Stout hats are not uncommon in pastoral, but it is hard to read this without recalling the 'plattid hiue of straw, | Which fortified her visage from the Sunne' in *A Louers Complaint* (8–9), and the more difficult not to conclude that Shakespeare's poem is a version of *pastourelle*, with the 'fickle maid' a country girl seduced by a more sophisticated, perhaps courtly, suitor.[5]

Such a role for the youth is standard in ballad literature. *Loue without Lucke: Or, The Maidens Misfortune* has the full received panoply of wandering 'I', pastoral landscape in which 'lowd Ecchos are ringing', and an overheard weeper abandoned by that most dashing of lovers, a 'young Captaine'. *The Desperate Damsells Tragedy* by Martin Parker provides an errant narrator, 'a meddow faire, | and in a shade' a lamenter, 'spyed' on by the reporting 'I'. The abandoned 'maide' wrings her hands, deploring the 'false lad' who with 'speeches faire' robbed her of her 'dearest Jewell'. Occasionally the victim is rescued. Part 1 of *The Wofull Complaint of a Loue-*

---

[1] e.g. *A Loue-Sick Maids Song, Lately Beguild, By a Run-Away Louer that Left Her with Childe*; *The Distressed Virgin: Or, The False Young-Man, and the Constant Maid*; *The Lovely Northerne Lasse*; *Loues Lunacie: Or, Mad Bessies Fegary*.

[2] But see e.g. Martin Parker's — — — —: *Or, Cupid's Wrongs Vindicated*.

[3] e.g. *A Maydens Lamentation for a Bedfellow* and *The Louing Virgins Complaint: Or, Her Des[i]re to Obtaine the Loue of a Young Man*.

[4] e.g. *The Tragedie of Phillis, Complaining of the Disloyal Loue of Amyntas* with *The Complaint of the Shepheard Harpalus*.

[5] Cf. the 'foolish fickle state' of the betrayed speaker in *The Maidens Complaint of her Loves Inconstancie*.

Sicke Mayde has the neglected heroine urging 'maydens all, example take |
By me that am in griefe'; but then 'The young man's kinde reply' makes
everything good. More typical is the drift of *The Diseased Maiden Louer*, a
popular and early text reprinted here from the Pepys Collection. In it, as in
A Louers Complaint, the 'I' lies down to eavesdrop on a riverbank lament,
and he watches a maiden turn despair into prettiness by gathering flowers
and rushes—like Ophelia, and the Gaoler's Daughter in *The Two Noble
Kinsmen*—before dying of a broken heart. When challenged by the narrator,
her lover proves recalcitrant. He has found, he says, 'a loue more faire',
adding (with a whiff of hard pastoral) 'Besides, she is her Fathers heire'.
Apparently shaken, the 'I' rebukes him with the thought that such behaviour
will make maids 'stop their eares vnto our plaints, | And call us Deuils
seeming Saints' (cf. *A Louers Complaint*, 316–18). Given the run of poems to
which *The Diseased Maiden Louer* belongs, however, it scarcely needs the
'faithlesse' youth's 'example' to bring that message home.

It would distort these ballads to insist on narrative outline at the expense
of the patterns of knowledge, absence, and secrecy which shape their plaintful music. Discussing a late and well-known piece, 'Early one morning, just
as the sun was rising | I heard a maid sing in the valley below', J. H. Prynne
picks out the embedded address—'Oh, don't deceive me, Oh never leave
me'—by which the singer reveals events. 'If her exclamation is an
apostrophe', he observes,

> it is presented as addressed not to the unknown hearer who is present unbeknown,
> but to the deceiver who is deliberately absent and who is all too well known to her
> and yet not at all to the only person who hears. Yet neither the first auditor of her
> song, nor we the auditors of the outer, framing narrative, know who either of them
> is or was; the main narrative's past tense back-shifts, into an unascertainable
> remove, the immediacy of the heard lament, preserving its piercing moment as
> something also beyond present knowledge.[6]

This is persuasive not least because, beyond the relations of listening and
reading-in which modulate poems like 'Als i me rode . . .', it hears the
'remove' of what is sung. For all his narrative control, the 'I' of framed
complaint is less qualified to know the validity of what he mediates than the
speaker and her absent addressee. As a consequence of that absence the
plainant becomes rapt within processes of lament which might yield her
false solicitude (such as sustaining the illusion that the lover is there to be
addressed). Even so, the authority of the narrator is more vulnerable to
doubts by virtue of a style of plaining which underlines the elsewhereness of
its field of application. From this gulf within the poem a problem of

---

[6] 'English Poetry and Emphatical Language', *Proceedings of the British Academy*, 74 (1988),
135–69, at p. 156.

intrusion follows which is not unrelated to the sexual importunities of the 'I'
in some 'female complaints'. Can the narrator's overhearing and sub-
sequently circulating the maid's song be disentangled from the (equally
masculine, invasive) wrong which she reports? In most poems this is not an
explicit issue; but that a risk of violation is registered somewhere in the
matrix out of which generic texts are realized is indicated, delicately, in the
lyric reproduced here from Gascoigne.

   'A Louing Lady Being Wounded in the Spring Time' offers a situation
familiar from broadsides. The wandering narrator (for once, in a boat)
hears, then eavesdrops on, a 'female' plainant in a riverbank garden. Puttenham, in a rare example of contemporary close reading of complaint,
objected to the periphrases with which this frame was opened[7]—a clear
misjudgement, since Gascoigne piles '*Aries*' on 'March', and adds '*Phœbus*
rayes' and '*Ver*' to show the poeticalness of a narrator who, after hearing the
lady's lament, will have a keener, more soberly depressed, sense of what
'wynter . . . spring' and the 'sunne' might signify. Certainly, at the turn of
plaint back to frame, there is a belated meeting of eyes in which, though the
awkwardness is mutual, the narrator most takes the shock:

> This sayed: she cast a glance and spied my face,
> By sight whereof, Lord how she chaunged hew?
> So that for shame, I turned backe a pace
> And to my home, my selfe in hast I drew . . .

'For shame' acknowledges wrong, and (more subtly) intimates that what the
'I' takes from the lady belongs to a set of reciprocating circumstances (she
blushes too) which place him in the same narrative as the lover whose
conduct she laments and which extend socially through the interaction of
his poem with its audience, giving food for complaint in plaint. For
Gascoigne declares, at the end of his lyric, 'Now Ladies you, that know by
whom I sing'. Implying a further frame, he educes his 'I' from the narrator's
and uses courtly intimacy between poet and audience to suggest that his
'shame' bears on experiences which, though deeply recessed in the poem,
are part of the world he shares with his auditors.

   Because this lyric was first printed in a Gascoigne collection which
purported to be a miscellany by various hands,[8] much could be said about
the perplexed relations it adumbrates between 'Gascoigne as editor', the
'poet' of its closing address, and the narrator's venturesome 'I'. Of larger
significance for 'female complaint', though, is the unusual and corrective

---

[7] *The Arte of English Poesie*, ed. Gladys Doidge Willcock and Alice Walker (Cambridge, 1936),
194, 258–9.

[8] *A Hundreth Sundrie Flowres Bounde vp in One Small Poesie* (1573); cf. 'An Absent Dame Thus
Complaineth' (P4ᵛ–Q1ʳ) and 'A Lady Being Wronged by False Suspect, and also Wounded by the
Durance of her Husband, Doth Thus Bewray hir Grief' (K1ᵛ–2ᵛ).

effect of that turn towards 'Ladies you'—a challenging obliquity reinforced by the insistence that these women 'know' more about the matter of the plaint than readers of the lyric. While these lines cannot prevent the poem from being construed, at least in the abstract, as a text which includes for the diversion of readers a framed 'female' audience as well as a plaintful subject/object, its being directed at the 'Ladies' in practice disrupts the assumption (implicit in much feminine love plaint) that male readers should enjoy the victim's woe in ways not only continuous with the 'pleyinge' of an errant narrator—hearing a 'mirie note' where there is grief—but with that of the treacherous lover. When the faithless youth of *The Diseased Maiden Louer* tells the narrator, 'I was not made for one alone, | I take delight to heare them moane', he anticipates and seems to share in the pleasure of a misogynistic reader, leafing promiscuously through ballads, perusing Ovid's gallery of heroines, or turning the pages of this anthology. There are said to be cultures in which plaint is a 'women's verbal genre' set apart in its own social space.[9] Few, if any, of the texts gathered here can claim such privilege for what the speaker says. Filtered through processes of copying, printing, and circulation largely commanded by male interests, 'female complaint' was directed towards a readership in which (though women bulked larger than is sometimes claimed) men predominated.[10] Feminine plaints might be dedicated to women (as in the case of Drayton's *Rosamond*), or be recommended to their attention by authors and translators (as with Wye Saltonstall's *Heroides*, below, p. 74), but there is no evidence that the subgenre was sustained by a sectional audience. A broadly male readership, with a corresponding range of interpretative 'performances', provided the final, collaborative frame assumed by poets around the subject/object of even unframed 'female'-voiced deploration. The writer who (like Gascoigne) wanted to question this arrangement did not write free-standing plaint but was forced to restructure the containment of the form.

'Now Ladies you, that know by whom I *sing* . . .' The naïvety of *The Diseased Maiden Louer* will, when 'sung', have turned into something more persuasive. Integral to 'Early one morning . . .' are the voices (reported and performing) which lend it tension and resonance. Links between music and complaint are of great antiquity. Keening, though a complex art, can sound like grief's own idiom. To wail and sob is to approach language through melopoeia. Much of the verse discussed thus far was originally set to music.

---

[9] See e.g. Joel Sherzer, ' A Diversity of Voices: Men's and Women's Speech in Ethnographic Perspective', in Susan U. Philips, Susan Steele, and Christine Tanz (eds.), *Language, Gender, and Sex in Comparative Perspective* (Cambridge, 1987), 95–120, esp. pp. 100, 105–6, 112–13.

[10] See e.g. Boffey, 'Women Authors and Women's Literacy'; David Cressy, *Literacy and the Social Order: Reading and Writing in Tudor and Stuart England* (Cambridge, 1980), 106, 145; Keith Thomas, 'The Meaning of Literacy in Early Modern England', in Gerd Baumann (ed.), *The Written Word: Literacy in Transition* (Oxford, 1986), 97–131, at pp. 116–17.

The Wife's Lament must have seemed less opaque when its sorrows were realized in a singing line. Early *planctus*—like the six composed by Abelard, and many of the *planctus Beatae Virginis Mariae*—were musical. Melodies survive for certain *lais* of Northern France, that secular branch of *planctus*, as they do for the troubadour *planh*. Disappointingly little music is extant for English medieval lyric, but several songs which survive with settings are Marian laments and love plaints. Even when not sung, complaint inclines to complicated stanzas, foregrounding musicality. As Shakespeare's 'fickle maid' reminds us, a 'tale' does not need melody to be 'sad tun'd' (4–5). Hence the audible ornateness of Chaucer's shorter plaints (so that he keeps Grandson's rhyme-scheme for *Venus*, remarking on its difficulty in English), and his declaring of the Knight in Black's lament: 'He sayd a lay, a maner song, | Withoute noote, withoute song.' It has become a convention to refer these lines (*Book of the Duchess*, 471–2) to Deschamps's discussion of the difference between the artificial music of sung poetry and the subtler melodiousness of words. As interesting is the fact that writing a 'compleynte' (464) prompts Chaucer to reiterate this distinction. Plaint carries a musical burden which, stronger than its speaking singer, develops its own momentum, exercises sway, and gives the discourse weight and fulness:

> For sorrow, like a heauie hanging Bell,
> Once set on ringing, with his own waight goes,
> Then little strength rings out the doleful knell . . .[11]

Not all readers are satisfied with such intrinsic harmony. The critical history of the Black Knight's lay demonstrates the divided effect of emotive woe, its emphasis encouraging some to insist on reference. For them, far from being resolved in acoustic elaboration, the 'compleynte' opens out into the life of John of Gaunt and death of Blanche his duchess. There is little doubt that Chaucer wrote this particular work with topicality in mind (just as Puttenham's discussion of 'A Louing Lady . . .' suggests knowledge of 'by whom' it was sung). But contexts are not poetry, and by the standards of medieval elegy *The Book of the Duchess* is reticent about the circumstances which precipitated it. Plaint is often vulnerable to forced readings *à clef*. With its busy rhetoric pointing to ill-defined hurts, it offers the goad of urgency and uncertainty of a puzzle. From the fifteenth century to the present—whether it is the scribe John Shirley taking *The Complaint of Mars* and *Venus* to be about illicit amours at court, or Richard Allan Underwood concluding that *A Louers Complaint* concerns Southampton's seduction of Elizabeth Vernon[12]—the genre has generated dubious speculation. Even

---

[11] *Lucrece*, 1493–5.
[12] Trinity College, Cambridge, MS R.3.20; *Shakespeare on Love: The Poems and the Plays. Prolegomena to a Variorum Edition of 'A Lover's Complaint'* (Salzburg, 1985), 132–69.

when explicitly historical, rehearsing the griefs of fallen princes, complaint
has found it hard to achieve exemplary relevance without exposing itself to
false decoding. The search for stories which could illuminate the reigns of
Edward VI and Queen Mary, and omission of subjects 'because their examples were not much to be noted' (as the compiler William Baldwin puts it),
led *Myrroure for Magistrates* authors to provide matter for an 'indoor sport'—
that of 'identifying', under given action, 'the persons and situations
reflected'.[13]

Woeful ballads should not be thought of as an afterglow of fifteenth-
century lyricism: they draw on lively currents in low culture. Peter Burke
sees 'the lament, the French *complainte*, the German *Klagen*' as belonging to
the basic 'stock of genres' through which popular culture was articulated.[14]
Especially when amatory or religious, such works found their way into the
Tudor miscellanies. From Tottel's *Songes and Sonettes* (1557) through *Englands Helicon* (1600), 'female complaints' recur.[15] At times they bend their
'sad tuning' towards a harsh directness:

> A Cruell Tiger all with teeth bebled,
> A bloody tirantes hand in eche degre,
> A lecher that by wretched lust was led,
> (Alas) deflowred my virginitee.

'The Complaint of a Woman Rauished . . .' has an alliterative vehemence
that puts it among the most compelling works in this anthology. Violence in
lyric plaint tends to be metaphorical: piercing eyebeams, broken hearts.
This text describes atrocities usually associated with the public stage or
prose fiction. More characteristic of the miscellanies is Surrey's 'Complaint
of the Absence of her Louer Being vpon the Sea', reprinted here (like the
'Woman Rauished') from Tottel. Its elegant stanzas of tetrameters and
trimeters, with longer closing lines, might not have the complexity of Chaucer's shorter plaints, but their continual interplay between patterns of stress
and quantity brings the speaker's 'moorning voyce' musically alive. Surrey's

---

[13] *The Mirror for Magistrates*, ed. Lily B. Campbell (Cambridge, 1938), 54–5.
[14] *Popular Culture in Early Modern Europe* (London, 1978), 120, 124.
[15] Tottel includes four 'female'-voiced plaints, two reprinted here. *The Paradyse of Daynty Deuises*
(1576) has M.D.'s 'A Lady Forsaken, Complayneth'. *A Gorgious Gallery, of Gallant Inuentions*
(1578) specializes in verse letters, such as 'A Letter Written by a Yonge Gentilwoman and Sent to
her Husband Vnawares (by a Freend of Hers) into Italy', replied to (in the Ovidian manner) and
associated not only with half a dozen male plaints but with 'The Lady Beloued Exclaymeth of the
Great Vntruth of her Louer'. Clement Robinson's *Handefull of Pleasant Delites* (1584) includes 'The
Complaint of a Woman Louer' and an unusual 'Lamentation of a Woman Being Wrongfully
Defamed'. Breton's *Bower* (1591) has plaints for Diana and Venus, while his *Arbor* (1597) adds 'A
Ladies Complaint for the Losse of her Loue' and (printed below) the 'Poeme of a Mayde Forsaken'. Notable in *Englands Helicon* (apart from texts collected here) is a poem about unhappy
marriage, 'The Nimph Dianaes Song'. Cf. Underwood's useful discussion, *Shakespeare on Love*,
49–59.

imagination can be sharply visual: in the vignette of the speaker at her
window, gazing upon scudding clouds and the 'grene waues' of the 'salt
flood' ('Lo, what a mariner loue hath made me'), there is a keen sense of
situation. But it seems indicative that a sung version should survive in an
early manuscript.[16] Time and again the Tudor plaints collected here succeed by chiming across levels of lyric activity in a kind of self-orchestration.
Texts like 'A Poeme of a Mayde Forsaken' (with its musical funeral of
birds) or Munday's 'Excellent Pastorall Dittie' (where a nymph sits 'Lute in
hand' to 'paint out her vnrest') aspire to the condition of Morley's madrigal
'Round, around . . .' (also printed here), where the abandoned maid, crying
'Hey hoe tro-ly-lo', vents a 'mirie note' of plaintful babble. Such texts
abstract the situation of the feminine persona and at worst exploit her as a
vehicle for plangency.

Englands Helicon, however, complicates matters by almost abolishing sexual difference. In its tuneful lyrics, contrasts enforced by the cruder broadsides — the harsh maleness of *The Louers Complaint for the Losse of his Loue*
and swooning pathos of *The Diseased Maiden Louer* — are melodiously lost.
Nymphs and swains alike experience love as a baffling desire which leads to
passive yearning. The elision goes deeper, yet is more immediate, than the
medieval ambivalence which allows the speaker of 'The man that I loued
. . .' to change gender by revision. It has not the mystical aura of the
feminized Christ in Middle English lyric quoting (as in male-voiced versions of *Canticus Amoris*) erotic lament from the Song of Solomon,[17] or
echoing in poems drawn from the *Improperia* (Good Friday reproaches) that
feminine Jerusalem who cries, at Lamentations 1: 12 (printed below), 'Is it
nothing to you, all ye that passe by? behold and see, if there be any sorrow
like vnto my sorowe'. Yet the effect of a plaint like Richard Barnfield's 'The
Sheepheards Ode' is extraordinary. In this *chanson dramatique* the narrator
overhears a 'Silly Swaine' bewail his love for the 'fayrest boy . . . faire
Ganimede' as well as a 'Lasse that did in beauty passe'. It is during the 1590s
that Edward II's lover, Piers Gaveston, becomes the controversial speaker
of one of Drayton's plaintful *Legends*. In a late ballad like *The Louing Virgins
Complaint*, the speaker will lament her failure to win a lad who is not just
handsome but an '*Adonis*', a beauty with 'rosie blushes' resembling '*Hermaphradite*'. The virgin blazons his 'rare complexion . . . his eyes
like lodestones' and 'His lockes of louely browne . . . euery one a snare'.
'Would I had neuer seene', she cries, 'those honey smiles so sweet.' There
is more than a trace in such lines, contemporary as they are with
Shakespeare, of the sexual ambivalence in *A Louers Complaint* (the youth's

---

[16] British Library Add. MS 30513.
[17] For texts see *Quia amore langueo*, ed. H. S. Bennett (London, 1937); a speculative context is
provided by Julia Kristeva, *Histoires d'amour* (Paris, 1983), 234–6.

face a bower for Venus, his voice 'maiden tongu'd'), of that fluidity in gender which seems not just overlaid from the Sonnets but grounded in the poem's enfolding masculine and feminine love plaints in a common language.

The primary feature of this idiom are apostrophe and antistrophe, epimone, ecphonesis—schemes of repetition and outburst—and, above all, echo and anaphora, figured start and clamorous finish of Shakespeare's poem, ubiquitous in *Englands Helicon*. For the 'dumpish' plainants of pastoral, enclosed and endstopped emotions generate a sense of the bounded, precipitating a realm of caves and hollows, glades, shorelines, riverbanks: an environment within which words are reflective by nature. Versions of this locus and its language can be found in bucolic from Theocritus to Frost, and they feature in Renaissance poetry through Spenserians even later than Shakespeare. Marina, for instance, near the start of William Browne's *Britannia's Pastorals*, abandoned by a faithless shepherd, laments among 'mountaines, fields, by watry springs, | Filling each caue with wofull ecchoings'.[18] Emotion is enlarged by these acoustics. Because the grievous idiom is virtually ungendered, the closest analogue of Shakespeare's 'fickle maid' in Browne turns out to be 'a musing lad' (2. 30–1). But it is through women speakers that poets realize most effectively the paradox which lends power to abandonment, as when Marina plains upon the willow-sprouting shore:

> O hearken then
> Each hollow vaulted Rocke, and crooked Den!
> And if within your sides one *Eccho* be
> Let her begin to rue my destinie!
> And in your clefts her plainings doe not smother,
> But let that *Eccho* teach it to another!
> Till round the world in sounding coombe and plaine,
> The last of them tell it the first againe ...   (2. 6)

Although the myth of Echo is more than double-sided, its urge to define and exceed containment with a device which lends singleness multiplicity, gives weakness the strength vocally to rebound from crags, and makes an isolated speaker the whole tongue of a world, helps explain not only its fascination as a fable but its association with the most dramatically enlargeable of laments: those uttered by 'female' personae.

But fascination for whom? Feminist theory has concerned itself with reading out of Echo's closure,[19] and it would be rash to take the blurred

---

[18] Books 1 [1613] and 2 (London, 1616), here 1. 3.
[19] See e.g. Caren Greenberg, 'Reading Reading: Echo's Abduction of Language', in Sally McConnell-Ginet, Ruth Borker, and Nelly Furman (eds.), *Women and Language in Literature and Society* (New York, 1980), 300–9.

gender of pastoral complaint as anticipating the transcended roles advo-
cated in some twentieth-century writing. Rather, it shows a dilution of
identity, the voluntary or forced withdrawal of a speaker from sexuality. Its
pathos is that of Cesario's 'willow Cabine' plaint, hollering and hallowing a
'name to the reuerberate hilles', to 'make the babling Gossip of the aire, |
Cry out'.[20] Within *Twelfe Night*, of course, Cesario is Viola, a plaintful 'male'
contains the feminine. Roland Barthes's claim 'In any man who utters the
other's absence *something feminine* is declared' would be treacherous if read
as prescriptive, yet its literary deductions are significant: 'Woman is faithful
(she waits) . . . It is Woman who gives shape to absence, elaborates its fiction
. . . the man who waits and suffers from waiting is miraculously feminized. A
man is not feminized because he is inverted, but because he is in love.'[21]
Among writers of the English Renaissance, Sidney explores this most
searchingly. As Cleophila makes towards Pamela's lodge in book 3 of the
Old Arcadia, she finds 'a cave, made as it should seem by nature in despite of
art'—an 'eorþsele' reminiscent of *The Wife's Lament*, 'framed out into many
goodly spacious rooms', yet dark and melancholy.[22] 'Sitting down in the first
entry of the cave's mouth', Cleophila complains. In this 'mouth' (the word is
repeated) voice provides the music which an anguished body orchestrates. It
vents, moreover, music which falls short of a womanish treble; for the singer
is actually Pyrocles, a 'hero' dressed as a 'heroine', reduced to this circumstance by his faithful love for Philoclea:

Instead of an instrument, her song was accompanied with the wringing of her
hands, the closing of her weary eyes, and even sometimes cut off with the swelling
of her sighs . . . But as she was awhile musing . . . she might afar off first hear a
whispering sound which seemed to come from the inmost part of the cave, and
being kept together with the close hollowness of the place, had (as in a trunk) the
more liberal access to her ears. And by and by she might perceive the same voice
deliver itself into musical tunes, and with a base lyre give forth this song:

> Hark, plaintful ghosts! Infernal furies, hark
> Unto my woes the hateful heav'ns do send . . .

Gynecia, loving Pyrocles, 'doth bear part with the complaints' in the cave.
'The same voice', echoing, is different. Becoming a listener, the confessor
finds (that same word, echoed) a confessor. The 'mouth' discovers an ear,
dialogue emerges (complaint as one-sided, frustrated, or introverted,
exchange), and a new branch of fabling is opened by the confessional motif.
Lament meanwhile gravitates towards the '*feminine*' position, becomes a
'Woman''s song, most itself in melopoeia. Hence Gynecia's music being,

---

[20] *Twelfe Night, Or What You Will* I. v (561, 565–7).
[21] *A Lover's Discourse: Fragments*, trans. Richard Howard (London, 1979), 13–14.
[22] *The Countess of Pembroke's Arcadia (The Old Arcadia)*, ed. Jean Robertson (Oxford, 1973),
179–81.

more elaborately than Cleophila/Pyrocles', harmonious. Once again adumbrating the poetics of a genre, Sidney retraces myth. In *Britannia's Pastorals* Pan's mistress—obliquely, Echo—amuses herself by ranging the woods and imitating bird-song. So sweetly vocal is her 'babling Gossip' that, from merest speech, from 'the repercussion of her tongue ... begun the *Art* | Which others (though vniustly) doe impart | To bright *Apollo*' (2. 96). This is the birth of Music out of the spirit of Echo. And Sidney registers it through an imagery which juxtaposes 'the cave's mouth' with a subterranean cochlea—'the close hollowness of the place ... as in a trunk' (that is, through a tube) enabling Cleophila/Pyrocles to hear Echo's lyre-strummed tones. As Bacon noted in *Sylva Sylvarum*, 'the instrument of sense hath a sympathy or similitude with that which giveth the reflexion ... so is the ear a sinuous cave, with a hard bone to stop and reverberate the sound ... like to the places that report echoes'.[23] Acoustics, in this account, start to sound inherently plaintful. The passage of speech from 'mouth' to 'sinuous cave' is a record of removedness, a 'report' of absence. For Sidney and other writers of the period, language projects affects through the 'instrument of sense' into an inwardness which lends each utterance 'base' undertones of ... complaint. The 'vogue of complaint poems about women', with which this discussion began, not only extends more richly into the 1590s than has been thought: it draws on deeper sources in the imaginary acoustics of the age.

3. *Complaint Reformed*

Another nameless plainant. She has clambered up the tree of state, and fallen at the height of her glory. A favourite of the king's, she was once the envy of the court. Among her glittering accomplishments were those of Echo: a resourceful singer, 'Scho countrafaitit all fowlis, les and more'. But now she regrets 'That euer [she] wes brocht in to the court', and, as death approaches, laments her faults. In a passage of lofty grandiloquence, the speaker sets out 'to complene' her 'fait Infortunate'. To clear a troubled conscience, she dictates 'Epystyll's, texts both grave and pithy, recorded by a *chanson d'aventure* poet lurking under a nearby hawthorn bush. Finally a canon, friar, and Benedictine approach, and to these the plainant makes confession. After bequeathing all her worldly goods, she dies leaving her heart to the king—and, instantly, has her body ravaged by those clerics in the guise of magpie, raven, and kite. For this is not some 'female'-voiced extract from *A Myrroure for Magistrates* but Sir David Lyndsay's

---

[23] Century 3. 282, in *The Works of Francis Bacon*, ed. James Spedding, Robert Leslie Ellis, and Douglas Denon Heath, 14 vols. (London, 1857–74), ii. 434.

ornithological fantasy *The Testament, and Complaynt of our Souerane Lordis Papyngo* (1530).[1]

Written to divert James V of Scotland, whose parrot had met an untimely death, and concerned to make play with Ovid on a similar theme (*Amores*, 2. 6) while out-lamenting Henryson's Cresseid, the poem is also scathingly addressed to abuses in the Church. Lyndsay's sympathy with reform is apparent in his satirical redeployment of motifs derived from Boccaccio's *De casibus virorum illustrium*: not only in the *Papyngo*, but in—shades of *Wulf and Eadwacer* as the lament of 'a female dog'—*The Complaint and Publict Confessioun of the Kingis Auld Hound, callit Bagsche* (1533–6), and *Tragedie of the Umquhyle Maist Reuerend Father Dauid . . . Archibyschope of Sanctandrous* (1547). Why would the stuff of medieval chronicle tragedy appeal to Lyndsay's reformed imagination? This question becomes the more intriguing when it is realized that Boccaccio, like his translator Lydgate (in the *Fall of Princes*), prefers inquest, debate, and other indirect modes[2] to 'publict confessioun'. Suggestively, Lyndsay's standing among Protestants is confirmed by an illustration in Bullein's *Dialogue both Pleasant and Piety-full* (1564) which shows him 'with a hammer of strong steele in his hande, breakyng a sonder the counterfeicte crosse kaies of Rome, forged by Antichriste'.[3] These are 'the keys of the kingdom of heaven' given to St Peter at Matthew 16. In medieval theology they were associated with the sacrament of confession supposedly granted to the priesthood by Christ: 'Whose soever sins ye remit, they are remitted unto them; and whose soever sins ye retain, they are retained' (John, 20: 23).

For reformers this was heretical. Luther and Calvin maintained that corruption ran so deep that to catalogue one's faults to a priest was impossible. Faith in the Word and its promise of remission was the only means to forgiveness, and such recourse was open to all believers. 'The keys have not been given to St Peter but to you and me', insisted Luther.[4] So far from being established by Christ, Calvin declared, auricular confession was a 'snare' set by Innocent III.[5] Luther pressed for a simpler rite, one which could be conducted by laymen. Calvin, inspired by David as Psalmist and by the example of the Pauline Church, argued on the one hand for general confession by congregations and on the other for recognition by penitents

---

[1] *The Works of Sir David Lindsay of the Mount 1490–1555*, ed. Douglas Hamer, 4 vols. (Edinburgh, 1931–6), i. 56–90.

[2] For feminine exceptions in the *Fall* see 'The lettre of compleynt of Canace to hir brothir', Dido's short lament, the admixture of monologue from Brunhilde (below, p. 35), 'the greuous compleynt of Lucrece'.

[3] Cf. W. Murison, *Sir David Lyndsay: Poet and Satirist of the Old Church in Scotland* (Cambridge, 1938), p. xii.

[4] 'The Sacrament of Penance, 1519', trans. E. Theodore Bachmann, in *Luther's Works*, gen. eds. Jaroslav Pelikan and Helmut T. Lehmann, 55 vols. (St Louis, 1958–), xxxv. 3–22, at p. 16.

[5] *The Institution of Christian Religion*, trans. Thomas Norton (1561), 3. 4. 7, fo. 139ᵛ.

'that the secret corners of their euels are so depe, that thei can not be throughly disclosed'. The penitent 'crieth out with Dauid', Calvin adds, 'Who vnderstandeth his errours? Lord cleanse me from my hidden sinnes.'[6] Fifteenth-century piety had been infused with the language of the Psalter. Yet there are differences between the taxonomies of guilt characteristic of late medieval writing and the psalm-steeped idiom of Catherine Parr (that influential female plainant) in *A Lamentacioun or Complaynt of a Sinner* (1547), or the psychological development of Wyatt's version of the seven penitential psalms.[7] In pre-Henrician manuals we confront a 'whole sea of laws and impossible questions about "cases of sins" '[8]—anonymous instances, often spiritually curious. Parr, by contrast, wrote her treatise 'to confesse and declare to the world, how ingrate, negligent, unkynde, and stubberne, I haue bene to god my Creatour' (Λ1^v), and included within its articulately first-person text 'A christian complaint' sueing for forgiveness (D6^r). In Wyatt the same impulses are carried further, towards dramatic projection and innerness, and Christian complaint takes on the properties of what is called (in the wake of Boccaccio) *de casibus* tragedy.

Wyatt's David, indeed, set back and scrutinized by the narrator, resembles Edward IV, Locrinus, Vortiger, and those other adulterous and faulty monarchs—become so repentant with hindsight—examined in the generation after Wyatt by Baldwin, Higgins, and Blenerhasset. His psalms anticipate (still more evidently than the *Tragedie of the Umquhyle Maist Reuerend Father Dauid*) the 'tragedies' and 'complaintes' of *A Myrroure for Magistrates*, whose suppression under Queen Mary is suggestive. It would be wrong to imply that the *Myrroure* format was somehow unacceptable to Catholics. Cavendish's *Metrical Visions* employ the conventions of historical monologue independently of Baldwin and his fellows, yet its author was loyal to Rome.[9] But then, Cavendish's relative failure in this mode (comparing, for example, his *'Historye/Cardinalis Eboracensis'* with the same events in the *Life and Death of Cardinal Wolsey*) might be symptomatic. The confessional way of telling history was peculiarly well adapted to presenting a Protestant view, for it gave immediacy to a David figure, the fallen prince as Everyman. Post-Reformation readers will have known David as a speaker of 'complaints' from the title of psalms (e.g. 69, 90, 102) in the Great, Geneva, and 1611 Bibles.[10] When Francis Seager went beyond his paraphrase of *Certayne Psalmes* (1553) to write *Richard Plantagenet Duke of Glocester* (part of

---

[6] Ibid. 3. 4. 18, fo. 143^v; cf. Ps. 19: 12 and (in the margins of Norton's text) 19: 31.

[7] Nos. 6, 32, 38, 51, 102, 130, and 143 in English Bibles.

[8] Luther, 'A Discussion on How Confession Should Be Made, 1520', trans. Eric W. and Ruth C. Gritsch, in *Luther's Works*, xxxix. 23–47, at p. 33.

[9] His feminine plainants are Anne Boleyn, Katherine Howard, Viscountess Rochford, the Countess of Salisbury, Lady Jane Grey.

[10] They will also have been familiar with his 'lamentation' over Saul and Jonathan (2 Sam. 1: 17–27) and Absalom (18: 33), passages often echoed and alluded to in complaint.

the 1563 *Myrroure*), he remained within a kind. As though to underline his continued relevance, Calvin's exemplary penitent claims a *de casibus* role in Munday's *Mirrour of Mutabilitie* (1579). The speaker of this *Complaint of King David*, 'attired in the weeds of a Gentleman . . . drying the tristfull teares which flowed from the fountayne of his eyes with a handkertcher' (B4ᵛ), is not historically or socially distant, but a man who might be the reader, a plainant in doublet and ruff: someone, as in Wyatt, to identify and 'cry out' with.

Medieval penitential literature comprised far more than manuals. Doctrine could be discoursed within a structure of story-telling (as in *The Parson's Tale*), or prompt a moral fable (e.g. *The Pardoner's Tale*). In Gower penitential process structures an entire work, *Confessio Amantis*, while the *Gawain* poet draws on it for his techniques of characterization. Among the medieval lyrics can be found model confessions. Buried in the notes of preachers are lyric fragments drawn from 'women's songs . . . and lovers' complaints'.[11] Because they cover a greater range of exemplary emotions than male-voiced lyrics—from flighty 'fickleness' to destitute abandonment—'female complaints' proved useful to those preaching repentance. But there is a difference between the medieval cleric saying of the Magdalene 'Item amor revelat, ut ipsa publice confitetur', then quoting a lyric to illustrate her flight from the world,[12] and the post-Reformation poet thinking his way into a figure to generate 'publict confessioun'. The distinctive appearance of the *Myrroure for Magistrates* speaker (Blenerhasset's Ebbe accompanied by '51 Nunnes . . . hauing all their noses and vpper lippes flead of'), and his or her narrative singularity, are largely absent from medieval plaint. Texts like Chaucer's *Venus* motivate plaining as an activity, and only then precipitate their subjects, whereas, in later works, the speaker's relation to language is primarily at issue in the poem. When using prosopopoeia ('an excellent figure'), wrote Abraham Fraunce in 1588, 'Wee must diligentlie take heede, that the person thus represented haue a speach fit and conuenient for his estate and nature.'[13] It is no accident that John Higgins, adding episodes to the *Myrroure for Magistrates*, should have pioneered the use of inverted commas for direct speech, distinguishing the plainant's discourse from that of narrator and compiler.

This is not indiscriminately to prize the complaint reformed. The fifteenth-century 'Lament of the Duchess of Gloucester' is not inferior to the same speaker's plaint in the *Myrroure for Magistrates*. Thomas More's hybrid 'Lamytacyon off Quene Elyzabeth', which follows the duchess's lament in Balliol College MS 354, is a work of gravity and cumulative force. Much

---

[11] Siegfried Wenzel, *Preachers, Poets, and the Early English Lyric* (Princeton, 1986), 230–2, 226.
[12] 'Love shows itself openly, just as she makes a public confession': Wenzel, *Preachers*, p. 227.
[13] *The Arcadian Rhetorike*, G2²ʳ.

verse composed in the wake of the *Myrroure* must always have seemed flat, and arguably those plaints which draw most directly on penitentialism run the acutest risk of tedium.[14] Yet by insisting on a view of the world in which each life had its own trajectory, the reformers revived complaint as the medium through which such lives could authoritatively be described: from within. Like its precursors, Tudor plaint elaborated distressful exempla. More than what went before, it traced chains of action and reaction. In Munday's *Mirrour of Mutabilitie*, writes Willard Farnham, 'one will read far before he finds any mention of Fortune at all. . . . mutability has turned into a dramatic progress from cause to effect.'[15] Overstated though this is (neglecting the reform of 'Fortune' into Divine Providence), it points up psychological consequences. Self-explicating yet to itself obscure (for its deepest 'corners' remained unsearchable), introverted rather than taxonomic, and exclamatory (with David) when unkennelling its guilt, oppressed by doubts about justification and election rather than by fear of Fortune, the plaintful self emerged from the Reformation as a soliloquizer—like Hamlet, in fact, returned from Luther's Wittenberg, with a 'cause' assumed for each 'effect, | Or rather say . . . defect' in him.[16]

Against this guilty background, the most striking thing about plaintful women in Tudor poetry is their lack of 'defect'. The proportion of virtuous to wicked (saintly Hellina, faithful Penelope, chaste Lucrece)[17] is far higher than with masculine plainants, even though admirable men begin to figure in late editions of the *Myrroure*. Moreover, as the plaints of Mistress Shore (by Thomas Churchyard) and Daniel's Rosamond collected here show, *de casibus* women can be 'fallen' yet sympathetic. As victims of guile and frailty, they tug at the heart-strings in the way a Richard III cannot. Subtly defensive, Jane Shore plays up the wickedness of that king (who humiliated her after the death of her lover, Edward IV), and uses the big measures of rhyme royal—'fittest for a graue discourse'[18]—to impress the reader with her wise counsel. Daniel's Rosamond, who cites Churchyard's heroine in the first lines of her plaint, extends the art of self-exculpation with keenly etched accounts of her betrayal, diminishing guilt. To read these poems in the light of Lydgate and Lyndsay is to suspect that their success derives

[14] e.g. 'The Wordes of Tormented Tantalus' in Richard Robinson's *The Reward of Wickedness* (1574), tricked out with marginal references to the Church fathers on confession.

[15] *The Medieval Heritage of Elizabethan Tragedy* (Berkeley, 1936), 308–9.

[16] II. ii (1129–30).

[17] Blenerhasset celebrates Hellina in his additions to the *Myrroure*, Peter Colse perpetrates *Penelopes Complaint: Or, A Mirrour for Wanton Minions* (1596). For Shakespeare's heroine in this context see Heather Dubrow, 'A Mirror for Complaints: Shakespeare's *Lucrece* and Generic Tradition', in Barbara K. Lewalski (ed.), *Renaissance Genres: Essays on Theory, History, and Interpretation* (Cambridge, Mass., 1986), 399–417.

[18] Gascoigne, *Certayne Notes of Instruction Concerning the Making of Verse or Ryme in English* (1575), in *Elizabethan Critical Essays*, ed. G. Gregory Smith, 2 vols. (Oxford, 1904), i. 46–57, at p. 56.

from their finding, in male exploitation and female self-suborning, a post-Reformation substitute for the force of 'fait Infortunate'. Instead of suffering at the hands of Fortune, poets in the line of the *Myrroure* dramatize the 'effect' of being subject to 'causes'—and find in woman and her 'unruly' eroticism (as it was termed) the most vulnerable instance.

The consequence is a special kind of vitality, dependent on weakness. Usually unable to exculpate themselves by an appeal to events which they have initiated, feminine characters discover what can be said of and for their motives. Passivity is relative, retribution insistent; suffering can seem to demonstrate the existence of wrongs not admitted by plainants. In Churchyard, though to a provocatively lesser extent in Daniel, sinfulness runs through 'female complaint' as an explanation of misfortune. Yet the very idea of 'explaining' becomes, given the change in 'mutability', problematic. To glance back at Lydgate[19] is to be reminded that plainants are 'plaintiffs', 'effects' of others' 'causes' presenting quasi-legal 'causes'. The ghosts interviewed by Bochas (the *Fall*'s name for Boccaccio) are all untrustworthy, but those of women are particularly deceitful. Like a lawyer or judge, Bochas calls evidence against them, trying to elicit 'confessioun'. Though the *Myrroure* ghost narrates without interrogation, the question of judgement is never far away. With Baldwin in his Prefaces it is made explicit. Evidence is brought out and laid before the reader: even literally, in the form of epistles.[20] But the speaker's appeal to constraints receding within—from Jane Shore's 'Who can withstand a puissaunt kynges desyre?' to 'The rypest wittes are soonest thralles to love' (89, 147)—becomes the stuff of plaint, and 'effects' express 'causes' by a quasi-legal, as well as psychological, manœuvre. 'Case' in the penitential sense (above, p. 25), merging with *de casibus* and psychological 'causation', intersects at this point with legal 'case' and 'cause'. Certainly plaint appealed to Renaissance readers trained to think of rhetoric (following Cicero and *Ad Herennium*) as an adjunct of law.[21] 'Euery matter' of writing, claimed Thomas Wilson, can be 'contained in one of . . . fower causes'; or again, '*There are three kindes of causes or Orations*'.[22] The chances are that Polonius's quibbling about Hamlet's 'cause', 'effect', and 'defect' derives (though he uses no art at all) from Wilson—the only rhetorician to leave his mark on the quarto which

[19] His persistent relevance is indicated by A. S. G. Edwards, 'The Influence of Lydgates's *Fall of Princes c.*1440–1559: A Survey', *Mediaeval Studies*, 39 (1977), 424–39.

[20] *Parts Added to 'The Mirror for Magistrates'*, ed. Lily B. Campbell (Cambridge, 1946), 195–7.

[21] See e.g. Richard J. Schoeck, 'Rhetoric and Law in Sixteenth-Century England', *Studies in Philology*, 50 (1953), 110–27; 'Lawyers and Rhetoric in Sixteenth-Century England', in James J. Murphy (ed.), *Renaissance Eloquence: Studies in the Theory and Practice of Renaissance Rhetoric* (Berkeley, 1983), 274–91.

[22] *Wilson's 'Arte of Rhetorique' 1560*, ed. G. H. Mair (Oxford, 1909), 7–8, 11.

brought *A Louers Complaint* to the world.[23] 'Causation' of this kind makes it difficult but appropriate for the reader to judge how far plaintful speakers were responsible for their downfall. The persona casts her monologue in an idiom which, as in Shakespeare, has a quasi-legal colour ('the verdict', 'precedent', 'from iudgement stand aloofe!'), and which makes apparent the 'design'—in both structural and manipulative senses—of her 'explanation'.

So persuasive can such figures become that, in poems like *Shores Wife* and *The Complaint of Rosamond*, repentance provides its own grace and the reader answers 'confessioun' with absolution. This at least was Drayton's doubt when reviewing the genre in *Matilda* (1594). Blenerhasset's Hellina had begun her monologue by saying that women were neglected by *de casibus*.[24] Over the next two decades the pace of complaint-writing was such[25] that (as we have noticed with Daniel's Rosamond) poets began to opt for initial stanzas in which figures wondered why, when others had been noticed, they were not yet themselves immortalized. In this spirit Matilda says that Rosamond, though 'highly graced', was a sinner, and the poet misguided 'who strives to stellifie her name'[26] While virtue is passed over, she grumbles, '*Shores* wife is in her wanton humor sooth'd'. Unlike these royal courtesans, Matilda explains, she fled King John to a nunnery and (under further pressure) took poison upon the thought: 'Faith finds free passage to Gods mercy seat, | Repentance carries heavens eternall kayes'.[27] Hearing of her death, John, a tyrant for love like David, protests (the doubting Protestant) against heaven's 'Predestinating this untimely death', then rues his words and appeals for 'grace': 'O let Repentance, just revenge appease' (995 ff.). The male lament enfolded by Matilda's monologue could not be more frankly 'reformed': it employs the kind of psalmic rhetoric which appears in Hunnis's 'Complaint of a Sinner', or William Birch's sonnet-cycle of the same title. Such emphases are characteristic even of belatedly post-Reformation plaint. Daniel's Rosamond chides the 'credulous deuout ... ignorance' associated with Godstow nunnery. Drayton's Gaveston details the 'many a Trentall said' in 'blind devotion' for his repose, and, in one of the strangest passages of complaint, continues his narrative beyond the point of death to assure the efficacy of grace: 'Even

[23] He seems to have transmitted Erasmus's letter on breeding to the early sonnets; see e.g. Katharine M. Wilson, *Shakespeare's Sugared Sonnets* (London, 1974), 146–7.

[24] *Parts Added*, ed. Campbell, 412.

[25] Before the efflorescence of 1592–6 note esp. *The Disorded Life, of Bianca Maria, Countesse of Celaunt, in Forme of her Complainte*, 'Cressids Complaint', and 'The Pitious Complaint of Medea' in George Whetstone's *The Rock of Regard* (1576), Churchyard's *A Pitefull Complaint, in Maner of a Tragedie, of Seignior Anthonio dell Dondaldoes Wife* in *A Generall Rehearsall of Warres* (1579), revised as *A Tragicall Discourse of a Dolorous Gentlewoman* in Churchyard's *Challenge* (1593).

[26] *Matilda. The Faire and Chaste Daughter of the Lord Robert Fitzwater*, 29, 32, in *The Works of Michael Drayton*, ed. J. William Hebel, Bernard H. Newdigate, and Kathleen Tillotson, 5 vols. (Oxford, 1931–41), i. 209–46.

[27] Explicit in the edition of 1596: stanza 151, in *Works*, ed. Hebel *et al.*, v. 37.

thus my soule . . . By true contrition flyes to him alone . . . And by repentance, finds a place of rest'.[28]

When Drayton wrote about King John, David provided a model. Speaking for Matilda posed difficulties of another order, since exemplary female
sinners were few. Mary Sidney's consummate handling of loss and exile in
psalm paraphrases like the one printed below —

> You that of Musique make such showe,
> Come sing vs now a Sion laie.
> O no! wee haue nor voice, nor hand,
> For such a song in such a land —

should not obscure the paucity of scriptural plainants for female emulation.
Women might ponder David in their devotions, like Catherine Parr, or be
compared with him polemically (as in Mary Sidney's dedication of her
Psalms to Queen Elizabeth), but a fuller, quasi-dramatic identification with,
for example, David's love for Bathsheba would have struck contemporaries
as problematic. An exemplar such as Munday's Jezebel might offer direct
instruction; but her warnings against 'Vanitie' lack the energetic interest of a
David torn between love and duty, divine favour and sexual desire — and she
is, symptomatically, the only feminine plainant in the *Mirrour of Mutabilitie*.
Women were thought responsive readers of others' sorrow. Shakespeare
adapts a commonplace when Lucrece's woes are divined by her maid and
that 'counterfaite of her complayning' weeps in sympathy (1269). When
they wrote for Mary Sidney the complaints collected here, Daniel and
Spenser will have been able to count on empathy from their dedicatee. But
what kind of exemplary figuring could male poets best provide for women
concerned to 'cry out' their sins? The most lyrical of plainants in Scripture
requires wary handling by a moralist (Song of Solomon, 3: 1–5, 5: 6–6: 3);
'Rachel weeping for her children' (Jeremiah, 31: 15 ff.) can be allegorically
applied, but is a type of bereavement, not sin; the most popular feminine
exemplar in this period, Susannah (in the Apocrypha),[29] is not an evident
object of meditation for those guilty rather than sinned against.

These reservations help explain the prominence of one lamenter: Mary
Magdalene. Commonplace in medieval sermons, she persists in poems of
spiritual grief from the pseudo-Chaucerian *Lamentatyon of Mary Mag-
daleyne* — also known as her *Complaynte* (1520/6) — through Southwell
(1594) and John Sweetnam (1617) to Crashaw. But the reformers' relative
neglect of the Virgin lent her renewed significance. The production of such
texts as *The Lamentacyon of Our Lady* (1509–10?) dwindled, and the sorrows

---

[28] ll. 1589–97, in *Works*, ed. Hebel *et al.*, i. 157–207.
[29] See e.g. Götz Schmitz, *Die Frauenklage: Studien zur elegischen Verserzählung in der englischen
Literatur des Spätmittelalters und der Renaissance* (Tübingen, 1984), 174–93.

of Mary were pushed to the recusant margin—as in *The Rosarie of Our Ladie, Otherwise Called Our Ladies Psalter* (1600), a closely ordered prayer-book contrasting with psalmic devotions in the style of Parr. Increasingly conspicuous are texts like *The Blessed Weeper* (1601): a rhyme-royal dream vision by Nicholas Breton, in which the Magdalene, fusing penitent grief with the language of erotic lament, bewails 'the losse, or lacke of her deere loue'.[30] Even among recusant writers, narratives framed into immediacy were cultivated. I.C.'s *Saint Marie Magdalens Conversion* (1603), for example, invokes Helen, Troilus and Cressida, '*Rychards* stratagems for the english crowne … *Tarquins* lust, and lucrece chastitie', and sets those Shakespearian exemplars aside (yet aligns itself with them) to celebrate in complaint 'A womans warre with her selfe-appetite' (A3ʳ). Male poets and readers could attempt to identify with the Magdalene,[31] but I.C.'s depiction more evidently encouraged women to share in this 'warre'. His freshly handled motifs of witchcraft, sinful poison, town against country, speech vs. silence, reverberation ('The woodes the babling *Ecco* entertaine, | Which eache worde iterates and makes one twaine', C1ᵛ), prompt comparison with amorous poems like *A Louers Complaint*. The overlap is unsurprising. Gervase Markham appears, for example, to have published *Marie Magdalens Lamentations* alongside *The Blessed Weeper* in 1601, followed in the year of Shakespeare's poem, 1609, by *The Famovs Whore, or Noble Curtizan: Conteining the Lamentable Complaint of Pavlina*. While the former makes empathetic the stricken grief of a saint, the latter displays a contemporary Magdalene revelling in the language of repentance. There is little to choose, in the poems' closing phases, between Paulina's pious admonitions and Magdalene's assurance of Christ: 'He can the ruines of thy soule repaire' (H2ᵛ).

Markham's metaphor is notable, since the idea of Daniel's Rosamond or Shakespeare's maid owing something to Mary Magdalene seems less unlikely than what can be more securely demonstrated: their debts, as ruined cities, temples, palaces (a recurrent figuring in 'female complaint'), to Lamentations. Ascribed to Jeremiah, but uttered in part by a ravaged Jerusalem with 'filthiness … in her skirts' (1: 9), this book supplemented the Psalms in private devotion, and featured (as during the Anglo-Saxon period) in the liturgy for Holy Week. For Catholics it elucidated the plight of a Church reduced by 'affliction'. When Southwell's St Peter speaks of 'everlasting matter of complaint', the grieving he has in mind extends

---

[30] *A Diuine Poeme Divided into Two Partes: The Rauisht Soule, and The Blessed Weeper*, D4ᵛ. Breton had already addressed himself to this subject: *Marie Magdalens Loue* (1595) analyses John 20: 1–18 and appends an address to the repentant soul; *Maries Exercise* (1597), a reformed equivalent of *Our Ladies Psalter*, incorporates prayers centred on the weeper's situation.

[31] See e.g. G. Ellis, *The Lamentation of the Lost Sheep* (1605)—a poem heavily indebted to Breton's (?) *Passion of a Discontented Minde*—E2ʳ⁻ᵛ.

'Beyond the panges which *Jeremy* doth paint'.[32] For Protestants Lamentations was, if anything, still more significant. As the cry of a chosen people
returning to God, the complaint of a repentant city, it offered an instance of
general confession to complement David's heart-searchings. The verses of
chapter 1 printed here appealed to poets and musicians as text which might
be fruitfully (like the Psalms) paraphrased and sung,[33] art adding to the
beauty of the original as it could not to the Lord's plain word. The title
'lamentation' was given along with 'complaint' to psalm-resembling can-
ticles—as in 'The Lamentation of a Sinner' and 'Humble Complaint of a
Sinner' in John Dowland's *Whole Booke of Psalmes.* Popular religious
literature shows the terms becoming interchangeable.[34] Such a blurring of
nomenclature was encouraged by Jeremiah. In manuscript headings of the
Fall of Princes the term 'complaint' had been used to describe 'jeremiads . . .
diatribes against sin'.[35] Reformation Jeremiads are often 'complaints', but
also 'laments'[36]—in part, no doubt, because Lamentations follows from
Jeremiah, and could be taken to show the kind of penitence which preaching might stir in London or Cambridge or some other lapsed outpost of
Zion. So familiar a plainant was Jerusalem that to seek a spiritual analogue
for Shakespeare's 1609 quarto is to contemplate the devotional relationship
between the Psalms and Lamentations.

That the former helped shape the Sonnets is agreed, whether or not one
accepts the numerological argument that the poems follow the pattern of
the Vulgate.[37] Equally apparent is the debt of *A Louers Complaint* to *The
Ruines of Time.*[38] Such is the controversy surrounding Spenser's poem
(printed below), however, that its alignment with Lamentations has been
blurred. Many take the plainant, a 'Woman sitting sorrowfullie' beside the
Thames—figure of the ruined city of Verulamium—to speak for the poet.
And there are indeed passages, after the *chanson d'aventure* opening, in
which she expresses Spenserian concerns. Against Verlame's praise of William Camden, her lament for the Dudleys, the celebration of Sidney, recent

---

[32] 'Saint Peters Complaint', in *The Poems of Robert Southwell, S.J.*, ed. James H. McDonald and
Nancy Pollard Brown (Oxford, 1967), ll. 38–40.

[33] e.g. Thomas Drant's 'The Wailings of the Prophet Hieremiah Done into Englyshe Verse', in
Medicinable Morall (1566); the *Lamentations of Jeremie* dedicated by Christopher Fetherstone (1587);
settings by Byrd and Tallis.

[34] e.g. the 'female'-voiced *Lamentinge of a Yonge Mayde Who by Grace ys fully Stayde* (1566–7) and
Excellente Ballad Conteyning a Lamentacon Fygurativelie Mente by all People but Spoken by Eve (1580).

[35] David Edwin Craun, 'The *De Casibus* Complaint in Elizabethan England, 1559–1593' (diss.
Princeton, 1971), 18.

[36] e.g. *A Complaint of the Churche, against the Barbarous Tiranny Executed in Fraunce* (1562); *A
Complaynt agaynst the Wicked Enemies of Christ* (1564); *The Lamentacyon of a Christen agaynst the Cytye
of London* by Henry Brinkelow (1545).

[37] See Alastair Fowler, *Triumphal Forms: Structural Patterns in Elizabethan Poetry* (Cambridge,
1970), 183–97.

[38] *The Sonnets and 'A Lover's Complaint'*, ed. John Kerrigan (Harmondsworth, 1986), 390–1.

scholarship has set her association with the Rome of Antichrist. But is it the case that Verulam takes a corrupt pride in those visions of worldly vanity which lie at the heart of the poem? Contemporary reaction, such as that of I.O. (probably John Ogle), in his *Lamentation of Troy* (1594), seems to have found the city sympathetic.[39] To pursue a hostile reading any distance is to overlook the Saxon associations of Verulam, and its importance in the growth of a native Church. It is to neglect the running comparison, which at times becomes troublingly explicit, between the now ruined satellite of Rome and that other new Troy, London, which flanks 'siluer streaming *Thamesis*' (2). And it is, above all, to slight the context provided by the collection of *Complaints* which *The Ruines of Time* opens. Like Jane Shore, Elstred, and Rosamond, Verlame is a flawed speaker. She recovers her past with a poignancy which might, as Drayton feared with Churchyard's and Daniel's heroines, seduce an unguarded reader. Yet, as surely as the fallen 'Ierusalem rememb[ering] . . . all her pleasant things that she had in the dayes of old' (1: 7), Verlame is punished ('does penance'; the words are cognate) while being comforted. In her, the breast-beating pain (that other lexical branch of 'penitence') of 'plaint' enacts an acknowledgement of guilt.

The poem also returns us to Lyndsay and Lydgate, to complaint as historical narrative: its praise of the antiquary Camden is not aberrant. In *De casibus virorum illustrium* and (even more) the *Myrroure*, plainants do not simply describe their own crimes and sufferings but testify to the divinely directed movement of events. For early humanists *historia* was a category of rhetoric in which instruction was effected by invoking figures from the past. Complaint gave voice to these exemplars, whose authority gave weight to their advice. The necromantic and prosopopoeic devices of the genre could satisfy that desire to hear 'dead men speake', to 'call to counsel those that are dead and gone', which makes early modern historiography so persistently 'oral' in its metaphors.[40] In this light Spenser's interest in *Ruines* and 'moniments', explicit from the start of his poem, is striking. For the words are used again of Camden, who recovers 'simple veritie, | Buried in ruines', though 'Time' makes 'moniments obscure' (171–2, 174). The growing sense of history's pastness in the Elizabethan period seems to have been nurtured by the 'bare rwn'd quires' of pillaged monasteries:[41] living,

---

[39] Plaint need not personify such grand cities; see the laments of a market town in Suffolk ('God in his ire | For sinne hath consumed me, Beckles, with fire') in *A Collection of Seventy-Nine Black-Letter Ballads and Broadsides, Printed in the Reign of Queen Elizabeth*, prefaced by Joseph Lilly (London, 1867), 78–84.

[40] John Hoskyns, 'Direccions for Speech and Style' (*c.*1599), and George Benson, *A Sermon Preached at Paules Crosse the Seaventh of May MDCIX* (1609), quoted by D. R. Woolf, 'Speech, Text, and Time: The Sense of Hearing and the Sense of the Past in Renaissance England', *Albion*, 18 (1986), 159–93, at p. 183.

[41] Shakespeare, Sonnet 73. See e.g. Margaret Aston, 'English Ruins and English History: The

dwindling evidence of that England which (for better or worse) had pre-ceded the Reformation.[42] Rosamond does not just describe the misplaced piety of Godstow nunnery: she depicts it as, symbolically, a ruin. Moreover, both her complaint and *The Ruines of Time* have the place-centredness of antiquarianism, the past understood in relation to locality.[43] This is the larger context—one which matters to complaint as late as Pope—in which Verlame's lament should be understood. Voicing a Roman past, limited in wisdom yet instructive for all that, Verlame is a figure of history, of ruin and place, of 'moniments' so worn that she needs a poet's help to be read. Yet by seeing (and speaking for) her, the male poet became a contriver of mean-ings. What needs discussion, before repentance is further pursued, is what was 'seen' in 'female complaint'.

4. *Double Standards*

Bochas is musing in his study. Enter a feminine 'ymage', stridently 'Froward', hair 'vntressid' (like a thousand plainants) and a nature so 'doubil' that being divides:

> Partid on tweyne of colour and corage,
> Hir riht[e] side ful of somer flours,
> The tothir oppressid with wyntris stormy shours.[1]

What can the poet, 'pale in his visage', make of this 'monstruous' spectacle? Wearing 'Wachet bleuh of feyened stedfastnesse', the figure bears 'liht greene for chaung and doubilnesse'. Dull as an ass yet swift as a swallow, crooked and upright, both coward and warrior, 'Now was she mannyssh, now was she femynyne'—strangest vision of androgyny. The scene is one of Lydgate's most intense, at the start of book 6 of the *Fall of Princes*, and one of those most lovingly elaborated from his French prose source. Doubtless this is so not least because it presented an imaginary situation which shaped the best part of his writing. Here is Bochas, respected auctor, among his books with 'penne on honde', confronting fickle 'Fortune'. Here is the enticing but unpredictable other, the contradictory matter of *de casibus*, to be grasped and won for art. Lydgate inherits assumptions which correlate, through literary history from Virgil onwards, the 'variable' shifts of Fortune and female nature, and in doing so suggests a gravitational pull towards

Dissolution and the Sense of the Past', *Journal of the Warburg and Courtauld Institutes*, 36 (1973), 232–55.

[42] See e.g. Keith Thomas, *The Perception of the Past in Early Modern England* (London, 1983), 9–23.

[43] Cf. Leland's *Laboryouse Journey and Serche ... for Englandes Antiquities* (1549), Lambarde's *Perambulation of Kent* (1576), Harrison's 'Description of Britaine', prefixed to Holinshed's *Chronicles* (1577), Stow's *Survay of London* (1598), as well as Camden's *Britania* (1586).

[1] *Fall of Princes*, 6. 1–84, ed. Henry Bergen, 4 vols. (London, 1924–7), iii. 675–7.

feminine subjects/objects. Significantly, though, he does this with a hint that gender does not quite inhere. Whence the 'mannyssh' aspect of this plainant? Why is Bochas, 'object' of this intrusion, rendered as passive and 'full pale' as a maid? Lydgate and his auctor, with busy pens scribbling over the horizon of what they know, are aware of masculine dread grafted into their vision of the feminine.

Certainly a character such as Brunhilde, who appears near the end of the *Fall of Princes*, compounds womanly, Fortune-like, and—as she wrests the argument from Bochas—masculine traits.[2] With 'Hir her vntressid' and 'weeping eyen', she at first seems the epitome of passive suffering. But she quickly shows characteristics of that 'Fortune' whose effects she indexes. Both 'vntressid' figures are 'Froward', both 'cruel' though alluring, and both (above all) 'Double'. 'Variable' and 'Partid', Bochas insists, women ('tauht' by 'Nature') present a creditable aspect even when at fault. So sharp is the goad of misogyny that, having first admitted to 'Knowyng nothing' about Brunhilde's life, Bochas refutes her 'compleynt' by imputing duplicity. 'I was youe in mariage | To Sigibert', she begins; but Bochas objects. Sigibert was slain in battle, she avers; but Lydgate's Boccaccio interjects, 'Nat so'. He was 'moordred in sothnesse | Oonli be occasioun of your doubilnesse'. There is strong resistance to the encroachment on male initiative, a pre-emptive dislike for what is 'seen' as 'doubil'. Boccaccio and Lydgate use the narrator to rationalize disagreements in their sources. Divergence between the 'Cronicles' could be turned to advantage by making argument part of the poem. The resulting aggregate, however, holds more interest than the sum of its parts because it does less than transcend them. Friction between its evidences reveals the shape of Bochas's prejudice in ways which tell us about 'female complaint' in general. Indeed Lydgate, being so artless, is more absorbingly contradictory than Boccaccio. He does not simply reproduce the inconsistencies of his auctor. With fruitful clumsiness he derives a 'Lenvoye' summarizing Brunhilde as a 'Maistresse of moordre', 'Double of hir tunge', and then adds a coda of his own stressing the 'maner of ambiguite' which filled Bochas as he digested the 'confessioun that she hirsiluen tolde'. The effect is to point up uncertainties within framing 'authority' which imply more than could be deduced from 'Als i me rode . . .'. The passage helps explain why, even in enclosed *chansons* where feminine monologue is uncontested by a narrator, it is difficult for the other to be 'seen' as other than the 'Partid' figure whose 'confessioun' implies guilt.

It is not so paradoxical that those male-authored 'female complaints' which make explicit the presence of an observer should be those which have it in them to be most intelligent about the feminine:

[2] 9. 162–532, ed. Bergen, iii. 923–33.

From off a hill whose concaue wombe reworded,
A plaintfull story from a sistring vale
My spirrits t' attend this doble voyce accorded,
And downe I laid to list the sad tun'd tale,
Ere long espied a fickle maid full pale
Tearing of papers, breaking rings atwaine,
Storming her world with sorrowes wind and raine.

No sooner does the narrator of *A Louers Complaint* 'espy' the speaker than she is defined as morally 'variable' ('fickle' like medieval Fortune). Full of opposites, she is young but wrinkled with 'sear'd age', 'Her haire nor loose nor ti'd' displays both 'careless[ness]' and 'pride'. Shakespeare's 'ymage' may not be the bifold 'monstruous' thing recorded by Lydgate, but its body-straining distortions—vehement gestures, eyeballs spinning like planets, 'shriking ... wo, | In clamours of all size both high and low'—are disconcerting as well as antithetical. The question the poet raises, more consciously than Lydgate, is how much of this fickleness lies in the eye of the beholder. For the Shakespeare Concordance associates 'fickle' not only with 'Fortune' and false femininity, but derangement of the senses, particularly sight. Faulconbridge, for instance, scorns the 'outward eye of fickle France' and Henry IV speaks of 'some fine colour, that may please the eye | Of fickle Changelings'.[3] 'Fickleness' emerges in the 'I', or between the 'eye' (a quibbling equivalent) and its 'object'; the state of being 'variable' is integral to the means by which an 'ymage' is perceived. Complaint becomes a kind of *Myrroure* writing because its phenomenal field is specular—seen through what Sonnet 126 condensedly calls a 'fickle glass'.

An exchange in *Troylus and Cressida*, III. iii, points up the antiquity and continued centrality of specular theses. Drawing on an unnamed book, Ulysses asserts that 'man ... Cannot make boast to haue that which he hath; | Nor feeles not what he owes, but by reflection' (1949–52), and Achilles responds with an idea that goes back to Plato's *Alcibiades*, 132 D–E: 'speculation turnes not to it selfe, | Till it hath trauail'd, and is mirrored there | Where it may see it selfe'.[4] Self-confirming 'speculation' resembles sight. 'Imaginative' in an etymological sense (*imago* as 'mirror'), it is subject, Ulysses adds, to what it 'receiues and renders backe'. Where is the feminine in this process? The exchange lends force to the claim, radically formulated by Irigaray in *Speculum de l'autre femme*, that 'man''s thought since Plato (*Alcibiades*, 132 D–E, is cited)[5] has fabricated 'women' as other, images reflected into life rather than possessors of the gaze-directing 'eye' from which 'man' is confirmed. 'Woman', in this view, 'has no gaze, no discourse

---

[3] *The Life and Death of King Iohn*, II. i (904); *The First Part of Henry the Fourth*, V. i (2712–13).
[4] 1961–3; 'mirrored' is the standard emendation of Q/F 'married'.
[5] Trans. Gillian C. Gill, *Speculum of the Other Woman* (Ithaca, 1985), 327 n. 47.

for her specific specularization that would allow her to identify with herself (as same)—to return into the self—or break free of the natural specular process that now holds her'.[6] Certainly when 'woman' changes her mind in Shakespeare, allows herself to appear 'fickle' ('tauht' by 'Nature', shaped by 'natural specular process'), the result can be a fracture in being, a 'doubilnesse' articulated by the dislocation in male identity both dependent and visited upon her:

> O madnesse of discourse!
> That cause sets vp, with, and against [it selfe,
> By-fould] authoritie: where reason can reuolt
> Without perdition, and losse assume all reason,
> Without reuolt. This is, and is not, *Cressid* ...   (3139–43)

Troilus' fraught seeing—in this most extreme 'espying' of a 'fickle maid', outside Calchas' tent—of his and another man's object ('this is *Diomids Cressida* ... *Cressid* is mine', 3134, 3151) is 'doubil'. Any 'cause' uttered by or for this other would be 'Partid', because 'authoritie' (in the enclosing frame) perceives the figure as seamlessly 'By-fould'. Troilus acknowledges that this division is inward as well as perceived, registering the reflective self-recognition that

> Within my soule, there doth conduce a fight
> Of this strange nature, that a thing inseperate,
> Diuides more wider then the skie and earth:
> And yet the spacious bredth of this diuision,
> Admits no Orifex for a point as subtle
> As *Ariachnes* broken woofe to enter ...   (3144–9)

Applying a feminine image to himself, Troilus conflates Arachne with Ariadne. One school of theory, tangled in his eyestrings (*theoria*, 'looking at ... speculation'), takes this crux's 'mind-twisting reversal of the sexes' as saying more about tropes than gender, construes '*Ariachnes* ... woofe' as an 'aporetical figure in Shakespeare's tapestry of citations ... merging an image of the clue to the pattern with an image of the breaking and loss of the pattern'.[7] This risks overlooking the perplexity of who has abandoned whom. Left in that isolation from which (to recall Barthes) 'the other's absence' is 'utter[ed]', Troilus finds a thread of mythically 'female' experience in his hand. However 'feminized', though, he remains male, and the man of legend tied to Arachne/Ariadne is the Theseus who, with the latter's thread in his hand, got in and out of the labyrinth and, eventually,

---

[6] Irigaray, *Speculum*, trans. Gill, 224.

[7] J. Hillis Miller, 'Ariachne's Broken Woof', *Georgia Review*, 31 (1977), 44–60, at p. 57; Elizabeth Freund, ' "Ariachne's Broken Woof": The Rhetoric of Citation in *Troilus and Cressida*', in Patricia Parker and Geoffrey Hartman (eds.), *Shakespeare and the Question of Theory* (London, 1985), 19–36, at p. 20.

abandoned her. Discussing '*Ariachne*', Nancy K. Miller insists on the need
to value Arachne's weaving over Ariadne's anguish—the 'trope' (as she puts
it elsewhere) 'of a *penultimate* masochism, the always renewable figure of
feminine suffering'.[8] She asks, 'When the critic follows the thread handed
to him by the "woman in the text" . . . whose powers do we admire? The
man who entered to kill, or the woman who allowed him to exit alive?'
'Entered to kill' is nicely pejorative, but it may not go far enough:

> Heere I inclos'd from all the world a sunder,
> The Minotaure of shame kept for disgrace:
> The monster of fortune, and the worlds wonder,
> Liu'd cloystred in so desolate a case:
> None but the King might come into the place,
>   With certaine maides that did attend my neede,
>   And he himselfe came guided by a threed.

As Daniel's Rosamond knows, in the plaint reprinted here (477–83), the
tale of Theseus and Ariadne can be 'seen' as casting 'imagined' woman in
the 'monstrous' role of Minotaur—a 'By-fould' figure to be hunted, seduced, destroyed. 'This is familiar Hate to Smile and Kill', cries Adriadne in a
poem by William Cartwright (also reproduced here). For her, in a deathly
conceit, Theseus is 'Proud of two Conquests *Minotaure*, and Me'.

   Though Shakespeare, Daniel, and Cartwright use 'female'-voiced plaint
in ways which raise questions about what is 'seen', they do not relinquish
the overarching male perspective from which that construction takes place.
Perhaps the closest approach to demolishing the received structure comes
in Ephelia's 'Beneath a spreading Willows shade'. The poem, printed
below, comes from a collection of *Female Poems on Several Occasions* (1679)
which includes an admixture of male work;[9] but there is nothing 'doubtful'
about this piece. On the contrary, what it boldly does is place the author's
persona, as plainant, under a willow at the source of a field of sight. Instead
of being found and reported by a masculine 'I', 'kind *Ephelia*' recounts her
story from an angle which ties the narrator to a point of view that starts from
loss. This standing within and without the frame might be less commanding
than being in dominant view of an other subject/object, but it combines a
version of the 'authoritative' position with inward knowledge of what
belongs (in a poem like 'Early one morning . . .') to the recessed 'remove'.
Remarkably, however, though Ephelia tells us that 'her Faithless Swain',

---

   [8] 'Arachnologies: The Woman, the Text, and the Critic', in Nancy K. Miller (ed.), *The Poetics of Gender* (New York, 1986), 270–95, at pp. 282–6; ' "I's" in Drag: The Sex of Recollection', *The Eighteenth Century*, 22 (1981), 47–57, at p. 56.
   [9] See e.g. *Kissing the Rod: An Anthology of Seventeenth-Century Women's Verse*, ed. Germaine Greer, Susan Hastings, Jeslyn Medoff, and Melinda Sansone (London, 1988), 279. Contrast Maureen Mulvihill, ' "Ephelia" (fl. *c.*1678–82)', in Janet Todd (ed.), *Dictionary of British Women Writers* (London, 1989), 227–8.

Strephon, wooed a new love on a 'neighb'ring Plain', she does not do so with reference to the one sense which might reveal this—sight. For discovery to be made, Strephon has to lead his acquisition 'near | Th' Unlucky, Fatal Willow' where Ephelia sits, and even so is heard, not seen. Ephelia's response to betrayal, moreover, is to make a spectacle of herself ('rudely tar[ing] | Her Garland first, and then her Hair') before beginning to speak. It is as though abandonment can be visualized from the stance of Ephelia-as-reporter, but not through Ephelia-in-the-poem's eyes. The controlling perspectives of 'female complaint' begin to seem male, regardless of attributed gender. The plainant (as in this poem) will be 'seen' but does not appear to look, and she operates instead through the faculty in which women are supposedly expert—too much so, sexist cliché would say—that of speech. It is from the energy of sight, back to the power of what is said and heard, that we now must turn.

5. A Louers Complaint

Another scenario, or the same. Wooed by a youth of charm and breeding, and bound to him by vows and tokens—though not as yet by church ceremony—a maiden succumbs and is seduced. We meet her in the company of a 'reuerend man' whose comforting presence elicits admissions of guilt. The aura of 'confessioun' is, though, partly misleading. For the spiritual 'father' is not what he seems, but a man of public affairs who has fled the 'ruffle' of court for the sake of reflective detachment. As the unhappy character describes her sensual fault, it becomes touchingly apparent that she still loves the youth who caused her fall. In keeping with his role, the 'reuerend man' urges her to distinguish penitence from fear of shame. 'I doe confesse it, and repent it (Father)', she says: 'I doe repent me, as it is an euill, | And take the shame with ioy.' For this is not the 'fickle maid' of *A Louers Complaint*, or at all events not only her, but Juliet in *Measure for Measure*, II. iii (985, 991–2), confessing the affair with Claudio.

Now that *A Louers Complaint* has been recovered from Chapman and wrested from Shakespeare's juvenilia,[1] it begins to relate to a series of middle-period plays. Connections between the false youth and Bertram have been remarked, along with the shared predicament of Desdemona, Ophelia, and 'fickle maid'.[2] More striking than congruities in character, though, is the spiritual density of the poem and its reliance on confessional

---

[1] See the work of Kenneth Muir, MacD. P. Jackson, and Eliot Slater listed by Kerrigan in *Sonnets and 'A Lover's Complaint'*, 66.

[2] Roger Warren, 'Why Does it End Well? Helena, Bertram, and the Sonnets', *Shakespeare Survey*, 22 (1969), 79–92; ' "A Lover's Complaint", "All's Well", and the Sonnets', *Notes and Queries*, 215 (1970), 130–2; Underwood, *Shakespeare on Love*, 66–73, 76–8; *Sonnets and 'A Lover's Complaint'*, ed. Kerrigan, 393–4.

monologue—traits which associate it with Elsinore and Angelo's Vienna. When Claudius disgorges his crimes in the chapel, or Hamlet turns his mother's eyes into her soul, or Laertes forgives the Prince for killing Polonius (his sins already remembered in Ophelia's orisons, or at least in her plaintful ballads), tragedy takes shape around a set of penitential situations. And when *Measure for Measure* enmeshes its characters in moral perplexity, contriving 'cases of conscience' as delicate as anything in William Ames and Jeremy Taylor, it does so in a context established by the Duke's close listening, judging, blessing, and absolving—by his maintaining even when not disguised as a 'reuerend man' the role and authority of confessor. The Prince is a kind of anti-Duke: his soliloquies are open and subject to the world of the play, yet at crucial junctures (such as the chapel scene) the motives of others are opaque to him. Vincentio, more intrusively, agitates souls to provoke confession. He comes nearer than anyone else in the comedy to rooting out people's motives, yet his soliloquies are inflexibly apophthegmic, as though nothing he hears does more than reinforce the assurance with which, in the final act, he judges and absolves. In *A Louers Complaint*, where the 'reuerend man' is a decisive catalyst but not a figure whose personality colours the poem, something close to unimpeded confession unfolds, and the psychological complexities of that process are, in greater detail than in the plays, explored.

Given the views of Luther and Calvin, the status of 'confessioun' for Shakespeare's audience and readers might seem predictable. But the Duke's disguise is theologically complicated. He may act under false pretences, but Protestant doctrine makes him as effective as any 'reuerend man' so long as he incites remorse—which he evidently does with Juliet. Luther said that a sinner could be reconciled by 'a brother or a neighbour . . . in the house or in the fields',[3] a statement which must affect one's view of the 'fickle maid' 's outburst to her local herdsman, leaning on his 'greyned bat'. Auden's quip, 'since the British Isles went Protestant | A church confession is too high for most', is true, yet not so deeply as what follows: 'still confession is a human want.'[4] Many Elizabethans sought such help from their pastors, who were required by the *Boke of Common Prayer* to urge communicants with unquiet consciences to 'come to me, or some other discrete and learned minister' for 'gostly counsail, aduise, and comfort'.[5] Perhaps surprisingly, the Sarum formula for absolution survives through the 1549, 1552, and 1661 versions of 'The Ordre for the Visitacion of the

---

[3] Quoted from the *Babylonian Captivity* by John Bossy, 'The Social History of Confession in the Age of the Reformation', *Transactions of the Royal Historical Society*, 5th ser. 25 (1975), 21–38, at p. 27.

[4] 'Letter to Lord Byron', in *The English Auden: Poems, Essays and Dramatic Writings 1927–1939*, ed. Edward Mendelson (London, 1977), 169.

[5] *The English Rite: Being a Synopsis of the Sources and Revisions of the Book of Common Prayer*, ed. F. E. Brightman, 2 vols. (London, 1915), ii. 673.

Sicke'.[6] The persistence of Catholic beliefs, and that 'popular Pelagianism' upon which elevated arguments about 'justification' hardly impinged,[7] contributed to a state in which confession was an understood, if not always accepted, spiritual benefit. 'Most of the clergy felt wistful about the disappearance of the confessional',[8] and, while few in the Established Church would have accepted the kind of sacerdotal claims which emerged among Laudians, there was sympathy with the view that a 'reuerend man' could assist a sinner's reconciliation.

As its title insists, *A Louers Complaint* is amorous. Whatever the importance of 'confessioun' and repentance elsewhere, this poem is about love. Yet here is a concealed source, in Spenser's part of Van der Noot's *A Theatre for Worldlings*:

> Hard by a rivers side, a wailing Nimphe,
> Folding hir armes with thousand sighs to heauen
> Did tune hir plaint to falling rivers sound,
> Renting hir faire visage and golden haire,
> Where is (quod she) this whilome honored face?
> Where is thy glory and the auncient praise,
> Where all worldes hap was reposed,
> When erst of Gods and man I worship was?[9]

The speaker is Rome, in a sonnet derived from Du Bellay, expressing for Protestant readers both the 'monstruous' nature and wished-for 'regret' of that city of Antichrist. Her plaint, compressing into fifteen lines concerns developed in *The Ruines of Time*, contributes to a cycle of texts which culminates in a vision of the heavenly city. This grounding in scriptural poetry helps explain why 'feind' and 'Cherubin', 'grace' and 'tempter', should resonate so powerfully in Shakespeare's poem, and why it should be interested in such Church questions as—further reminder of *Measure for Measure*—convent life, a seduced and 'sacred Nunne'. But *A Theatre for Worldlings* also matters because of its emblematic method. Each of the sonnets begins from a crude but effective woodcut. Rome in 'Hard by a rivers side' is a woeful maid (Fig. 2), seated in a semi-rustic landscape, city conventionally in the background,[10] arms crossed in a posture of grievance.

---

[6] Ibid. 828–9.

[7] See e.g. Christopher Haigh, 'The Continuity of Catholicism in the English Reformation', in Haigh (ed.), *The English Reformation Revised* (Cambridge, 1987), 176–208, esp. p. 180; P. G. Lake, 'Calvinism and the English Church 1570–1635', *Past and Present*, 114 (1978), 32–76, at p. 33.

[8] Keith Thomas, *Religion and the Decline of Magic: Studies in Popular Beliefs in Sixteenth- and Seventeenth-Century England* (1971; repr. Harmondsworth, 1978), 187.

[9] *The Yale Edition of the Shorter Poems of Edmund Spenser*, Sonnet 8, ed. William A. Oram *et al.* (New Haven, 1989), 477. The 1569 title-page is strenuously religious: *A Theatre wherein Be Represented as wel the Miseries and Calamities that Follow the Voluptuous Worldlings, as also the Greate Ioyes and Plesures which the Faithfull Do Enioy*. Cf. *The Visions of Bellay*, 10.

[10] The scene reconstructs, by symbolic means, a familiar locus; see e.g. the Marian lament 'As

2. Rome, from Jan van der Noot, trans. Edmund Spenser, *A Theatre for Worldlings* (1569)

Spenser's sonnet is read as the voice of this 'ymage'; perception moves from eye to tacit ear. The 'fickle maid' is depicted in a similar way, by use of the scheme called 'icon', in Shakespeare's opening stanzas. His blocks of visual description provide an 'ymage' as distorted, expressive, and thick with information as anything in Ripa's *Iconologia*. The maid offers an emblem of grief before engaging the reader with her 'sad tun'd tale'.

Like Spenser's Rome, moreover, she inhabits 'a theatre for worldlings'. Set between 'concaue wombe' and 'sistring vale', 'reworded' by echoes, the speaker has been placed in an arena of the kind described by Bacon: 'Where echoes come from several parts at the same distance, they must needs make (as it were) a quire of echoes, and so make the report greater, and even a continued echo; which you shall find in some hills that stand encompassed, theatre-like.'[11] There might even be a deep coincidence between ruined Rome and this kind of 'theatre', given that Renaissance editions of Vitruvius

Reson Rywlyde my Rechyles mynde', in *Religious Lyrics of the XVth Century*, ed. Carleton Brown (Oxford, 1939), 8–13, at ll. 5–6: 'I met a mayde at þe citeys ende, | snobbynge & syȝynge sche wes ny schente'.

[11] *Sylva Sylvarum*, Century 3. 253, in *Works*, ed. Spedding *et al.*, ii. 428.

engrave images of classical architecture reverting to decay, sprigged with trees and grasses, as though crossed with guide-books to the dilapidated city.[12] Admittedly *De architectura* urges that resonance be cultivated in theatres to the exclusion of distracting echoes. During the Renaissance, however, the treatise was read with a difference and echoes were judged attractive: 'Vitruvian architecture was not thought to have aimed at acoustic purity per se, but at effects more baroque.'[13] Echo scenes, widely current in court entertainments, and prized among *cognoscenti* after the device's success in Guarini's *Pastor Fido* (1589), reinforced the connection between 'rewording' and the dramatic idea. While our first reaction to the maid's 'doble voyce' might be to recall those plaints in which the speaker calls upon other lovers to lend their voices in a chorus of grief,[14] early readers, attuned to the theatricality of the genre,[15] might have thought in terms of a well-known playwright writing for a paper stage.

The literature of echoes does not, in any case, begin with Renaissance Vitruvius. In Virgil the riverbank famously reverberates Orpheus' dying song; Ovid's Ariadne hears the seashore answer 'Theseus'.[16] An ample medieval corpus lies behind Albanact's obscurity in the *Myrroure*: 'With Ecco so did halfe his wordes rebounde, | That scarce at first the sence might well appeare.'[17] Bound up with Fame and Rumour, 'Ecco' could connote confusions running deeper than acoustic muddle. Fama, in *Metamorphoses*, 12, lives in a house of sounding brass which repeats and doubles ('refert iteratque') what it hears (46–7). When Warwick assures Henry IV that the number of rebels is exaggerated, he quibblingly says: 'Rumor doth double, like the Voice, and Eccho, | The numbers of the feared.'[18] Where does this leave the 'doble voyce' heard in Shakespeare's printed 'quire of echoes', the quarto of 1609? However enticingly they strike the ear—quasi-theatrical resonance making the reader an eager listener—the plaintful maid's words are registered as difficult and potentially false. Writing about American popular culture, Lauren Berlant declares:

To the extent that women employ the complaint as a mode of self-expression, it is an admission and a recognition both of privilege and powerlessness: it is a powerful

---

[12] See e.g. the elevations used in 5. 6, 'De conformatione theatri faciendi' and 'Della conformatione del Theatro', of the Venetian *De Architectvra Libri Decem* (1567) and *I Dieci Libri Dell' Architettvra*, ed. and trans. Daniel Barbaro (1584).

[13] Joseph Loewenstein, *Responsive Readings: Versions of Echo in Pastoral, Epic, and the Jonsonian Masque* (New Haven, 1984), 59.

[14] e.g. the opening lines of Surrey's 'Complaint of the Absence of her Louer . . .' (below, p. 126).

[15] Cf. Jane Shore's 'so step I on the stage . . .' (in the 1587 prose link, given in *Mirror*, ed. Campbell, 372); Thomas Middleton, *The Ghost of Lucrece*, A3^{r-v}, C3^r.

[16] *Georgics*, 4. 523–7; *Heroides*, 10. 17–24.

[17] *Parts Added*, ed. Campbell, 45.

[18] *The Second Part of Henry the Fourth*, III. i (1517–18).

record of patriarchal oppression, circumscribed by a knowledge of woman's inevitable delegitimation within the patriarchal public sphere . . .

For it is not the woman who first calls her self-articulation a complaint, a whine, a plea: rather, the patriarchal social context in which she makes her utterance hystericizes it for her, even before she speaks.[19]

Unpack 'hystericizes' and you find (as early readers knew through Latin) ὑστέρα, 'concaue wombe'. Shakespeare indicates that the 'context' of the maid's 'utterance' pre-emptively endangers what is said. The received landscape of complaint (realm of Spenser, William Browne) takes a 'voyce' and makes it 'doble', generating pathos but exposing 'woman''s grievance to dismissal as 'babling Gossip'. Just as Shakespeare presents the (as yet unknown) 'maid' as 'fickle', 'By-fould', 'monstrous'—ostentatiously following convention to cast doubt on its perspective—so he brings out the problematic way in which a plaining 'woman' will be heard. The speaker does not 'call her self-articulation' *A Louers Complaint*; it is the poet, figured in the 'I', and 'reuerend man'—evidence of the 'patriarchal' sphere (of labour, ministry, and writing) around her—who bring definition to what is heard.

Yet the situation (this being Shakespeare) is more complicated. For any voice, echoing, might properly invite doubt. Near the start of the Act III temptation scene, Othello says to Iago, 'thou ecchos't me; | As if there were some Monster in thy thought' (1713–14)—echoing, by any measure, calculated to deceive. It is important to recognize the subtlety of the possible falsehood. 'From off a hill whose concaue wombe reworded . . .' The *Oxford English Dictionary* gives no clear instance before the nineteenth century of 'reworded' meaning (as we use it) 'put into different words'. But that is not what echoes do. They pluck words out of context and return them partially, entering dialogue at an inopportune moment, or with a hollowness which rings like doubt. '*Words reported againe have as another sound, so another sense*', Montaigne notes.[20] Even if the 'fickle maid' reports truth, she might not report 'the whole truth' (whatever that means), or the circumstances which make it so. We should resist the prompting of 'doble' either wholly to credit what she says or to judge her account mendacious. Apart from anything else, too much clarity would overlook the speaker's desire to recover in monologue the pleasures of lost intercourse, bending his and her words into a harmony which makes each seem to cite the other.

During Shakespeare's lifetime 'report' could be used in both music and poetry to mean 'echo', as in Breton's 'Report Song in a Dreame, Betweene a Sheepheard and his Nimph'. This reinforces the conceptual aptness of the 'fickle maid' 's resonant setting for the 'reworded' speech of the youth.

[19] 'The Female Complaint', *Social Text*, 19–20 (1988), 237–59, at p. 243.
[20] *Essays*, trans. Florio, introd. L. C. Harmer, 3 vols. (London, 1965), iii. 321.

But the chiming of landscape with 'report' cannot substitute for missing testimony. Iago's half-truths must become full lies to rationalize his 'rewording', because drama accommodates those alternative points of view which challenge him. In *A Louers Complaint*, by contrast, the partiality and irresolution of monologue prevent truth and falsehood being tested. The poem moves in a sphere of credibility and credulity, where suasive words hold sway. Rhetoric is part of the 'question' as well as the vehicle of this poem. As she recites the gilded words with which the youth, it is said, betrayed her, the maiden dazzlingly persuades us to mistrust only somewhat less her own persuasion. The compounding of voice furthers this; especially in the 1609 edition, where lines are not distributed between speakers by inverted commas, the 'maiden tongu'd' plainant (to use her description of him of her) loses herself in the youth's eloquence, becomes a mouthpiece of his duplicity. The very title contributes: Elizabethan and Jacobean usage weights 'Louer' so heavily towards the male that early readers must have felt the poem delivering its promise as the young man's discourse emerged.[21] As the quarto pages turn, the initial woodcut-like impression fades, and the reader becomes absorbed in argument.

Characterized even physically by images of rhetorical accomplishment (she has 'haire' that 'Proclaimd', his 'termlesse skin' confidently 'brag'd'), the lovers come to seem almost aspects of what is said. To this extent resembling Lucrece, the 'fickle maid' has none of the hinted reserves (for all her possible rationalizing) which allow us to divine shadowy depths in the characters of mature Shakespeare. Almost a parody of the Ciceronian orator, she presents her 'cause' in disarray rather than with 'countenance ... comelilie and orderlie composed', 'the eyes verie diligentlie' disciplined.[22] Certainly the youth, by the maid's report, has an inner life inseparable from the fertility of rhetorical invention:

> In him a plenitude of subtle matter,
> Applied to Cautills, all straing formes receiues,
> Of burning blushes, or of weeping water,
> Or sounding palenesse: and he takes and leaues,
> In eithers aptnesse as it best deceiues ...   (302–6)

'Matter', 'straing formes', 'aptnesse' are words which, in Shakespeare, bear on art. With such terms forward, the poem plots the realization of argument as well as an unhappy love story. Starting from significant but inexplicit objects ('A thousand fauours ... Of amber, christall and of bedded Iet'), it offers increasingly legible tokens—'Posied gold and bone', 'letters sadly

---

[21] Cf. *Sonnets and 'A Lover's Complaint'*, ed. Kerrigan, 393, on the broadside *A Louers Complaint Being Forsaken of his Loue* (probably a source); further 'Louers Complaint' poems with masculine personae can be found in e.g. Breton's *Bower* and *Arbor* (three in this miscellany alone).

[22] Fraunce, *Arcadian Rhetorike*, K1ʳ⁻ᵛ, citing Sidney's woeful Gynecia in useful parallel.

pend in blood'—until the maid begins to speak, and what we have seen is explained. Acoustically the enclosed chime and final couplet of rhyme royal, rising to a moment of fullness within the stanza before furthering the voice to a pointed or elegiac conclusion, give definition to what is declared. That tendency to refrain and keening repetition which had been part of complaint since Old English secures longer rhythms of persuasion, voiced through seven-line units which the breath can just sustain into completed arcs of sound. Not least because of the legal language which stiffens the poem, the plaintful lover's voice ('male' and/or 'female') seems to precipitate, in the quarto's 'folded schedulls', a 'bill' or 'testament' of the kind presented at a Parliament of Love, or ecclesiastical court, before the 'fickle maid' is roused to the almost operatic vehemence of her conclusion.

This movement towards clarity should not be overstated. The 'deepe brain'd sonnets' at the heart of the poem, which, along with tears, desire, pride, and a set of more obscure motives, prompt the maiden's downfall,[23] remain as unread as the 'Posied' rings and 'letters . . . pend in blood' which are, in the opening stanzas, broken, torn, and flung into the mire. Whereas letters are printed in *A Myrroure for Magistrates* to advance and authenticate the narrative, epistolary 'contents' are no more than implied in *A Louers Complaint*. Even the 'Napkin' strayed in from the world of *Othello*, whose 'conceited charecters' the maid is 'often reading' as the poem begins, goes unglossed. Initially a reader might feel that only an arrogantly 'fickle maid' would discard such pricey and heartfelt tokens as gold rings, blood-written letters, and the equivalent of a Gucci scarf. Sympathy follows, when we learn how they have been emotionally traded, but it cannot be secure. Rather as when Troilus rends Cressida's letter in Shakespeare's play, the maiden's rage is understandable but (by concealing evidence) troubling. On the other hand, in quasi-legal terms, the tokens also damage the accused. The gift of a ring was often thought to seal an agreement of pre-contract.[24] The 'fickle maid''s submission to the youth, after his granting of the tokens, takes her closer to the pregnant Juliet's situation than might at first appear. And, of course, the tokens are erotic. Gifts laden with erotic associations are ubiquitous in complaint (especially its pastoral variety), where they are hoarded as substitutes for the lover. Throwing them away is a painful expiation. Oenone's 'Bracelets' of Paris's 'hair', in the Ovidian paraphrase by Aphra Behn reproduced here, are a typical synecdoche. Silvio's 'Faun', with bell and chain, in Marvell's 'Nymph Complaining . . .' (also printed), carries animation of the gift to a bizarre extreme.

Destroying these tokens might, even so, be wise. Rings, sonnets, and

[23] *Sonnets and 'A Louers Complaint'*, ed. Kerrigan, 17–18.
[24] Ralph A. Houlbrooke, *Church Courts and the People During the English Reformation, 1520–1570* (Oxford, 1979), 60–1.

papers can charm as ominously as a young man's tears. When the maid cries, 'Oh father, what a hell of witch-craft lies, | In the small orb of one perticular teare' (288–9), her metaphors are not idle. Egeus in *A Midsommer Nights Dreame* claims that Demetrius has 'bewitch'd' Hermia with 'bracelets of thy haire, rings, gawdes', while Brabantio says that Othello ('Damn'd as thou art') has 'enchaunted' Desdemona 'with foule Charmes ... Drugs or Minerals' and 'witch-craft'.[25] Both are wrong, but audiences would not have found their beliefs absurd.[26] The 'fickle maid' calls the youth—more than 'Damn'd'—a 'feind' (317), and there is a suggestive parallel to his speaking through her in the African belief that a jilted girl will sicken—be 'full pale', wrenched in limbs, eyeballs rolling—because she has been 'entered' by the spirit of her lover.[27] For early readers, the 'reuerend man' would be in a position resembling that of an exorcist. Like Dr Pinch in *The Comedie of Errors* and the Master Parson sent to cure Malvolio, however, he confronts a state of mind in which possession ('Lo, how hollow the fiend speakes within him ... Pray God he be not bewitch'd') blurs into mental illness ('he's mad').[28] Discussing the changes modifying African ideas of 'entering', I M Lewis explains that 'young western-educated Somalis today describe such cases of young women's possession, in the Shakespearian idiom of "love-sickness" '.[29] The 'fickle maid' belongs to a period in which supernatural explanations were giving way to a recognizably medical analysis of the 'loveris maladye | of Hereos',[30] as she demonstrates by invoking, after 'witch-craft', physicians' argot to describe the youth's tears. It is language advanced enough to anticipate the *Oxford English Dictionary* on 'drop' by a hundred and twenty years:[31] 'our drops this diffrence bore, | His poison'd me, and mine did him restore' (300–1). The tears are not just (in Brabantio's phrase) 'Drugs or Minerals' in liquid form. They are 'infected moysture' (323), and the maid, drinking them through eager eyes, becomes a *Diseased Maiden Lover*. In the ballad-title 'diseased' means 'disturbed, robbed of *ease*'; but the idea of 'love-sickness' is not excluded. Making greater play with visible symptoms of distress, Shakespeare's maid 'complains' in a sense emergent in Jacobean English ('To give sign of physical suffering or pain'),[32] so that his title-word *Complaint* begins to claim—what

---

[25] I. i (35–46); I. ii–iii (281–93, 397–401).

[26] Cf. e.g. Middleton's *The Witch*, II. ii, where Almachildes wins Amoretta by thrusting a charmed ribbon into her bosom, promptly losing her when it is dropped.

[27] I. M. Lewis, *Ecstatic Religion: A Study of Shamanism and Spirit Possession*, 2nd edn. (London, 1989), 65.

[28] *Twelfe Night, Or What You Will*, III. iv (1614, 1624, 1658).

[29] *Ecstatic Religion*, 66.

[30] Michael MacDonald, *Mystical Bedlam: Madness, Anxiety, and Healing in Seventeenth-Century England* (Cambridge, 1981), 149, 198–231; see above, pp. 5–6.

[31] Cf. *Sonnets and 'A Lover's Complaint'*, ed. Kerrigan, 422.

[32] *OED*, s.v., verb, 4a.

again the dictionary does not pick up until a century later—the meaning 'bodily ailment, indisposition, disorder'.

There was no shortage of 'diseased' maids. The casebooks of Richard Napier, a clergyman and physician who treated more than two thousand patients between 1597 and 1643, show that 'Lover's quarrels, unrequited love, and double-dealing accounted for the emotional turmoil of 141 persons, about two-thirds of whom were young women.'[33] In every class ('Jilted lovers', 'Seduced and betrayed', 'Marriage broken off'), women come out worse than men in his notes. 'Desertion by the male partner' was 'a classic' form of family disintegration; the seduction and banishment of female servants was frequent; 'a host' of those lodging near the Globe, in Southwark, were single women, pregnant or with children.[34] Complaint for many was a descant to begging in the streets. Affluent readers of cony-catching pamphlets learnt to mistrust the 'miserable complainte' of 'manerly' beggars, the vagabond women who 'wyll most lamentably demaunde your charity, and wyll quickly shed salte teares, they be so tender harted'.[35] A few of those 'Left' could mourn in security, like Mariana in the moated grange, 'bestow'd . . . on her owne lamentation, which she yet wears for [Angelo's] sake'.[36] Others were desperate, and suicide was a real possibility:[37] what the Gaoler's daughter attempts and is rescued from in *The Two Noble Kinsmen* (IV. i), and what Ophelia succeeds in doing (unless the water came to her), is a risk which the stream-haunting 'fickle maid' runs.

Many doctors perceived the correlation between women's experience and mental distress. Like the physician who attends the Gaoler's Daughter, they decided that disappointed love caused 'mopishness' and (higher up the social scale) 'melancholy'. It wasted the blood by overheating it with passion, or drained its vital warmth with grief. Sorrow, wrote Sir Thomas Elyot, is *'the mother and daughter of melancholy'*.[38] His imagery is interesting, since physiological explanation could take a decidedly female turn. Following Edward Jorden's example in *A Briefe Discourse of a Disease Called the Suffocation of the Mother* (1603), some doctors claimed that mental distress was caused by the womb's tendency to wander and come into proximity with the heart. Men could be afflicted with what Lear calls *'Hysterica passio'*, the

---

[33] *Mystical Bedlam*, 88–9.

[34] A. L. Beier, *Masterless Men: The Vagrancy Problem in England 1560–1640* (London, 1985), 52, 25; Paul Slack, *Poverty and Policy in Tudor and Stuart England* (London, 1988), 103.

[35] John Awdeley (?), *The Fraternitye of Vacabondes* (1575), A3ᵛ–4ʳ; Thomas Harman, *A Caueat for Commen Cursetors Vulgarly Called Vagabondes* (1567), C2ʳ.

[36] *Measure for Measure*, III. i (1446–50).

[37] Michael MacDonald, 'The Inner Side of Wisdom: Suicide in Early Modern England', *Psychological Medicine*, 7 (1977), 565–82, esp. pp. 569, 580; cf. Richard L. Greaves, *Society and Religion in Elizabethan England* (Minneapolis, 1981), 531–7, esp. p. 536.

[38] *Castle of Helth* (1541), fo. 64; quoted by Lawrence Babb, *The Elizabethan Malady: A Study of Melancholia in English Literature from 1580–1642* (East Lansing, 1951), 24.

'Mother' that 'swels vp toward my heart',[39] but the illness was typically female. Gynaecological disorders, especially those associated with child-birth, were so wretchedly frequent that disturbance of the uterus became only too ready an explanation for unruly or depressive behaviour in women. When Berlant writes of the complaining female voice being 'hystericized', the term can be given a literal edge. The voice of Shakespeare's discon-solate maid reaches us from a 'concaue wombe' which is somatic in connotation.

Fetishes of lost love, insidiously charmed, the 'fickle maid' 's tokens are still more deeply involved with what Lydgate and Lyndsay call 'confes-sioun'. Raffaele Pettazzoni has pointed out both that sexual irregularity is '*The* sin, the sin which takes the first place in confession among uncivilised peoples', and that 'Confession is continually linked to eliminatory prac-tices'—to purging, vomiting, discarding, and impassioned expression 'in the proper sense of the Latin *exprimere*, to press out, to extract by pressure'.[40] Construed from this angle, *A Louers Complaint* deals with the primal matter of confessional utterance, reified in emotionally charged tokens and in a clotted rhetoric thickened by guilt, vented before its 'reuerend man'. The almost visceral impulse to 'confessioun' is, of course, not unrelated to the poem's quasi-legal language. As the Catechism of Trent makes clear, a confessor will decide before offering absolution whether the penitent has inwardly earned it. 'Penance' is a 'tribunal' inciting 'self-accusation'; but 'priests are, evidently, appointed judges of the matter'.[41] The pronounce-ments of Trent on this subject, though scarcely approved reading in Shakespeare's England, are instructive. Because of changes in confession associated with the name of Cardinal Borromeo—away from public shriving towards the analytic privacy of the confessional—Catholic writings become peculiarly alert to the way a sinner's psychology can recoil to her or his undoing. Not that Protestants needed telling that repentance was difficult to sustain. In a sermon called *Loues Complaint*, preached in the year that Shakespeare's poem was published, William Holbrooke declared 'Without repentance, damnation' and urged his auditor to keep 'always before thine eyes, and in thy heart' such plaintful exemplars as Christ's tears over Jerusalem, the weeping 'people of God in *Ezekiels* time', and Jeremiah's laments.[42] It was, and is, no simple matter genuinely to repent. And in Shakespeare's poem the final stanzas show regret in danger of unravelling itself. Many plaints have the same shape; a loved object is dismissed, only for desire to surge back. Only rarely, however, does the presence of a

---

[39] II. iv (1328–9), emending '*Historica*'.

[40] *Essays on the History of Religions*, trans. H. J. Rose (Leiden, 1967), 49–50.

[41] *The Catechism of the Council of Trent*, trans. J. Donovan (Dublin, 1829), 'On the Sacrament of Penance', 251–95, at pp. 272–3.

[42] 3 Dec. 1609, Paul's Cross, published 1610, C4^{r-v}.

crypto-clerical interlocutor seal the analogy with thwarted repentance.[43]

More vividly than any previous poem, *A Louers Complaint* dramatizes the emotional difficulties of 'confessioun'. Those tokens, shattered and cast aside, are laden with associations which stir the love regretted. Since to shed them is to throw part of oneself, and the other, away, the spirit revolts at purgation. The maid's language then 'expresses' a dangerous element of eroticism, betraying (since contrition should be dumbstruck)[44] the repentance it advances; self-accusation, requiring 'report' (an insistence on the individual 'cause', entailing that 'doble voyce'), also fosters remembrance until, in the closing phase of the poem, recapitulation becomes re-capitulation: 'Aye me I fell, and yet do question make, | What I should doe againe for such a sake' (321–2). The Tridentine authorities warn against 'The pride of some, who seek by vain excuses to justify or extenuate their offences'.[45] But Shakespeare refuses to disentangle self-justification ('Who young and simple would not be so louerd?') from the intractable problem of honesty. To be true to her experience (seeking spiritual 'reconciliation'), the 'fickle maid' must recoil into a rapt subjectivity which excludes us:

> O that infected moysture of his eye,
> O that false fire which in his cheeke so glowd:
> O that forc'd thunder from his heart did flye,
> O that sad breath his spungie lungs bestowed,
> O all that borrowed motion seeming owed,
> Would yet againe betray the fore-betrayed,
> And new peruert a reconciled Maide.   (323–9)

Hence the disappearance of the narrating 'I' and 'reuerend man' in Shakespeare's almost unparalleled refusal to close the frame, and the felt pointlessness of complaint: both lamentation's crying over the irreversible (its not advancing the speaker to acceptance but intensifying her loss), and the text's failure to draw a moral.

'All *de casibus* complaints include a homiletic admonition, prominently placed at the conclusion of the tale', declares a standard account: 'they are exemplary narratives intended to save their readers from misfortune, as well as laments designed to elicit pity.'[46] A train of plaintfulness runs from the *Myrroure* to Shakespeare, yet *A Louers Complaint* is not bound by this didacticism. Unlike *The Diseased Maiden Louer* and the other broadsides, it promulgates no forthright moral. Its heroine stands late in generic history (as surely as Drayton's Matilda and I.C.'s Magdalene, who make this

---

[43] In medieval literature the clearest example is not in English, but Dafydd ap Gwilym's 'Y Bardd a'r Brawd Llywd': *Selected Poems*, trans. Rachel Bromwich, 2nd edn. (Harmondsworth, 1985), 150–3.

[44] For this commonplace see e.g. Chute, *Beawtie Dishonoured Written under the Title of Shores Wife* (1593), E3ᵛ: 'For when true penitence doth begin . . . shame in hidden silence doth conceal.'

[45] *Catechism*, trans. Donovan, 283.   [46] Craun, *'De Casibus* Complaint', 27.

explicit), and she is also, within her poem, placed near the end of a chain of plaintful and hortatory discourses (the 'end' being *A Louers Complaint* itself). Yet these heterogeneous texts—'folded schedulls', 'deepe brain'd sonnets', 'precepts', and the like—either offer fruitless admonition or seduce in ways which depend less on their 'contents' than on love's prompting. The problematic nature of 'example' cuts deep:

> But ah who euer shun'd by precedent,
> The destin'd ill she must her selfe assay,
> Or forc'd examples gainst her owne content
> To put the by-past perrils in her way?
> Counsaile may stop a while what will not stay:
> For when we rage, aduise is often seene
> By blunting vs to make our wits more keene.   (155–61)

The stanza is not just complicated because what it says pre-echoes what the youth has argued: 'When thou impressest what are precepts worth | Of stale example?' (267–8). 'Rage' is a fierce emotion, and the lines are urgent with images of blocking, shoving, and the sharpness of a scheming knife. As the poem reaches this pass, her/his condition seems at once intensely that of linguistic 'doubilnesse' and directed by feelings which reduce words to frippery. A powerful undertow keeps threatening to 'rage' through, and it finally—where 'a homiletic admonition' is most expected—breaks down syntax in exclamation, leaving the poem fully cadenced yet on the edge of incoherence. The poet and 'reuerend man' are swept away by this emergent, dramatically passionate impulse. Shakespeare, though, is alert to 'the connection between apostrophe and embarrassment'.[47] There is more than a hint of absurdity in the maid's invocation of the youth's charms. 'O' this, and 'O' that—woeful for the speaker yet with potentially ludicrous overtones of orgasmic excess—pushes to a point where extremes meet the conventional rhetoric of complaint. In place of articulate 'example', Shakespeare writes towards perplexity. What I.C., Drayton, and the rest sensed when creating their heroines, that they gained force as persuasive individuals by losing exemplary clarity, is transformed by the dramatist into a 'characteristic' truth. Shakespeare the sonneteer considers from another stance an anxiety central to his sequence: can speaking of love ever free one from its tangles? And the 'reuerend man' elicits a monologue inseparable from the 'grammar of repentance'.

[47] See Jonathan Culler, 'Apostrophe', in *The Pursuit of Signs: Semiotics, Literature, Deconstruction* (London, 1981), 135–54, at p. 140.

6. *Complaint Enlarged*

The lively sophistication of Renaissance genre theory has only recently
found an answering subtlety in students of Tudor and Stuart literature.
When Hallett Smith linked *A Louers Complaint* to the 'vogue of complaint
poems about women in the 1590's', he was confirmed in this straitened
perspective by assumptions, very much of his period, which discounted the
rhetoric of kinds for the sake of poems as ends in themselves. Thanks
especially to Alastair Fowler,[1] we now have a more plausibly discursive, as
well as historically variable, sense of the way genre contributed to writing.
Poems belong to kinds or 'species' (to use Renaissance terms) not only by
variation within formulae—relations tending to pastiche and parody—but
through 'family resemblances' which hold between otherwise unlike texts.
Except when dying, genres rarely develop by direct routes. They branch,
revert, and (frequently in the seventeenth century) generate 'mixed' forms.
To say that a poem like *A Louers Complaint* participates in a set of traditions
can imply more about what it leads readers to expect than about its fabrica-
tion from received ingredients. Other works appearing at the same time as
Shakespeare's, and later for at least a century, share traits with his poem
without there being conduits of influence. They do so in ways which shift
the centre of gravity of complaint. The processes of this change are difficult
to chart not least because plaint can behave more like a 'mode' than a
'genre'. As a tone of voice, array of topoi, or local effect of structure—some
way of framing narrative, a lyric hiatus—it contributes to kinds which have
their own family histories.

Lady Mary Wroth's prose romance *Urania* (1621), for instance, is punctuated by verse plaints which answer, and often match in beauty, those in
Sidney's works. Sometimes the effect of replying is explicit: the poet will
take a male-voiced lament such as 'What changes here . . .', which
denounces female infidelity with dejected cynicism, and rewrite it for an
abandoned 'lady'.[2] Less pointedly, the song from the cave episode of
Arcadia discussed above (pp. 22–3), which climaxes with Pyrocles/
Cleophila finding a woeful poem on a stone table in Gynecia's retreat, is
recalled in the opening pages of Wroth's narrative, where Urania finds
'Here all alone in silence . . .' (another plaint as 'pseudo-document') in a
cell carved inside a rock. As Wroth's uncle, Sidney exercised a peculiarly
intimate influence over her writing, and *Urania* seems to analyze this

---

[1] *Kinds of Literature: An Introduction to the Theory of Genres and Modes* (Oxford, 1982).
[2] 'Certain Sonnets', 28, in *The Poems of Sir Philip Sidney*, ed. William A. Ringler, jun. (Oxford,
1962), 157–8; *The Poems of Lady Mary Wroth*, ed. Josephine A. Roberts (Baton Rouge, 1983),
206–8.

burden, by looking for the 'answer' in echo while 'imitating' feminine plaint. Certainly the poem reproduced here exposits with crystalline inwardness, and does not appear to succumb to, the claustrophobia of 'female' lament:

> Vnseene, vnknowne, I here alone complaine
> To Rocks, to Hills, to Meadowes, and to Springs,
> Which can no helpe returne to ease my paine,
> But back my sorrowes the sad Eccho brings.
> Thus still encreasing are my woes to me,
> Doubly resounded by that monefull voice . . .

Early readers took pleasure in such poems out of, as well as in, context. The indexing of '*Byblis . . . querelae*' and '*Bradamant . . . her complaynt*' in narratives as unlike as the 1584 *Fabularum Ovidii Interpretatio* and Harington's *Orlando Furioso in English Heroical Verse* (1591) shows that they expected to be able to pluck out plaints like plums. Verse emulating Ovid or Ariosto could dispense with story-telling and concentrate on what was most valued. Thus the short erotic epics incorporate much formal lament. Sometimes—as with *Scyllaes Metamorphosis* by Lodge—fable seems the merest thread for stringing plaints together. In more ambitious narratives the mode is equally active. Having 'included four plaintive eclogues in *The Shepheardes Calender* ("Januarye," "June," "November," "December")' and 'used the genre for Alcyon's monologue in *Daphnaida*', the author of *The Ruines of Time* 'assigned complaints to characters such as Arthur, Britomart, Cymoent, Timias, Scudamour, and, most strikingly, Dame Mutabilitie' in *The Faerie Queene*.[3] In canto iv of Book III 'a small anthology of lyric complaints' is 'arranged so as to compose a cumulative protest against the ineluctable accidents and the dreaded certainties that make human beings finally vulnerable and subject to destiny'.[4] *Paradise Lost* deploys the mode with more extended structural purpose. Before the forbidden fruit is plucked, Adam and Eve never soliloquize; transgression precipitates a series of plaints which advance through confessional rhetoric to psalmic lament, adding to the tragic harmonies of books 9 and 10.[5]

The spread and continuity of plaintful writing after Shakespeare is, though, such as to baffle exposition. Much turgid discourse can be found in David Murray's *Tragicall Death of Sophonisba* (1611), in *Fortunes Fashion*,

---

[3] Ronald Bond, introduction to *Complaints*, in *Shorter Poems of Edmund Spenser*, ed. Oram *et al.*, 217–22, at pp. 218–19. At least the 'October' eclogue (where Cuddie 'complayneth of the contempte of Poetrie' ['Argument']) should be added; cf. Richard Barnfield's 'The Complaint of Poetrie' attached to *The Encomium of Lady Pecunia: Or, The Praise of Money* (1598).

[4] Georgia Ronan Crampton, 'Spenser's Lyric Theodicy: The Complaints of *The Faerie Queene* III. iv', *English Literary History*, 44 (1977), 205–20, at pp. 221, 205.

[5] See e.g. Barbara K. Lewalski, *'Paradise Lost' and the Rhetoric of Literary Forms* (Princeton, 1985), esp. pp. 244–53.

Pourtrayed in the Troubles of the Ladie Elizabeth Gray by Thomas Sampson (1613), and Henry Reynolds's *Ariadne's Complaint* (1628). A lusher train of sentiment runs through Stuart pastoral into eighteenth-century bucolic, both in sheep-keeping vein—Nicholas Rowe, Prior, Ambrose Philips—and in such subgeneric works as Diaper's *Nereides: Or, Sea-Eclogues* (e.g. 11). For educated readers these plaints were but one branch of a wider literature, in Italian, French, and Spanish, of which the parent stem was Neo-Latin.[6] Lamenting maids persist in ballads and miscellanies.[7] Whether pastoral[8] or city-based,[9] late broadsides deliver a message of pathos and (increasingly) comedy.[10] Post-Restoration political satire makes ample use of the kind.[11] 'Female laments pervade the early issues of *The Gentleman's Magazine*.'[12] Plaints purportedly written by criminals between repentance and execution were continuously published. Pepys gathers them in the 1680s and 1690s: they are not just a Tudor phenomenon, though those now best known—such as the *Complaint and Lamentation of Mistress Arden of [Fev]ersham in Kent*—are read for their links with the Elizabethan stage. More largely penitential are the paraphrases of Psalms and Lamentations which (along with versions of the Song of Solomon) proliferated in the seventeenth century. Political turmoil gives them new relevance to public affairs. *A Bottle of Holy Teares: Or, Jeremies Threnes and Lamentations* (1645) calls itself 'Very suitable for these times' and applies the two passages of Scripture printed here to the distresses of civil war: 'Is it nothing to you, that the Land mourns, the Church hangs up her Harp on the Willow trees. Sion sorrowes, *England* and *Ireland* are bidding farewell to their broken hart-strings, behold and see if there be any sorrow like *Englands* sorrow' (p. 2).[13]

---

[6] See e.g. W. Leonard Grant, *Neo-Latin Literature and the Pastoral* (Chapel Hill, NC, 1965), esp. chs. 2, 8, 10.

[7] e.g. the 'fickle maid' of *The Maidens Complaint of her Loues Inconstancie* who returns, updated in stanza-form, in Cotgrave's *Wits Interpreter*.

[8] e.g. *The Lamentation of Cloris for the Unkindness of her Shepherd*; *The Perjur'd Swain: Or, The Damsels Bloody Tragedy*; *Bleeding Lovers Lamentation: Or, Fair Clorindas Sorrowful Complaint for the Loss of her Unconstant Strephon*.

[9] e.g. *The Distressed Damsels: A Dolefull Ditty of a Sorrowful Assembly of Young Maidens that were Met together near Thames-Street, to Bewail the Loss of their Loves which were lately Press'd away to Sea*; cf. 'The Disconsolate Girl for the Loss of her Love, lately Prest to Sea' in *London Drollery* (1673).

[10] e.g. *The Maids Complaint for Want of a Dil Doul*; *The Maids Hue and Cry After a Husband: Or, The Damosels Complaint*; *Hey Ho, for a Husband: Or, The Willing Maids Wants Made Known*. Cf. 'The Widows Complaint' (a dialogue) in *Wits Interpreter*.

[11] e.g. *The Bully Whig: Or, The Poor Whores Lamentation for the Apprehending of Sir Thomas Armstrong*; or, dealing with court scandal, *The Dutchess of Monmouth's Lamentation*; *Mrs Nelly's Complaint* (on Nell Gwyn); *A Dialogue between the D[uchess] of C[leveland] and the D[uchess] of P[ortsmouth] at their Meeting in Paris: With the Ghost of Jane Shore*.

[12] Ellen Pollak, *The Poetics of Sexual Myth: Gender and Ideology in the Verse of Swift and Pope* (Chicago, 1985), 71.

[13] Anna Kasket, '"How Like a Widow?": Lamentations in English Literature of the 1640s' (typescript), 5. Cf. *The Lamentations of the Prophet Jeremiah Paraphras'd, Suitable to the Exigencies of these Times* (1647).

Because Lamentations 1: 12 ('behold and see . . .') traditionally figured in crucifixion poetry, the same text could be used in mourning for Charles, king and martyr. Pamphlets and ballads repeatedly echo Lamentations in the wake of his execution. Yet it would require another anthology to trace the diffusion of scriptural plaint through works of politics and piety— Crashaw's profound debt to Marian lament, for instance, his translating Remond's 'Alexias: The Complaint of the Forsaken Wife . . .'. More urgently relevant to the development of those strains which interest us here is the impact of the larger genre upon drama, petitionary grievance, and song.

Renaissance tragedy, for example, shows the impress of *A Myrroure for Magistrates* in contexts (bereavement, family betrayal, loss of state) which shadow but do not coincide with the shapes of love lament. One reason why the work of Baldwin and his fellows looms large is that earlier English drama offered playwrights few models for feminine grief. Marian *planctus* in the mystery plays are a partial and (especially in the Towneley cycle) affecting exception, yet, despite the performance of some miracle drama after the Reformation, the Virgin's griefs—above all those centred on the *pietà*, which lacked scriptural warrant—could not directly contribute to the London stage. Another plainant in miracle plays, the Magdalene, survived longer. Lewis Wager's *Life and Repentaunce of Marie Magdalene* (1566) is familiar; more remarkable is Nicholas Grimald's *Christus Redivivus* (1543), which mingles Ovidian plaint and scriptural paraphrase for the saint in rhetorical Latin.[14] There were, of course, classical precedents. Euripides' *Medea*, 465–519, was followed by Seneca and Buchanan. In general Neo-Latin tragedy is lavish with laments. Dido, in William Gager's play of that title—splendidly staged at Christ Church, 1583—mourns Aeneas' departure, then takes her life with much Virgilian plangency. Aurora begins Joseph Crowther's *Cephalus et Procris* (acted in Oxford, 1625–8) with a lament that her love for Cephalus is not returned.

But examples from academic drama are easily found. More interesting is the question they raise about the stageworthiness of grief. How far does Senecan convention distance and make manageable the high-flown anguish which, in a case like Constance's (*King Iohn*, III. iv), teeters on the brink of bathos? It is difficult to know whether the queen's 'vntressid' hair, her entangled grief and blame, owe more to dramatic or non-theatrical complaint. Yet much hangs, tonally, on this difference. Constance stirs mild impatience when her lines are read in the 1623 Folio, as she might if encountered in the *Myrroure*. Performance makes her altogether trying— the more so because we are moved; and audiences are tempted to agree

[14] e.g. the outcrying and epistrophic B2ʳ; cf. the longer lament of III. iv as Mary approaches the tomb.

with Pandolph's 'You hold too heynous a respect of greefe' (1475). All voluble distress is hard to sustain in performance: Lear presents some of the same problems for an actor as Constance. But the switch-off point for audiences is imminent when 'hystericized' femininity forces itself on the attention. Those ballads sung by Desdemona and Ophelia begin to seem significant: ways of evoking pathos that do not alienate sympathy from the characters. Likewise, when Julia, abandoned by Proteus, describes 'Julia''s grief to Silvia, she allusively recalls playing 'the womans part' in an interlude based on Ovid: '*Ariadne,* passioning | For *Theseus* periury and vniust flight'.[15] This is one reason why Lavinia's grieving in *Titus Andronicus* is such an inspired compromise with patriarchy. Robbed of hands, she cannot 'thumpe' the 'hollow prison' of her 'breast', 'strike' down her woeful 'hart': Andronicus' 'right hand ... Is left' to do this for her. Ravaged of her tongue, she is a 'Speechlesse complayne[n]t' whom Titus feels he must 'interpret'.[16] Lavinia is deprived of the primary instruments of plangency, her griefs are mediated by the Father. Yet despite as well as because of Titus' (and her uncle's) appropriation, her woes take hold of an audience. Silent plaint, legible wrongs—unignorable yet unable to insist—make deep grief (proverbially wordless) the idiom of her violated body.

This is not to say that when sorrow is fluently self-declaring it lacks theatrical interest. On the contrary, complaint is problematic because stagey before it is staged. The breast-beating lamenter's tendency to play to an audience (even if only of one) makes her or his grief, within bounds, innately dramatic. This was grasped by those Renaissance commentators on Ovid's *Heroides* who emphasized the ludic force of the poems in ways which—since we have a less expository sense of drama—can seem wishful. Prompted by a passage in *Ars amatoria* (3. 343–6) distinguishing between the soft recitation of *Amores* and the stronger delivery appropriate to the heroines' letters, aware of lines in the *Tristia* which might imply their dance-related performance (2. 515–20, 5. 7. 25–30), and encouraged by the knowledge that Ovid had written a tragedy about Medea, critics celebrated the *Heroides* ('generally granted to be the most perfect piece of Ovid') in terms inseparable from their sense that he 'had a genius most proper for the Stage'.[17] The problem for playwrights following him was to secure the limits within which his sort of complaint could be ludic but not ludicrous. Hence the reinforced framing of Fletcher—a dramatist generally wary of monologue and more interested in active than grieving women—in *The Maides Tragedy*, II. ii, that famous scene (extracted in this anthology) where Aspatia, jilted by her lover, instructs her women in needlework.

---

[15] *The Two Gentlemen of Verona*, IV. iv (1979, 1986–7).   [16] III. ii (1459–66, 1488–91).

[17] From Dryden's 'Preface' to *Ovid's Epistles, Translated by Several Hands* (1680) and *Of Dramatick Poesie, An Essay* (1668): in *The Works of John Dryden*, gen. ed. H. T. Swedenberg, jun. (Berkeley, 1956–), i. 109–19, at p. 114; xvii. 8–81, at p. 30.

Antiphila has embroidered Ariadne abandoned by Theseus, but with 'colours' (according to her mistress) 'not dull and pale enough':

> Doe it againe, by me the lost *Aspatia* . . .
> Suppose I stand vpon the Sea breach now
> Mine armes thus, and mine haire blowne with the wind,
> Wilde as the place she was in; let all about me
> Be hearers of my story; doe my face,
> If thou hadst euer feeling of a sorrow,
> Thus, thus, *Antiphila*; make me looke good girle
> Like sorrowes monument . . .

Insisting that Ariadne be modelled after her, Aspatia bases herself the more closely on *Heroides*, 10, for there Ariadne, indebted to Catullus' version of herself (64), '*plays* the abandoned heroine'.[18] The potential difficulty of shifting from paper stage to Jacobean performance is made to contribute to the awkward anguish of the scene without betraying Ovid's tone. Monopolizing pity, engrossing it as self-pity, Aspatia, transfixing her onstage auditors, frees the larger theatre audience to respond to her articulate way with grief. Old images can be revived; the pathetic fallacies of *Heroides* and Catullus are lent fresh significance by signifying *as* tropes for the sufferer. The artifice of plaint is evident, but the effect of suffering is solidified by our recognition that it embraces itself. Above all, as Aspatia mobilizes her rhetoric to talk as much about as through complaint, she aspires towards eloquent silence: 'make me looke . . . Like sorrowes monument'. The disposition of her limbs, hair, and face strives for a hurt numbness that speaks (as with Lavinia) beyond words. Aspatia moves into an impersonality of extravagant feeling; T. S. Eliot's use of the speech as an epigraph (to 'Sweeney Erect') is not accidental. Her grief becomes 'ecstatic' in the original sense of passionate self-estrangement, and this takes her as near as Renaissance theatre can to the 'suffering extasie' (*A Louers Complaint* 69) of the 'fickle maid'. Beside a character like Penthea in *The Broken Heart*—whose name is glossed by Ford as '*Complaint*'—this is perhaps a figure whose plangency rather punctuates than informs the play. Yet Aspatia is not the less powerful a presence for withdrawing like a baroque statue into the vortex of emotion, set back from the intrigue all around her.

Complaint is not always individuating. Even Aspatia wants 'all' her women 'about' her, to reflect and contain her 'sorrow'. Though grief isolates and obsesses, simplifying relations with the world until sufferers see their own woe everywhere, its language has a harmonizing amplitude which can draw victims together. Drama is peculiarly well equipped to explore the dynamics of this—as in *Richard the Third*, where female mourners are reconciled by shared loss. Queen Elizabeth enters II. ii with an Aspatia-like

---

[18] Jacobson, *Ovid's 'Heroides'*, 224.

apartness and dishevelment, '*her haire about her ears*', and she is quick to resist the Old Duchess of York's involvement in grief: 'Giue me no helpe in Lamentation, | I am not barren to bring forth complaints' (1306, 1340–1). Yet the Duchess will not be denied, and in a cumulative, anaphoric speech urges that the woes devolve upon her: 'I am the Mother of these Greefes . . . I am your sorrowes Nurse, | And I will pamper it with Lamentation' (1354–61). Similar estrangement characterizes the first phase of iv. i, yet Anne of Gloucester's lament at Crookback's malice towards her (2545–66) prompts 'Poor heart . . . I pittie thy complaining' from Elizabeth, to which Anne and the Old Duchess respond. Earlier in the play (i. iii) we have seen Elizabeth at odds with Queen Margaret. But these central scenes crescendo towards the full swell of iv. iv, where Margaret joins Elizabeth and the Old Duchess in a tirade of 'copious . . . exclaimes' (2907).[19] The patterned rhetoric of early Shakespeare is magnificently adapted to sustain the anguish of this scene, spiralling towards imprecation. But the late plays can be equally drawn to choric distress, as in Shakespeare's depiction of the widowed queens at the start of *The Two Noble Kinsmen*. Both the history and tragicomedy show groups of women waylaying authority. Elizabeth and the Old Duchess seek to harrow the King surrounded by his '*Traine*' (2908 ff.); the queens in black cut across Theseus' procession, interrupting his nuptials. In drama great impact can be gained from this juxtaposition: male power and hierarchy on the one hand, collective distress, 'female'-voiced, on the other. Shakespeare returns to it variously, in the 'Complaint' of Isabella and Mariana against Angelo at the Duke's formal return into Vienna, or, to equally decisive effect, in the pressing forward of the Widow and Diana to the King of France: 'Both suffer vnder this complaint we bring, | And both shall cease, without your remedie.'[20]

Stylized feminine grief remained a potent resource of drama beyond the span of this anthology, through such 'She-Tragedies' as Rowe's *Jane Shore* (1714). When George Lillo, in a prologue to *The London Merchant* (1731), surveyed the achievements of Restoration drama, he saw Melpomene not as some lofty farouche creature in buskins but a woman who 'complains | In . . . moving Strains'. Other subgenres were as persistent. The medieval corpus of 'Complaint against the Times' has vigorous Tudor offshoots[21] which flourish through and beyond the seventeenth century.[22] Pamphlets in

---

[19] Cf. Nicole Loraux, *Les Mères en deuil* (Paris, 1990), 9–18.

[20] *Measure for Measure*, v. i (2628); *All's Well, that Ends Well*, v. iii (2882–3).

[21] See e.g. Whitney R. D. Jones, *The Tudor Commonwealth 1529–1559* (London, 1970), chs. 6–9; Patrick Collinson, *The Religion of Protestants: The Church in English Society 1559–1625* (Oxford, 1982), 199–205, 220–6.

[22] e.g. B. Spenser, *Vox Civitatis: Or, London's Complaint* (1625); Alexander Ross, *Englands Threnodie: Or, A Briefe and Homely Discoverie of Some Jealousies and Grievances, under which the Kingdom at Present Groaneth, Affectionately Tendred by Lady Anglia* (1648); *The Complaint of Liberty and Property against Arbitrary Government* (1681). But social grievance is inextricable from religion;

this category are often petitions to the authorities. Enough survive to make it clear that they came in waves and could proceed in relays, plaint countered by further grievance. If it is not always easy to be sure that similarly titled tracts go together, this is because they adopt a level of reference which is often strikingly vague. In a founding discussion of σχετλιασμός, Aristotle had said, 'To express in general terms what is not general is especially suitable in complaint', recommending that 'One should even make use of common and frequently quoted maxims . . . for because they are common, they seem to be true.'[23] Unwittingly Aristotelian, the authors of popular petitions gravitate to consensual truisms and verses from Scripture. There are continuities between their style and what Coriolanus scorns in the plebs, when they 'sigh'd forth Prouerbes | That Hunger-broke stone wals: that dogges must eate | That meate was made for mouths.' 'With these shreds', he says 'They vented their Complainings', and delivered 'a petition' which was 'granted them' (I. i; 218–23).

Closer to the cut-and-thrust of sexual politics, the Elizabethan and Jacobean *querelle des femmes* is prosecuted in a rhetoric that owes so much to legal disputation—'testimony', 'arraignment', 'complaint'—that pamphlets like *Iane Anger her Protection for Women* (against those *that Complaine so to bee Ouercloyed with Womens Kindnesse*) draw plaint as protest[24] into the formality of quasi-legal pleading. The decorum of the dispute[25] arguably licensed its displays of 'anger'. Rather as codes of 'spirit' possession and mourning give female grievance temporary scope in traditional societies,[26] so this exchange could express feminine resentment in ways which were hard-hitting yet less dismissible than 'scolding'. As it happens, women's propensity to 'scold', a central issue in the pamphlet-war, caused heightened alarm during the late sixteenth and early seventeenth centuries. An 'epidemic of scolding' and possible 'crisis in gender relations' has been inferred from troubled court

---

see e.g. *Englands Complaint to Jesus Christ, against the Bishops Canons* (1640); *Complaints Concerning Corruptions and Grievances in Church-Government* (1641); Edmund Hickeringill, *The Fourth Part of Naked Truth: Or, The Complaint of the Church to Some of her Sons for Breach of her Articles* (1682). Roger Lonsdale makes late instances accessible in *The New Oxford Book of Eighteenth Century Verse* (Oxford, 1984), 342–3, 658–9, 788–90, 830–1.

[23] *Rhetoric*, 2. 21, 1395ª 8 ff., trans. John Henry Freese, *The 'Art' of Rhetoric* (London, 1926), 284–5.

[24] Cf. Betty Travitsky, 'The Lady Doth Protest: Protest in the Popular Writings of Renaissance Englishwomen', *English Literary Renaissance*, 14 (1984), 255–83.

[25] Cf. Linda Woodbridge, *Women and the English Renaissance: Literature and the Nature of Womankind, 1540–1620* (Urbana, 1984), esp. chs. 3–5; Katherine Usher Henderson and Barbara F. McManus (eds.), *Half Humankind: Contexts and Texts of the Controversy about Women in England, 1540–1640* (Urbana, 1985), pt I.

[26] See e.g. Lewis, *Ecstatic Religion*, 66–78 (persuasively modified by Janice Boddy, *Wombs and Alien Spirits: Women, Men, and the Zār Cult in Northern Sudan* (Madison, Wis., 1989), ch. 4); Anna Caraveli, 'The Bitter Wounding: The Lament as Social Protest in Rural Greece', in Jill Dubisch (ed.), *Gender and Power in Rural Greece* (Princeton, 1986), 169–94.

records and the spread of cucking-stools.[27] On many an alehouse bench, in this view, village Volumnias rallied gossips with the cry, 'Leaue this faint-puling, and lament as I do, | In Anger'.[28] Indubitably women 'prophets' composed Jeremiads,[29] and, during the stresses and opportunities of the interregnum, used plaint and petition as vehicles of protest. As early as 1642, Milton writes of 'the meanest artizans . . . also women . . . assembling with their complaints'.[30] These texts invited pastiche and parody because they posed such a threat to the convention that political process belonged to enfranchised gentlemen.[31] It was bad enough that groups like waggoners aired their grievances by publishing 'complaints' (numbers survive), worse that 'scolding' women should challenge the commonwealth or kingdom of the family by penning unclassical *querelae*. The terms in which mock plaints are cast make them, more than any other kind of writing, support Felicity Nussbaum's claim that 'the threat to the established order brought about by the Civil War and the Interregnum must have played a significant role in encouraging the eruption of satire against lustful, proud, and inconstant women in the late seventeenth century'.[32] Topical complaints, often keenly misogynistic though put in women's mouths, survive in enough quantities from the 1670s and 1680s to suggest a buoyant output. One of the more genial,[33] *The Maids Complaint against the Batchelors* (1675), is reprinted in this anthology. Its author makes some 'shrewd' hits at male folly, but risks little and (arguing from men's self-interest) subverts less. A suspicion of complacency in such plaintful 'defences' of women can only be streng-thened by the case of Richard Ames, who slipped easily from writing anti-feminist pamphlets to *Sylvia's Complaint, of her Sexes Unhappiness* (1692)—

[27] D. E. Underdown, 'The Taming of the Scold: The Enforcement of Patriarchal Authority in Early Modern England', in Anthony Fletcher and John Stevenson (eds.), *Order and Disorder in Early Modern England* (Cambridge, 1985), 116–36, at pp. 120, 122.

[28] *Coriolanus*, IV. ii (2567–8).

[29] e.g. Lady Eleanor Douglas, *Sions Lamentation* (1649); Martha Simmonds, *A Lamentation for the Lost Sheep* (1655); Jean Bettris, *A Lamentation for the Deceived People of the World* (1657); Dorothy White, *A Lamentation unto this Nation* (1660); and, merging into threats, Hester Biddle, *Wo to the Towne of Cambridge* (166?); Judith Boulbie, *A Warning and Lamentation over England* (1679); and the aptly named Isabel Wails, *A Warning to the Inhabitants of Leeds* (1685).

[30] *An Apology against a Pamphlet Call'd a Modest Confutation of the Animadversions*, 40, quoted by Patricia Higgins, 'The Reactions of Women, with Special Reference to Women Petitioners', in Brian Manning (ed.), *Politics, Religion and the English Civil War* (New York, 1973), 184.

[31] e.g. *The Petition of the Weamen of Middlesex* (1641); *The Virgins Complaint for the Loss of their Sweethearts* (1642/3); *The Mid-Wives Just Petition: Or, A Complaint of Divers Good Gentlewomen of that Faculty* (1643); *The Widdowes Lamentation for the Absence of their Deare Children, and Suitors* (1643); *The Mid-Wives Just Complaint* (1646); *The Maids Petition* (1647)—sometimes read as an authentic appeal by women; *A Remonstrance of the Shee-Citizens of London* (1647); *The City-Dames Petition* (1647).

[32] *The Brink of All We Hate: English Satires on Women, 1660–1750* (Lexington, 1984), 9.

[33] Cf. e.g. *The Whores Petition to the London Prentices* (1668); *The Women's Petition against Coffee: Representing . . . the Grand Inconveniencies Accruing to their Sex from the Excessive Uses of that Drying, Enfeebling Liquor* (1674); *The Womens Complaint against Tobacco: Or, An Excellent Help to Multiplica-tion* (1675); *The Petition of the Widows: For the Use of the Wide-O's of London* (1693).

an extremely late and condescending example of 'I'-framed *chanson d'aventure*.

Musical versions of complaint reach back, as we have seen, to the troubadour *planh* and early *planctus Beatae Virginis Mariae*. Even briefly to sketch the development of *Marienklagen*, ballad-tunes, settings of the Psalms and Lamentations in later centuries would be a substantial and uncertain labour. In England plaintful lyrics are abundant in late Tudor and Jacobean song-books.[34] Popular throughout the seventeenth century, these ayres and madrigals fill collections of the sort used by Pepys.[35] The effect of music in such cases can be contrarily to condense or qualify. Much depends on the method of setting—lute-song, dialogue, canon—and, not just audibly, on the extent to which performance implies involvement with the suffering subject. A single female singer, the focus of admiration in a room full of gentlemen, will come closer to dramatizing the typical love plainant than a raucous band clinking their pots. At one extreme, music refines grief into the elegiac sweetness described by Coprario.[36]

> Musicke though it sweetens paine
> Yet no whit empaires lamenting:
> But in passions like consenting
> Makes them constant that complaine:
> And enchantes their fancies so,
> That all comforts they disdaine,
> And flie from ioy to dwell with woe.

At the other, sociable chiming counterpoints sorrow. The sixty-sixth canon of Ravenscroft's *Pammelia* (1609) might read like plaint's epitome:

> Musing mine owne selfe all alone,
> I heard a maid making great mone
> With sobs and sighes, and many a grieuous [groan],
> For that for that for that her maidenhead was gone.

But, as the insistent repetitions of its last line suggest, there is a rising tide of glee in performance. Mingled tones were not the preserve of the musically

[34] For salient traits see *English Madrigal Verse*, ed. E. H. Fellowes, 3rd edn. rev. Frederick W. Sternfeld and David Greer (Oxford, 1967): Thomas Bateson, 1618, xi, xix, xxii–xxiii; William Byrd, 1589, xxiii, xxvii; Michael East, 1606, ix–x; Giles Farnaby, 1598, iii; John Hilton, 1627, xxiv; George Kirbye, 1597, xii–xiii; Henry Lichfild, 1613, xi; Thomas Morley, 1593, ix, xii, xiii; Francis Pilkington, 1613, xiv, 1624, v; John Ward, 1613, xxiii–xxiv; Thomas Weelkes, 1597, ix, xvii; John Wilbye, 1598, xvi–xvii, xix, xxvi–xxvii, 1609, xxxiv; Nicholas Yonge, 1588, xlviii–xlix; Henry Youll, 1608, ix; John Attey, 1622, xii; Thomas Campian, c.1618b, i; Michael Cavendish, 1598, xvi; John Dowland, 1597, xiv; Robert Dowland, 1610, i; George Handford, 1609, ii, v, vii; Robert Jones, 1601, xi, 1609, ii; Francis Pilkington, 1605, xi, xv.

[35] e.g. John Playford's compilation, *Select Ayres and Dialogues* (1659), 1, 4–5, 6, 10, 13 (a late, four-stanza version of *The Diseased Maiden Louer*), 19, 25, 29, 40, 41, 52, 58, 80–1, 82–3, 100. Pepys took a copy on the voyage which brought back the restored Charles II.

[36] *Funeral Teares* (1606), B1ᵛ.

sophisticated. The Clown in *The Winters Tale* is remembering subtitles from
broadsides when he says 'I loue a ballad but euen too well, if it be dolefull
matter merrily set downe.'[37]

Complaints could be melodiously protracted. No Middle English text
rivals Machaut's 'Tels rit au main qui au soir pleure', which has a single
tune for thirty-six sixteen-line stanzas—and never repeats a rhyme. Yet
Patrick Hannay's Jacobean sprawl, *The Nightingale*, provides one melody for
an even greater hundred and five (also sixteen-line) stanzas. He is rewarded
for persistence by reproduction (Fig. 3), though this exposes for all to see
the misogynistic ineptitude with which his opening lines sabotage his
plainant. Again, nothing survives from medieval England to compare with
the *Ordo Rachelis* in the Fleury Prayerbook. Yet spiritual plaints could be
sung at length during Shakespeare's lifetime. Elizabeth Grymeston's *Mis-
celanea. Meditations. Memoratives* (1604) prints an eight-page 'Morning
Meditation, with sixteene sobs of a sorrowfull spirit, which she vsed for a
mentall prayer, as also an addition of sixteen staues of verse taken out of
Peter's complaint; which she vsually sung and played on the winde instrument' (D4^v–E4^r). The idea of 'sobbing' out plaint was commonplace—as in
Hunnis's metaphrase of the penitential psalms, *Seuen Sobs of a Sorrowfull
Soule for Sinne*, published with music in 1579—and this suggests the emotive way in which the genre was read aloud. 'In ... lamentation', wrote
Fraunce, 'the voyce must be full, sobbing, flexible, interrupted.'[38] Reading
aloud need not imply performance to an audience. Yet some texts were
presented thus. Quasi-operatic laments go back to the *Carmen Grenfel-
lianum* (second century BC), a female-voiced παρακλαυσίθυρον or 'plaint
at the lover's door', partly in agitated choriambics. During the seventeenth
century, however, monodic lament gained impressive prominence. Influential, and suggestive by virtue of its later adaptation to fit a sacred text, is
Monteverdi's *Lamento d'Arianna* of 1608. Other voicings of that subject
quickly followed from Severo Bonini and Possenti.[39] In England an early
analogue is Henry Lawes's setting of the Cartwright *Ariadne* reproduced
below. Shaped at first by the divagations of texts, the *lamento* developed,
through the 1620s and 1630s, more evidently formal patterns; but it
remained (like complaint in pastoral drama) a vehicle for single, virtuosic
voices. In *stile recitativo* or, as often, over a tetrachord ostinato bass,[40] either
in chamber-song or as part of larger dramatic works, the mode burgeoned
in Italy and France 'to the point where some operas contain as many as four
lamenti spread over their three acts'.[41] Declamatory plaints were sung in

---

[37] IV. iv (2013–14).   [38] *Arcadian Rhetorike*, I2^v.

[39] Ellen Rosand, 'Lamento', in Stanley Sadie (ed.), *The New Grove Dictionary of Music and
Musicians*, 20 vols. (London, 1980).

[40] The initiative is, again, Monteverdi's: *Lamento della nimfa* (published 1638).

[41] Rosand, 'Lamento'.

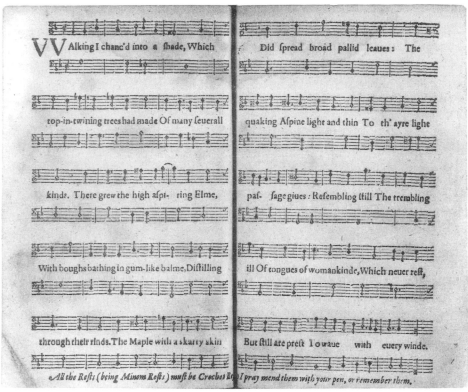

3. 'Walking I chanc'd into a shade', from Patrick Hannay, *The Nightingale. Sheretine and Mariana* (1622)

England at musical entertainments throughout the 1640s and 1650s. When the influence of continental taste began to register more grandly, in opera, they became high points of anguish — as with the final recitative and song of Purcell's Dido, or 'The Plaint' ('O let me weep, for ever weep') in Act V of *The Fairy Queen*.

7. *Wit and Distress*

The form's operatic links are illuminated, in jest, by Henry Carey. Satirizing Italianate fads in music, he wrote 'The Beau's Lamentation for the Loss of Farrinelli' and (a poem collected here) 'A Sorrowful Lamentation for the Loss of a Man and No Man'. The latter, odd footnote to androgyny in complaint, extravagantly bemoans the departure from the London stage of Senesino, a renowned castrato. Such parodic manipulation becomes familiar, from 'My Lady's Lamentation and Complaint against the Dean' by Swift to Sheridan's lyrical 'To Laura', but Carey displays to full advantage the early eighteenth-century capacity to indulge what is mocked. As in Gay's pastoral laments 'Panthea' and 'Araminta', 'Molly's Complaint' by Carey (for instance) does not so much court as digest absurdity. It is self-aware in ways which defuse scepticism. Grief in such poems has the clarity of wit, is not an object of mirth. In *The Beggar's Opera* lament is burlesqued by the means which lend it intensity. Gay's *Shepherd's Week* develops such potentially anxious topics as: the fetishism of tokens (their interchange-ability resembling that of lovers); the closeness of grief to grievance, curs-ing, and (given lament's drift to incantation) witchcraft.[1] His success is not that of a satirist triumphing over an exhausted genre, but of a poet negotiat-ing highly charged matter with a dexterity only possible within conventions exhaustively known.

Gay's effects are delicate, but the bases of his humour broad. The maidens of complaint play with fire then repine. This lays them open to a serves-you-right hilarity. Poems of this sort go back to the Sir Johns and Jolly Jankins of medieval lyric—the kind of poem represented here by 'Þis enþer day I mete a clerke'.[2] Even when less ribald, amorous plaint facilitates—with its detached narrators and readers—amusement at another's misfortune. But there are several sources of humour. Strategic laughter can get complaints heard, or elicit them from troubled speakers.[3] 'Regret', almost by definition, recalls something happier than the present. As Aristotle points out, the absorption of the lover in a beloved is such that 'even when his absence is painful, there is a certain amount of pleasure even in mourning and lamentation; for the pain is due to his absence, but there is pleasure in remembering and, as it were, seeing him and recalling his actions and personality'.[4] What do the lovers of plaint, meanwhile, remem-ber? The erotic adventures dealt with by the genre are often comic because social rules were transgressed by the passion recalled. Then again, the kind can pander to kitsch voyeurism. Erotically yearning, sexually frail (as her story reveals) and usually in alluring *déshabillé*, the feminine plainant, all flowery in a meadow, resembles the objects of soft porn. Parody has related fun (it might be said) in those poems which make it 'The Maids Complaint' that she remains a maid.[5] The milder varieties of pornography have a comedy (for smugly detached male readers) intrinsic to their derivativeness —clichés of posture and invitation—and the familiarity of the dishevelled,

---

[1] This motif is as old as Theocritus 2.

[2] The earliest 'female complaint' in English with comic undertones seems to be 'Atte ston castinges my lemman i ches', cited in a 12th-cent. sermon; cf. Peter Dronke, 'On the Continuity of Medieval English Love-Lyric', in Edward Chaney and Peter Mack (eds.), *England and the Continen-tal Renaissance: Essays in Honour of J. B. Trapp* (Woodbridge, 1990), 7–21, at pp. 10–11.

[3] Gail Jefferson, 'On the Organisation of Laughter in Talk about Troubles', in J. Maxwell Atkinson and John Heritage (eds.), *Structures of Social Action: Studies in Conversation Analysis* (Cambridge, 1984), 346–69.   [4] *Rhetoric*, 1. 11, 1370^b 23–8, trans. Freese, 284–5.

[5] e.g. the poem of that title in *London Drollery*.

typical speaker of plaint can feed this. Further reflection suggests that the
very idea of falsetto production, of a male author deigning to flute the
'female voice', is misogynistically risible. Certainly an array of factors is
needed to explain why feminine texts in the genre, even when non-parodic,
have an unfocused comic air which needs dispersing by poets seeking
pathos. The awkward humour of even Shakespeare's poem—as when the
old man, propelled on his 'greyned bat', sits *comely* distant' beside the
'fickle maid'—functions in a field of embarrassment enriched by the erotic
and moral disadvantages with which love plaint burdens its subjects.

Above all, lament can seem absurd because it does not recover what is
lost. In Shakespeare we are told repeatedly that 'Plaints' are 'Bootlesse',
that 'it bootes not to complaine'.[6] The Nurse in *Romeo and Juliet* is the kind
of exponent calculated to make plangency ridiculous. 'O Lamentable day',
she cries at Juliet's false death—that we know her to be alive sharpens the
comedy—'O wo, O wofull, wofull, wofull day, | Most lamentable day, most
wofull day . . . O day, O day, O day, O hatefull day.'[7] The Nurse is so
haplessly ridden by plaint as to make persuasive the austere mirth extracted
from lament (a few lines later) by the Friar: 'though fond Nature bids all vs
lament, | Yet Natures teares are Reasons merriment'.[8] As the example of
the Nurse reminds us, plaining is more ridiculous because of its tendency to
magnify beyond focus and go *on*. The self-denial of Lucrece to her rela-
tives, 'my laments would be drawn out too long, | To tell them all with one
poor tired tong' (1616–17), comes rather late for readers who know that
'Sometime' her grief 'too much talke affords' (1106), that 'time doth wearie
time with her complayning' (1570). In *Venus and Adonis* Shakespeare is drily
sceptical about the kind of lamenting amplitude which features so largely in
A Louers Complaint. Venus, rejected by Adonis, 'beates her heart, whereat it
grones, | That all the neighbour caues . . . Make verball repetition of her
mones' (829–31). Out of this concave-wombed landscape, inevitably, a
'doble voyce' sounds: 'Passion on passion, deeply is redoubled, | Ay me, she
cries, and twentie times, wo, wo, | And twentie ecchoes, twentie times crie
so' (832–4). Protraction has its pleasures; the copiousness of Tudor plaint
when most solemnly confident suggests a tolerance, in early readers, for
length. But Shakespeare is capable of registering the bludgeoning effect of
lament. Of Venus, he remarks:

> Her song was tedious, and out-wore the night,
> For louers hOures are long, though seeming short . . .
>> Their copious stories oftentimes begunne,
>> End without audience, and are neuer donne.   (841–6)

---

[6] *The Third Part of Henry the Sixt*, II. vi (1303); *The Life and Death of King Richard the Second*, III. iv
(1826).   [7] IV. v (2608–32).
[8] IV. v (2662–3), accepting the usual emendation of 'some Nature', from F2.

The 'theatre' of *A Louers Complaint* stands empty, as it were, its galleries resonant in the moonlight. The 'reuerend man' and wandering 'I' went home to bed hours ago, and Venus is attended by a flat 'quier of ecchoes' that (with the help of a recurrent rhyme-scheme) become the kind of listeners who, buttonholed by a bore, stop listening and mutter 'O dear, how dreadful': 'She says tis so, they answer all tis so, | And would say after her, if she said no' (840, 851–2).

More difficult to characterize is the ingrained tonal wit which comes from derivativeness in the genre. Shakespeare clearly enjoys, for instance, the 'reuerend man' 's Spenserian trappings—somewhat arch even in 1609. As later and more assiduously in *The Shepherd's Week*, there is a clutter of objects (like that 'bat') indicating rustic innocence, and an archaic elevation of idiom, which, when related to social impropriety, become urbane and droll. Knowingness can play across subtler linguistic fields. In Marvell, above all, inevitability and knowingness interact in ways which make feeling a wit of style without its affectingness being quite compromised. Loss is rendered by verbal contours which the verse rather rehearses than presents. In 'The Nymph Complaining . . .' (printed here) especially, the speaker strikes a note of absorbed but impersonal, typological though individually cadenced, self-positing. 'I have a Garden of my own . . .' Marian *planctus* and lyricism from the Song of Solomon might be audible in that line, but they do not define what the nymph might be. It would be more than usually tautological to say that the poem itself defines her: this is a voice in search of identity, finding out elements (familiar to 'her' reader) of what precipitates a plaintful subject. Many texts in the kind include speakers schooled in apt rhetoric: the princes of the *Myrroure*, accustomed to audiences and familiar with the shocks of Fortune; the various feminine plainants—Jane Shore, Matilda—aware of what has been said about their predecessors. In 'The Nymph Complaining . . .', by contrast, interest grows between the speaker's discovery of plaint and the attunement assumed in the reader. 'Report' in *A Louers Complaint* and elsewhere is uncertain because of the ingenuity of the plaintant. In Marvell the opposite seems true on account of the nymph's insecurity in language. She gives back Sylvio's voice with more confidence than she places in her own words, and what reverberates through the silences of the poem is the anxiety of an innocence with much to relate but minimal powers of deduction:

> Unconstant *Sylvio*, when yet
> I had not found him counterfeit,
> One morning (I remember well)
> Ty'd in this silver Chain and Bell,
> Gave it to me: nay and I know
> What he said then; I'me sure I do.

>   Said He, look how your Huntsman here
>   Hath caught a Faun to hunt his *Dear*.

The anger of earlier plaints has been so refined away that rigour is felt most in the desire to 'report' aright. Blame often feels constrained in 'female complaint'. This reflects, it might be thought, the conditions which make language richer in terms for abusing women than men.[9] But Marvell raises poverty to a fine art. This is the most rarefied complaint in the anthology, grief with no centre in grievance. It is a poem unhelpfully substantiated even by allegory. Unframed, unglossed, its voice approaches definition by aspiring to silence. For what will be left in the garden, according to the nymph, is a dumb icon of suffering, 'my unhappy Statue . . . cut in Marble'. Analogues might be found for this in the Greek Anthology's associating love plaints and animal elegies with so many texts which describe sculpture, or in *pietà* lyrics centred on statues. More simply and affectingly relevant is Fletcher's Aspatia, imagining herself 'sorrowes monument'. There is poignant plausibility in the impulse towards a wordlessness which will make both plainants enduringly themselves lamenting. But the purified self-pity in Marvell would not be so touching without a sense that the nymph is numbed by loss because her warm and sentient life is ebbing with the blood of the fawn. An imaginative fusion of nymph with love token is often remarked. It is as though the dying creature, as the only sign of mutuality left, carries the symbolic burden of bringing the nymph and Sylvio together one last time. The emotional alchemy of this is unique, but in so far as the nymph becomes prosopopoeic of her fawn Marvell has precedents in English. There are laments by birds and their bereft keepers,[10] or, stranger and closer, the plaints against the huntsman ascribed to Hart, Hare, Fox, and Otter in Turberville's (unless it is Gascoigne's) *Noble Arte of Venerie or Hunting* (1575). But then, to think of Turberville in such a context is to recall another set of plaints: those of *Heroides*, which he was the first to translate fully into English. It is to the genre in epistolary form that we must penultimately turn.

8. *'To charme a sacred Nunne'*

Paris in 1669 saw the publication of five texts which would carry complaint beyond drama, pastoral lyric, and other high Renaissance genres into the world of the novel. Ostensibly penned by a Portuguese nun seduced and

---

[9] See e.g. David Graddol and Joan Swann, *Gender Voices* (Oxford, 1989), 111–19.

[10] e.g. Philomel's sorrows in Gascoigne, *Complaynt of Phylomene* (1576), the closing lyric of *The Passionate Pilgrime* ('As it fell vpon a Day'), or Martin Parker, *The Nightingale Warbling Forth Her Own Disaster* (1632); 'Complaint of a Friend of his Hauing Lost his Dove', in Turberville, *Epitaphes, Epigrams, Songs and Sonets, with a Discourse of the Friendly Affections of Tymetes to Pyndara his Ladie* (1567), S1r–v.

abandoned by a French cavalier, *Les Lettres portugaises* elaborate with elegance and intricacy a mode in danger of fossilizing. Throughout the eighteenth century, the constraints and pangs of Mariane would remain compelling. Two hundred years later Rilke was moved to ask, 'What else happened to the Portuguese nun, save that inwardly she became a spring?'[1] That most scholars—unlike Rilke—now think the texts not the work of a nun but of Gabriel-Joseph de Lavergne de Guilleragues has given a fresh twist to arguments about the letters' femininity rather than diminished their appeal.[2] Politically *Les Lettres* remain live: in the cavalier's insouciant command and nun's self-aware self-defeat they provide points of departure for the radically questioning *Novas cartas portuguesas* (1972). They do so not least by making colonialism (French power, Portuguese subjection) available as a subtext. Ovid had been alert to the barbarian status of Colchian Medea, Thracian Hero; in the many eighteenth-century Heroidean letters of Yarico—an Indian maid sold into slavery by her European lover—cultural difference and exploitation become sentiment-stirring obsessions.[3]

But the initial vogue is the extraordinary thing: not just in France, where *Les Lettres* emerge from a developed literature,[4] but European-wide. In England the translation reproduced here was printed ten times by 1740; a poetic version ran through half a dozen editions from 1709. Disconcerting originality is not the way to cult status. The cavalier is an updated knight of *pastourelle*. Like *A Louers Complaint* or *Matilda*, *Les Lettres* set cloistered faith against masculine perfidy. Rhetorically they move from clamour through retrospection—that narrative challenge of complaint, to produce a story backwards from the griefs which end it—into forensic self-analysis, redeploying outburst and echo. As surely as in Daniel or Shakespeare, artfulness becomes entangled with feeling: the book's eventual publication bound with Ovid's *Art of Love . . . Dedicated to the Ladies* is no accident. 'It is not Love alone that begets Love', the nun discovers: 'there must be Skill, and Address; for it is Artifice, and not Passion, that creates Affection.' The letters are varied by snapshots of the suitor and typical scenes of love: a balcony, the estranging sea. There is the familiar wrestle with tokens,

---

[1] Lawrence Lipking, *Abandoned Women and Poetic Tradition* (Chicago, 1988), 162.

[2] For debate and analysis see e.g. Miller, ' "I's" in Drag: The Sex of Recollection'; Peggy Kamuf, *Fictions of Feminine Desire: Disclosures of Heloise* (Lincoln, Nebr., 1982), ch. 2; Linda S. Kauffman, *Discourses of Desire: Gender, Genre, and Epistolary Fictions* (Ithaca, NY, 1986), ch. 3.

[3] See the *Inkle and Yarico Album*, ed. L. M. Price (Berkeley, 1937).

[4] See e.g. Gabrielle Verdier, 'Gender and Rhetoric in Some Seventeenth-Century Love Letters', *Esprit créateur*, 23 (1983), 45–57; Janet Gurkin Altman, 'The Letter Book as a Literary Institution 1539–1789: Toward a Cultural History of Published Correspondences in France', *Yale French Studies*, 71 (1986), 17–62; Katharine A. Jensen, 'Male Models of Feminine Epistolarity; Or, How to Write Like a Woman in Seventeenth-Century France', in Elizabeth C. Goldsmith (ed.), *Writing the Female Voice: Essays on Epistolary Literature* (London, 1989), 25–45.

letters, a picture: can the nun discard or return them? Above all the epistles revive what is stylistically received: 'a series of emotional complaints, strikingly like the *Heroides* in tone and method'.[5]

Encouraged by the example of Chaucer, the letter had become 'the main conventional form' of love lyric 'during the fifteenth century'.[6] But the Ovidian impulse evident in a text such as the 'Letter of Dido to Eneas' (foisted on Chaucer by Pynson) would consolidate the kind.[7] Whether the measure is translation,[8] imitation and parody,[9] even song,[10] the *Heroides* became hugely influential. One explanation for this lies in the upper forms of grammar schools. After probably reading some Ovid in English, and learning to construe parts of the *Heroides*, boys were expected to acquire the Roman poet's style. Erasmus begins 'Exercitatio et Imitatio' in his *Opus conscribendis epistolis* (1552) by saying that students should emulate Ovid's Helen dissuading Paris from adultery, Penelope writing to Ulysses, Acontius to Cydippe. The sort of 'imitation' he envisages is centred on male correspondents: Antenor, Linus, Menelaus. But it could not be undertaken without an understanding of Ovidian femininity. Erasmus helps us see how a poet such as Shakespeare must have assimilated in the schoolroom classical techniques of 'female' characterization. That he read *Heroides* at school seems certain. Along with *Metamorphoses*, they are the Ovidian texts he most deploys. Indeed we glimpse Elizabethan teaching at work in *The Taming of the Shrew*, III. i, where Lucentio wooingly misconstrues 'Penelope to Ulysses' for his pupil Bianca. Preparing *Heroides*, 1, she is clearly near the start of her course, and reading a text decorously apt for such a proper young lady.

---

[5] Robert Adams Day, *Told in Letters: Epistolary Fiction before Richardson* (Ann Arbor, 1966), 36.

[6] *Secular Lyrics of the XIVth and XVth Centuries*, ed. Robbins, 286.

[7] Cf. Julia Boffey, 'Richard Pynson's *Book of Fame* and the *Letter of Dido*', *Viator*, 19 (1988), 339–53; and, more largely, Heinrich Dörrie, *Der heroische Brief: Bestandsaufnahme, Geschichte, Kritik einer humanistisch-baroken Literaturgattung* (Berlin, 1968), esp. chs. B and C.

[8] After Turberville's clumsy version of 1567, reprinted half a dozen times, the epistles were most importantly Englished before Dryden by Wye Saltonstall (1636) and John Sherburne (1639).

[9] Anticipated by some of the letters of Tymetes and Pyndara in Turberville's *Epitaphes, Epigrams, Songs and Sonets*, the line of emulation spirals from Drayton's *Englands Heroicall Epistles* (1597), Daniel's 'Octauia to ... Marcus Antonius', and Samuel Brandon's—appended to his *Tragicomeodi of the Vertuous Octavia* (1598)—through Donne's 'Sapho to Philaenis' and Wither's (distinctly readable) *Elegiacall Epistle of Fidelia to her Vnconstant Friend* (1615) as far as David Crauford's *Ovidius Britannicus* (1703) and Pope's *Eloisa to Abelard*. A mock invocation of Penelope to Ulysses appears in Sir John Mennys's and James Smith's *Wit Restor'd* (1658); the 1682 edition of *Wit and Drollery* garnishes the 'Complaint of *Penelope*' with cod-erudite footnotes; nine years earlier Alexander Radcliffe had published (as 'Naso Scarronnomimus') *Ovidius Exulans, Or, Ovid Travestie*; his *Ovid Travestie, A Burlesque* was a hit, and expanded through several editions.

[10] From time to time, reading 'cantetur' at *Ars Amatoria*, 3. 345, literally, scholars have argued that Ovid meant his epistles to be sung. Nor was epistolary music a 16th-cent. innovation in English (see e.g. Boffey, *Manuscripts of English Courtly Love Lyrics*, 72–3). Even so, it is curious to find the first lines of 'Penelope to Ulysses' in William Byrd's *Psalmes, Sonets, and Songs of Sadnes and Pietie* (1588).

Young women, as well as grammar-school boys, were exposed, then, to
Ovid's epistles. Humanist education introduced them, for the first time in
literary history, to highly valued 'female complaint' at the heart of the
cultural mainstream. Formal 'imitation' by women survives from as early as
Isabella Whitney's lively *Copy of a Letter, Lately Written in Meeter, By a Yonge
Gentilwoman: To her Vnconstant Louer* (*c.* 1567), and it persists as a pedagogic
subgenre into the eighteenth century.[11] Female poets are among the most
formidably accomplished Ovidians of this period. Aphra Behn's 'Paraphrase on Oenone to Paris', printed here from *Ovid's Epistles, Translated
by Several Hands* (1680), is a glittering and impassioned performance. The
1712 edition of Dryden's volume adds Anne Wharton's 'Penelope to
Ulysses', a text already varied by Anne Killigrew and published as a 'frag-
ment' (itself a relatively new and ponderable phenomenon) in her posthu-
mous *Poems* (1686). Significantly, though, women writers such as Katherine
Philips were creating modes of feminine epistle which could make the
Heroidean formulae seem stilted. Dorothy Osborne, most obviously, has
read Ovid[12] but eschews his idiom, just as she knows from ballad complaint
how to put her tongue in cheek when a suitor marries another: 'What a
multitude of Willow garlands shall I weare before I dye, I think I had best
make them into fagotts this cold weather.'[13] Especially after the Restoration,
female epistle glances away from Ovidian patterns, or negotiates them
obliquely. Thus the letters of Ephelia to J.G. deploy situations and strategies inherited from *Heroides*[14] without following a classical format. As has
often been pointed out, the stylistic energies of Ovid and his imitators most
evidently issue in the irregular practices of prose fiction. To pursue the
development of the novel through such writers as Aphra Behn and Eliza
Haywood is to find the *Heroides* (and *Lettres portugaises*) everywhere visible
yet their conventions far from duplicated.[15]

Attitudes to the female letter contained a double bind: excelling male
epistolary writers in their empathy, elevation, and refinement (it was said),
women could not display this superiority because publishing their emotional
secrets was indiscreet. The demand for 'female' epistles was therefore
satisfied by creative forgery. This extended the range of male authors, laid
bare women's secrets (proving them far from discreet after all), and tacitly

[11] e.g. 'Julia to Ovid', written in adolescence by Lady Mary Wortley Montagu.
[12] *The Letters of Dorothy Osborne to William Temple*, ed. G. C. Moore Smith (Oxford, 1928), 131.
[13] Ibid. 84.
[14] 'First Farewel to J.G.', 'To J.G. in Absence', 'The Unkind Parting', and others, in *Female
Poems on Several Occasions* (London, 1679), 12, 15, 67–9.
[15] e.g. Behn's *Love Letters between a Nobleman and His Sister* (1683–7); Delariviere Manley, *Letters
Written by Mrs. Manley, to Which is Added a Letter from a Suppos'd Nun in Portugal ... in Imitation of
the Nun's Five Letters in Print by Colonel Pack* (1696); Eliza Haywood, translated from Edme
Boursault, *Letters from a Lady of Quality to a Chevalier* (1721); Jane Barker, 'The Heroick Cavalier',
in *A Patch-Work Screen* (1723).

refuted the notion that they were—even in this specialized department —better writers than men. Yet impersonation of this kind resembles cross-dressing in that, while it can annex and travesty, it can also be experimental and enriching. A poet such as Drayton—robustly traditional in his attitudes—shows himself so aware of male injustice when writing heroical epistles that his adopting a feminine persona cannot be dismissed as merely invasive or a sham. In the thumping self-exculpation of William de la Pole against the measured solicitude of his correspondent Queen Margaret, or in the vulgarity of Edward IV, celebrating Shore's wife in terms of the citizens' wealth he affects to despise, *Englands Heroicall Epistles* expose modes of egotism and competitiveness which depend on peculiarly male axes of power. No final distinction can be maintained between poet and moralist. But while Drayton's notes to, for instance, the epistle of Mistress Shore (printed here) are astringent, the text makes evident the unfairness of men, who flatter their way to adultery and then 'lay the fault on beauty, and on vs', who marry young wives, enjoy and then neglect them, 'And yet still preaching abstinence of meate, | When he himselfe, of euery Dish will eate' (102, 131–2). It matters that, following the pattern of the late *Heroides*, this is written in reply. In exchanges such as Edward's with Jane Shore, the 'report' dialogue of *A Louers Complaint* is, as it were, laid out in 'doble' columns. The texts are partly simplified by becoming, to that extent, immediate; yet, alert to self-deception, the unfolded 'schedulls' articulate a difficult interaction between speakers addressing images of themselves and each other.

While those plaints which centre in reported speech foreground the imaginary acoustics by which words are changed when broadcast, works in the Heroidean strain (problematic one stage earlier) create highly charged relations between author and subject. Epistolary plaints lack—as we have seen—the analytic machinery of frames because to write another's 'voice' is distancing in ways which penning 'her' script is not. The involvement of writer with 'writer' no doubt encouraged poets like Behn and Wharton to translate Ovid and (especially in the former's free 'Paraphrase') make his plaints their own. As the example of *Eloisa to Abelard*—with which this introduction will end—suggests, it also incited male authors, more than spoken plaint, to explore the scope and limits of their identification with 'female' personae. In most texts, it follows, inscription becomes a locus of concern. Ovid's feminine subjects are already eager to depict the scene from which their letters proceed. Here is the Canace of *Heroides* 11, rendered by Dryden in 1680:

> If streaming blood my fatal Letter stain,
> Imagine, er'e you read, the Writer slain:

> One hand the Sword, and one the Pen employs,
> And in my lap the ready paper lyes.
> Think in this posture thou behold'st me Write . . .   (1–5)

The sleight of time is effective: reading the page we half-expect it to be stained, and the fact that it is not enforces the immediacy which makes 'the ready paper' still not filled. The provisionality of writing takes force from a threat of closure, the pen sinisterly foreshadowing the sword, as ink suggests blood. Canace wills herself on to the letter, held (in her 'lap') at the centre of sexuality. English poets recognize and pay tribute to Ovid's suave violence by investing traditional conceits (cheeks pale as paper, blood the banner of desire) with what hovers about their original, pushing epistles towards the extremity at which 'letters' are indeed 'pend in blood' (*A Louers Complaint*, 47). When that happens, what gets said is less impressive than its scribbled physicality. Beyond or before their communicative force these texts are quasi-bloodied objects (written from very self) that become fetishistic. Between lovers script draws on the power elsewhere associated with bracelets of hair, a stricken fawn. The epistle extends the person, and physical intimacy with letters (each one a point where lovers touch) is repeatedly invoked—as at the start of *Eloisa to Abelard*, where the plaintive 'must kiss the name' on Abelard's missive.

A parody of Dryden's Canace in *The Wits Paraphras'd* (1680) brings out the significance of bodily intimacy:

> If menstruous Bloud can make a spot,
> Imagine I am gone to pot.
> One hand employs my Pen, alas!
> With t' other hand I scratch my A— —
> In that same posture now I write,
> Just as my Father us'd to sh— —
> Wou'd he were present with his Nose,
> T' extract the Essence of my close;
> That he might see while I am feigning
> To die, what mouths I make with straining.   (pp. 9–10)

Canace, Canace, Canace shits, as a strain of satire derived from Juvenal 6 is crossed with Ovid. But Canace also bleeds. A plaintive pen blots the paper with uterine gore, and (like a 'menstruous woman' in Scripture)[16] Canace is set apart. It is as though the power of authorship, issuing from a 'concaue wombe', provoked a need to travesty. The persistently low level of female literacy in the period (above, p. 17 n. 10) underlines the paranoia of this reaction, however much the emergence of well-read Ovidians like Bianca, and apparent improvement in women's access to reading and writing

---

[16]   e.g. the Jerusalem of Lamentations, 1: 17 (below, p. 226).

(especially in cities) during the seventeenth century,[17] might 'explain' it.
What Susan Gubar diagnoses from bemonstered women in Swift and the
other Scriblerians is relevant: 'The representation of male dread of women
and, more specifically, of male anxiety over female control and artistry'.[18]
Satire takes from Ovid the shock of incest (Canace is writing to her brother-
lover), and insists on the affront to patriarchy in references which scatolo-
gize *Heroides*. Natural functions airbrushed out of male fantasies about
fragrant femininity are violently reinscribed and produced as evidence
against female nature.

Usually, in epistolary plaint, fascination with the female body is less
hatefully registered. Drayton, for instance, finds physical experience written
in Lady Jane Gray's 'numbers':

> As Teares doe fall and rise, Sighes come and goe,
> So doe these numbers ebbe, so doe they flow.
> These briny Teares doe make my Incke looke pale,
> My Incke clothes Teares in this sad mourning vale,
> The letters mourners, weepe with my dim Eye,
> The Paper pale, griev'd at my miserie.[19]

The movement of pentameters becomes that of breath and weeping; tears
and ink puddle mournfully on the page, image the writer's face. Compared
with the rhetorical arc of a rhyme-royal stanza, the couplets of Drayton and
his Heroidean successors seem more pointedly recorded, yet they also have
a potential for greater discursive fluency. While they typically fall into
antithesis within a line or couplet, they can reach beyond the to and fro of
their returns—far beyond the seven-line harmony of rhyme royal—in an
ebb and flow of grief. As for Lady Jane's anxiety about ink and paper: it is
not a chance allusion. The opening lines of *Rosamond to King Henrie the
Second* (printed below) suggest factors integral to the topic. The legible
thereness of a letter has implications for honour. At one point in Drayton's
chief source, Daniel's *Complaint of Rosamond*, fame is discounted as 'Breath
of the vulgar' (263), transient and removed. This would hardly persuade in
a plaint which enfamed by writing. More than speech, script makes a
complainant present in the world. The letter, an exchangeable record of
her, is subject to circulation and debasement. Hence that anxiously
perceived resemblance between those faults which Rosamond thinks can be
read from her person and the lettering of the epistle which declares and
reflects this to Henry.

It would be wrong to overstate these poems' anticipation of that 'writing

---

[17] See e.g. Cressy, *Literacy and the Social Order*, 145–9, though his statistics need some
discounting.

[18] 'The Female Monster in Augustan Satire' *Signs*, 3 (1977), 380–94, at p. 380.

[19] ll. 25–30, in *Works*, ed. Hebel *et al.*, ii. 296.

with the body' celebrated by some feminist theory. But there is in parts of
Drayton a ranging through somatic contexts which serves to retrace the
difficulty of claiming language. Heroidean plaint could be commended to
female readers because its 'subject' has 'a just relation' to the experiences
'of Ladies and Gentlewomen'.[20] More searchingly, it provided linguistic
tools for analysing obstacles between them and expression. 'Griefe stops my
words', Lady Jane Gray writes from her prison, 'and I but strive in vaine',

> When through my Lips, my Heart thrusts forth my Woes.
> But then the Dores that make a dolefull sound,
> Drive backe my Words, that in the noyse are drown'd,
> Which somewhat hush'd, the Eccho doth record,
> And twice or thrice reiterates my Word . . .   (8–14)

Plaintful resonance here returns to a bodily order of limits which when
extroverted constitutes a crypto-Gothic realm of vaults and dungeons.[21]
Extraordinary, yet passed over in criticism, are the lines of Drayton's Elinor
Cobham,

> Glad here to kennell in a Pad of Straw;
> And like an Owle, by Night to goe abroad,
> Roosted all day within an Ivy Tod,
> Among the Sea-Cliffes, in the dampie Caves,
> In Charnell-Houses, fit to dwell in Graves. . . .
> So pin'd away, that if thou long'st to see
> Ruines true Picture, onely look on mee.[22]

Epistolary complaint, in this guise, moves towards the psychoanalytic
fabling of Irigaray, in which to 'look on me' in language is to 'Picture'
woman in Echo's cave, within a 'bony cavernous socket' which 'encloses the
eye. An inside-out socket . . . in which the gaze is swallowed up in a vault.
Projection sphere for the *hystera protera* . . . All is organized into cavities,
spheres, sockets, chambers, enclosures, simply because the speculum is put
in the way.'[23] The seventeenth century begins to explore the cells and
caverns of sensibility, the bodily speleology which makes each eye, like the
'hollow trunk' of the ear, 'an organ'—in Mandelstam's phrase—'that pos-
sesses its own acoustics'.[24]

---

[20] From Saltonstall's dedication to his translated *Heroides*.
[21] Cf. Gillian Beer, ' "Our Unnatural No-voice": The Heroic Epistle, Pope, and Women's
Gothic', *The Yearbook of English Studies*, 12 (1982), 125–51.
[22] ll. 158–62, 173–4, in *Works*, ed. Hebel *et al.*, ii. 219–20.
[23] *Speculum*, trans. Gill, 254–5.
[24] Quoted by Henry Gifford, 'Mandelstam and the Journey', in *Journey to Armenia*, trans. Sidney
Monas (San Francisco, 1979), 5–34, at p. 27.

9. *In the 'concaue wombe'*

At a radical level of representation this places 'female complaint' on a male
side (inside/out) of the 'speculum', even when written by women about
'woman'—as in Aphra Behn's 'The Reflection' (printed below). Certainly
there are reasons to feel that love plaint, as it develops *c.*1300 to 1729, is 'an
essentially masculine mode, predicated on a sado-masochistic sexual
dynamic'.[1] Objections to the kind are made in the seventeenth century.
Anne Wharton might be an Ovidian translator, but she writes 'To
Melpomene against Complaint'. Jane Barker offers vigorous counsel 'To
Ovid's Heroines in his Epistles':

> Bright *Shees*, what Glories had your Names acquir'd,
> Had you consum'd those whom your Beauties fir'd,
> Had laugh'd to see them burn, and so retir'd:
>
> Then they could ne'er have glory'd in their shames,
> Either to *Roman*, or to *English* Dames,
> Had you but warm'd, not melted in their flames.[2]

True, there is no shortage in European literature of ladies clad in 'the
Armour of . . . scorn' (as Barker puts it), a stereotype flourishing on the
'other' side of the looking-glass less threateningly than an Ovidian heroine
reaching emotional melt-down. The *Heroides* licensed excess, and even
Rochester purported to be shocked by the poems' unladylike vehemence.[3]
As Gillian Beer says: 'heroic epistle may be, for the reader, consolatory
more than distressing: our participation in the heroine's extremity allows us
to enjoy a commanding rhetoric'.[4] Yet, while reading in 'female complaint',
the impression grows that, especially beyond the Heroidean conventions
which underpin the female writer's (with the 'writer' 's) authority, the subgenre frustrates as well as enables women authors. In a case like Ephelia's
'Beneath a spreading Willows shade' it was possible to show at least
diagrammatically how lines of power are thwarted for a non-male framing
'I' that would claim generic space. To read poems like Behn's 'The Reflection' or—another poem collected here—Jane Barker's 'The Complaint',
with a sense of the articulate intensity of other parts of their *œuvres*, is to
suspect that, in so far as the kind retains its guiding features, it offers
different opportunities to each sex and gives less scope to those female
writers who were, at just this time (and in related modes, such as familiar
epistle), reinventing literature.

[1] Germaine Greer, correspondence.   [2] *Poetical Recreations* (1688), 28–9.
[3] 'Answer to a Paper of Verses Sent Him by Lady Betty Felton and Taken out of the Translation
of Ovid's "Epistles," 1680'.
[4] ' "Our Unnatural No-voice" ', 128.

Complicating, at this point, is the interchangeability of masculine and feminine. Aphra Behn writes almost as meltingly about Amintas abandoned by Sylvia ('The Complaint' and 'Song. To Pesibles Tune') as she does about Serena in 'The Reflection'. Barker also cross-dresses; as well as 'The Complaint' given here, her *Poetical Recreations* include an attractive plaint-song involving '*Corydon* . . . laid | I' th' shady Myrtle *Grove*'. If a 'sado-masochistic . . . dynamic' operates, it is one that can subordinate 'male' characters. A poem such as Anne Killigrew's 'The Complaint of a Lover' will posit an 'I' whose gender seems to waver between that of the poet and a subject whose masculinity is barely sustained. Set in 'a Cave . . . Th' entrance hid with dismal Yew', the persona inhabits a landscape of 'hollow Rocks' and '*Eccho*' which, if anything, images the feminine. Killigrew's tenebrous lyric shows continuities with those male-authored Elizabethan plaints in which masculine lovers take on, by virtue of their circumstance, androgynous properties. What students of eighteenth-century fiction call 'the feminization of the male subject', that process which Stephen Greenblatt has thwartedly sought to trace back into the cross-dressing of Rosalind and Viola, in part develops ('from a search for the hidden penis in women to a search for the hidden womb in men')[5] through the inside/out cave-dwelling of complaint.

It needs to be recalled that withdrawn, even morbid sensitivity of the kind celebrated by Killigrew was becoming, during the century of 'Il Penseroso', positively regarded, and also that philosophic 'melancholy' and its equivalents ('hypochondria', 'vapours', 'spleen') had 'merged' by 1700 with 'hysteria'.[6] The lyric subject not only grew 'reflective' (Behn's title 'The Reflection' implies that change), it was increasingly thought of as privileged by feminine sensibility. Melancholics were said to haunt 'grots, caves, and other hidden cels of the earth' and liked 'to walk alone . . . betwixt Wood and Water, by a Brook side'[7]—classic theatres of complaint. The chiaroscuro places of 'thought' (which could itself mean 'depressive anxiety') were sketched, painted, and—as in the illustration to Gay's 'Wednesday: Or, the Dumps' (Fig. 6)—affectionately mocked. The landscape of imagination, of the *imago* or replication into creative fecundity, came to incorporate a 'concaue wombe'. Increasingly this held in generic branches beyond love plaint. Anne Killigrew's 'The Miseries of Man', for instance, which anticipates such reveries as Young's *The Complaint: Or, Night Thoughts*, does so by setting a plaintful woman beneath a 'Hill' in Arcady:

---

[5] 'Fiction and Friction', in *Shakespearean Negotiations: The Circulation of Social Energy in Renaissance England* (Oxford, 1988), 66–93, at p. 87 and n. 36.

[6] Babb, *Elizabethan Malady*, 28 and n. 53.

[7] Thomas Walkington, *The Optick Glasse of Humors*, 3rd edn. (1639), 132; Richard Burton, *The Anatomy of Melancholy*, ed. A. R. Shilleto, 3 vols. (London, 1926–7), i. 452; quoted by Babb, *Elizabethan Malady*, 132, 35.

Close at its mossie Foot an aged Wood,
Compos'd of various Trees, there long has stood,
Whose thick united Tops scorn the Sun's Ray,
And hardly will admit the Eye of Day.
By oblique windings through this gloomy Shade,
Has a clear purling Stream its Passage made,
The *Nimph*, as discontented seem'd t' ave chose
This sad Recess to murmur forth her Woes.

   To this Retreat, urg'd by tormenting Care,
The melancholly *Cloris* did repair,
As a fit Place to take the sad Relief
Of Sighs and Tears, to ease oppressing Grief.
Near to the Mourning *Nimph* she chose a Seat,
And these Complaints did to the Shades repeat.

The privileging of feminine intelligence is explicit. Matted with vegetation and shrouded from sight, the 'sad Recess' needs little psychoanalytic ingenuity to yield its gender. Pope gently mocks this kind of female emblem in his 'gloomy Cave of *Spleen*'.[8] But its potency in the period helps explain the menstrual blotting administered in *The Wits Paraphras'd*. Killigrew could have deployed the incipiently feminine 'I' of her 'Complaint of a Lover', but a fully 'reflective' maiden ('in solidarity' with a 'discontented' nymph) is now judged more effective for voicing 'Man''s miseries.

Where this vein of sentiment emerged from is difficult to determine. A good claim can be made, however, for Du Bellay's musings among the antiquities of Rome, translated by Spenser. *Ruines of Rome* was little read after the 1600s; it does not appear to have contributed to a pensive cult in England as the original did in France. Other Latin and Italian sources feed Antonio's melancholy in the echo scene of *The Duchess of Malfy* (v. ii) — 'I doe love these auncient ruynes . . .' — and Inigo Jones's vista of classical decay in *Prince Henry's Barriers*. Even so, it seems that later poets found, in the work which first developed Du Bellay's sonnets, *The Ruines of Time*, discourses of dilapidation which could enrich their Augustan vision. Our knowledge of Spenser's influence after the Restoration remains rudimentary. But it looks as though the ruin-prompted meditative poetry which runs from Thomson's encounter with 'the fair majestic POWER | Of LIBERTY' amid the detritus of Rome[9] as far as Childe Harold in the Colosseum has roots in the female-imaginary counsel of shattered Verulamium. Here is John Dyer, in a 'theatre-like' arena (to recall Bacon and Vitruvius), set in the sort of 'concaue wombe' which lends poetic resonance:

---

[8] *The Rape of the Lock*, 4. 11–88.
[9] *Liberty, A Poem*, part I, 'Antient and Modern Italy Compared', 25–6, in *'Liberty', 'The Castle of Indolence', and Other Poems*, ed. James Sambrook (Oxford, 1986), 43.

> Amid the tow'ry Ruins, huge, supreme,
> Th' enormous *Amphitheatre* behold,
> Mountainous Pile! o'er whose capacious Womb
> Pours the broad Firmament its varied Light;
> While from the central Floor the Seats ascend
> Round above Round, slow-wid'ning, to the Verge,
> A Circuit vast and high; nor less had held
> Imperial *Rome*, and her attendant Realms,
> When drunk with Rule she will'd the fierce delight,
> And op'd the gloomy Caverns ...[10]

Writing with the eye of a painter, Dyer sweeps the mind up to a bound of light then down to the 'Caverns' of the Colosseum in which Rome kept her tyrannous secrets. Political criticism, not unlike Thomson's Whiggish vision, is integrated into a scene which gives what Elinor Cobham calls 'Ruines true picture' a 'capacious Womb'.

The creative possibilities which Dyer draws on find fuller scope in a writer whose politics are rather different, a poet for whom, still more clearly, Gothic represents the dark obverse of neo-classical achievement. Pope is the author to end this introduction (and the anthology) with because *Eloisa to Abelard* so consummately draws together the materials of earlier complaint. A 'sacred Nunne', as in Drayton's *Matilda* or Shakespeare, Eloisa addresses an absent lover who is also a 'reuerend man'. Rhapsodic and forensic by turns, her rhetoric, informed by *Heroides*, derives from a paraphrase of Héloïse's letters shaped by *Les Lettres portugaises*. These medieval epistles appealed to the antiquary in Pope, and his poem makes much of locale: as in *The Ruines of Time*, the past speaks from place—something not lost on those early readers who went in pilgrimage to the site of Eloisa's nunnery. Loss is the epistle's obsession, erotic loss so absolute that love lament merges with elegy. In Renaissance literary theory complaint had overlapped with threnody.[11] Even in the short measures of song-books, the kind turned lovers into ghosts fancifully flitting through texts of their own own despair.[12] Eloisa, more largely intimate with shades, comes to resemble —like the 'heroine' of *A Wife's Lament*—a *revenant*. It was a fortuitous printer's error which made these famous lines first read 'Propt in', not 'on':

> See in her Cell sad *Eloisa* spread,
> Propt on some tomb, a neighbour of the dead!
> In each low wind methinks a Spirit calls,
> And more than Echoes talk along the walls.   (305–8)

[10] *The Ruins of Rome* (1740), 8–9.

[11] Perusing Sébillet's 'De la Deploration, et Complainte', in *Art Poétique Francoys* (1548), Spenser found material on epitaphs as well as eclogues. In ch. 23 of Puttenham, as read by Shakespeare, 'The forme of Poeticall lamentations' includes 'funerall songs' as well as songs bewailing 'true loue lost or ill bestowed'.

[12] e.g. *English Madrigal Verse*, ed. Fellowes: John Ward, 1613, xxi; Thomas Watson, 1590, iii, xiii; Robert Jones, 1605, xiii.

We are, inevitably, among 'Echoes', sounds acoustically rendered expressive. It has been said of *The Wife's Lament*: 'As in response to Alexander Pope's admonition that "the sound must seem an Echo to the sense," the vocabulary and resultant tone of the poem are . . . suited to the theme and tradition of suffering through separation.'[13] However dubiously 'swift *Camilla*', in 'An Essay on Criticism', 'skims along the Main',[14] Pope's efforts at enactment find in the 'tradition of suffering through separation' conventions which readers take as 'echoing' pathos. Eloisa's bereft couplets, turned back and forth, realize (as surely as the 'doble' tropes of *A Louers Complaint*) plaintful solipsism, desire reaching out and rebounding from its *paysage intérieur*. Amplifying the excesses they curb, harmonizing extremity, Pope's rhymes enforce scenic closures—'awful cells', 'moss-grown domes', 'grots that eccho'—in endstopped measures that reverberate lament.

Quotation from Crashaw, signalled at line 212, reminds us of another strain: that sequence of Magdalene and Marian plaints which runs through recusant poetry. Eloisa is not snared by sexuality like the 'Nun, | Or Sister sanctified' in Shakespeare, of whom it is said: 'Religious loue put out religions eye' (*A Louers Complaint*, 250). Her 'Religious loue' is eroticized, and it finds thrilling focus on the figure who should 'reconcile' her to God. It is hard enough for the 'fickle maid' to extricate herself from desire while addressing the 'reuerend man'. Eloisa pours out her feelings to a confessor who is also her lover. Her passage on the difficulty of repentance (163–96) goes back with unabated force to twelfth-century spiritual plaint, to Héloïse's second letter. Concurrently Pope transcends stereotypes of the cloister in post-Restoration plaint: locus of frustration, as in *Five Love Letters from a Nun to a Cavalier*, yet also orgiastic excess (e.g. *The Nunns Complaint against the Fryars*). Even more than Crashaw, Pope finds absurdity in religious eroticism; but his jests are strangely tender. The author of 'The Lamentation of Glumdalclitch, For the Loss of Grildrig' and 'Mary Gulliver to Captain Lemuel Gulliver' could guy plaintful rhetoric when he chose. Fused into hopeless craving, comedy in *Eloisa to Abelard* is inextricable from pity. The emasculation of Abelard makes the poem a vulnerable elegy to desire, as when Eloisa cries 'Give all thou canst—and let me dream the rest' (124). Criticism has judged these deft, pained touches to be connected with the poet's Eloisan yearning and (given his sickly, diminutive size) Abelard-like stuntedness.[15] Certainly Eloisa's coda implicates the author:

> And sure if fate some future Bard shall join
> In sad similitude of griefs to mine,

---

[13] Renoir, 'A Reading Context for *The Wife's Lament*', 239.

[14] ll. 364–73; cf. Samuel Johnson, *Lives of the English Poets*, ed. Arthur Waugh, 2 vols. (Oxford, 1906), ii. 315.

[15] See e.g. Maynard Mack, *Alexander Pope: A Life* (New Haven, 1985), 319–31.

> Condemn'd whole years in absence to deplore,
> And image charms he must behold no more,
> Such if there be, who loves so long, so well;
> Let him our sad, our tender story tell . . .   (361–6)

Heroic epistles do not conventionally end thus. The lines highlight, with defensive levity, what Pope has invested in the 'story'. Securing the identification latent in any writer's involvement with a Heroidean subject, they paradoxically deflect the poem away from Ovidian 'imitation' into more plural relations with 'the tradition of suffering through separation'. For Pope has 'predecessors in the Elizabethan "Complaint" '[16] for this self-in-imagined-subject conclusion.

This autobiographical tactic, which anticipates Romantic patterns of disclosure, depends on a compounding with femininity. Significantly, the second edition both illustrates Eloisa's authorial ecstasy (Fig. 4) and foregrounds Pope's debt to female lament, by printing one of his sources, Elizabeth Rowe's 'Upon the Death of her Husband'. It is worth contrasting this self-implication with the difference enforced between poet (through his 'I') and feminine subject/object in earlier framed plaints. In Shakespeare's 1609 quarto, for instance, the confessional idiom of many sonnets ('Let me confesse . . .', 'Sinne of selfe-loue . . .'), modulated through *'feminine'* grievance ('Beshrew that heart . . .'), is opened to scrutiny in the complaint which follows. Quasi-dramatic method allows the quarto's 'I' to be observed, in *A Louers Complaint*, learning from another's performance. Pope's warmer involvement, willingly assimilable to Barthes's dictum, 'in any man who utters the other's absence *something feminine* is declared', makes deeper claims. Especially when read through the long perspective of generic history, *Eloisa to Abelard* seems to seek quickening in 'the hidden womb in men'. Despite anecdotes to the contrary, it could not be mistaken for the work of a female poet. Male interest in feminine 'sensibility', nurtured by complaint, perhaps made it easier for women's writing to find readers after the Restoration. But the potential of the subgenre remained circumscribed. Some of Aphra Behn's poems (such as 'On the First Discovery of Falseness in Amintas') fruitfully think through—before sidestepping—the kind. That texts like her 'Oenone to Paris' were misogynistically burlesqued indicates that male writers felt a threat from women's plaintful poetry. In Matthew Stevenson's 'Sapho to Phaon', for example—reprinted in this anthology—the archetypal female poet, committed to women's experience, is debased by doting on a man and her vital eroticism is 'exposed' in all its seaminess. It comes as no surprise to learn that Behn was

---

[16] *The Twickenham Edition of the Poems of Alexander Pope*, ed. John Butt *et al.*, 11 vols. (1939–69), ii, ed. Geoffrey Tillotson, 326.

4. Eloisa, frontispiece to the second edition (1719) of Alexander Pope, *Eloisa to Abelard*

sometimes called 'Sappho'. If, up to a point, the development of women's writing after the fifteenth century was encouraged by 'female complaint', the subgenre was embedded in belying and bemonstering relations which framed texts reinforced and which Heroidean texts could not dismantle, and which directed the energies of the form into male constructions of femininity.

The emergence of women into plaintful writing, and, as significantly, their sceptical dialogue with it (in such poems as Barker's 'To her Lovers Complaint. A Song'), helped make 'female complaint', after Pope, a dispersed phenomenon. The structural and rhetorical conventions of *chansons d'aventure* and 'sad tun'd' speech, the exemplary figures (Ariadne, Dido, Magdalene) and claustrophobic landscapes, were developed beyond recognition. It is true that complaint as narrowly defined lingered in occasional and popular writing,[17] while its modal offshoots in prose fiction left a legacy to high culture. And there is evidence that, in the late eighteenth and early nineteenth centuries, plangent varieties of feminine language were praised and condescended to by male authors and critics. Some such shift in temper encouraged the late appearance of poems like Wordsworth's 'Complaint of a Forsaken Indian Woman', 'Laodamia' (drawing on *Heroides*), and, famously, Tennyson's early lyrics: 'Mariana', 'Mariana in the South', 'Oenone' (further debt to Ovid). It would be an inflated account of the kind, however, which claimed more than scattered passages in Arnold, Browning, or Hopkins, Elizabeth Barrett Browning and Christina Rossetti. Later women poets have sometimes tested complaint (Marina Tsvetayeva is the obvious example), and though male authors seem increasingly eager to concede that—as Paul Durcan drily puts it—'The Pietà's Over',[18] occasional 'female'-voiced pieces are still written in the genre by men.[19] But these are the exceptions. Only 'an obsession' with 'abandoned women' would so insist on the survival of the type as to fault, say, *The Waste Land* because 'Tiresias's monotone drowns out a host of such women: the Countess Marie; Philomela; poor Lil; the typist forsaken by her carbuncular clerk and "glad it's over"; the Thames daughter unresentful "after the event"; and she who fiddles music on her hair.'[20]

What this lively claim, in practice, suggests (Tiresias saying so little in the poem) is the range of female miseries which modernist verse can admit without an androgynized poet figure becoming an emblem, and mouth, of complaint. Eliot's greatest contemporary offers a still more revealing exam-

[17] See e.g. the dozen (often comic) 'female'-voiced poems catalogued under 'Complaint', 'Lament', and 'Lamentation' by D. F. Foxon, *English Verse 1701–1750: A Catalogue of Separately Printed Poems with Notes on Contemporary Collected Editions*, 2 vols. (Cambridge, 1975).

[18] *The Berlin Wall Café* (Belfast, 1985), 54–5.

[19] e.g. Ian Hamilton, 'Complaint', in *Fifty Poems* (London, 1988), 15.

[20] Lipking, *Abandoned Women*, pp. xvi, 113.

ple. The Crazy Jane poems of Yeats have behind them an Ophelian figure made fashionable by 'Monk' Lewis. Very much a product of late eighteenth-century feminine plangency, she flits through ballads and melodramas 'chaunt[ing her] love-lorn ditty' and telling passers-by, 'Henry fled: with him for ever | Fled the wits of Crazy Jane!'[21] Yeats's changes are remarkable. Abusive, mocking, earthy, sexually unrepentant, his Crazy Jane expresses an antagonism to patriarchal sterility which partly vents the poet's hostility to censorship in the Free State but which more radically harnesses his excitement in, and anxiety at, feminist agitation. For it is feminism, above all, which puts the subgenre in doubt. Adrienne Rich has grievances; she does not write complaint. Michèle Roberts composes a novel about the Magdalene without succumbing to the forcefield of lament.[22] A great deal of creative work at the moment attempts to expunge or elude the male 'seeing' linguistically ingrained in female self-explication. So this seems a good time for anthologizing work from a kind which imposes and exposes these constraints. Most readers will respond sceptically to a poem like *The Diseased Maiden Louer*, approach *A Louers Complaint* with doubts. Clearly the value of such texts is contingent on our awareness of the factors which influenced their production and which, differently, inform our reading. Reconstructing those circumstances, beyond the sweep of literary history, and determining how they might be negotiated, would be another day's work. What is clear for now is that, though 'female complaints' might disturb and warn us in ways rather different from those envisaged by their authors, they still have the power to involve us, as men and as women (even as men and women), with their 'motiues of . . . woe'.

[21] M. G. Lewis, *Poems* (London, 1812), 24–5.
[22] *The Wild Girl* (London, 1984), 98, 102–3.

The Anthology

I

Medieval Lyrics

THESE poems were composed over a period of at least two centuries. The earliest, 'Als i me rode . . .' (*c.* 1300), is written in the margin of a legal manuscript. The pair which seem latest, and which might be female-authored (above, p. 10), 'What so men seyn' and 'My woofull hert . . .' (late fifteenth century?), appear in a miscellany circulated in the Midlands. Tonally they are as different as their provenance and date. 'Y louede a child . . .' and 'Þis enþer day . . . ' are unframed fourteenth-century laments; while the former makes it possible for us to sympathize with the speaker, the latter is blithe and mocking. In 'A Balade, Sayde by a Gentilwomman . . .' John Lydgate (?1370–1449) has not only given unusual retrospective reach to his subject but atypically allowed her to express the frustrations of a would-be wooer. The remaining text, a dream vision of the Virgin, might seem apart from the rest. But as its title in the manuscript edited here —*Canticus Amoris*—suggests, it resembles love plaint in its depiction of a figure who implores the human soul with a refrain drawn from the Song of Solomon. Echoes of that book were only one means by which erotic and sacred interacted in medieval lyric. Religious texts were fitted to the tunes of love songs. An amatory tenor could be used in a sacred motet. Look up 'Als i me rode . . .' in a collection of medieval poems and you are as likely to be referred to a *chanson* centred on the *pietà* (first published by Richard Kele, 1542–6) or Five Joys of Mary (British Library Harley MS 2253) as you are to the poem printed below. Mention of Kele's *Christmas Carolles* serves as a reminder that, though medieval poetry was little read in the Tudor period, various fourteenth- and fifteenth-century lyrics were known throughout the span of this anthology. Of the texts given here only 'Y louede a child . . .' is known to have been set to music: it is keyed in manuscript to the tune of 'Bryd on brere . . .' (which can be found in E. J. Dobson and F. Ll. Harrison (eds.), *Medieval English Songs* (London, 1979), 269). 'Sayde', qualifying the title of Lydgate's 'Balade', rules out music. Beyond that, nothing is certain, though 'Þis enþer day . . .' and 'Als i me rode . . .' strike the ear with the sound of lost melodies.

'Als i me rode þis endre dai'

Nou sprinkes þe sprai,
   Al for loue icche am so seek
Þat slepen i ne mai.

Als i me rode þis endre dai
   O mi pleyinge,   5
Seih i hwar a litel mai
   Bigan to singge:
   'Þe clot him clingge,
Wai es him i louue-longinge
   Sal libben ai,   10
      Nou sprinkes, &c.'

Son icche herde þat mirie note,
   Þider i drogh;
I fonde hire in an herber swot
   Vnder a bogh   15
   With ioie inogh.
Son i asked, 'þou mirie mai
   Hwi sinkes tou ai?'
      'Nou sprinkes þe sprai,

Þan answerde þat maiden swote   20
   Midde wordes fewe:
'Mi lemman me haues bihot
   Of louue trewe;
   He chaunges a newe.
Ʒiif i mai, it shal him rewe   25
   Bi þis dai,
      Now sprinkes, &c.'

---

1 *Nou sprinkes þe sprai*: now the twig sprouts (with new leaf, buds, a typical vernal opening)   2 *icche*: I   *seek*: sick   3 *ne mai*: cannot   4 *þis endre dai*: recently, the other day   5 *O mi pleyinge*: amusing myself, at play   6 *mai*: maid   8 *Þe clot him clingge*: may he go to his grave (where clods of earth will grasp him)   9–10 *Wai es him . . . libben ai*: woeful is the person who lives always in love-longing   12 *Son icche herde*: as soon as I heard   13 *drogh*: went, drew myself   14 *herber swot*: sweet arbour, pleasant bower   17 *Son*: at once   18 *sinkes tou ai*: do you continually sing   21 *Midde*: with   22 *lemman*: lover   *me haues bihot*: has promised me   25–6 *Ʒiif i mai . . . dai*: if I can help it, he'll regret it (pay for the wrong) this very day

'Y louede a child of þis cuntre'

Were it vndo þat is ydo
I wolde bewar.

Y louede a child of þis cuntre,
And so y wende he had do me;
Now myself þe soþe y see,   5
 Þat he is far.
  Wer it undo þat is ido, &c.

He seyde to me he wolde be trewe,
And chaunge me for none oþur newe;
Now y sykke and am pale of hewe,   10
 For he is far.
  Were it undo, &c.

He seide his sawus he wolde fulfille,
Þerfore y lat him haue al his wille;
Now y sykke and morne stille,   15
 For he is far.
  Wer it undo, &c.

'Þis enþer day I mete a clerke'

A, dere god, qwat I am fayn,
For I am madyn now gane.

Þis enþer day I mete a clerke,
And he was wylly in hys werke;
He prayd me with hym to herke,   5
 And hys cownsell all for to layne.
  A, dere god, qwat I am fayn, &c.

1 *vndo . . . ydo*: undone . . . done 2 *bewar*: be cautious in future, beware 3 *child of þis cuntre*: young man of this district 4 *wende*: thought, believed 5 *soþe*: truth 9 *none oþur newe*: no other new person 10 *sykke*: sigh 13 *sawus*: promises

1 *qwat I am fayn*: how worthless I am *gane*: obliging, pliant 3 *Þis enþer day*: recently, the other day *clerke*: cleric 5 *herke*: listen 6 *layne*: conceal, store up in my mind

I trow he cowd of gramery,
I xall now telle a good skyll wy;
For qwat I hade siccurly,　　　　　　　　　　10
　　To warne hys wyll had I no mayn.
　　　A, dere god, qwat I am fayn, &c.

Qwan he and me browt un us þe schete,
Of all hys wyll I hym lete;
Now wyll not my gyrdyll met—　　　　　　15
　　A, dere god, qwat xal I sayn?
　　　A, dere god, qwat I am fayn, &c.

I xall sey to man and page
Þat I haue bene of pylgrymage;
Now wyll I not lete for no rage　　　　　　20
　　With me a clerk for to pleyn.
　　　A, dere god, qwat I am fayn, &c.

CANTICUS AMORIS

In a tabernacle of a toure,
As I stode musyng on the mone,
A crouned quene most of honoure
Apered in gostly syght ful sone.
She made compleynt thus by hyr one,　　　5
For mannes soule was wrapped in wo,
'I may nat leue mankynde allone,
Quia amore langueo.

'I longe for loue of man, my brother,
I am hys voket to voyde hys vyce;　　　　　10
I am hys moder, I can none other,

8 *trow he cowd of gramery*: am convinced he knew about magic spells　　　9 *skyll*: reason, way of evidencing　　　10 *siccurly*: safely, surely　　　11 *warne*: refuse　　　*mayn*: strength 13 *browt un us þe schete*: brought us together on the sheet, went to bed together　　　14 *lete*: allowed　　　18 *page*: youth　　　20 *rage*: passion

1 *tabernacle of a toure*: tower's niche, alcove　　　4 *ful sone*: all at once　　　5 *by hyr one*: on her own　　　8 *Quia amore langueo*: because I languish for love (from S. of S. 2: 5, 5: 8) 10 *voket to voyde hys vyce*: advocate for the annulment of his evil, intercessor

Why shuld I my dere chylde dispyce?
Yef he me wrathe in diuerse wyse,
Through flesshes freelte fall me fro,
Yet must me rewe hym tyll he ryse,   15
Quia amore langueo.

'I byd, I byde in grete longyng;
I loue, I loke when man woll craue;
I pleyne for pyte of peynyng;
Wolde he aske mercy, he shuld hit haue.   20
Say to me, soule, and I shal saue,
Byd me my chylde and I shall go;
Thow praydc mc ncucr but my son forgauc,
Quia amore langueo.

'O wreche, in the worlde I loke on the,   25
I se thy trespas day by day,
With lechery ageyns my chastite,
With pryde agene my pore aray.
My loue abydeth, thyne ys away;
My loue the calleth, thow stelest me fro.   30
Sewe to me, synner, I the pray,
Quia amore langueo.

'Moder of mercy I was for the made,
Who nedeth hit but thow allone?
To gete the grace I am more glade   35
Than þow to aske hit. Why wilt þou noon?
When seyd I nay, tel me, tyll oon?
Forsoth neuer yet to frende ne foo.
When þou askest nought þan make I moone,
Quia amore langueo.   40

'I seke the in wele and wrechednesse,
I seke the in ryches and pouerte,
Thow man, beholde where þy moder ys,
Why louest þou me nat syth I loue the?

13 *wrathe*: anger   *wyse*: ways   14 *fall me fro*: fall away from following me   15 *rewe*: pity   17 *byd . . . byde*: pray . . . wait   18 *craue*: desire, ask   19 *pyte of peynyng*: for pity at suffering   21 *Say*: speak, give the word   23 *but my son forgaue*: without my son forgiving   28 *pore aray*: humble attire   31 *Sewe*: sue, make plea   36 *wilt þou noon*: do you want none   37 *tyll oon*: to anyone   39 *make I moone*: I complain   41 *wele*: prosperity   44 *syth*: since

Synful or sory now euere thow be,   45
So welcome to me there ar no mo.
I am thy suster, ryght trust on me,
Quia amore langueo.

'My childe ys outlawed for thy synne,
Mankynde, ys bette for thys trespasse;   50
Yet prykketh myne hert þat so ny my kynne
Shuld be dysseased. O sone, allasse,
Thow art hys broþer, hys moder I was;
Thow sokyd my pappe, thow louyd man so
Thow dyed for hym, myne hert he has,   55
Quia amore langueo.

'Man, leue thy synne þan for my sake,
Why shulde I gyf þe þat þou nat wolde?
And yet yef thow synne som prayere take
Or trust in me as I have tolde.   60
Am nat I thy moder called?
Why shulde þou flee me? I loue the soo,
I am thy frende; I helpe, beholde,
Quia amore langueo.

'Now sone,' she sayde, 'wylt þou sey nay   65
Whan man wolde mende hym of hys mys?
Thow lete me neuer in veyne yet pray.
Than, synfull man, see thow to thys.
What day þou comest, welcome thow ys,
Thys hundreth yere yef thow were fro.   70
I take the ful fayne, I clyppe, I kysse,
Quia amore langueo.

'Now wol I syt and sey nomore,
Leue and loke with grete longyng;
When man woll calle I wol restore,   75
I loue to saue hym, he ys myne hosprynge,

---

50 *bette*: scourged, beaten   51 *prykketh*: grieves, it pierces   52 *dysseased*: distressed
54 *sokyd my pappe*: sucked at my breast   58 *þat þou nat wolde*: what you do not want
66 *mys*: wrong-doing, amiss   70 *Thys hundreth yere yef thow were fro*: if you had been away,
neglecting me, this past century   71 *ful fayne*: gladly   *clyppe*: embrace   74 *Leue*: cease

No wonder yef myne hert on hym hynge;
He was my neyghbore what may I doo?
For hym had I thys worshippyng
And therfore *Amore langueo*.   80

'Why was I crouned and made a quene?
Why was I called of mercy the welle?
Why shuld an erþly woman bene
So hygh in heuen aboue aungelle?
For þe, mankynde, þe truþe I telle: 85
Þou aske me helpe and I shall do
Þat I was ordeyned, kepe þe fro helle,
Quia amore langueo.

'Nowe man, haue mynde on me foreuer,
Loke on þy loue þus languysshyng.   90
Late vs neuer fro other disseuere,
Myne helpe ys þyne oune, crepe vnder my wynge.
Thy syster ys a quene, þy broþer ys a kynge,
Thys heritage ys tayled; sone come þerto:
Take me for þy wyfe and lerne to synge   95
Quia amore langueo.'

JOHN LYDGATE

A BALADE, SAYDE BY A GENTILWOMMAN WHICHE LOUED A MAN OF GRET ESTATE

Allas, I wooful creature,
Lyving betweene hope and dreed,
Howe might I þe woo endure,
In tendrenesse of wommanhede,

---

77 *hynge*: hang   91 *fro other disseuere*: separate from each other   94 *heritage is tayled*:
your inheritance is entailed, secured for you and your successors   *sone*: quickly

In langoure ay my lyff to leede,   5
And sette myn hert in suche a place,
Wher as I, by liklyhede,
Am euer vnlyke to stonde in grace.

Þer is so gret a difference
Tweene his manheed and my symplesse,   10
Þat daunger by gret vyolence
Haþe me brought in gret distresse;
And yit in verray sikurnesse,
Þoughe my desyre I neuer atteyne,
Yit withoute doubleness   15
To love him best I shal not feyne.

For whane we were ful tendre of yeeris,
Flouring booþe in oure chyldheede,
Wee sette to nothing oure desyres,
Sauf vnto playe, and tooke noon heede,   20
And gaderd flowres in þe meede,
Of youþe þis was oure moost pleasaunce,
And love þoo gaf me for my meede
A knotte in hert of Remembraunce,

Which þat neuer may beo vnbounde,   25
Hit is so stedfast and so truwe,
For alwey oone I wol beo founde
His womman, and chaunge for no nuwe.
Wolde God þe sooþe þat he knewe,
Howe offt I sighe for his saake,   30
And he me list not onys ruwe,
Ne yyveþe no force, what yvell I make.

5 *langoure*: emotional enfeeblement   10 *symplesse*: humbleness (her social and gender *difference*), inexperience, naïvety   11 *daunger*: power, dominance (often used of a lady's indifference to a lover, relations here reversed)   13 *sikurnesse*: truth   15–16 *withoute doubleness . . . I shall not feyne*: when I offer to *love him best* I won't be engaged in any feigning or duplicity   20 *Sauf*: except, save   21 *meede*: meadow   22 *moost pleasaunce*: greatest delight   23 *meede*: reward   24 *knotte in hert*: like some knotted handkerchief, a token of *Remembraunce*, also imaging distress of *hert* and its bondage   27 *alwey oone*: constant, always the same   29 *sooþe*: truth   31 *he me list not onys ruwe*: he is not inclined to give me pity, he shows no compassion   32 *yyveþe no force, what yvell I make*: takes no account of how bad my state is

His poorte, his cheere, and his fygure
Beon euer present in my sight,
In whos absence eeke I ensure,   35
I cane neuer be gladde ne light:
Fore he is my chosen knyght,
Þaughe hit to him ne beo not kouþe,
And so haþe he beon boþe day and night,
Truly fro my tendre youþe.   40

Emprynted in myn Inwarde thought,
And alwey shal til þat I deye,
Out of myn hert he parteþe nought,
Ne neuer shal, I dare weel seye.
Ilis loue so soore me dooþe werreye,   45
God graunt hit tourne for þe best!
For I shal neuer, I dare wel sey,
Withoute his love lyve in rest.

A trouthe in tendre aage gonne,
Of loue with longe perseueraunce,   50
In my persone so sore is ronne,
Þat þer may beo no varyaunce;
For al myne hertes souffysaunce
Is, wheþer þat I waake or wynk,
To haue hooly my Remembraunce   55
On his persone, so mychil I thynk!

'What so men seyn'

What so men seyn
Loue is no peyn
To them, serteyn,
   Butt varians.
For they constreyn   5
Ther hertis to feyn,
Ther mowthis to pleyn
   Ther displesauns.

---

33 *poorte*: bearing   *cheere*: manner, temper (especially as visible in the face)   35 *ensure*: assure   36 *light*: i.e. of heart   38 *kouþe*: truly known   49 *trouthe*: pledge *tendre aage*: youth   52 *varyaunce*: change of mind   53 *souffysaunce*: satisfaction 54 *wynk*: sleep   56 *mychil*: much, greatly

---

1 *What so*: whatever

Whych is in dede
Butt feynyd drede,   10
So god me spede,
    And dowbilnys;
Ther othis to bede,
Ther lyuys to lede,
And proferith mede   15
    New fangellnys.

For when they pray,
Ye shall haue nay;
What so they sey
    Beware for shame.   20
For euery daye
They waite ther pray
Wherso they may,
    And make butt game.

Then semyth me   25
Ye may well se
They be so fre
    In euyry plase,
Hitt were pete
Butt they shold be   30
Begelid, parde,
    Withowtyn grase.

'My woofull hert thus clad in payn'

My woofull hert thus clad in payn
Wote natt welle what do nor seyn,
    Longe absens greuyth me so.

For lakke of syght nere am I sleyn;
All Ioy myne hert hath in dissedeyn,   5
    Comfort fro me is go.

13 *bede*: bid, offer   15 *proferith mede*: offer as reward, give in payment   30 *Butt*: unless
31–2 *Begelid . . . grase*: deceived, by God, mercilessly
2 *wote*: knows

Then thogh I wold me owght complan
Of my sorwe and grete payn,
 Who shold comforte me do?

Ther is no thynge can make me to be fayn,   10
Butt the syght of hym agayn
 That cawsis my woo.

None butt he may me susteyn;
He is my comfort in all payn;
 I loue hym and no moo.   15

To hym I woll be trywe and playn,
And euyr his owne in serteyn,
 Tyll deth departe us to.

My hert shall I neuer fro hym refrayn;
I gaue hitt hym withowte constrayn,   20
 Euyr to contenwe so.

7 *owght*: thoroughly, excessively   10 *fayn*: glad   17 *in serteyn*:   certainly, truly

2

Geoffrey Chaucer, Of Quene Annelida and False Arcite (c.1372–1380), Edited by William Thynne (1532)

THE date and textual history of this delicately accomplished poem are uncertain. Most scholars assume that it started as an experiment with the matter of Boccaccio's *Teseida*, the work which later provided a source for *The Knight's Tale*. In that part of *The Canterbury Tales* Annelida is not mentioned, and Chaucer (*c.*1343–1400) focuses on Arcite's passion for Emelye, sister of Ypolita. Recently it has been wondered whether the variousness of *Annelida* might not be the product of scribal intervention. According to one view the received text was forged out of distinct parts—a section of narrative (1–210) followed by Annelida's letter (211–357)—only the second of which is likely to be by Chaucer. The poem is given here, however, in the compound form known to writers from Lydgate to Pope and beyond. This means preserving a final stanza generally considered non-authorial. The text is edited from William Thynne's *Workes of Geffray Chaucer* (1532)—almost the first, and perhaps the most influential, of collected Chaucers. Thynne took great care over *Annelida*, comparing and emending manuscripts before sending his copy to the printer. Later editors in the period of this anthology—notably Thomas Speght (1598, 1602)—remained close to his text. Variants between Thynne's *Annelida* and the manuscript-based version of modern editors (as represented by *The Riverside Chaucer*) are selectively recorded in the textual notes. That the poem was a valued part of the Chaucer canon during the fifteenth century is evident from the manuscript tradition. It is more difficult to assess its status in the sixteenth and seventeenth centuries, though Shakespeare was not the only reader to have been prompted by the organization of Chaucer editions to read *Annelida* in conjunction with *The Knight's Tale*—source for *A Midsommer Nights Dreame* and *The Two Noble Kinsmen*.

OF QUENE ANNELIDA AND FALSE ARCITE

O thou feirs god of armes Mars the rede
That in thy frosty countre called Trace
Within thy grisly temples ful of drede
Honoured arte as patron of that place
With the Bellona Pallas ful of grace   5
Be present, and my songe contynewe and gye
At my begynnynge thus to thee I crye

For it ful depe is sonken in my mynde
With pytous herte in Englysshe to endyte
This olde story, in latyn whiche I fynde   10
Of quene Annelyda and false Arcite
That elde, which al can frete and byte
And it hath freten many a noble story
Hath nyghe deuoured out of our memory

Be fauourable eke thou Polymnia   15
On Pernaso that with thy systers glade
By Elycon, not farre from Crisa
Singest with voyce memorial in the shade
Vnder the laurer, which that may not fade
And do that I my shyp to hauen wynne   20
First folowe I Stace, and after hym Corynne

Iamque domos patrias Cithice post aspera gentis   21a
Prelia laurigero subeunte Thesea curru   21b
Letifici plausus missusque ad sidera vulgi   21c

---

2 *Trace*: Thrace   5 *the Bellona Pallas*: unless *Pallas ful of grace* is a distinct clause (making the goddess of war and *Pallas* two objects of address led by 'thee'), *Bellona* is an adjective qualifying (and stressing the warlike qualities of) *Pallas*   6 *gye*: guide   9 *endyte*: compose   12 *elde*: outdating age, the irresistible passage of time   *frete*: gnaw upon   15 *eke*: also *Polymnia*: one of the nine Muses, *systers glade*   16 *Pernaso*: Parnassus, like that other mountain *Elycon* (Helicon) and the town of *Crisa* ('Cirrea' in manuscript, port of 'Crissa'), is a haunt of the Muses   19 *laurer*: laurel (of poetic accomplishment)   20 *do*: ensure   21 *Stace*: Statius, author of the *Thebaid*   *Corynne*: see Introduction, p. 5   21a–c *Iamque domos . . . ad sidera vulgi*: Statius, *Thebaid*, 12. 519–21, paraphrased in 22–8

Whan Theseus with warres longe and grete
The aspre folke of Cithe hath ouercome
The Laurer crowned in his chayre golde bete
Home to his countre houses is ycome   25
For whiche the people blysful al and some
So cryden, that to the sterres it wente
And hym to honouren dyd al her entente

Before this duke, in signe of victorie
The trompes come, and in his baner large   30
The ymage of Mars, and in token of glorie
Men might se of tresour many a charge
Many a bright helme, and many a spere and targe
Many a fressh knight, and many a blisful route
On horse and on foote, in all the felde aboute   35

Ipolyta his wyfe, the hardy quene
Of Cithya, that he conquered had
With Emelie her yonge suster shene
Fayre in a chare of golde he with him lad
That al the grounde about her chare she sprad   40
With brightnesse of beautie in her face
Fulfylled of largesse and of grace

With his triumphe and laurer corowned thus
In al the floure of fortunes yeuyng
Lete I this noble prince Theseus   45
Towarde Athenes in his way rydyng
And fonde I wol in shortly for to bring
The slye way of that I gan to write
Of quene Annelida and false Arcyte

Mars that through his furyous course of yre   50
The olde wrathe of Iuno to fulfyl
Hath set the peoples hertes both on fyre
Of Thebes and Grece, and euerich other to kyl

23 *aspre*: fierce   *Cithe*: Scythia   25 *countre houses*: houses of his district   28 *dyd al her*
entente: fulfilled their intention   32 *charge*: load   34 *blisful route*: happy crowd
38 *shene*: bright   43 *triumphe*: victory procession   44 *yeuyng*: bounty   47 *fonde*:
attempt   48 *slye way*: deceitful conduct   51 *olde wrathe of Iuno*: her long-standing anger
against Thebes was prompted by Jupiter's affairs with women of the city, Semele and Alcmene
53 *euerich other*: each other, everyone on the other side

With blody speares rested neuer styl
But throng now here nowe there amonge hem bothe   55
That eueryche other slew, so were they wrothe

For whan Amphiorax and Tydeus
Ipomedon, and Partynope also
Were deed, and slayne proude Campaneus
And whan the wretched thebans brethern two   60
Were slayne, and kyng Adrastus home ago
So desolate stode Thebes and so bare
That no wight coude remedye of his care

And whan the olde Creon gan espye
How that the bloode royal was brought adoun   65
He helde the cytee by his tyrannye
And dyd the gentyls of that regyoun
To ben his frendes, and dwel in the toun
So what for loue of him, and what for awe
The noble folke were to the towne ydrawe   70

Amonge al these Annelyda the quene
Of Ermonye, was in that towne dwellyng
That fayrer was than the sonne shene
Throughout the world so gan her name spring
That her to se had euery wight lyking   75
For as of trouthe is there none her lyche
Of al the women in this worlde ryche

Yonge was this quene, of twenty yere olde
Of myddle stature, and of suche fayrenesse
That nature had a ioye her to beholde   80
And for to speken of her stedfastnesse
She passed hath Penelope, and Lucresse
And shortly if she shal ben comprehended
In her might nothyng ben amended

---

55 *throng*: pressed, hastened   57–9 *Amphiorax . . . Campaneus*: heroes of the siege of Thebes
(that of the Seven against Thebes) which followed the exile of Oedipus   60 *brethern two*:
Eteocles and Polynices   61 *Adrastus*: king of Argos, leader of the Seven besieging
Thebes   *ago*: was gone   72 *Ermonye*: Armenia   74 *gan . . . spring*: did flourish
76 *as of trouthe*: truly

This Theban knight eke sothe to sayne 85
Was yonge, and therto withal a lusty knight
But he was double in loue, and nothing playne
And subtyl in that crafte ouer any wight
And with his connyng wan this lady bright
For so ferforthe he gan her trouthe assure 90
That she him trusteth ouer any creature

What shulde I sayne, she loueth Arcyte so
That whan that he was absent any throwe
Anon her thought her herte brast a two
For in her syght to her he bare him lowe 95
So that she wende haue al his herte yknowe
But he was false, it nas but fayned chere
As nedeth not suche crafte men to lere

But neuerthelesse ful mykel besynesse
Had he, er that he might his lady wynne 100
And swore he wolde dyen for distresse
Or from his wytte he sayd he wolde twynne
Alas the whyle, for it was routhe and synne
That she vpon his sorowes wolde rewe
But nothing thinketh the false as doth the trewe 105

Her fredom founde Arcyte in suche manere
That al was his, that she hath moche or lyte
Ne to no creature made she chere
Further than it lyked to Arcyte
There was no lacke, with which he might her wyte 110
She was so ferforthe yeuen him to please
That al that lyked him, dyd her ease

There nas to her no maner letter sent
That touched loue, from any maner wight
That she ne shewed him or it was brent 115
So playne she was, and dyd her ful might

90 *ferforthe*: far   *gan her ... assure*: did promise her   93 *any throwe*: at or for any time
94 *brast*: burst, broke   95 *lowe*: humbly   96 *wende haue ... yknowe*: thought she had
full knowledge of his heart   97 *chere*: manner, temper   98 *lere*: learn   99 *ful
mykel besynesse*: very much to do   102 *from his wytte ... twynne*: go out of his mind
103 *routhe*: a pitiful thing   105 *nothing ... as*: not at all like   106 *fredom founde*:
liberality provided for   107 *lyte*: little   109 *lyked to*: pleased   110 *wyte*: blame
112 *lyked him*: pleased him   *dyd her ease*: satisfied her   115 *or*: before   *brent*: burnt

That she nyl hyde nothyng from her knight
Leste he of any vntrouthe her vpbreyde
Without bode his herte she obeyde

And eke he made him ialous ouer her   120
That what that any man had to her sayde
Anon he wolde prayen her to swere
What was that worde, or make him yuel apayde
Than wende she out of her wytte haue brayde
But al was but sleyght and flaterye   125
Without loue he fayned ielousye

And al this toke she so debonairly
That al his wyl, her thought it skylful thyng
And euer the lenger she loued him tenderly
And dyd him honour as he were a kyng   130
Her herte was to him wedded with a ryng
For so ferforthe vpon trouthe is her entent
That where he gothe, her herte with him went

Whan she shal eate, on him is so her thought
That wel vnneth of meate toke she kepe   135
And whan she was to her rest brought
On him she thought alway tyl that she slepe
Whan he was absent, priuely dothe she wepe
Thus lyueth fayre Annelyda the quene
For false Arcyte, that dyd her al this tene   140

    This false Arcyte, of his newfanglenesse
For she to him so lowly was and trewe
Toke lesse deynte for her stedfastnesse
And sawe another lady proude and newe
And right anon he clad him in her hewe   145
Wote I not whether in whyte, reed, or grene
And falsed fayre Annelyda the quene

---

119 *bode*: hesitation   123 *make him yuel apayde*: conduct himself like someone badly treated
124 *wende she . . . brayde*: believed she would go mad, be started out of her wits   127 *debon-airly*: courteously   128 *skylful*: reasonable, just   129 *euer the lenger*: increasingly with time   132 *ferforthe*: much   134 *shal*: ought to   135 *wel vnneth . . . kepe*: she paid scarcely any attention to food   140 *tene*: harm   143 *deynte*: delight   145 *right anon*: immediately   *hewe*: colour (of a specific favour, or imagined lovers' heraldry)
146 *Wote*: know

But neuerthelesse, great wonder was it none
Though he were false, for it is the kynde of man
Sythe Lamek was, that is so longe agone   150
To be in loue as false as euer he can
He was the first father that began
To louen two, and was in bigamye
And he founde tentes first, but if men lye

   This false Arcyte, somwhat muste he fayne   155
Whan he was false, to coueren his traytorie
Right as an horse, that can both byte and playne
For he bare her in honde of trecherye
And swore he coude her doublenesse espye
And al was falsnesse that she to him ment   160
Thus swore this thefe and forth his way he went

Alas, what herte might endure it
For routhe or wo, her sorowe for to tel
Or what man hath the connyng or the wyt
Or what man might within the chambre dwel   165
If I to him rehersen shal the hel
That suffreth fayre Annelida the quene
For false Arcyte, that dyd her al this tene

She wepeth, wayleth, and swouneth pitously
To grounde deed she falleth as a stone   170
Crampyssheth her lymmes crokedly
She speketh as her wytte were al agone
Other colour than asshen hath she none
Ne none other worde speketh she moche or lyte
But mercy cruel herte myn Arcyte   175

And thus endureth, tyl that she was so mate
That she ne hath foote, on which she may sustene
But forth languisshing euer in this estate
Of which Arcyte hath neyther rothe ne tene

---

149 *kynde*: nature   150 *Lamek*: the first bigamist (Gen. 4: 19)   154 *he founde tentes first*:
according to Gen. 4: 20, however, his son Jabal established the use of tents   *but if*: unless
157 *playne*: be playful   158 *bare her in honde*: accused her   160 *ment*: said
171 *Crampyssheth*: contorts   176 *mate*: exhausted, disconsolate   178 *But forth*: but she
must continue   *estate*: condition   179 *rothe ne tene*: pity nor sorrow

His herte was els where newe and grene   180
That on her wo, ne deyneth him not to thinke
Him recketh neuer whether she flete or synke

   This newe lady holdeth him so narowe
Up by the bridel, at the staues ende
That euery worde he dred it as an arowe   185
Her daunger made him both bowe and bende
And as her luste, made him turne or wende
For she ne graunted him in her lyuyng
No grace, why that he hath lust to synge

But droue him forthe, vnneth lyst her knowe   190
That he was seruaunt vnto her ladyshyp
But leste he were proude, she helde him lowe
Thus serueth he, without meate or syp
She sente him nowe to lande, and nowe to shyp
And for she yaue him daunger al his fyl   195
Therfore she had him at her owne wyl

   Ensample of this, ye thrifty women al
Take hede of Annelyda and false Arcyte
That for her lyst him, her dere herte cal
And was so meke, therfore he loued her lyte   200
The kynde of mannes herte is to delyte
On thing that straunge is, also god me saue
For what they may not get, that wold they haue

   Nowe turne we to Annelyda ayen
That pyneth day by day in languisshyng   205
But whan she sawe that her ne gate no geyn
Vpon a day ful soroufully wepyng
She cast her for to make a complaynyng
And with her owne hande she gan it write
And sente it to her theban knight Arcyte.   210

---

182 *flete*: swim   183 *narowe*: straitly   184 *at the staues ende*: either in training, tied to a pole, or pulling a wagon strenuously, strained at the shafts' *ende*   186 *daunger*: disdain   187 *as her luste*: at her whim   188 *her lyuyng*: the way she lived   189 *why . . . to synge*: for which he would want to sing (because cheerful)   190 *vnneth lyst her knowe*: she hardly deigned to acknowledge   199 *for her lyst him . . . cal*: because it pleased her to call him   202 *straunge*: distant   *also*: as   206 *ne gate no geyn*: got no gain, made no progress

¶ The Complaynt of Annelyda to False Arcyte

So thyrled with the poynt of remembraunce
The swerde of sorowe, whet with false plesaunce
Myn herte bare of blysse, and blacke of hewe
That turned is to quakyng al my daunce
My sewerte in waped countenaunce   215
Sens it auayleth nought to ben trewe
For who so trewe is, it shall her rewe
That serueth loue, and dothe her obseruaunce
Alway to one, and chaungeth for no newe

I wote my selfe as wel as any wight   220
For I loued one, with al myn hert and might
More than my selfe, an hundred thousande syth
And called him my hertes lyfe, my knight
And was al his, as ferre as it was right
And whan that he was glad, than was I blythe   225
And his disease was my dethe as swythe
And he ayen, his trouthe hath me plight
For euermore his lady me to kythe

Nowe is he false alas, and causeles
And of my wo he is so routhles   230
That with a worde him lyst not ones dayne
To bring ayen my sorouful herte in pees
For he is caught vp in an other lees
Right as him lyst he laugheth at my payne
And I ne can myn herte not restrayne   235
For to loue him yet alway neuertheles
And of al this I not to whom to playne

And shulde I playne, alas the harde stounde
Vnto my foe, that yaue myn herte a wounde
And yet desyreth that myn harme be more   240
Nowe certes ferther wol I neuer be founde

---

211 *thyrled*: pierced   212 *plesaunce*: delight   215 *sewerte*: security   *waped*: stunned (as though struck)   222 *syth*: times   226 *swythe*: quickly   228 *kythe*: acknowledge 233 *lees*: snare   237 *not*: do not know   238 *stounde*: condition   241 *certes*: certainly   *ferther*: elsewhere (with someone else)

None other helpe, my sores for to sounde
My desteny hath shaped so ful yore
I wol none other medicyne ne lore
I wol ben aye there I was ones bounde 245
That I haue sayd, be sayd for euermore

Alas, where is become your gentylnesse
Your wordes ful of plesaunce and humblesse
Your obseruaunce in so lowe mancre
Your awayting, and your besynesse 250
On me, that ye called your maystresse
Your souerayne lady in this worlde here
Alas, is there neyther worde ne chere
Ye vouchsafe vpon myn heuynesse
Alas your loue, I bye it al to dere 255

Now certes swete, though that ye
Thus causelesse the cause be
Of my deedly aduersyte
Your manly reason ought it to respyte
To slee your frende, and namely me 260
That neuer yet in no degre
Offended you, as wisly he
That al wote, of wo my soule quyte

But for I was so playne Arcyte
In al my workes moche and lyte 265
And was so besy you to delyte
Myn honour saue, meke, kynde, and fre
Therfore ye put in me this wyte
Alas, ye retche not a myte
Though that the swerde of sorowe byte 270
My woful herte, through your cruelte

---

242 *sounde*: heal   243 *so ful yore*: such a long time ago   244 *wol*: desire
258 *deedly*: deadly to me   259–60 *ought it to respyte | To slee*: should withhold itself from the
killing of   261 *in no degre*: in any way   262–3 *as wisly … quyte*: as surely as he that
knows all may free my soul of woe   267 *Myn honour saue*: except that I did not compromise
my honour *kynde, and free*: sympathetic and generous   268 *wyte*: blame   269 *retche
not a myte*: care not a jot

My swete foe, why do ye so for shame
And thynke ye that furthered be your name
To loue a newe, and ben vntrewe aye
And put you in slaunder nowe and blame   275
And do to me aduersyte and grame
That loue you moste, god thou woste alwaye
Yet turne ayen, and yet be playne some daye
And than shal this that nowe is mys ben game
And al foryeue, whyle I lyue maye   280

Lo herte myn, al this is for to sayne
As whether shal I pray or els playne
Whiche is the way to done you to be trewe
For eyther mote I haue you in my chayne
Or with the dethe ye mote departe vs twayne   285
There bethe none other meane wayes newe
For god so wysely on my soule rewe
As verely ye sleen me with the payne
That mowe ye se vnfayned on myn hewe

For thus ferforth haue I my dethe sought   290
My selfe I murder with my priuy thought
For sorowe and routhe of your vnkyndnesse
I wepe, I wayle, I faste, al helpeth naught
I weyue ioy that is to speke of aught
I voyde company, I flye gladnesse   295
Who may auaunt her better of heuynesse
Than I, and to this plite haue ye me brought
Without gylte, me nedeth no wytnesse

And shulde I pray, and weyuen womanhede
Nay rather dethe, than do so foule a dede   300
And aske mercy and gyltlesse, what nede
And if I playne what lyfe I lede

---

275 *slaunder*: ill repute   276 *grame*: anguish   277 *god thou woste*: as, by Heaven, (or 'as
well') you know   279 *mys*: amiss   *ben game*: appear sport, be laughed at as a mis-
adventure   280 *foryeue*: forgive   284 *mote*: must   285 *departe*: separate
286 *meane*: moderate   287 *For . . . rewe*: So may God in his wisdom take pity on my soul
289 *mowe ye*: you are able to   294 *weyue*: relinquish   295 *voyde*: shun   296 *auaunt*:
boast   299 *pray*: supplicate

You recketh not, that knowe I out of drede
And if I vnto you myn othes bede
For myn excuse, a scorne shal be my mede   305
Your chere floureth, but it wol not sede
Ful longe agon I might haue taken hede

For though I had you to morowe agayne
I might as wel holde April from rayne
As holde you to maken stedfast   310
Almighty god, of trouthe the souerayne
Wher is the trouth of man, who hath it slayne
She that hem loueth, shal hem fynde as fast
As in a tempest is a rotten maste
Is that a tame beest, that is aye fayne   315
To renne away, whan he is leste agaste

    Nowe mercy swete, if I missay
Haue I aught sayd out of the way
I not, my wytte is al away
I fare as dothe the songe of chaunteplure   320
For nowe I playne, and nowe I pley
I am so mased that I dey
Arcyte hath borne away the key
Of al my worlde, and my good auenture

For in this worlde there nys no creature   325
Walkyng in more discomfyture
Than I, ne more sorowe endure
For if I slepe a furlonge way or twey
Than thynketh me that your fygure
Before me stante clad in asure   330
Efte to profre a newe assure
For to ben trewe, and mercy me to prey

---

303 *out of drede*: without doubt   304 *bede*: offer   306 *Your chere ... not sede*: your demeanour blossoms with promises which won't come to fruition   315 *aye fayne*: always inclined   319 *not*: know not   320 *the songe of chaunteplure*: 13th-cent. French poem contrasting the sorrows after death which follow a life of sinful pleasure ('sing ... weep'), shorthand in later usage for the way joys lead to woe or vice versa   322 *mased*: confused 324 *auenture*: fortune   328 *a furlonge way*: couple of minutes, time needed to walk a furlong   330 *asure*: azure (blue was the colour of constancy)   331 *Efte to profre*: to offer again

The longe nyght, this wonder syght y drie
That on the day for suche affray I dye
And of al this right naught iwys ye retche   335
Ne neuermore myn eyen two ben drie
And to your routhe, and to your trouthe I crye
But welaway, to ferre ben they to fetche
Thus holdeth me my destyne a wretche
But me to rede out of this drede or gye   340
Ne may my wyt (so weake is it) not stretche

Than ende I thus, sythe I may do nomore
I yeue it vp for nowe and euermore
For I shal neuer efte putten in balaunce
My sykernesse, ne lerne of loue the lore   345
But as the swan, I haue herde say ful yore
Ayenst his dethe wol synge in his penaunce
So synge I here the destenye and chaunce
Howe that Arcyte Annelyda so sore
Hath thrilled with the poynt of remembraunce   350

    Whan that Annelyda this woful quene
Hath of her hande written in this wyse
With face deed, betwyxe pale and grene
She fel a swoune, and sythe she gan to ryse
And vnto Mars auoweth sacrifyse   355
Within the temple, with a sorouful chere
That shapen was, as ye may plainly here.

---

333 *drie*: experience   334 *on the day for suche affray I dye*: I long for day because of this fearful
shock   335 *iwys*: indeed   *retche*: care   339 *holdeth*: keeps   340 *me to rede . . . or
gye*: to talk, argue, find a way out of this distress or guide myself   345 *sykernesse*: safety   *lore*:
knowledge   347 *Ayenst*: in preparation for   350 *thrilled*: equivalent to 211 *thyrled*
354 *sythe*: afterwards   *gan to*: did   356 *chere*: bearing, mood   357 *shapen was*: took
shape

3

Thomas Churchyard,
Shores Wife (1563)

THE career of Churchyard (*c.* 1520–1604), as a soldier of fortune and on the fringes of court, passed through decades of vicissitude. In the literary field too his work fluctuated in public esteem and responded, in its way, to change. Certain of these shifts of taste are written into *Shores Wife*—aptly, for a poem so concerned with life's variableness. First penned, if *Churchyard's Challenge* (1593) can be believed, during the reign of Edward VI, it did not appear in print until the 1563 edition of *A Myrroure for Magistrates*. The work won applause, but then fell (along with the *Myrroure*) into the shadows. It was Churchyard's revision of the piece thirty years later for the *Challenge* which found Mistress Shore a new audience. Inlaying large blocks of text, the poet did some damage to his narrative structure, and (though the textual notes record points at which material was added in 1593) the work is edited here from the *Myrroure*. Jane Shore would loom large in poetry and drama at least until Rowe's tragedy (1714), named after her. On stage and page alike she found opportunities to exculpate herself and denounce Richard III for the misery which followed the death of her lover, Edward IV. It is a tribute to her eloquence in Churchyard that the 1587 *Myrroure* should have her say: 'since without blushing I haue so long beene a talkatiue wench, (whose words a world hath delighted in) I will now goe on boldly with my audacious manner'. Complaint in the line of Lydgate often figured unreliable speakers. What makes Churchyard's poem absorbing is the way Jane Shore's rhetorical character, essential to the doubts we have about her, is integrated into her impressive deployment of such Tudor topics as Worldly Ambition or the Miseries of Enforced Marriage.

SHORES WIFE

Among the rest by Fortune overthrowen,
I am not least, that most may wayle her fate:
My fame and brute abrode the world is blowen,
Who can forget a thing thus done so late?
My great mischaunce, my fall, and heauye state,   5
Is such a marke whereat eche tounge doth shoote,
That my good name is pluckt vp by the roote.

This wandryng worlde bewitched me with wyles,
And wonne my wittes wyth wanton sugred ioyes,
In Fortunes frekes who trustes her when she smyles,   10
Shal fynde her false, and full of fyckle toyes,
Her tryumphes al but fyl our eares wyth noyse,
Her flatteryng gyftes are pleasures myxt wyth payne.
Yea al her wordes are thunders threatnyng rayne.

The fond desire that we in glory set,   15
Doth thirle our hartes to hope in slipper happe,
A blast of pompe is all the fruyt we get,
And vnder that lyes hidde a sodayne clappe:
In seeking rest vnwares we fall in trappe.
In groping flowers wyth Nettels stong we are,   20
In labouring long, we reape the crop of care.

Oh darke deceyt with paynted face for showe,
Oh poysoned baite that makes vs egre styll,
Oh fayned frende deceyuing people so,
Oh world of thée we can not speake to yll,   25
Yet fooles we are that bende so to thy skyll,
The plage and skourge that thousandes dayly feele,
Should warne the wise to shonne thy whyrling whele.

---

3 *brute*: loud renown   *blowen*: i.e. by Fame's trumpet (cf. 45–6)   4 *late*: recently
6 *marke*: target   8 *wandryng*: full of error   10 *frekes*: caprices   14 *thunders
threatnyng rayne*: big promises which augur something unpleasant   15 *fond desire . . . set*:
foolish hope that we fix   16 *thirle*: bind, pierce   *slipper happe*: slippery chance
17 *blast*: mere gust   18 *clappe*: shock of misfortune   26 *thy skyll*: the (crafty) way you do
things   28 *thy whyrling whele*: that of *Fortune*

But who can stop the streame that runnes full swyft?
Or quenche the fyer that crept is in the strawe? 30
The thirstye drinkes, there is no other shyft,
Perforce is such, that nede obeyes no lawe,
Thus bound we are in worldly yokes to drawe,
And can not staye, nor turne agayne in tyme,
Nor learne of those that sought to hygh to clyme. 35

My selfe for proofe, loe here I nowe appeare,
In womans weede with wepyng watered eyes,
That bought her youth and her delyghtes ful deare,
Whose lowde reproche doth sound vnto the skyes
And byds my corse out of the grave to ryse, 40
As one that may no longer hide her face,
But nedes must come and shewe her piteous case.

The shete of shame wherein I shrowded was
Did move me ofte to playne before this daye,
And in mine eares dyd ryng the trumpe of brasse, 45
Which is defame that doth eche vice bewraye.
Yea though ful dead and lowe in earth I laye,
I heard the voyce of me what people sayd,
But then to speake alas I was affrayed.

And nowe a time for me I see preparde, 50
I heare the lives and falles of many wyghtes:
My tale therfore the better may be heard,
For at the torche the litle candle lightes.
Where Pageantes be, small thinges fil out the sightes.
Wherefore geve eare, good Baldwyn do thy best, 55
My tragedy to place among the rest.

Because that truthe shal witnesse wel with thee,
I wil rehearse in order as it fell,
My life, my death, my dolefull destenie,
My wealth, my woe, my doing every deale, 60

31 *shyft*: expedient   32 *Perforce is such*: it is and must be the case   34 *staye*:
linger   *turne agayne*: go back   39 *Whose lowde reproche*: blame of whom   42 *case*:
bodily person, condition, state of affairs, suit (what she can say for herself)   43 *The shete of
shame ... was*: her shroud recalls the *shete* of *penaunce* worn by adulterers (cf. 308)
46 *bewraye*: reveal   51 *I heare the lives and falles of many wyghtes*: i.e. in the *Myrroure* itself
55 *good Baldwyn*: the poet William Baldwin (*c.*1515–63), chief compiler of *The Myrroure for Magistrates*, appears as a linking figure addressed by its historical personages   57 *witnesse wel with*:
be accounted good evidence by   60 *every deale*: each detail

My bitter blisse, wherein I long dyd dwell:
A whole discourse of me Shores wife by name,
Now shalt thou heare as thou hadst sene the same.

Of noble bloud I can not boast my byrth,
For I was made out of the meanest molde,   65
Myne heritage but seven foote of earth,
Fortune ne gave to me the gyftes of golde:
But I could bragge of nature if I would,
Who fyld my face with favour freshe and fayer,
Whose beautie shone like Phebus in the ayer.   70

My shape, some sayd, was seemely to eche sight,
My countenaunce did shewe a sober grace,
Myne eyes in lookes were never proved lyght,
My tongue in wordes were chaste in every case,
Myne eares were deafe, and would no lovers place, 75
Save that (alas) a prynce dyd blot my browe,
Loe, there the strong did make the weake to bowe.

The maiestie that kynges to people beare,
The stately porte, the awful chere they showe,
Doth make the meane to shrynke and couche for feare, 80
Like as the hound, that doth his maister knowe:
What then, since I was made vnto the bowe:
There is no cloke, can serve to hyde my fault,
For I agreed the fort he should assaulte.

The Egles force, subdues eche byrd that flyes,   85
What mettal may resist the flaming fyre?
Doth not the sonne, dasill the clearest eyes,
And melt the ise, and make the frost retire?
Who can withstand a puissaunt kynges desyre?
The stiffest stones are perced through with tooles, 90
The wisest are with princes made but fooles.

65 *molde*: both 'clay' and 'pattern'   66 *but seven foote of earth*: only enough land to be buried in (common *heritage*, it is said, of even the least of men)   69 *favour*: graces of *Fortune*, comeliness 70 *Phebus*: Apollo, god of the sun   73 *lyght*: immodest   75 *deafe*: i.e. to lovers' enticements   *place*: gratify (with listening); old form of 'please', though *place* as 'offer preferment' was emerging   76 *blot my browe*: i.e. with shame; also 'darkened my mood', since a 16th-cent. *browe* is seat of emotions in the countenance   79 *awful chere*: dread-inspiring mien 80 *couche*: lie down   82 *made vnto the bowe*: brought into compliancy (involving archery as well as bodily bowing of submission)

Yf kynde had wrought my forme in common frames,
And set me forth in coloures black and browne,
Or beautie had bene parched in Phebus flames,
Or shamefast waies had pluckt my fethers downe,   95
Then had I kept my name and good renowne:
For natures gyftes was cause of all my griefe.
A pleasaunt pray entiseth many a thiefe.

Thus woe to thee that wrought my peacocks pryde
By clothing me with natures tapistrye,   100
Woe wurth the hewe wherein my face was dyed,
Whych made me thinke I pleased everye eye:
Like as the sterres make men beholde the skye,
So beauties showe doth make the wise ful fond,
And bringes free hartes ful oft to endeles bond.   105

But cleare from blame my frendes can not be found,
Before my time my youth they did abuse:
In maryage, a prentyse was I bound,
When that meere love I knewe not howe to vse.
But wealaway, that can not me excuse,   110
The harme is mine though they deuysed my care,
And I must smart and syt in slaundrous snare.

Yet geve me leave to pleade my case at large,
Yf that the horse do runne beyond his race,
Or any thing that kepers have in charge   115
Do breake theyr course, where rulers may take place,
Or meat be set before the hungryes face,
Who is in fault? the offendour yea or no,
Or they that are the cause of all this wo?

92 *kynde*: nature   *wrought . . . in common frames*: made according to ordinary patterns, worked intricately on the same devices (e.g. looms) as average folk   93 *black and browne*: unfashionable *coloures* for hair and complexion   94 *parched in Phebus flames*: sun-tan was considered unattractive   95 *shamefast waies . . . downe*: virtuous conduct (which secures against shame) had chastened my vain beauty, prevented me from pluming myself   99 *pryde*: magnificence (as well as 'vanity')   100 *with natures tapistrye*: her most glorious weaving   101 *wurth*: befall   104 *fond*: doting and foolish   109 *meere*: pure, absolute   *vse*: habituate myself to   110 *wealaway*: ah woe (a generalized cry of lamentation)   111 *care*: circumstances, sorrow   112 *slaundrous snare*: the trap of bad report   114 *race*: 'herd, stud' and 'stamping-ground'   116 *breake theyr course*: abandon their territory and usual track, give up their regimen   *take place*: claim priority   117 *meat*: food   118 *the offendour*: i.e. the horse that understandably ranges, the hungry person who eats

Note wel what stryfe this forced maryage makes,   120
What lothed lyves do come where love doth lacke,
What scratting bryers do growe vpon such brakes,
What common weales by it are brought to wracke,
What heavy loade is put on pacientes backe,
What straunge delyghtes this braunch of vice doth brede   125
And marke what graine sprynges out of such a seede.

Compel the hawke to syt that is vnmande,
Or make the hound vntaught to drawe the dere,
Or bryng the free agaynst his wil in band,
Or move the sad a pleasaunt tale to heare,   130
Your time is lost and you are never the nere:
So love ne learnes of force the knot to knyt,
She serves but those that feele sweete fancies fyt.

The lesse defame redoundes to my disprayse,
I was entyste by traynes, and trapt by trust: 135
Though in my power remayned yeas or nayes,
Vnto my frendes yet nedes consent I must,
In every thing, yea lawfull or vniust:
They brake the boowes and shakte the trée by sleyght,
And bent the wand that might have growen ful streight.   140

What helpe in this, the pale thus broken downe,
The Deere must nedes in daunger runne astraye:
At me therfore why should the world so frowne,
My weakenes made my youth a prynces praye.
Though wysedome should the course of nature stay,   145
Yet trye my case who lyst, and they shal prove,
The rypest wittes are soonest thralles to love.

---

120 *this*: such a   122 *scratting*: scratching   *brakes*: heaps of brushwood, thickets
123 *common weales*: shared life between partners, welfare of kingdoms   *brought to wracke*: wrecked
124 *pacientes*: patience's   125 *straunge delyghtes*: alienating pleasures with those outside
wedlock   127 *vnmande*: unused to the presence of men (falconry term)   128 *drawe*:
follow the scent of, move towards without startling   131 *never the nere*: not a jot nearer your
object   133 *fancies fyt*: stirring of desire (with 'madness' available in *fyt*)   135 *traynes*:
plots, lures   140 *wand*: young shoot   141 *pale*: boundary paling   146 *trye my case*:
consider my circumstances, be in my shoes

What nede I more to cleare my selfe to much?
A kyng me wanne, and had me at his call:
His royall state, his pryncely grace was such,   150
The hope of will (that women seeke for all,)
The ease and wealth, the gyftes whych were not smal,
Besieged me so strongly rounde aboute,
My power was weake, I could not holde him out.

Duke haniball in all his conquest greate,   155
Or Ceaser yet, whose tryumphes did excede,
Of all their spoyles which made them toyle and sweat,
Were not so glad to haue so ryche a meade,
As was this prince when I to hym agreed.
And yelded me a prisoner willynglye,   160
As one that knew no way aweye to flee.

The Nightingale for all his mery voyce
Nor yet the Larke that stil delightes to syng,
Did never make the hearers so reioyce,
As I with wordes have made this worthy kyng: 165
I never iard, in tune was every stryng,
I tempered so my tounge to please his eare,
That what I sayd was currant every where.

I ioynde my talke, my gestures, and my grace
In wittie frames that long might last and stand,   170
So that I brought the kyng in such a case,
That to his death I was his chiefest hand.
I governed him that ruled all this land:
I bare the sword though he did weare the crowne,
I strake the stroke that threwe the mightye downe.   175

148 *What nede I more ... to much?*: what further extenuation need I cite to more than exculpate myself?   151 *will*: being at liberty, wilfulness   156 *did excede*: were immense (and greater than Hannibal's)   166 *iard*: stuck at some issue, was discordant   168 *currant every where*: from the musical strain in *tempered* ('moderated, tuned for performance in different keys') comes 'transposed acceptably into everyone's discourse'; then 'cast and hardened' supports 'currency universally valid' (coinage *tempered* purely enough to retain its value everywhere)   170 *wittie frames ... stand*: long-memorable devices or tableaux, clever patterns of conduct that could for a long time dictate behaviour   172 *to his death*: until he died (parodic hints of the marriage vow)   174 *bare the sword*: exercised the power (cf. the *sword* which Justice wields in iconography, and that of Rom. 13: 4)

Yf iustice sayd that iudgement was but death,
With my sweete wordes I could the kyng perswade,
And make him pause and take therein a breath,
Tyl I wyth suyte the fawtors peace had made:
I knewe what waye to vse him in his trade,   180
I had the arte to make the Lyon meeke,
There was no poynt wherein I was to seeke.

Yf I did frowne, who then did looke awrye?
Yf I dyd smyle, who would not laugh outryght?
Yf I but spake, who durst my wordes denye?   185
Yf I pursued, who would forsake the flyght?
I meane my power was knowen to every wyght.
On such a heyght good hap had buylt my bower,
As though my swete should never have turnd to sower.

My husband then, as one that knewe his good,   190
Refused to kepe a prynces concubine,
Forseing the ende and mischiefe as it stoode,
Agaynst the king did never much repyne,
He sawe the grape whereof he dranke the wyne,
Though inward thought his hart did still torment,   195
Yet outwardly he seemde he was content.

To purchase prayse and winne the peoples zeale,
Yea rather bent of kinde to do some good,
I ever did vpholde the common weale,
I had delyght to save the gylteles bloud: 200
Eche suters cause when that I vnderstoode,
I did preferre as it had bene mine owne,
And helpt them vp, that might have bene orethrowne.

---

176 *iudgement was but death*: the punishment decided (for a particular crime) could only be death   178 *a breath*: giving stay of execution   179 *wyth suyte the fawtors peace had made*: by suing for grace had reconciled the offender with authority   180 *vse him in his trade*: take advantage of the way he did things   182 *no poynt wherein I was to seeke*: no matter in which I fell short of satisfying the king (nor in which my claims were unsatisfied)   183 *did looke awrye*: dared to attend to other things   187 *meane*: 'think, hold it to be the case' and 'tell you', as well as 'intend by this to say'   190 *knewe his good*: was prudent   198 *bent of kinde*: inclined by nature   199 *vpholde the common weale*: maintain the general good   202 *preferre*: put forward, recommend

My power was prest to ryght the poore mans wrong,
My handes were free to geve where nede requyred, 205
To watche for grace I never thought it long,
To do men good I nede not be desyred.
Nor yet with gyftes my hart was never hyred.
But when the ball was at my foote to guyde,
I played to those that fortune did abide. 210

My want was wealth, my woe was ease at wyll,
My robes were ryche, and braver then the sonne:
My Fortune then was farre above my skyll,
My state was great, my glasse did ever runne,
My fatal threede so happely was spunne, 215
That then I sat in earthly pleasures clad,
And for the time a Goddesse place I had.

But I had not so sone this lyef possest,
But my good happe began to slyp asyde.
And fortune then dyd me so sore molest, 220
That vnto playntes was tourned all my pride.
It booted not to rowe agaynst the tyde:
Myne oares were weke my hart and strength did fayle,
The wynd was rough I durst not beare a sayle.

What steppes of stryef belonge to highe estate? 225
The clymynge vp is doubtfull to indure,
The seate it selfe doth purchase priuie hate,
And honours fame is fyckle and vnsure,
And all she brynges, is floures that be vnpure,
Which fall as fast as they do sprout and spring, 230
And cannot last they are so vayne a thyng.

---

204 *prest*: prompt (with 'pressed' as 'gathered for action, enlisted' emergent)   205 *free*: ready, liberal   206 *watche for grace*: wait (even into the 'watches of the night') for royal favour   207 *desyred*: requested   210 *did abide*: were waiting on   211 *My want . . . at wyll*: rare happiness, when 'need' was obliterated by *wealth* and *woe* lost in *ease* on demand   212 *braver*: more bright and sumptuous   213 *skyll*: capacity, desert   214 *my glasse did ever runne*: good times kept coming like an hourglass with endless sand (the emendation 'over' would produce a more familiar image)   225 *steppes of stryef*: court life as a stairway of emulation and dispute   226 *doubtfull to indure*: full of pitfalls to get through, of uncertain outcome   227 *seate*: lofty position   228 *honours fame*: the renown that *honour* (advancement) brings

We count no care to catche that we do wyshe,
But what we wynne is long to vs vnknowen,
Til present payne be served in our dyshe,
We skarce perceyve whereon our gryefe hath growen: 235
What grayne proves wel that is so rashely sowen?
Yf that a meane dyd measure all our deedes,
In stead of corne we should not gather weedes.

The setled minde is free from Fortunes power,
They nede not feare who looke not vp aloft,   240
But they that clyme are carefull every hower,
For when they fall they light not very softe:
Examples hath the wysest warned ofte,
That where the trees the smallest braunches bere,
The stormes do blowe and have most rigor there.   245

Where is it strong but nere the ground and roote?
Where is it weake but on the hyghest sprayes?
Where may a man so surely set his foote,
But on those bowes that groweth lowe alwayes?
The litle twigges are but vnstedfast stayes,   250
Yf they breake not, they bend wyth every blast,
Who trustes to them shal never stand full fast.

The wynde is great vpon the hyghest hilles,
The quiete life is in the dale belowe,
Who treades on yse shal slide agaynst theyr wylles,   255
They want no care that curious artes would knowe.
Who lives at ease and can content him so,
Is perfect wise, and settes vs all to scoole,
Who hates this lore may wel be called a foole.

What greater gryefe may come to any lyfe,   260
Than after sweete to taste the bitter sower?
Or after peace to fall at warre and stryfe,
Or after myrth to have a cause to lower?

---

232 *count no care*: spare no effort   233 *to vs vnknowen*: because we cannot know what the
desired thing entails until it has been lived with   240 *aloft*: i.e. to *highe estate*   241 *care-*
full: full of woes   242 *light*: alight   244 *where*: i.e. at the top   256 *They want no*
care . . . would knowe: those who pursue arcane lore (court intrigue compared with learned and
magical *artes*) have every woe

Vnder such proppes false Fortune buyldes her bower,
On sodayne chaunge her flitting frames be set,   265
Where is no way for to escape her net.

The hastye smart that Fortune sendes in spyte
Is hard to brooke where gladnes we imbrace,
She threatens not, but sodaynly doth smyte,
Where ioye is moste there doth she sorowe place.   270
But sure I thinke, this is to strange a case,
For vs to feele such gryefe amyd our game,
And know not why vntil we taste the same.

As earst I sayd, my blisse was turnde to bale,
I had good cause to weepe and wring my handes,   275
And showe sad cheare with countenaunce full pale,
For I was brought in sorowes woful bandes:
A pyrrye came and set my shippe on sandes,
What should I hide, or colour care and noye?
Kyng Edward dyed in whom was all my ioye.   280

And when the earth receyved had his corse,
And that in tombe, this worthye prince was layd,
The world on me began to shewe his force,
Of troubles then my parte I long assayed:
For they, of whom I never was afrayed,   285
Vndyd me most, and wrought me such despyte,
That they bereft from me my pleasure quyte.

As long as life remaynd in Edwardes brest,
Who was but I? who had such frendes at call?
His body was no sooner put in chest,   290
But wel was him that could procure my fall:
His brother was mine enemy most of all
Protector then, whose vice did stil abound,
From yll to worse tyll death dyd him confound.

---

265 *flitting frames*: both 'transitory dispensations, fleeting patterns of life' (*Fortune* is *set* for, or
'fixed' *On*, a career of *sodayne change*) and (in a rarer sense of *frames*) 'subtly moving snares' (which
are *set* to be triggered *On* a movement of *sodayne change*, *Fortune* dropping the victim into the next
line's *net*   267 *hastye*: rapidly following *gladnes*   269 *threatens not*: gives no warning
271 *to strange a case*: too bewildering a state of affairs   273 *why*: what rationale its coming
has   274 *bale*: sorrow, suffering   276 *cheare*: spirits   278 *pyrrye*: gust of wind
279 *noye*: hurt, annoy   286 *despyte*: sharp wrong   290 *chest*: coffin (still current in
dialect)

He falsely fayned, that I of counsayle was   295
To poyson him, which thing I never ment,
But he could set thereon a face of brasse,
To bring to passe his lewde and false entent,
To such mischiefe this Tyrantes heart was bent.
To God, ne man, he never stoode in awe,   300
For in his wrath he made his wyll a lawe.

Lord Hastinges bloud for vengeauns on him cries,
And many moe, that were to long to name:
But most of all, and in most wofull wise
I had good cause this wretched man to blame.   305
Before the world I suffred open shame,
Where people were as thicke as is the sand,
I penaunce tooke with taper in my hand.

Eche iye did stare, and looke me in the face,
As I past by the rumours on me ranne,   310
But Patience then had lent me such a grace,
My quiete lookes were praised of every man:
The shamefast bloud brought me such colour than,
That thousandes sayd, which sawe my sobre chere,
It is great ruth to see this woman here.   315

But what prevailde the peoples pitie there?
This raging wolfe would spare no gylteles bloud.
Oh wicked wombe that such yll fruite did beare,
Oh cursed earth that yeldeth forth such mud,
The hell consume all thinges that dyd the good,   320
The heavens shut theyr gates against thy spryte,
The world tread downe thy glory vnder feete.

I aske of God a vengeance on thy bones,
Thy stinking corps corrupts the ayre I knowe:
Thy shameful death no earthly wyght bemones,   325
For in thy lyfe thy workes were hated so,

---

295 *of counsayle was*: secretly intended, belonged to a conspiracy   297 *set thereon a face of brasse*: brazen out his charge   298 *lewde*: wicked   308 *I penaunce tooke ... hand*: see 43 and n.   316 *what prevailde*: how availed   319 *mud*: often used in 16th-cent. English of human dregs, moral pollutants

That every man dyd wyshe thy overthrowe:
Wherefore I may, though percial nowe I am,
Curse every cause whereof thy body came.

Woe wurth the man that fathered such a childe: 330
Woe worth the hower wherein thou wast begate,
Woe wurth the brestes that have the world begylde,
To norryshe thée that all the world dyd hate.
Woe wurth the Gods that gave thée such a fate,
To lyve so long, that death deserved so ofte.   335
Woe wurth the chaunce that set thee vp alofte.

Ye Princes all, and Rulers everychone,
In punyshement beware of hatreds yre.
Before ye skourge, take hede, looke well thereon:
In wrathes yl wil yf malice kyndle fyre,   340
Your hartes wil bourne in such a hote desire,
That in those flames the smoake shal dym your sight,
Ye shal forget to ioyne your iustice ryght.

You should not iudge til thinges be wel deserned,
Your charge is styll to mainteyne vpryght lawes,   345
In conscience rules ye should be throughly learned,
Where clemencie byds wrath and rashenes pawes,
And further sayeth, stryke not wythout a cause,
And when ye smite do it for Iustice sake,
Then in good part eche man your skourge wil take.   350

Yf that such zeale had moved this Tyrantes minde,
To make my plague a warning for the rest,
I had small cause such fault in him to finde,
Such punishement is vsed for the best:
But by yll wil and power I was opprest.   355
He spoyled my goodes and left me bare and poore,
And caused me to begge from dore to dore.

What fall was this, to come from Princes fare,
To watche for crummes among the blinde and lame?
When almes was delt I had a hungry share,   360
Bycause I knewe not howe to aske for shame,

328 *percial*: partial   330 *wurth*: befall   338 *beware of hatreds yre*: eschew the rage of hatred   343 *ioyne*: impose   345 *charge*: task   356 *spoyled*: pillaged   360 *hungry share*: so little that I was left hungry

Tyll force and nede had brought me in such frame,
That starve I must, or learne to beg an almes,
With booke in hand, and say S. Dauids psalmes.

Where I was wont the golden chaynes to weare,   365
A payre of beades about my necke was wound,
A lynnen clothe was lapt about my heare,
A ragged gowne that trayled on the ground,
A dishe that clapt and gave a heavie sound,
A stayeng staffe and wallet therewithal,   370
I bare about as witnesse of my fal.

I had no house wherein to hyde my head,
The open strete my lodging was perforce,
Ful ofte I went al hungry to my bed,
My fleshe consumed, I looked like a corse,   375
Yet in that plyght who had on me remorse?
O God thou knowest my frendes forsooke me than,
Not one holpe me that suckered many a man.

They frownde on me that faund on me before,
And fled from me that followed me ful fast,   380
They hated me, by whom I set much store,
They knewe ful wel my Fortune dyd not last,
In every place I was condemnd and cast:
To pleade my cause at barre it was no boote,
For every man dyd tread me vnder foote.   385

Thus long I lyved all weary of my life,
Tyl death approcht and rid me from that woe:
Example take by me both maide and wyfe,
Beware, take heede, fall not to follie so,
A myrrour make of my great overthrowe: 390
Defye this world, and all his wanton wayes,
Beware by me, that spent so yll her dayes.

---

366 *payre of beades*: set of rosary beads   369 *dishe that clapt*: clapdish, begging-bowl with a lid
(carried by lepers and paupers, and clapped to announce their approach)   *heavie*: doleful
370 *stayeng*: supporting   *wallet*: bag for provisions   380 *ful fast*: very closely
383 *cast*: thrown aside   384 *at barre*: in law

4

Renaissance Lyrics

THIS group begins with a monologue by the Earl of Surrey (?1517–47). An example of epistolary plaint diverted into lyric, it is based on Serafino's 'Quella ingannata, afflicta . . .', which has behind it 'Phyllis to Demophoon', *Heroides*, 2. The text is taken from Richard Tottel's *Songes and Sonettes* (1557). From the second edition of that miscellany comes 'The Complaint of a Woman Rauished, and also Mortally Wounded', a remarkable poem of unknown authorship. Though the genre elsewhere discourses on rape, as in Gascoigne's *Complaynt of Phylomene*, this poem's concentration is unique. The poem by Gascoigne (*c.*1543–77) which follows is less extended than *Phylomene*; but it probes the authority of the masculine narrator in ways which reveal much about the controlling structures of 'female complaint' (above, pp. 16–17). Three lyrics from Elizabethan anthologies are included: the anonymous 'Poeme of a Mayde Forsaken', 'An Excellent Pastorall Dittic' by Anthony Munday (1560–1633), and 'The Nimph Seluagia . . .' by Bartholomew Young (1560–1612). The 'Poeme of a Mayde Forsaken', perhaps by Richard Edwards (?1523–66), comes from Nicholas Breton's selection, *The Arbor of Amorous Deuises* (1597). 'Oenones Complaint' might be added to this group, for it appeared, beside the poems of Munday and Young, in *Englands Helicon* (1600). The text given here, though, is taken from *The Araygnement of Paris* (1584), an entertainment for Elizabeth I by George Peele (1556–96). Like Surrey's lyric, Peele's is an epistolary distillation; it condenses material from *Heroides*, 5, paraphrased in this anthology by Aphra Behn. Compare, especially, lines 90–6 and 282–5 of her text. Finally, two songs: 'Round, around . . . ' from the second edition of *Madrigals to Foure Voices* by Thomas Morley (1557/8–1602), and *The Diseased Maiden Louer*, written anonymously in the early seventeenth century. No melody survives for the latter; Morley's music is most accessible in Thomas Morley, *First Book of Madrigals (1594)*, ed. Edmund H. Fellowes, rev. Thurston Dart (London, 1966), 104–8. In the ballad-title *Diseased* means 'without *ease*', though suggestions of a malady are not excluded (above, p. 47). The text is printed from a copy in the Pepys Collection at Magdalene College, Cambridge. The woodcut which heads the broadside is reproduced opposite the poem. A variant edition reads *Deceased . . .* While most plaints express what has been called 'a *penultimate* masochism' (above, p. 38), a few, such as this one, complete their action in death.

HENRY HOWARD, EARL OF SURREY

COMPLAINT OF THE ABSENCE OF HER LOUER
BEING VPON THE SEA

O Happy dames, that may embrace
The frute of your delight,
Help to bewaile the wofull case,
And eke the heauy plight
Of me, that wonted to reioyce   5
The fortune of my pleasant choyce:
Good Ladies, help to fill my moorning voyce.
   In ship, freight with rememberance
Of thoughts, and pleasures past,
He sailes that hath in gouernance   10
My life, while it wil last:
With scalding sighes, for lack of gale,
Furdering his hope, that is his sail
Toward me, the swete port of his auail.
   Alas, how oft in dreames I se   15
Those eyes, that were my food,
Which somtime so delited me,
That yet they do me good.
Wherwith I wake with his returne,
Whose absent flame did make me burne.   20
But when I find the lacke, Lord how I mourne?
   When other louers in armes acrosse,
Reioyce their chiefe delight:
Drowned in teares to mourne my losse,
I stand the bitter night,   25
In my window, where I may see,
Before the windes how the cloudes flee.
Lo, what a mariner loue hath made me.
   And in grene waues when the salt flood
Doth rise, by rage of winde: 30
A thousand fansies in that mood
Assayle my restlesse mind.

10 *in gouernance*: under his guidance, steered (cf. Latin *gubernaculum* 'rudder') on the sea of life
12 *gale*: breeze   14 *auail*: safety, profit   22 *in armes acrosse*: embracing (cf. lines 1–2)
26 *In my window*: as though on the bridge of a ship, resembling *her Louer*.

Alas, now drencheth my swete fo,
That with the spoyle of my hart did go,
And left me but (alas) why did he so?   35
   And when the seas waxe calme againe,
To chase fro me annoye.
My doutfull hope doth cause me plaine:
So dreade cuts of my ioye.
Thus is my wealth mingled with wo,   40
And of ech thought a dout doth growe,
Now he comes, will he come? alas, no no.

THE COMPLAINT OF A WOMAN
RAUISHED, AND ALSO
MORTALLY WOUNDED

A Cruell Tiger all with teeth bebled,
A bloody tirantes hand in eche degre,
A lecher that by wretched lust was led,
(Alas) deflowred my virginitee.
And not contented with this villanie,   5
Nor with th' outragious terrour of the dede,
With bloody thirst of greater crueltie:
Fearing his haynous gilt should be bewrayed,
By crying death and vengeance openly,
His violent hand forthwith alas he layed   10
Vpon my guiltles sely childe and me,
And like the wretch whom no horrour dismayde,
Drownde in the sinke of depe iniquitie:
Misusing me the mother for a time,
Hath slaine vs both for cloking of his crime.   15

---

1 *bebled*: blood-stained   2 *eche degre*: every way   11 *sely*: simple, innocent

GEORGE GASCOIGNE

A LOUING LADY BEING WOUNDED
IN THE SPRING TIME, AND
NOW GALDED EFTSONES WITH THE
REMEMBRANCE OF THE SPRING, DOTH
THERFORE THUS BEWAYLE

This tenth of March when *Aries* receyu'd,
Dan *Phœbus* rayes, into his horned head:
And I my selfe, by learned lore perceyu'd,
That *Ver* approcht, and frostie wynter fled.
I crost the *Thames*, to take the cherefull ayre,   5
In open feeldes, the weather was so fayre.

And as I rowed, fast by the further shore,
I heard a voyce, which seemed to lament:
Whereat I stay'd, and by a stately dore,
I left my Boate, and vp on land I went.   10
Till at the last by lasting payne I found,
The wofull wight, which made this dolefull sound.

In pleasaunt garden (placed all alone)
I saw a Dame, who sat in weary wise,
With scalding sighes, she vttred all hir mone,   15
The ruefull teares, downe rayned from hir eyes:
Hir lowring head, full lowe on hand she layed,
On knee hir arme: and thus this Lady sayed.

Alas (quod she) behold eche pleasaunt greene,
Will now renew, his sommers liuery,   20
The fragrant flowers, which have not long bene seene,
Will florish now, (ere long) in brauery:
The tender buddes, whom colde hath long kept in,
Will spring and sproute, as they do now begin.

TITLE *Galded*: galled, stung   *Eftsones*: again, a second time   *Remembrance of the Spring*: spring
acting as a reminder   1–4 *when Aries . . . Ver approcht*: the sun enters *Aries*, zodiacal constellation of the ram (hence *horned*), on 21 Mar., and with it comes *Ver*, the spring   12 *wight*:
person   14 *wise*: manner   17 *lowring*: mournful, woefull in bearing   21 *not long*:
i.e. not since last summer

But I (alas) within whose mourning mynde,   25
The graffes of grief, are onely giuen to growe,
Cannot enjoy the spring which others finde,
But still my will, must wyther all in woe:
The cold of care, so nippes my ioyes at roote,
No sunne doth shine, that well can do them boote.   30

The lustie *Ver*, which whillome might exchange
My griefe to ioy, and then my ioyes encrease,
Springs now elsewhere, and showes to me but strange,
My winters woe, therfore can neuer cease:
In other coasts, his sunne full clere doth shyne,   35
And comfort lends to eu'ry mould but myne.

What plant can spring, that feeles no force of *Ver*?
What flower can florish, where no sunne doth shyne?
These Bales (quod she) within my breast I beare,
To breake my barke, and make my pyth to pyne: 40
Needs must I fall, I fade both roote and rynde,
My braunches bowe, at blast of eu'ry wynde.

This sayed: she cast a glance and spied my face,
By sight wherof, Lord how she chaunged hew?
So that for shame, I turned backe a pace   45
And to my home, my selfe in hast I drew:
And as I could hir woofull wordes reherse,
I set them downe in this waymenting verse.

Now Ladies you, that know by whom I sing,
And feele the wynter, of such frozen wylls: 50
Of curtesie, yet cause this noble spring,
To send his sunne, aboue the highest hilles:
And so to shyne, vppon hir fading sprayes,
Which now in woe, do wyther thus alwayes.

Spreta tamen viuunt.

26 *graffes*: grafts (which begin to sprout in spring)   30 *do them boote*: help them
33 *showes*: appears   35 *coasts*: regions   36 *mould*: earth (continuing the figure of graft-
ing and growth, with a likely quibble on 'bodily form')   39 *Bales*: afflictions, sorrows
41 *rynde*: bark   47 *as I could*: as far as I could recall, as best I could manage   48 *waymenting*: lamenting   49 *that know by whom I sing*: though *The Hundreth Sundrie Flowres* at times
hints topicality without seeming genuinely allusive, it has been suggested that the poem connects
with circumstances in the Montague family (noble patrons of Gascoigne, with holdings in Southwark along the Thames)   51 *Of*: for the sake of   MOTTO: *Spreta tamen viuunt*: this
phrase (roughly 'they live despite disdain') tags and groups several poems around 'A Louing Lady'

GEORGE PEELE
OENONES COMPLAINT

From *The Araygnement of Paris*

Melpomene, the muse of tragicke songes,
With moornefull tunes in stole of dismall hue,
Assist a sillie Nymphe to wayle her woe,
And leaue thy lustie companie behinde.

Thou luckles wreath, becomes not me to weare   5
The Poplar tree for triumphe of my loue.
Then as my ioye my pride of loue is lefte,
Be thou vncloathed of thy louelie greene.

And in thy leaues my fortune written bee,
And them some gentle winde let blowe abroade,   10
That all the worlde may see how false of loue,
False Paris hath to his Oenone bene.

A POEME OF A MAYDE FORSAKEN

As late I lay within an Arbor sweete,
The ayre to take amongst the flowers faire:
I heard a Mayd to mourne and sorely weepe,
That thither vsd to make her oft repayre.

Alas, poore wench, quoth she, drownd in despaire,   5
What folly fond doth breed me my vnrest:
Will spitfull loue increase continuall care,
To worke her wrath on me aboue the rest.

And will she still increase my sorrowing sighes,
With pinching paine of heart, with torments torne: 10
Are these rewards, or are they *Cupids* slights,
To kill the heart which is with sorrowes worne?

3 *sillie*: simple, innocent

Then witnes beare, you woods and wasts about,
You craggie rockes, with hilles and valleyes low,
Recording birds, you beasts both strong and stout,   15
You fishes deafe, you waues that ebbe and flow.

Heere haue in minde that loue hath slaine a hart
As true as trueth vnto her froward friend,
Whose dying death shal shew her faithfull parte,
What so my dearc hath alwayes of me deemd.   20

The red brest then did seeme to be the Clarke,
And shrowded her vnder the mosse so greene,
He calles the birds each one to sing a parte:
A sight full strange and worthy to be seene,

The Larke, the Thrush and Nightingale,   25
The Linnets sweete, and eke the Turtles true,
The chattering Pie, the Iay, and eke the Quaile,
The Thrustle-Cock that was so blacke of hewe.

All these did sing the prayse of her true heart,
And mournd her death with dolefull musick sound: 30
Each one digged earth, and plyed so their part,
Till that she was close closed vnder ground.

ANTHONY MUNDAY

AN EXCELLENT PASTORALL DITTIE

A Carefull Nimph, with carelesse greefe opprest,
    Vnder the shaddow of an Ashen tree:
With Lute in hand did paint out her vnrest,
    Vnto a Nimph that bare her companie.
        No sooner had she tuned euery string: 5
        But sob'd and sigh'd, and thus began to sing.

15 *Recording*: repeating phrases of song (as *the Thrush* characteristically does), with a suggestion that the maid's mourning is echoed   20 *What so*: whatever   *deemd*: judged   27 *Pie*: magpie   28 *Thrustle-Cock*: blackbird   32 *close*: secretly, intimately

1 *Carefull*: full of woe   *carelesse greefe*: sorrow which takes no heed of anything else

Ladies and Nimphs, come listen to my plaint,
  On whom the cheerefull Sunne did neuer rise:
If pitties stroakes your tender breasts may taint,
  Come learne of me to wet your wanton eyes.   10
    For Loue in vaine the name of pleasure beares:
    His sweet delights are turned into teares.

The trustlesse shewes, the frights, the feeble ioyes,
  The freezing doubts, the guilefull promises:
The feigned lookes, the shifts, the subtill toyes,   15
  The brittle hope, the stedfast heauines.
    The wished warre in such vncertaine peace:
    These with my woe, my woes with these increase.

Thou dreadfull God, that in thy Mothers lap,
  Doo'st lye and heare the crie of my complaint,   20
And seest, and smilest at my sore mishap,
  That lacke but skill my sorrowes heere to paint:
    Thy fire from heauen before the hurt I spide,
    Quite through mine eyes into my brest did glide.

My life was light, my blood did spirt and spring,   25
  My body quicke, my hart began to leape:
And euery thornie thought did prick and sting,
  The fruite of my desired ioyes to reape.
    But he on whom to thinke, my soule still tyers:
    In bale forsooke, and left me in the bryers.   30

Thus Fancie strung my Lute to Layes of Loue,
  And Loue hath rock'd my wearie Muse a-sleepe:
And sleepe is broken by the paines I proue,
  And euery paine I feele dooth force me weepe.
    Then farewell fancie, loue, sleepe, paine, and sore: 35
    And farewell weeping, I can waile no more.

---

8 *On whom . . . neuer rise*: she claims never to have experienced a day which was not, from the
outset, woeful   9 *taint*: touch   19 *dreadfull God . . . thy Mothers lap*: Cupid dandled by
Venus   25 *light*: gay   27–8 *euery thornie thought did prick . . . to reape*: eagerness is
proverbially 'on thorns' (agitated and eager) *to reape* life's benefits and harvest its *fruite*
29 *tyers*: labours, exhausts itself (with a hint of feeding)   30 *In bale forsooke*: abandoned me
when things were bad, *left* me in woe   33 *proue*: experience

BARTHOLOMEW YOUNG
THE NIMPH SELUAGIA HER SONG

Sheepheard, who can passe such wrong,
    And a life in woes so deepe?
Which to liue is to too long,
    As it is too short to weepe.

Greeuous sighs in vaine I wast,   5
    Leesing my affiance, and
I perceaue my hope at last
    With a candle in the hand.

What time then to hope among
    Bitter hopes, that neuer sleepe?   10
When this life is to too long,
    As it is too short to weepe.

This greefe which I feele so rife,
    (Wretch) I doo deserue as hire:
Since I came to put my life   15
    In the hands of my desire.

Then cease not my complaints so strong,
    For (though life her course dooth keepe:)
It is not to liue so long,
    As it is too short to weepe.   20

TITLE *Seluagia*: 'selvage' is borderland, a marginal tract, so the name implies that rustic, exiled condition incident to the typical abandoned *Nimph*   1 *passe*: survive, silently endure (even, with reference to the lover and glance at Lam. 1: 12, 'pass by')   3–4 *Which to liue . . . to weepe*: a *life* so deeply woeful is *too long* to be endured but *too short* for enough tears to be shed to lament it properly   6 *Leesing*: losing   *affiance*: betrothal   8 *With a candle in the hand*: from Luke 15: 8, perhaps, suggesting penitence and prayers for the dead (possibly also with a bawdy innuendo) 14 *hire*: recompense

5. Woodcut from *The Diseased Maiden Louer* (early seventeenth century)

THOMAS MORLEY

'Round, around about a wood as I walkt'

Round, around about a wood as I walkt,
  Late in the euening, so faire, so fresh and gay,
Vnder a hathorne tree, I heard a prettie maide that talkt,
A pretty merrie maide that long before had walkt,
  Hey hoe tro-ly-lo heauie hart quoth shee,   5
  My louely louer, hath disdained mee.

THE DISEASED MAIDEN LOUER

Being a pleasant new court Song:
To an excellent new tune,
Or to be sung to the tune of *Bonny Nell*

As I went forth one Summers day,
To view the Meddowes fresh and gay,
A pleasant Bower I espi'd,
Standing hard by a Riuers side:
  And in't I heard a Mayden cry,   5
  Alas, there's none ere lou'd like I.

I couched close to heare her moane,
With many a sigh and heauie groane,
And wisht that I had beene the wight,
That might haue bred her hearts delight: 10
  But these were all the words that she,
  Did still repeat, none loues like me.

Then round the Meddowes did she walke,
Catching each flower by the stalke,

---

3 *hathorne*: hawthorn

TITLE *Diseased*: see above, p. 47   *Bonny Nell*: the tune (well known to Jacobean readers) is lost

Such as within the Meddowes grew,   15
As *Dead-mans thumbe*, and *Hare-bell* blue:
   And as she pluckt them, still cryde she,
   Alas, there's none ere lou'd like me.

A bed therein she made to lie:
Of fine greene things that grew fast by,   20
Of *Poplers*, and of *Willow* leaues,
Of *Sicamore* and *Flaggy* sheaues:
   And as she pluckt them, still cryde she,
   Alas, there's none ere lou'd like me.

The little *Lark-foote* shee'd not passe,   25
Nor yet the flowers of *Three-leau'd grasse*,
Which Milkemayds *Honny Succles* phraise,
The *Crowes foot*, nor the yellow *Crayse*,
   And as she pluckt them, still cride she,
   Alas, there's none ere lou'd like me.   30

The pretty *Dasie* which doth show
Her loue to *Phœbus*, bred her woe,
Who ioyes to see his chearefull face,
And mournes when he is not in place,
   Alacke, alacke, alacke, quoth she,   35
   There's none that euer lou'd like me.

The Flowers of the sweetest sent,
She bound them round with knotted *Bent*,
And as she layd them still in bands,
She wept, she wayl'd, and wrung her hands,   40
   Alas, alas, alas, quoth she,
   There's none that euer lou'd like me.

False man, quoth she, forgiue thee heauen,
As I doe wish my sinnes forgiuen,

---

16 *Dead-mans thumbe*: local name (chiefly West Country) for *Orchis mascula*, so named from the shape of its tubers   22 *Flaggy sheaues*: bundles of flag, iris   25 *Lark-foote*: now commonly known as larkspur   26 *Three-leau'd grasse*: meadow trefoil, clover   27 *phraise*: term, call   28 *Crowes foot*: usually applied to the buttercup, though *Crayse* covers that; can describe a range of geraniums, hyacinths, and the like (with leaves or flowers resembling claws) *Crayse*: rustic name for buttercup   31–2 *show | Her loue to Phœbus* (by opening in sunlight) 38 *Bent*: sedge, rushes, reeds

In blest *Elizium* I shall sleepe,   45
When thou with periur'd soules shalt weep
  Who when they liu'd, did like to thee,
  That lou'd their Loues as thou dost mee.

When she had fild her Apron full,
Of such sweet Flowers as she could cull,   50
The greene leaues seru'd her for a Bed,
The Flowers pillowes for her head,
  Then down she lay, ne're more did speake,
  Alas, with loue her heart did breake.

The Faithlesse Louer

To the same tune

When I had seene this Virgins end,   55
I sorrowed as became a friend,
And wept to see that such a Mayd
Should be by faithlesse loue betrayd.
  But woe (I feare) will come to thee,
  That was not true in loue as shee.   60

The Birds did cease their Harmony,
The harmelesse Lambs did seeme to cry,
The Flowers they did hang their head,
The Flower of Maydens being dead,
  Whose life by death is now set free,   65
  And none did loue more deare then shee.

The bubbling brookes did seeme to moane,
And Eccho from the Vales did groane;
Diana's Nimphs did ring her knell,
And to their Queene the same did tell,   70
  Who vowed by her chastitie,
  That none should take reuenge but she.

When as I saw her corps were cold,
I to her Louer went, and told
What chance vnto this Mayd befell,   75
Who sayd, I am glad she sped so well,
  D'ee thinke that I so fond would bee,
  To loue no Mayde but onely shee?

I was not made for one alone,
I take delight to heare them moane: 80
When one is gone, I will haue more:
That man is rich, that hath most store,
   I bondage hate, I must liue free,
   And not be ty'd to such as shee.

O Sir, remember, (then quoth I)   85
The power of Heauens All-seeing eye,
Who doth remember vowes forgot,
Though you denie you know it not:
   Call to your minde this Mayden free,
   The which was wrong'd by none but thee.   90

Quoth he, I haue a loue more faire,
Besides, she is her Fathers heire,
A bonny Lasse doth please my minde,
That vnto me is wondrous kinde:
   Her will I loue, and none but she,   95
   Who still shall welcome be to me.

False-minded man that so would proue,
Disloyall to thy dearest Loue,
Who at her death for thee did pray,
And wisht thee many a happy day.   100
   I would my Loue would but loue me,
   Euen halfe so well as shee lou'd thee.

Faire Maydens will example take,
Young-men will curse thee for her sake:
They'l stop their eares vnto our plaints,   105
And call vs Deuils seeming Saints:
   They'l say to day, that we are kinde,
   To morrow of another minde.

5
Edmund Spenser, The Ruines of Time
(1591)

THIS poem is almost an anthology in itself. Elegy, political satire, *chanson d'aventure*, 'Complaint against the Times', visionary rapture derived from Revelation: all find scope in its structure. In terms of the collection which it opens this hybrid effect is justified. *The Ruines of Time* introduces most of the topics and methods which Spenser (*c.*1552–99) will use in *Complaints* (1591). But it is likely too that the eclecticism indicates an erratic genesis. After a dedication to Mary Sidney, Countess of Pembroke (here omitted), *The Ruines of Time* recalls an encounter with the Genius of Verulamium, Roman precursor of St Albans. While this episode develops a sonnet by Du Bellay translated by Spenser in the late 1560s (above, pp. 41–2), the second phase of the poem, celebrating the life and lineage of Spenser's patron, the Earl of Leicester, probably draws on the poet's lost *Stemmata Dudleiana* (mentioned in a letter of 1580). Prompted by the death of one scion of the Dudleys, the poet Sir Philip Sidney, in 1586, Spenser then addresses himself to the question of art. Lines 344–490 mourn the neglect of the Muses in England, *c.*1590, and celebrate the power of verse. Throughout the poem, paraphrase from Ecclesiastes emphasizes the frailty of human endeavour. Yet when Spenser asks, at line 413, 'how can mortall immortalitie giue'?, he casts doubt on the claims he is making for the eternizing force of poetry. Perhaps it would be more accurate to say that the dilapidated city makes these claims, while the poem's 'I' grows towards a juster view. At all events, a new turn is taken at line 490: Verlame disappears and pagan vision is replaced by Christian allegory. During the 1590s and 1600s sonnet-sequences would precede complaints in linked structures: Daniel's *Rosamond* follows *Delia* in 1592, *A Louers Complaint* succeeds Shakespeare's Sonnets in 1609. Spenser varies this, since the lament of Verulamium gives way to fourteen double stanzas of rhyme royal. These not only amount, overall, to a macrosonnet, but are, as paired seven-line units, each a lyric sonnet. Always interested in numerology, Spenser uses the insistent seven-ness to formulate stanzas describing the futile glory of the Seven Wonders of the World. After a sometimes cryptic series of images drawn from the Old Testament and classical history, Spenser returns to Sidney. Figured by

a swan, a harp, an ebony coffer, and other devices, his life unfolds as a
heavenly pageant. The poem's closing lines imagine Sidney's apotheosis,
while, in a doleful envoi, Spenser recalls the 'siluer streaming' Thames
which began the poem, soliciting 'some few siluer dropping teares' from the
Countess of Pembroke.

THE RUINES OF TIME

It chaunced me on day beside the shore
Of siluer streaming *Thamesis* to bee,
Nigh where the goodly *Verlame* stood of yore,
Of which there now remaines no memorie,
Nor anie little moniment to see,   5
By which the trauailer, that fares that way,

This once was she, may warned be to say.

There on the other side, I did behold
A Woman sitting sorrowfullie wailing,
Rending her yeolow locks, like wyrie golde,   10
About her shoulders careleslie downe trailing,
And streames of teares from her faire eyes forth railing.
In her right hand a broken rod she held,
Which towards heauen shee seemd on high to weld.

Whether she were one of that Riuers Nymphes,   15
Which did the losse of some dere loue lament,
I doubt; or one of those three fatall Impes,
Which draw the dayes of men forth in extent;
Or th' auncient *Genius* of that Citie brent:
But seeing her so piteouslie perplexed,   20
I (to her calling) askt what her so vexed.

1 *on*: one   2–3 *Thamesis . . . of yore*: though Thames runs another way, some 16th-cent.
antiquaries believed it once passed Verulamium; see 141–7   12 *railing*: gushing
13 *broken rod*: symbolizing lost authority   17 *doubt*: am uncertain   17–18 *those three
fatall Impes . . . extent*: the Fates (*Impes* as 'spirits, petty fiends'), who spin (*draw* thread *forth*) and
determine the *extent* of men's lives before cutting them off   19 *brent*: burnt

Ah what delight (quoth she) in earthlie thing,
Or comfort can I wretched creature haue?
Whose happines the heauens enuying,
From highest staire to lowest step me draue,   25
And haue in mine owne bowels made my graue,
That of all Nations now I am forlorne,
The worlds sad spectacle, and fortunes scorne.

Much was I mooued at her piteous plaint,
And felt my heart nigh riuen in my brest   30
With tender ruth to see her sore constraint,
That shedding teares awhile I still did rest,
And after did her name of her request.
Name haue I none (quoth she) nor anie being,
Bereft of both by Fates vniust decreeing.   35

I was that Citie, which the garland wore
Of *Britaines* pride, deliuered vnto me
By *Romane* Victors, which it wonne of yore;
Though nought at all but ruines now I bee,
And lye in mine owne ashes, as ye see: 40
Verlame I was; what bootes it that I was,
Sith now I am but weedes and wastfull gras?

O vaine worlds glorie, and vnstedfast state
Of all that liues, on face of sinfull earth,
Which from their first vntill their vtmost date   45
Tast no one hower of happines or merth,
But like as at the ingate of their berth,
They crying creep out of their mothers woomb,
So wailing backe go to their wofull toomb.

Why then dooth flesh, a bubble glas of breath,   50
Hunt after honour and aduauncement vaine,
And reare a trophee for deuouring death,
With so great labour and long lasting paine,
As if his daies for euer should remaine?
Sith all that in this world is great or gaie,   55
Doth as a vapour vanish, and decaie.

27 *of all Nations . . . forlorne*: out of all realms and peoples (in the Bible *Nations* are 'gentile races') I am the most wretched; *forlorne* is coloured by its old sense 'destroyed'   32 *rest*: continue   36–7 *garland . . . Of Britaines pride*: wreath made from the vain splendour of defeated Britain (as worn by *Victors* in *Romane* games or triumphs)   40 *ashes*: remains, dust (cf. Gen. 18: 27), charred residue   41 *that*: what   42 *wastfull*: barren, rubble-strewn   45 *vtmost date*: absolute end, limit   47 *ingate*: entrance

Looke back, who list, vnto the former ages,
And call to count, what is of them become:
Where be those learned wits and antique Sages,
Which of all wisedome knew the perfect somme: 60
Where those great warriors, which did ouercomme
The world with conquest of their might and maine,
And made one meare of th' earth and of their raine?

What nowe is of th' *Assyrian* Lyonesse,
Of whome no footing now on earth appeares?   65
What of the *Persian* Beares outragiousnesse,
Whose memorie is quite worne out with yeares?
Who of the *Grecian* Libbard now ought heares,
That ouerran the East with greedie powre,
And left his whelps their kingdomes to deuoure?   70

And where is that same great seuen headded beast,
That made all nations vassals of her pride,
To fall before her feete at her beheast,
And in the necke of all the world did ride?
Where doth she all that wondrous welth nowe hide?   75
With her own weight down pressed now shee lies,
And by her heaps her hugenesse testifies.

O *Rome* thy ruine I lament and rue,
And in thy fall my fatall ouerthrowe,
That whilom was, whilst heauens with equall vewe   80
Deignd to behold me, and their gifts bestowe,
The picture of thy pride in pompous shew:
And of the whole world as thou wast the Empresse,
So I of this small Northerne world was Princesse.

---

57 *who list*: whoever wants to   58 *call to count*: reckon up   63 *one meare*: a single
thing (there was *one* empire), *one* boundary (their *raine* was commensurate with *The world*), a
battlefield-like mire (as in 'water mere', quibbling on *raine*)   64–8 *Assyrian Lyonesse* . . .
Persian Beares . . . Grecian Libbard: the three powers which dominated Israel, according to commentaries on the dream in Dan. 7: 1–8, the fourth beast of that passage being identified with Rome
through verses in Revelation (cf. 71 and n.)   65 *footing*: track, print   68 *Libbard*:
leopard (here Alexander the Great)   71 *seuen headded beast*: Rome and its Church in Protestant readings of Rev. 13   74 *in the necke of*: i.e. yoking nations like beasts   76 *weight*: as
often, implying wordly power and authority   77 *heaps*: i.e. of ruins, overruling 'piles of wealth'
80 *equall*: even-handed (and 'matching my good fortune with Rome's')

To tell the beawtie of my buildings fayre,   85
Adornd with purest golde, and precious stone;
To tell my riches, and endowments rare
That by my foes are now all spent and gone:
To tell my forces matchable to none,
Were but lost labour, that few would beleeue,   90
And with rehearsing would me more agreeue.

High towers, faire temples, goodly theaters,
Strong walls, rich porches, princelie pallaces,
Large streetes, braue houses, sacred sepulchers,
Sure gates, sweete gardens, stately galleries,   95
Wrought with faire pillours, and fine imageries
All those (ô pitie) now are turnd to dust,
And ouergrowen with blacke obliuions rust.

Theretoo for warlike power, and peoples store,
In *Britannie* was none to match with mee,   100
That manie often did abide full sore:
Ne *Troynouant*, though elder sister shee,
With my great forces might compared bee;
That stout *Pendragon* to his perill felt,
Who in a siege seauen yeres about me dwelt.   105

But long ere this *Bunduca* Britonnesse
Her mightie hoast against my bulwarkes brought,
Bunduca, that victorious conqueresse,
That lifting vp her braue heroïck thought
Boue womens weaknes, with the *Romanes* fought,   110
Fought, and in field against them thrice preuailed:
Yet was she foyld, when as she me assailed.

85, 87, 89 *tell*: describe, count up   95 *galleries*: a new interest in collecting art-objects was
giving the word its modern connotations   96 *imageries*: works of art, statuary, 'graven
images'   98 *rust*: decay   99 *peoples store*: abundance of people   101 *abide*:
endure   102 *Ne Troynouant ... sister*: not New-Troy (i.e. London, supposedly founded by
those fleeing the sack of Ilium), though older and related   104 *stout Pendragon*: the bold
British king Uther, who recovered the city from Saxons   106 *long ere this Bunduca*: Boudica,
many years before *Pendragon*'s campaign   112 *Yet was she foyld*: apparently not true, though
the city recovered from its defeat

And though at last by force I conquered were
Of hardie *Saxons*, and became their thrall;
Yet was I with much bloodshed bought full deere,   115
And prizde with slaughter of their Generall:
The moniment of whose sad funerall,
For wonder of the world, long in me lasted;
But now to nought through spoyle of time is wasted.

Wasted it is, as if it neuer were,   120
And all the rest that me so honord made,
And of the world admired eu'rie where,
Is turnd to smoake, that doth to nothing fade;
And of that brightnes now appeares no shade,
But greislie shades, such as doo haunt in hell   125
With fearfull fiends, that in deep darknes dwell.

Where my high steeples whilom vsde to stand,
On which the lordly Faulcon wont to towre,
There now is but an heap of lyme and sand,
For the Shriche-owle to build her balefull bowre: 130
And where the Nightingale wont forth to powre
Her restles plaints, to comfort wakefull Louers,
There now haunt yelling Mewes and whining Plouers.

And where the christall *Thamis* wont to slide
In siluer channell, downe along the Lee,   135
About whose flowrie bankes on either side
A thousand Nymphes, with mirthfull iollitee
Were wont to play, from all annoyance free;
There now no riuers course is to be seene,
But moorish fennes, and marshes euer greene.   140

Seemes, that that gentle Riuer for great griefe
Of my mishaps, which oft I to him plained;
Or for to shunne the horrible mischiefe,
With which he saw my cruell foes me pained,

---

116 *prizde with*: equal in price to (cost them), won as a prize   120–33 *Wasted it is . . . Plouers*:
informed by Isa. 34   124 *shade*: image, trace   125 *greislie shades*: gruesome ghosts
128 *towre*: get up high to spot its prey   130 *Shriche-owle*: in the Bible an unclean bird
(probably equivalent to the English barn-owl) of ill omen   133 *Mewes*: gulls   135 *chan-nell*: stream (not only the bed in which it flows)   *Lee*: meadow, fallow land   140 *moorish*:
boggy, spongy

And his pure streames with guiltles blood oft stained, 145
From my vnhappie neighborhood farre fled,
And his sweete waters away with him led.

There also where the winged ships were seene
In liquid waues to cut their fomie waie,
And thousand Fishers numbred to haue been, 150
In that wide lake looking for plenteous praie
Of fish, which thcy with baits vsdc to bctraic,
Is now no lake, nor anie fishers store,
Nor euer ship shall saile there anie more.

They all are gone, and all with them is gone, 155
Ne ought to me remaines, but to lament
My long decay, which no man els doth mone,
And mourne my fall with dolefull dreriment.
Yet it is comfort in great languishment,
To be bemoned with compassion kinde, 160
And mitigates the anguish of the minde.

But me no man bewaileth, but in game,
Ne sheddeth teares from lamentable eie:
Nor anic liucs that mcntioneth my name
To be remembred of posteritie, 165
Saue One that maugre fortunes iniurie,
And times decay, and enuies cruell tort,
Hath writ my record in true-seeming sort.

Cambden the nourice of antiquitie,
And lanterne vnto late succeeding age, 170
To see the light of simple veritie,
Buried in ruines, through the great outrage
Of her owne people, led with warlike rage,
Cambden, though time all moniments obscure,
Yet thy iust labours euer shall endure. 175

146 *vnhappie neighborhood*: sad and unlucky company   151 *lake*: watercourse (a word now dialectal with a different root from *lake* as 'enclosed water')   158 *dreriment*: dismalness   163 *lamentable*: mournful   166 *maugre*: despite   167 *tort*: injury   168 *true-seeming*: seemly and truthful, persuasive   169–70: *Cambden . . . succeeding age*: the *Britannia* (1586) of William Camden had 'fostered' an interest in the realm's *antiquitie* and illuminated more recent times (into which he was also researching)   170–1 *lanterne . . . To see the light*: makes play with the proverbial folly of holding a candle to see the sun   174 *moniments*: here, more than 5 and 179, 'written records, muniments'

But whie (vnhappie wight) doo I thus crie,
And grieue that my remembrance quite is raced
Out of the knowledge of posteritie,
And all my antique moniments defaced?
Sith I doo dailie see things highest placed,　　　　180
So soone as fates their vitall thred haue shorne,
Forgotten quite as they were neuer borne.

It is not long, since these two eyes beheld
A mightie Prince, of most renowmed race,
Whom *England* high in count of honour held,　　　　185
And greatest ones did sue to gaine his grace;
Of greatest ones he greatest in his place,
Sate in the bosome of his Soueraine,
And *Right and loyall* did his word maintaine.

I saw him die, I saw him die, as one　　　　190
Of the meane people, and brought foorth on beare,
I saw him die, and no man left to mone
His dolefull fate, that late him loued deare:
Scarse anie left to close his eylids neare;
Scarse anie left vpon his lips to laie　　　　195
The sacred sod, or *Requiem* to saie.

O trustlesse state of miserable men,
That builde your blis on hope of earthly thing,
And vainly thinke your selues halfe happie then,
When painted faces with smooth flattering　　　　200
Doo fawne on you, and your wide praises sing,
And when the courting masker louteth lowe,
Him true in heart and trustie to you trow.

---

181 *fates . . . haue shorne*: see 17–18 and n.　　　184 *A mightie Prince*: Robert Dudley, Earl of Leicester (?1532–88), courtier, patron of the arts, and supporter of the Protestant cause, had blood-links with the royal line　　　188 *Sate in the bosome of his Soueraine*: Leicester was a favourite, and for some time potential husband, of Queen Elizabeth; Spenser ignores the breach which followed the Earl's marriage to the Countess of Essex in 1578　　　189 *Right and loyall . . . maintaine*: his promises and undertakings were supported by *Droict et Loyal*, his motto　　　190–1 *as one* | *Of the meane people*: after leading an anti-Spanish force to the Low Countries, Leicester died impoverished; he was buried 'like a commoner'　　　200 *painted*: attractive, deceitful (hints of cosmetic decadence at court)　　　202 *courting masker*: falsely wooing deceiver (who behaves like a masquer)　　*louteth*: bows

All is but fained, and with oaker dide,
That euerie shower will wash and wipe away,   205
All things doo change that vnder heauen abide,
And after death all friendship doth decaie.
Therefore what euer man bearst worldlie sway,
Liuing, on God, and on thy selfe relie:
For when thou diest, all shall with thee die.   210

He now is dead, and all is with him dead,
Saue what in heauens storehouse he vplaid:
His hope is faild, and come to passe his dread,
And euill men now dead, his deeds vpbraid:
Spite bites the dead, that liuing neuer baid.   215
He now is gone, the whiles the Foxe is crept
Into the hole, the which the Badger swept.

He now is dead, and all his glorie gone,
And all his greatnes vapoured to nought,
That as a glasse vpon the water shone,   220
Which vanisht quite, so soone as it was fought:
His name is worne alreadie out of thought,
Ne anie Poet seekes him to reuiue;
Yet manie Poets honourd him aliue.

Ne doth his *Colin*, carelesse *Colin Cloute*,   225
Care now his idle bagpipe vp to raise,
Ne tell his sorrow to the listning rout
Of shepherd groomes, which wont his songs to praise:
Praise who so list, yet I will him dispraise,
Vntill he quite him of this guiltie blame: 230
Wake shepheards boy, at length awake for shame.

204 *oaker*: the yellow-brown pigment, ochre, was used for cosmetics and to dye masque costumes
205 *shower*: of adversity, stripping *away* false shows of friendship   212 *in heauens . . . vplaid*:
see Matt. 6: 20   214 *now dead*: referring to Leicester   215 *that liuing neuer baid*: which
never dared bark (like a cur) at the *dead* man when alive   216–17 *the Foxe is crept . . . the Badger
swept*: William Cecil, Lord Burghley (a devious and squalid fox taking over the badger's set),
advanced his power at court after Leicester's death   220 *as a glasse*: with a mirror-like
gleam   225 *carelesse Colin Cloute*: the pastoral persona of Spenser, 'cheerful' and so 'neglectful' of Leicester   226 *vp to raise*: to rouse, lift and swell into use, raise a tune on
228 *groomes*: fellows   230 *quite*: acquits

And who so els did goodnes by him gaine,
And who so els his bounteous minde did trie,
Whether he shepheard be, or shepheards swaine,
(For manie did, which doo it now denie)   235
Awake, and to his Song a part applie:
And I, the whilest you mourne for his decease,
Will with my mourning plaints your plaint increase.

He dyde, and after him his brother dyde,
His brother Prince, his brother noble Peere,   240
That whilste he liued, was of none enuyde,
And dead is now, as liuing, counted deare,
Deare vnto all that true affection beare:
But vnto thee most deare, ô dearest Dame,
His noble Spouse, and Paragon of fame.   245

He whilest he liued, happie was through thee,
And being dead is happie now much more;
Liuing, that lincked chaunst with thee to bee,
And dead, because him dead thou dost adore
As liuing, and thy lost deare loue deplore.   250
So whilest that thou, faire flower of chastitie,
Dost liue, by thee thy Lord shall neuer die.

Thy Lord shall neuer die, the whiles this verse
Shall liue, and surely it shall liue for euer:
For euer it shall liue, and shall rehearse   255
His worthie praise, and vertues dying neuer,
Though death his soule doo from his bodie seuer.
And thou thy selfe herein shalt also liue;
Such grace the heauens doo to my verses giue.

Ne shall his sister, ne thy father die,   260
Thy father, that good Earle of rare renowne,
And noble Patrone of weake pouertie;
Whose great good deeds in countrey and in towne

233 *bounteous minde*: abundant intellect and generosity of temperament   *did trie*: experience, put to
the test   234 *shepheard ... shepheards swaine*: differing ranks perhaps develop the allegory
beyond poets to pastors of the Church, bishops and below, nurtured by Leicester   236 *to his
Song ... applie*: sing a musical line in his threnody   239 *his brother*: Ambrose Dudley, Earl of
Warwick (who *dyde* in 1590)   240 *Prince ... noble Peere*: see 184 and n.   244 *dearest
Dame*: Anne Russell, his last wife   250 *deplore*: lament   260 *his sister ... thy father*:
Mary Dudley (mother of Sir Philip Sidney and the Countess of Pembroke) and Francis Russell,
2nd Earl of Bedford (both dead)

Haue purchast him in heauen an happie crowne;
Where he now liueth in eternall blis,   265
And left his sonne t' ensue those steps of his.

He noble bud, his Grandsires liuelie hayre,
Vnder the shadow of thy countenaunce
Now ginnes to shoote vp fast, and flourish fayre
In learned artes and goodlie gouernaunce,   270
That him to highest honour shall aduaunce.
Braue Impe of *Bedford*, grow apace in bountie,
And count of wisedome more than of thy Countie.

Ne may I let thy husbands sister die,
That goodly Ladie, sith she eke did spring   275
Out of this stocke, and famous familie,
Whose praises I to future age doo sing,
And foorth out of her happie womb did bring
The sacred brood of learning and all honour;
In whom the heauens powrde all their gifts vpon her.   280

Most gentle spirite breathed from aboue,
Out of the bosome of the makers blis,
In whom all bountie and all vertuous loue
Appeared in their natiue propertis,
And did enrich that noble breast of his,   285
With treasure passing all this worldes worth,
Worthie of heauen itselfe, which brought it forth.

His blessed spirite full of power diuine
And influence of all celestiall grace,
Loathing this sinfull earth and earthlie slime,   290
Fled backe too soone vnto his natiue place,

266 *his sonne*: Edward Russell, the 3rd Earl (and, as 267 says, Francis Russell's grandson)   *ensue*:
follow, provide the sequel to   268 *Vnder ... countenance*: sheltered by your approval and
authority (with a complimentary hint of family likeness, *shadow* as 'image')   272 *Impe*: scion,
shoot   *in bountie*: in goodness, surrounded by benefits   273 *count ... Countie*: value
wisedome more than Bedfordshire   274 *thy husbands sister*: the *sister* of 260   277 *praises*:
virtues, encomium   279 *brood*: offspring (Sir Philip and Mary Sidney, who in turn gave
'parentage', 'nativity', in distinctively Spenserian senses of *brood*, to *learning and all honour*)
281 *Most gentle spirite*: Sir Philip Sidney   282 *the makers blis*: God's clemency, divine
felicity   284 *natiue propertis*: unalloyed condition, place where they most belonged
289 *influence*: that which flows down (in astrological theory) from the heavens   291 *too soone*:
Sir Philip Sidney (1554–86) was only in his thirties when he died from wounds incurred at the
battle of Zutphen

Too soone for all that did his loue embrace,
Too soone for all this wretched world, whom he
Robd of all right and true nobilitie.

Yet ere his happie soule to heauen went   295
Out of this fleshlie goale, he did deuise
Vnto his heauenlie maker to present
His bodie, as a spotles sacrifise;
And chose, that guiltie hands of enemies
Should powre forth th' offring of his guiltles blood: 300
So life exchanging for his countries good.

O noble spirite, liue there euer blessed,
The worlds late wonder, and the heauens new ioy,
Liue euer there, and leaue me here distressed
With mortall cares, and cumbrous worlds anoy.   305
But where thou dost that happines enioy,
Bid me, ô bid me quicklie come to thee,
That happie there I maie thee alwaies see.

Yet whilest the fates affoord me vitall breath,
I will it spend in speaking of thy praise,   310
And sing to thee, vntill that timelie death
By heauens doome doo ende my earthlie daies:
Thereto doo thou my humble spirite raise,
And into me that sacred breath inspire,
Which thou there breathest perfect and entire.   315

Then will I sing, but who can better sing,
Than thine owne sister, peerles Ladie bright,
Which to thee sings with deep harts sorrowing
Sorrowing tempered with deare delight,
That her to heare I feele my feeble spright   320
Robbed of sense, and rauished with ioy,
O sad ioy made of mourning and anoy.

---

296 *goale*: jail (of the body, and world of the flesh)   299–300 *guiltie hands . . . guiltles blood*:
implies a Christlike sacrifice   301 *exchanging . . . good*: bartering his *life* in exchange for *good*
done to *his countrie* (and 'changing *mortal* for eternal *life*')   311 *timelie*: as ordained
314 *that sacred breath*: of the Lord, inspiration to Christian poets   317 *thine owne sister*: Mary
Sidney, Countess of Pembroke

Yet will I sing, but who can better sing,
Than thou thy selfe, thine owne selfes valiance,
That whilest thou liuedst, madest the forrests ring,   325
And fields resownd, and flockes to leap and daunce,
And shepheards leaue their lambs vnto mischaunce,
To runne thy shrill *Arcadian* Pipe to heare:
O happie were those dayes, thrice happie were.

But now more happie thou, and wretched wee,   330
Which want the wonted sweetnes of thy voice,
Whiles thou now in *Elisian* fields so free,
With *Orpheus*, and with *Linus* and the choice
Of all that euer did in rimes reioyce,
Conuersest, and doost heare their heauenlie layes,   335
And they heare thine, and thine doo better praise.

So there thou liuest, singing euermore,
And here thou liuest, being euer song
Of vs, which liuing loued thee afore,
And now thee worship, mongst that blessed throng   340
Of heauenlie Poets and Heroes strong.
So thou both here and there immortall art,
And euerie where through excellent desart.

But such as neither of themselues can sing,
Nor yet are sung of others for reward,   345
Die in obscure obliuion, as the thing
Which neuer was, ne euer with regard
Their names shall of the later age be heard,
But shall in rustie darknes euer lie,
Vnles they mentiond be with infamie.   350

What booteth it to haue been rich aliue?
What to be great? what to be gracious?
When after death no token doth suruiue,
Of former being in this mortall hous,

324 *valiance*: worth, valour   328 *Arcadian*: pastoral; glances at Sir Philip Sidney's *Arcadia*   332 *Elisian fields*: haunt of blessed souls in the classical underworld   333 *Orpheus*: type of Sidney, since his songs charmed and animated nature *Linus*: another ancient representative of song, said to be a son of Apollo and Psamathe, or Amphimarus and Urania, and sometimes described as Hercules' music-teacher   341 *Poets and Heroes*: complimenting Sidney as both writer and soldier   349 *rustie darknes*: the mouldering *obliuion* of 98   354 *this mortall hous*: the *goale* of 296, including the 'worldly condition' of Eccles. 12: 3–7

But sleepes in dust dead and inglorious,   355
Like beast, whose breath but in his nostrels is,
And hath no hope of happinesse or blis.

How manie great ones may remembred be,
Which in their daies most famouslie did florish;
Of whome no word we heare, nor signe now see,   360
But as things wipt out with a sponge to perishe,
Because they liuing, cared not to cherishe
No gentle wits, through pride or couetize,
Which might their names for euer memorize.

Prouide therefore (ye Princes) whilst ye liue,   365
That of the *Muses* ye may friended bee,
Which vnto men eternitie do giue;
For they be daughters of Dame memorie,
And *Ioue* the father of eternitie,
And do those men in golden thrones repose,   370
Whose merits they to glorifie do chose.

The seuen fold yron gates of grislie Hell,
And horrid house of sad *Proserpina*,
They able are with power of mightie spell
To breake, and thence the soules to bring awaie   375
Out of dread darkenesse, to eternall day,
And them immortall make, which els would die
In foule forgetfulnesse, and nameles lie.

So whilome raised they the puissant brood
Of golden girt *Alcmena*, for great merite,   380
Out of the dust, to which the *Œtæan* wood
Had him consum'd, and spent his vitall spirite:
To highest heauen, where now he doth inherite
All happinesse in *Hebes* siluer bowre,
Chosen to be her dearest Paramoure.   385

---

356 *breath but in his nostrels*: with no hope of eternal life, echoing Isa. 2: 22   361 *wipt out*: i.e.
from the slate of life   363 *gentle wits*: the poets who make *names* last   *through pride or*
couetize: because they vainly thought themselves unforgettable, or were too stingy to patronize the
arts   368 *Dame memorie*: Mnemosyne   371 *glorifie*: for scriptural resonances see Rom.
8: 17   373 *sad*: because *Proserpina* was condemned to spend part of each year as goddess of
the underworld   374 *They able are*: like Christ harrowing *Hell*   378 *forgetfulnesse*:
oblivion   380 *golden girt Alcmena*: Hercules' mother with a Senecan epithet   381–2 *dust,*
to which . . . spirite: the body of Hercules was *consum'd* on a pyre of wood from Mount Oeta
384 *Hebes siluer bowre*: Hercules' celestial wife is Hebe, cup-bearer to the gods

So raisde they eke faire *Ledæs* warlick twinnes,
And interchanged life vnto them lent,
That when th' one dies, th' other then beginnes
To shew in Heauen his brightnes orient;
And they, for pittie of the sad wayment,   390
Which *Orpheus* for *Eurydice* did make,
Her back againe to life sent for his sake.

So happie are they, and so fortunate,
Whom the *Pierian* sacred sisters loue,
That freed from bands of impacable fate,   395
And power of death, they liue for aye aboue,
Where mortall wreakes their blis may not remoue:
But with the Gods, for former vertues meede,
On *Nectar* and *Ambrosia* do feede.

For deeds doe die, how euer noblie donne,   400
And thoughts of men do as themselues decay,
But wise wordes taught in numbers for to runne,
Recorded by the Muses, liue for ay;
Ne may with storming showers be washt away,
Ne bitter breathing windes with harmfull blast,   405
Nor age, nor enuie shall them euer wast.

In vaine doo earthly Princes then, in vaine
Seeke with Pyramides, to heauen aspired;
Or huge Colosses, built with costlie paine;
Or brasen Pillours, neuer to be fired,   410
Or Shrines, made of the mettall most desired;
To make their memories for euer liue:
For how can mortall immortalitie giue.

386 *Ledæs warlick twinnes*: the Dioscuri, Castor and Pollux (brothers of Leda), became the constellation Gemini and alternate with each other (according to some accounts) in the heavens
389 *orient*: rising (dawn-like), lustrous   390-2 *And they … his sake*: for Orpheus and Eurydice see Virgil's *Georgics*, 4. 453–527, and, for the mythic singer in the company of Hercules, Castor, and Pollux, *Aeneid*, 6. 119–23   390 *wayment*: lamentation   394 *Pierian sacred sisters*: the nine Muses   395 *impacable*: not pacifiable, unrelenting   397 *wreakes*: harms   399 *Nectar and Ambrosia*: drink and food of the gods   401 *thoughts of men*: their being remembered   402 *numbers*: verse, metre   404 *showers*: as at 205   405 *bitter breathing windes*: of calumny   408 *Pyramides … aspired*: lofty edifices … built up
409 *Colosses, built with costlie paine*: immense statues (cf. the *Giaunt* of 533–46), expensive and arduous to construct   410 *fired*: destroyed by fire   411 *metall most desired*: here, gold

Such one *Mausolus* made, the worlds great wonder,
But now no remnant doth thereof remaine: 415
Such one *Marcellus*, but was torne with thunder:
Such one *Lisippus*, but is worne with raine:
Such one King *Edmond*, but was rent for gaine.
All such vaine moniments of earthlie masse,
Deuour'd of Time, in time to nought doo passe.   420

But fame with golden wings aloft doth flie,
Aboue the reach of ruinous decay,
And with braue plumes doth beate the azure skie,
Admir'd of base-borne men from farre away:
Then who so will with vertuous deeds assay   425
To mount to heauen, on *Pegasus* must ride,
And with sweete Poets verse be glorifide.

For not to haue been dipt in *Lethe* lake,
Could saue the sonne of *Thetis* from to die;
But that blinde bard did him immortall make   430
With verses, dipt in deaw of *Castalie*:
Which made the Easterne Conquerour to crie,
O fortunate yong-man, whose vertue found
So braue a Trompe, thy noble acts to sound.

Therefore in this halfe happie I doo read   435
Good *Meliboe*, that hath a Poet got,
To sing his liuing praises being dead,
Deseruiug neuer here to be forgot,

414 *Mausolus*: his tomb, at Halicarnassus, was the original 'mausoleum'   416 *Marcellus ...
torne with thunder*: Plutarch reports temples struck by lightning when he attempted, irregularly, to
dedicate one to two gods   417 *Lisippus*: sculptor of Alexander   418 *King Edmond ...
rent for gaine*: the abbey at Bury St Edmunds was dissolved by Henry VII at the instigation
(according to Camden) of greedy counsellors   419 *masse*: suggests value in addition to bulk,
as at 491   421 *golden wings*: not, that is, the spotted plumes of disfame   426 *Pegasus*:
winged horse who carried the thunderbolt of Jupiter and symbolized immortality; his foot striking
Mt. Helicon, he created the Hippocrene ('horse's fountain'), haunt of the Muses, and so became
associated with inspiration   428-9 *Not to haue ... to die*: even being *dipt* in the Styx (one of
the rivers of the underworld, generically known by the name of the chief of them, *Lethe*) did not
make Achilles invulnerable; *lake* carries the unusual sense noted at 151, while the lines are further
complicated by associations between *Lethe* and forgetting (the attempt to *make* Achilles *immortall*
ironically steeped him in common oblivion)   430 *that blinde bard*: Homer   431 *deaw of
Castalie*: water, scattered droplets, from the Castalian spring on Mt. Parnassus, sacred to Apollo and
the Muses   432-4 *Easterne Conquerour ... to sound*: Alexander the Great's praise of Homer
for memorializing Achilles is often cited in 16th-cent. poetry   435 *halfe happie*: because living
though dead   436 *Meliboe*: Sir Francis Walsingham, whose death in 1590 was a blow to poets
and soldiers in the Dudley circle   *a Poet*: Thomas Watson, author of *Meliboeus* (1590), translated
from Latin in the same year

In spight of enuie, that his deeds would spot:
Since whose decease, learning lies vnregarded,   440
And men of armes doo wander vnrewarded.

Those two be those two great calamities,
That long agoe did grieue the noble spright
Of *Salomon* with great indignities;
Who whilome was aliue the wisest wight.   445
But now his wisedome is disprooued quite;
For he that now welds all things at his will,
Scorns th' one and th' other in his deeper skill.

O griefe of griefes, ô gall of all good heartes,
To see that vertue should dispised bee   450
Of him, that first was raisde for vertuous parts,
And now broad spreading like an aged tree,
Lets none shoot vp, that nigh him planted bee·
O let the man, of whom the Muse is scorned,
Nor aliue, nor dead be of the Muse adorned.   455

O vile worlds trust, that with such vaine illusion
Hath so wise men bewitcht, and ouerkest,
That they see not the way of their confusion,
O vainesse to be added to the rest,
That do my soule with inward griefe infest: 460
Let them behold the piteous fall of mee:
And in my case their owne ensample see.

And who so els that sits in highest seate
Of this worlds glorie, worshipped of all,
Ne feareth change of time, nor fortunes threate,   465
Let him behold the horror of my fall,

442–4 *Those two . . . indignities*: at Eccles. 26: 28 Solomon urges that men of arts and arms be
rewarded: 'There be two things that grieve my heart . . . a man of war that suffereth poverty; and
men of understanding that are not set by'   446–8 *But now . . . his deeper skill*: the *wisedome* of
Solomon (a biblical phrase) is now 'completely out of use' and (with some irony) 'utterly refuted' by
Burghley, *the Foxe* of 216, who, being 'intellectually *deeper*' and 'more profound in government' than
Solomon, 'pronounces on all things as he likes, governs and disposes by bending *all* according to his
will'; in the collected Spenser of 1611 this attack is less specific, *he* and (at 451) *him* becoming
'such', *him* and *O let the man* in 453–4 becoming 'them . . . O! let not those'   451 *first was
raisde for vertuous parts*: Burghley owed his advancement to his talents and virtue in public life
457 *ouerkest*: overcast, darkened in mind   458 *the way of their confusion*: perplexedly both 'the
just way, in their confused state', 'the way their confusion is leading'   459 *vainesse*: the 'vanity'
of Ecclesiastes, to which this phase of the poem is indebted

And his owne end vnto remembrance call;
That of like ruine he may warned bee,
And in himselfe be moou'd to pittie mee.

Thus hauing ended all her piteous plaint,   470
With dolefull shrikes shee vanished away,
That I through inward sorrowe wexen faint,
And all astonished with deepe dismay,
For her departure, had no word to say:
But sate long time in sencelesse sad affright,   475
Looking still, if I might of her haue sight.

Which when I missed, hauing looked long,
My thought returned greeued home againe,
Renewing her complaint with passion strong,
For ruth of that same womans piteous paine;   480
Whose wordes recording in my troubled braine,
I felt such anguish wound my feeble heart,
That frosen horror ran through euerie part.

So inlie greeuing in my groning brest,
And deepelie muzing at her doubtfull speach,   485
Whose meaning much I labored foorth to wreste,
Being aboue my slender reasons reach;
At length by demonstration me to teach,
Before mine eies strange sights presented were,
Like tragicke Pageants seeming to appeare.   490

I

I saw an Image, all of massie gold,
Placed on high vpon an Altare faire,
That all, which did the same from farre beholde,
Might worship it, and fall on lowest staire.
Not that great Idoll might with this compaire,   495
To which th' *Assyrian* tyrant would haue made
The holie brethren, falslie to haue praid.

---

481 *recording*: remembering   485 *doubtfull*: uncertain, obscure   491 *an Image . . . gold*:
given the underlying formula of Seven Wonders of the World, Phidias' statue of Zeus at Olympia
(enriched with motifs from the *Idoll* of Dan. 3: 1–18)   494 *on lowest staire*: into a stance of
deepest deference   495–7 *that great Idoll . . . to haue praid*: in Dan. 3: 1–18 Nebuchadnezzar
seeks to have Shadrach, Meshach, and Abed-nego worship an 'image of gold'

But th' Altare, on the which this Image staid,
Was (ô great pitie) built of brickle clay,
That shortly the foundation decaid,   500
With showres of heauen and tempests worne away,
Then downe it fell, and low in ashes lay,
Scorned of euerie one, which by it went;
That I it seing, dearelie did lament.

2

Next vnto this a statelie Towre appeared,   505
Built all of richest stone, that might bee found,
And nigh vnto the Heauens in height vpreared,
But placed on a plot of sandic ground:
Not that great Towre, which is so much renownd
For tongues confusion in holie writ,   510
King *Ninus* worke, might be compar'd to it.

But ô vaine labours of terrestriall wit,
That buildes so stronglie on so frayle a soyle,
As with each storme does fall away, and flit,
And giues the fruit of all your trauailes toyle,   515
To be the pray of Tyme, and Fortunes spoyle:
I saw this Towre fall sodainlie to dust,
That nigh with griefe thereof my heart was brust.

3

Then did I see a pleasant Paradize,
Full of sweete flowres and daintiest delights,   520
Such as on earth man could not more deuize,
With pleasures choyce to feed his cheerefull sprights;
Not that, which *Merlin* by his Magicke slights
Made for the gentle squire, to entertaine
His fayre *Belphœbe*, could this gardine staine.   525

499 *of brickle clay*: like the 'brittle' feet of that 'great image' which Nebuchadnezzar dreams of in Dan. 2: 31–5   502 *ashes*: dust of the ground (cf. 40 n., 517)   504 *dearelie*: grievously
505 *a statelie Towre*: the Pharos of Ptolemy II at Alexandria   508 *sandie ground*: see Matt. 7: 26–7   509 *that great Towre*: Babel; Gen. 11: 1–9   511 *King Ninus*: often credited with founding Babel, Nineveh, Babylon, though the Bible cites Nimrod   512 *wit*: intelligence   513 *soyle*: foundation, moral basis (and the *sandie ground* of 508)   514 *flit*: vanish   518 *brust*: bruised to pieces, burst   523–5 *which Merlin . . . Belphœbe*: cf. that garden to which *Belphœbe* and her damsels carry Timias in *The Faerie Queene*, III. v. 39–43
525 *staine*: outshine

But ô short pleasure bought with lasting paine,
Why will hereafter anie flesh delight
In earthlie blis, and ioy in pleasures vaine,
Since that I sawe this gardine wasted quite,
That where it was scarce seemed anie sight?   530
That I, which once that beautie did beholde,
Could not from teares my melting eyes with-holde.

4

Soone after this a Giaunt came in place,
Of wondrous power, and of exceeding stature,
That none durst vewe the horror of his face,   535
Yet was he milde of speach, and meeke of nature.
Not he, which in despight of his Creatour
With railing tearmes defied the Iewish hoast,
Might with this mightie one in hugenes boast.

For from the one he could to th' other coast,   540
Stretch his strong thighes, and th' Occæan ouerstride,
And reatch his hand into his enemies hoast.
But see the end of pompe and fleshlie pride;
One of his feete vnwares from him did slide,
That downe hee fell into the deepe Abisse,   545
Where drownd with him is all his earthlie blisse.

5

Then did I see a Bridge, made all of golde,
Ouer the Sea from one to other side,
Withouten prop or pillour it t' vpholde,
But like the coulored Rainbowe arched wide;
Not that great Arche, which *Traian* edifide,   550
To be a wonder to all age ensuing,
Was matchable to this in equall vewing.

---

533 *a Giaunt*: the Colossus of Rhodes   534 *wondrous power*: in strength and miraculous
speach   537–8 *Not he . . . Iewish hoast*: Goliath, whose high stature, scorning of the Jewish
army, and overthrow by David are related in 1 Sam. 17: 4–54   540–1 *to th' other coast . . .*
ouerstride: the Colossus was said to bestride the harbour-mouth, shore to shore, at
Rhodes   547 *a Bridge*: based on that of Xerxes, built across the Hellespont as part of his
campaign to punish the Greeks for their participation in the Ionian revolt   551 *that great*
Arche, which Traian edifide: bridge over the Danube, built by Apollodorus under the authority of
Traian   553 *equall*: unbiased

But (ah) what bootes it to see earthlie thing
In glorie, or in greatnes to excell,   555
Sith time doth greatest things to ruine bring?
This goodlie bridge, one foote not fastned well,
Gan faile, and all the rest downe shortlie fell,
Ne of so braue a building ought remained,
That griefe thereof my spirite greatly pained.   560

6

I saw two Beares, as white as anie milke,
Lying together in a mightie caue,
Of milde aspect, and haire as soft as silke,
That saluage nature seemed not to haue,
Nor after greedie spoyle of blood to craue: 565
Two fairer beasts might not elswhere be found,
Although the compast world were sought around.

But what can long abide aboue this ground
In state of blis, or stedfast happinesse?
The Caue, in which these Beares lay sleeping sound,   570
Was but earth, and with her owne weightinesse
Vpon them fell, and did vnwares oppresse,
That for great sorrow of their sudden fate,
Henceforth all worlds felicitie I hate.

¶Much was I troubled in my heauie spright,   575
At sight of these sad spectacles forepast,
That all my senses were bereaued quight,
And I in minde remained sore agast,
Distraught twixt feare and pitie; when at last
I heard a voyce, which loudly to me called,   580
That with the suddein shrill I was appalled.

556 *Sith*: since   561 *two Beares*: the dream becomes obscurer, as befits its probable politics; the Earls of Leicester and Warwick can be assumed, *Beares* of starry eminence ('the Great Bear' and 'Lesser Bear': cf. 616 and n.), an image prompted by the Dudley crest, which displayed a Bear and Ragged Staff   563 *aspect*: appearance   564 *saluage*: wild   571 *weightinesse*: of power, as at 76, and earthy mortality   572 *vnwares*: hints political treachery 577 *bereaued*: bereft of their usual power   579 *Distraught*: pulled asunder, agitated

Behold (said it) and by ensample see,
That all is vanitie and griefe of minde,
Ne other comfort in this world can be,
But hope of heauen, and heart to God inclinde;   585
For all the rest must needs be left behinde:
With that it bad me, to the other side
To cast mine eye, where other sights I spide.

1

¶Vpon that famous Riuers further shore,
There stood a snowie Swan of heauenly hiew,   590
And gentle kinde, as euer Fowle afore;
A fairer one in all the goodlie criew
Of white *Strimonian* brood might no man view:
There he most sweetly sung the prophecie
Of his owne death in dolefull Elegie.   595

At last, when all his mourning melodie
He ended had, that both the shores resounded,
Feeling the fit that him forewarnd to die,
With loftie flight aboue the earth he bounded,
And out of sight to highest heauen mounted: 600
Where now he is become an heauenly signe;
There now the ioy is his, here sorrow mine.

2

Whilest thus I looked, loe adowne the Lee,
I sawe an Harpe stroong all with siluer twyne,
And made of golde and costlie yuorie,   605
Swimming, that whilome seemed to haue been

583 *all is vanitie*: initial assertion of Eccles.   587 *other side* (of *Thamesis*, hinting like *further shore* in 589 the 'next world')   590 *a snowie Swan*: the first of several images of Sir Philip Sidney, here praising his short-lived poetic art (the *Swan* was thought to sing once, exquisitely, just before death) and purity   591 *gentle kinde*: noble and generous nature   593 *white Strimonian brood*: those swans on the River Strymon in Thrace which, according to the *Lament for Bion* (attributed in the 16th cent. to Moschus), mourned the death of that pastoral poet   594– 5 *There he . . . Elegie*: plaintful and elegiac elements in Sidney's verse (e.g. in *Arcadia*), swan-like anticipating his death (see 593n.)   598 *fit*: both 'paroxysm' and 'musical strain' 601 *signe*: punningly identifies the *heauenly* 'Cygnus' ('Swan' constellation) said to figure Sidney   603 *loe adowne the Lee*: lo, coming down the meadow (carried by the *Thamesis*); despite 135, *Lee* might here mean 'sheltered side of a river, under the bank'   604–7 *an Harpe . . . seene*: after charming beasts and trees with song (cf. 333 n.), *Orpheus* was dismembered and his lyre floated down the River Hebrus with his head (see *Metamorphoses*, 11. 50–5) making music; *Dan* means 'master' in respectful archaic usage

The harpe, on which *Dan Orpheus* was seene
Wylde beasts and forrests after him to lead,
But was th' Harpe of *Philisides* now dead.

At length out of the Riuer it was reard   610
And borne aboue the cloudes to be diuin'd,
Whilst all the way most heauenly noyse was heard
Of the strings, stirred with the warbling wind,
That wrought both ioy and sorrow in my mind:
So now in heauen a signe it doth appeare,   615
The Harpe well knowne beside the Northern Beare.

3

Soone after this I saw on th' other side,
A curious Coffer made of *Heben* wood,
That in it did most precious treasure hide,
Exceeding all this baser worldes good: 620
Yet through the ouerflowing of the flood
It almost drowned was, and done to nought,
That sight thereof much grieu'd my pensiue thought.

At length when most in perill it was brought,
Two Angels downe descending with swift flight,   625
Out of the swelling streame it lightly caught,
And twixt their blessed armes it carried quight
Aboue the reach of anie liuing sight:
So now it is transform'd into that starre,
In which all heauenly treasures locked are.   630

---

609 *Philisides*: Sidney, as the shepherd-knight of *Arcadia*   611 *diuin'd*: made divine
613 *strings . . . warbling wind*: after being an Orphic lyre, it becomes an Aeolian *Harpe*, sounded by
the *wind* that blows across its strings   616 *Harpe . . . the Northern Beare*: the constellations
Lyra and the Great Bear, closer in measures of renown than celestial distance; Spenser associates
Sidney's art with the Bear of the Dudley crest (see 561 and n.)   618 *curious Coffer made of
Heben wood*: elaborate coffin made of ebony; but 619–28 make Sidney's death-casket a place in
which (spiritual) *treasure* is stored, as in the *Coffer* which sometimes describes that *Arke* in which
God's covenant was kept (Exod. 25) and that basket from which Moses was taken (cf. *Two Angels*) by
Pharaoh's daughter and her maid (Exod. 2: 1–10); in classical myth the baby Perseus (cf. 646–9 and
n.) was similarly cast adrift in a chest   623 *pensiue*: despondent   629–30 *that starre . . .
are*: the *starre* which, being Sidney (there is a quibble on Latin *sidereus*, 'starry'), contains or
constitutes the *precious treasure* of 619 made *heauenly* (no more particular reference seems made,
unless some part of Lyra or Cygnus is intended)

4

Looking aside I saw a stately Bed,
Adorned all with costly cloth of gold,
That might for anie Princes couche be red,
And deckt with daintie flowres, as if it shold
Be for some bride, her ioyous night to hold: 635
Therein a goodly Virgine sleeping lay;
A fairer wight saw neuer summers day.

I heard a voyce that called farre away
And her awaking bad her quickly dight,
For lo her Bridegrome was in readie ray   640
To come to her, and seeke her loues delight:
With that she started vp with cherefull sight,
When suddeinly both bed and all was gone,
And I in languor left there all alone.

5

Still as I gazed, I beheld where stood   645
A Knight all arm'd, vpon a winged steed,
The same that was bred of *Medusæs* blood,
On which *Dan Perseus* borne of heauenly seed,
The faire *Andromeda* from perill freed:
Full mortally this Knight ywounded was,   650
That streames of blood foorth flowed on the gras.

Yet was he deckt (small ioy to him alas)
With manie garlands for his victories,
And with rich spoyles, which late he did purchas
Through braue atcheiuements from his enemies: 655
Fainting at last through long infirmities,
He smote his steed, that straight to heauen him bore,
And left me here his losse for to deplore.

631–7 *a stately Bed . . . summers day*: this visionary bridal alludes to the marriage of the Church with Christ in Rev. 19   633 *red*: taken   638 *voyce . . . farre away*: cf. Rev. 19: 5–7   639 *dight*: make ready, dress   640 *in readie ray*: arrayed and ready to come   646 *A Knight all arm'd*: Sir Philip Sidney at Zutphen   646–9 *a winged steed . . . freed*: Pegasus, invoked at 426, was generated from the blood of Medusa; her killer *Perseus, borne of heavenly seed* because Jupiter's son by Danae, rode the winged horse when freeing *Andromeda* from the rock to which she was tied for sacrifice to a sea-monster   656 *Fainting at last*: Sidney died a month after his wounding   657 *straight to heaven*: both *Perseus* and his *winged horse* (itself coming to symbolize immortality) changed into constellations

6

Lastly I saw an Arke of purest golde
Vpon a brazen pillour standing hie,   660
Which th' ashes seem'd of some great Prince to hold,
Enclosde therein for endles memorie
Of him, whom all the world did glorifie:
Seemed the heauens with the earth did disagree,
Whether should of those ashes keeper bee.   665

At last me seem'd wing footed *Mercurie*,
From heauen descending to appease their strife,
The Arke did beare with him aboue the skie,
And to those ashes gaue a second life,
To liue in heauen, where happines is rife: 670
At which the earth did grieue exceedingly,
And I for dole was almost like to die.

L: Envoy

Immortall spirite of *Philisides*,
Which now art made the heauens ornament,
That whilome wast the worlds chiefst riches;   675
Giue leaue to him that lou'de thee to lament
His losse, by lacke of thee to heauen hent,
And with last duties of this broken verse,
Broken with sighes, to decke thy sable Herse.

And ye faire Ladie th' honor of your daies,   680
And glorie of the world, your high thoughts scorne;
Vouchsafe this moniment of his last praise,
With some few siluer dropping teares t' adorne:
And as ye be of heauenlie off spring borne,
So vnto heauen let your high minde aspire,   685
And loath this drosse of sinfull worlds desire.

659–63 *Arke of purest golde . . . glorifie*: the subject is the return of Sidney's corpse to England; cf.
618 n.   661 *ashes*: the *dust* which flesh returns to (cf. 40 and n.)   *great Prince*: like Leicester
and Ambrose Dudley (cf. 184, 240), Sidney had some claim to the throne (though *Prince* could be
used of the mighty in general, without royal significance)   663 *glorifie*: praise as glorious
665 *Whether*: which of two   666 *Mercurie*: conductor of dead into the afterlife, also god of
learning and literary skills   672 *dole*: grief   EPILOGUE *L: Envoy*: the parting admonition
or address (from *envoyer* 'to send') of a poem   677 *hent*: snatched up   678–9 *broken . . .
Broken*: inadequate . . . interrupted

6

Samuel Daniel, The Complaint of Rosamond *(1592)*

THE story of Henry II's love for Rosamond Clifford, of his queen's jealousy and Rosamond's death by poison, was familiar in the sixteenth century. A series of chroniclers, starting with Giraldus Cambrensis and including Fabyan, Stowe, and (in 1592) Warner, had dealt with the subject. Daniel (1563–1619) variously modified his sources—introducing, for example, the guileful 'Matrone' who persuades Rosamond to be seduced (211–301), and elaborating into narrative (as is the fashion of 1590s short epics) the 'Casket richly wrought' sent by the king as gift and warning (372–413). His greatest innovation was the simple complicating one of describing events from Rosamond's point of view. Contemporaries were impressed, and the poem was reprinted with revisions in *Delia and Rosamond Augmented* (1594), and several later editions (fastidiously reworked), up to the *Whole Workes* (1623). Daniel's changes are too plentiful for collation in a volume such as this, but points of large insertion—chiefly affecting the role of Queen Eleanor—are indicated in the textual notes. The version of *The Complaint of Rosamond* given here was printed, in 1592, after the sonnet-sequence *Delia*. Its allusion to '*Delia*, left to adorne the West' at line 525 is usually taken as complimenting Daniel's dedicatee, Mary Sidney: the Countess of Pembroke is compared with the sonnet-mistress whose grace and pity Rosamond seeks at the start of the plaint. Help is sought because the plainant thinks she cannot otherwise reach Elysium. For some readers, like Drayton's Matilda (above, p. 29), the unredeemed nature of Rosamond was troubling. Certainly her repentance might be more wholehearted. Towards the end of the poem, where Complaint typically exhorts virtue, Rosamond seems more concerned with fame, with correcting the world's neglect. Throughout, she insists on her mortal beauty. And although she remarks on the naïvety of unreformed religion (above, pp. 29–30), her dubious talk of intercession and 'indulgence' (notably at 45–9) will have struck readers as complicating the already ambiguous, though elegantly articulate, texture of Daniel's poem.

THE COMPLAINT OF ROSAMOND

Out from the horror of infernall deepes,
My poore afflicted ghost comes heere to plaine it:
Attended with my shame that neuer sleepes,
The spot wherewith my kinde, and youth did staine it:
My body found a graue where to containe it,   5
 A sheete could hide my face, but not my sin,
 For Fame finds neuer tombe t' inclose it in.

And which is worse, my soule is nowe denied,
Her transport to the sweet Elisean rest,
The ioyfull blisse for ghosts repurified,   10
The euer springing Gardens of the blest.
Caron denies me waftage with the rest,
 And sayes my soule can neuer passe that Riuer,
 Till Louers sighes on earth shall it deliuer.

So shall I neuer passe; for how should I   15
Procure this sacrifice amongst the liuing?
Time hath long since worne out the memorie,
Both of my life, and liues vniust depriuing:
Sorrow for me is dead for aye reuiuing.
 Rosamond hath little left her but her name,   20
 And that disgrac'd, for time hath wrong'd the same.

No Muse suggests the pittie of my case,
Each penne dooth ouerpasse my iust complaint,
Whilst others are preferd, though farre more base:
Shores wife is grac'd, and passes for a Saint;   25

---

4 *kinde*: nature, gender 6 *sheete*: shroud (though *shame* prompts comparison with *Shores Wife*, 43) 7 *it*: sin and its ill *Fame* 9 *transport*: carriage, pleasing flight (of *ioyfull blisse*) *Elisean rest*: peace enjoyed by souls in Elysium 10 *repurified*: purged of sin, purified repeatedly (until rarefied) 12 *Caron*: the aged boatman, Charon, ships souls across the underworld *Riuer* Styx 14 *deliuer*: redeem (traditionally by paying a coin, an obolus, to Charon, though the *sighes* required here prettily square with *waftage*) 16 *sacrifice*: so called because the *sighes* are offered by mortals to superhuman powers 18 *liues vniust depriuing*: the unjust way life was taken from me 19 *for aye reuiuing*: beyond all recovery 22 *suggests*: prompts in favour of 24 *preferd*: advanced, chosen 25–7 *Shores wife . . . did such compassion finde*: alluding to Churchyard's poem, above

Her Legend iustifies her foule attaint;
   Her well-told tale did such compassion finde,
   That she is pass'd, and I am left behinde.

Which seene with griefe, my myserable ghost,
(Whilome inuested in so faire a vaile,   30
Which whilst it liu'd, was honoured of the most,
And being dead, giues matter to bewaile)
Comes to sollicit thee, since others faile,
   To take this taske, and in thy wofull Song
   To forme my case, and register my wrong.   35

Although I knowe thy iust lamenting Muse,
Toylde in th' affliction of thine owne distresse,
In others cares hath little time to vse,
And therefore maist esteeme of mine the lesse:
Yet as thy hopes attend happie redresse,   40
   Thy ioyes depending on a womans grace,
   So moue thy minde a wofull womans case.

Delia may happe to deygne to read our story,
And offer vp her sigh among the rest,
Whose merit would suffice for both our glorie,   45
Whereby thou might'st be grac'd, and I be blest,
That indulgence would profit me the best;
   Such powre she hath by whom thy youth is lead,
   To ioy the liuing and to blesse the dead.

So I through beautie made the wofull'st wight,   50
By beautie might haue comfort after death:
That dying fayrest, by the fayrest might
Finde life aboue on earth, and rest beneath:

26 *attaint*: stain, dishonour, legal condemnation   28 *pass'd*: granted passage by Charon (being '*pass'd* over by blame')   30 *inuested in so faire a vaile*: clothed in such a beautiful bodily garb (*vaile* implies cloistered innocence, as at 209, yet indicates seductive disguise, extending physical loveliness into suggestions of *faire* attire)   31 *of the most*: in the greatest degree   35 *forme*: frame in composition (and so, with a quibble on *case*, in which type was kept, and *register*, 'put into print') *my wrong*: the injury done me   36–7 *thy iust lamenting Muse ... distresse*: alludes to the sonnets to Delia (see headnote)   40 *attend*: await   41 *a womans grace*: Delia's favour   42 *moue thy minde ... case*: may an unhappy woman's predicament (and pleading of it) sway you   45–9 *merit ... indulgence ... blesse the dead*: with hints of unreformed religion, the *sigh* for Rosamond resembling prayers uttered or procured for those in purgatory   53 *life*: of good fame

She that can blesse vs with one happy breath,
   Giue comfort to thy Muse to doe her best,   55
   That thereby thou maist ioy, and I might rest.

Thus saide: forthwith mou'd with a tender care
And pittie, which my selfe could neuer finde,
What she desir'd, my Muse deygn'd to declare,
And therefore will'd her boldly tell her minde: 60
And I more willing tooke this charge assignd,
   Because her griefes were worthy to be knowne,
   And telling hers, might hap forget mine owne.

Then write quoth shee the ruine of my youth,
Report the downe-fall of my slippry state: 65
Of all my life reueale the simple truth,
To teach to others, what I learnt too late:
Exemplifie my frailtie, tell howe Fate
   Keepes in eternall darke our fortunes hidden,
   And ere they come, to know them tis forbidden.   70

For whilst the sunn-shine of my fortune lasted,
I ioy'd the happiest warmth, the sweetest heat
That euer yet imperious beautie tasted,
I had what glory euer flesh could get:
But this faire morning had a shamefull set;   75
   Disgrace darkt honor, sinne did clowde my brow,
   As note the sequel, and Ile tell thee how.

The blood I staind was good and of the best,
My birth had honor, and my beautie fame:
Nature and Fortune ioyn'd to make me blest,   80
Had I had grace t' haue knowne to vse the same:
My education shew'd from whence I came,
   And all concur'd to make me happy furst,
   That so great hap might make me more accurst.

---

58 *neuer finde*: within myself   59 *she desir'd*: Rosamond requested   65 *slippry state*: insecure exalted position   66 *simple*: with quibble on 'foolish'   68 *Exemplifie*: make exemplary *to others*   71 *sunn-shine*: as often in 16th-cent. poetry, imaging royal favour as the sun   72 *ioy'd*: enjoyed   75 *set*: dusk   78 *of*: derived from   81 *vse the same*: persevere in living through the benefits which *blest* me   82 *My education . . . I came*: I was well brought up and showed it (while genealogy and history taught me pride in descent, cf. 78–9, 329)

Happie liu'd I whilst Parents eye did guide,   85
The indiscretion of my feeble wayes:
And Country home kept me from being eyde,
Where best vnknowne I spent my sweetest dayes;
Till that my frindes mine honour sought to rayse,
   To higher place, which greater credite yeeldes,   90
   Deeming such beauty was vnfit for feeldes.

From Country then to Court I was preferr'd,
From calme to stormes, from shore into the deepes:
There where I perish'd, where my youth first err'd;
There where I lost the Flowre which honour keepes;   95
There where the worser thriues, the better weepes;
   Ah me poore wench, on this vnhappy shelfe
   I grounded me, and cast away my selfe.

For thither com'd, when yeeres had arm'd my youth
With rarest proofe of beautie euer seene: 100
When my reuiuing eye had learnt the truth,
That it had powre to make the winter greene,
And flowre affections whereas none had beene:
   Soone could I teach my browe to tyrannize,
   And make the world do homage to mine eyes.   105

For age I saw, though yeeres with cold conceit,
Congeald theyr thoughts against a warme desire,
Yet sigh their want, and looke at such a baite,
I saw how youth was waxe before the fire:
I saw by stealth, I fram'd my looke a lire,   110
   Yet well perceiu'd how Fortune made me then,
   The enuy of my sexe, and wonder vnto men.

Looke how a Comet at the first appearing,
Drawes all mens eyes with wonder to behold it:
Or as the saddest tale at suddaine hearing,   115
   Makes silent listning vnto him that told it:

---

88 *best vnknowne*: to happiest effect living obscurely   95 *Flowre*: of virginity   97 *shelfe*:
reef   101 *reuiuing*: rejuvenating   108 *Yet*: even so, still (after those *yeeres*)
110 *fram'd my looke a lire*: made my looks deceive (in a display of innocence), belying what I thought
116 *silent listning*: a pool of silence (all ears)

So did my speech when rubies did vnfold it;
  So did the blasing of my blush appeere,
  T' amaze the world, that holds such sights so deere.

Ah beauty Syren, fayre enchaunting good,   120
Sweet silent rethorique of perswading eyes:
Dombe eloquence, whose powre doth moue the blood,
More then the words, or wisedome of the wise:
Still harmonie, whose diapason lyes
  Within a brow, the key which passions moue,   125
  To rauish sence, and play a world in loue.

What might I then not doe whose powre was such?
What cannot women doe that know theyr powre?
What woman knowes it not I feare too much,
How blisse or bale lyes in theyr laugh or lowre?   130
Whilst they enioy their happy blooming flowre,
  Whilst nature decks her with her proper fayre
  Which cheeres the worlde, ioyes each sight, sweetens th' ayre.

Such one was I, my beautie was mine owne,
No borrowed blush which banck-rot beauties seeke: 135
The newfound-shame, a sinne to vs vnknowne,
Th' adulterate beauty of a falsed cheeke:
Vild staine to honor and to women eeke,
  Seeing that time our fading must detect,
  Thus with defect to couer our defect.   140

Impiety of times, chastities abator,
Falshod, wherein thy selfe, thy selfe deniest:
Treason, to counterfeit the seale of nature,
The stampe of heauen, impressed by the hiest.

117 *rubies*: her lips   118 *blasing*: with a quibble on 'blazoning', 'displaying as in her-aldry'   124 *diapason*: consonant octave   125 *key*: musical tonality (close in Elizabethan English to the *key* of a keyboard instrument and the *key which* can *moue* a lock)   126 *in*: into   129 *I feare too much*: (I am afraid they all know it too well)   132 *proper fayre*: own beauty   135 *banck-rot*: variant of 'bankrupt' (cf. Italian *banca rotta*) with useful hints of decay   137 *adulterate*: falsely mingled (paint and flesh, with 'adulterous' ready for 141)   138 *Vild*: vile   139 *detect*: bring to light   140 *with defect*: by a fault   141–7 *Impiety of times ... idolatrise*: all the things which use of cosmetics, or the cosmetic-user, can be called   141 *times*: the epoch   143 *seale of nature*: signs (in wax-like flesh) with which *nature* impresses her works   144 *the hiest*: God

Disgrace vnto the world, to whom thou lyest,   145
   Idol vnto thy selfe, shame to the wise,
   And all that honors thee idolatrise.

Farre was that sinne from vs whose age was pure,
When simple beautie was accounted best,
The time when women had no other lure   150
But modestie, pure cheekes, a vertuous brest:
This was the pompe wherewith my youth was blest;
   These were the weapons which mine honour wunne
   In all the conflicts that mine eyes begunne.

Which were not small, I wrought on no meane obiect;   155
A Crowne was at my feete, Scepters obaide mee:
Whom Fortune made my King, Loue made my Subiect,
Who did commaund the Land, most humbly praid mee:
Henry the second, that so highly weigh'd mee,
   Founde well by proofe the priuiledge of Beautie,   160
   That it hath powre to counter-maund all duetie.

For after all his victories in Fraunce,
Tryumphing in the honour of his deedes:
Vnmatch'd by sword, was vanquisht by a glaunce,
And hotter warres within his bosome breedes: 165
Warres whom whole Legions of desires feedes,
   Against all which my chastity opposes,
   The fielde of honour, vertue neuer loses.

No armour might bee founde that coulde defend,
Transpearcing rayes of Christall-pointed eyes:
No Stratagem, no reason could amend,   170
No not his age; yet olde men should be wise:
But shewes deceiue, outward appearance lyes;
   Let none for seeming so, thinke Saints of others,
   For all are men, and all haue suckt their Mothers.   175

146 *shame*: shaming to behold   147 *idolatrise*: idolatrous   160 *proofe*: trial, experience   *priuiledge*: right, dispensation   169 *defend*: protect against   170 *Christall-pointed*: fitted out ('appointed') with *Christall* (stock likeness for windowed *eyes*); *Transpearcing* also has *Christall* tip and make *pointed* the *rayes* (darts of love)   172 *should be*: ought to be (having had so much experience), are looked upon as being (though *shewes deceiue*)   174 *for seeming so*: because they (those *others*) seem *Saints*

Who would haue thought, a Monarch would haue euer
Obayed his handmaide, of so meane a state;
Vultur ambition feeding on his lyuer,
Age hauing worne his pleasures out of date:
But happe comes neuer or it comes too late,   180
    For such a daintie which his youth found not,
    Vnto his feeble age did chaunce allot.

Ah Fortune neuer absolutely good,
For that some crosse still counterchecks our luck:
As heere beholde th' incompatible blood,   185
Of age and youth was that whereon we stuck:
Whose loathing, we from natures brests do suck,
    As opposit to what our blood requires;
    For equall age doth equall like desires.

But mightie men in highest honor sitting,   190
Nought but applause and pleasure can behold:
Sooth'd in their liking, carelesse what is fitting,
May not be suffred once to thinke the' are old:
Not trusting what they see, but what is told.
    Miserable fortune to forget so farre,   195
    The state of flesh, and what our frailties are.

Yet must I needes excuse so great defect,
For drinking of the *Lethe* of myne eyes:
H' is forc'd forget himselfe, and all respect
Of maiestie whereon his state relyes: 200
And now of loues, and pleasures must deuise.
    For thus reuiu'd againe, he serues and su'th,
    And seekes all meanes to vndermine my youth.

---

178 *Vultur . . . on his lyuer*: Henry (a mock Prometheus) suffers from hopeful desire gnawing at the seat of sexual appetite   179 *worne . . . out of date*: ground down until they are past the point of expiration (*out of date* as a contract can become)   180 *happe*: a piece of good fortune   184 *counterchecks*: thwartingly answers   187 *Whose loathing*: deep distaste for which discrepancy   192 *Sooth'd in their liking*: reassured that whatever they like is appropriate   193 *suffred once*: at any time permitted   198 *Lethe*: river of forgetfulness   199–200 *forget . . . all respect | Of*: neglect everything that pertains to (and thus 'do without the deference due towards')   201 *deuise*: scheme   202 *su'th*: woos, pursues

Which neuer by assault he could recouer,
So well incamp'd in strength of chaste desires: 205
My cleane-arm'd thoughts repell'd an vnchast louer,
The Crowne that could commaund what it requires,
I lesser priz'd then chastities attires,
 Th' vnstained vaile, which innocents adornes,
 Th' vngathred Rose, defended with the thornes.   210

And safe mine honor stoode till that in truth,
One of my Sexe, of place, and nature bad,
Was set in ambush to intrap my youth,
One in the habit of like frailtie clad,
One who the liu'ry of like weakenes had.   215
 A seeming Matrone, yet a sinfull monster,
 As by her words the chaster sort may conster.

Shee set vpon me with the smoothest speech,
That Court and age could cunningly deuise:
The one autentique made her fit to teach,   220
The other learnt her how to subtelise:
Both were enough to circumuent the wise.
 A document that well may teach the sage,
 That there's no trust in youth, nor hope in age.

Daughter (saith she) behold thy happy chaunce,   225
That hast the lot cast downe into thy lap,
Whereby thou maist thy honor great aduaunce,
Whilst thou (vnhappy) wilt not see thy hap:
Such fond respect thy youth doth so inwrap,
 T' oppose thy selfe against thine owne good fortune,   230
 That points thee out, and seemes thee to importune.

---

204 *recouer*: capture (not always in 16th-cent. English 'regain')   206 *cleane-arm'd*: weaponed
with purity   212 *of place*: in her office   214 *in the habit . . . clad*: dressed as, and *inuested*
(as 30 puts it) with femininity (the moral *frailtie* of which was proverbial)   216 *Matrone*:
motherly person   217 *by her words . . . conster*: from what she said . . . construe   220 *autentique . . . fit*: qualified and able   221 *subtelise*: make nice or sophistical
distinctions (a new word in the 1590s)   223 *document*: piece of evidence   224 *trust*:
reliability   226 *That hast the lot . . . into thy lap*: which, in casting lots, has thrown the winning
token to you (with a hint of sexual consequences, as at 235)   229 *fond respect*: foolish caution
231 *points thee out*: indicates you (with a gesture ready to *importune*), picks you (by pricking a list),
'appoints' you over others

Doost thou not see how that thy King thy *Ioue*,
Lightens foorth glory on thy darke estate:
And showres downe golde and treasure from aboue,
Whilst thou doost shutte thy lappe against thy fate: 235
Fye fondling fye, thou wilt repent too late
    The error of thy youth; that canst not see
    What is the fortune that dooth followe thee.

Thou must not thinke thy flowre can alwayes florish,
And that thy beautie will be still admired: 240
But that those rayes which all these flames doe nourish,
Canceld with Time, will haue their date expyred,
And men will scorne what now is so desired:
    Our frailtyes doome is written in the flowers,
    Which florish now and fade ere many howers. 245

Reade in my face the ruines of my youth,
The wracke of yeeres vpon my aged brow:
I haue beene faire, I must confesse the trueth,
And stoode vppon as nice respects as thow;
I lost my time, and I repent it now; 250
    But were I to beginne my youth againe,
    I would redeeme the time I spent in vayne.

But thou hast yeeres and priuiledge to vse them,
Thy priuiledge doth beare beauties great seale:
Besides, the law of nature doth excuse them, 255
To whom thy youth may haue a iust appeale:
Esteeme not fame more then thou doost thy weale;
    Fame, whereof the world seemes to make such choyce,
    Is but an Eccho, and an idle voyce.

---

233 *darke estate*: obscure situation in life transmuting himself in an act of love   234 *showres downe golde*: as *Ioue* did upon Danae, *lot* of 226, and spurning love's action   235 *shutte thy lappe against thy fate*: failing to catch the eyebeams of 170   236 *fondling*: foolish little one   241 *rayes*: the 242 *Canceld . . . their date expyred*: as at 179, the *date* is that limit of a legal or commercial agreement which passes, and is *Canceld*, in *Time*   244 *Our frailtyes doome*: the necessary end of our fragile beauty (214 sheds its ethical burden)   247 *wracke*: ruin 249 *stoode vppon . . . as thow*: was just as fastidious as you are   252 *redeeme the time*: an echo of St Paul (Eph. 6: 15, Col. 4: 5) mischievously follows appeals to *repent* at 236–7 and 250   254 *Thy priuiledge . . . great seale*: Rosamond's right to *vse* her *yeeres* is a *priuiledge* as of *law* authenticated not under royal power (cf. 'the Great Seal of England') but by *beauties* authority   257 *weale*: prosperity   258 *such choyce*: so choosy a fuss

Then why should thys respect of honor bound vs,   260
In th' imaginary lists of reputation?
Titles which cold seueritie hath found vs,
Breath of the vulgar, foe to recreation:
Melancholies opinion, customs relation;
 Pleasures plague, beauties scourge, hell to the fayre,   265
 To leaue the sweete for Castles in the ayre.

Pleasure is felt, opinion but conceau'd,
Honor, a thing without vs, not our owne:
Whereof we see how many are bereau'd,
Which should haue rep'd the glory they had sowne,   270
And many haue it, yet vnworthy knowne.
 So breathes his blasts this many-headed beast,
 Whereof the wisest haue esteemed least.

The subtile Citty-women better learned,
Esteeme them chast ynough that best seeme so: 275
Who though they sport, it shall not be discerned,
Their face bewraies not what their bodies doe;
Tis warie walking that doth safliest goe.
 With shew of vertue, as the cunning knowes,
 Babes are beguild with sweetes, and men with showes.   280

Then vse thy tallent, youth shall be thy warrant,
And let not honor from thy sports detract:
Thou must not fondly thinke thy selfe transparent,
That those who see thy face can iudge the fact;
Let her haue shame that cannot closely act.   285
 And seeme the chast, which is the cheefest arte,
 For what we seeme each sees, none knowes our harte.

---

261 *imaginary lists of reputation*: spurious borders of social respectability, limits dreamt up by the merely reputable, fanciful catalogues (a sense just emergent in 1590s) of those judged accomplished   262 *Titles*: of virtue, honorific but without reward   263 *vulgar*: common people   *foe to recreation*: because harmless pastimes, keeping men's company and the like, are closed to those who would keep the *Titles*   264 *Melancholies opinion, customs relation*: these *Titles* are at the mercy of malcontents' judgement and of commonplace hearsay   266 *leaue the sweete for Castles in the ayre*: give up something pleasant for fantasies (e.g. about heavenly mansions)   268 *without*: outside   269 *bereau'd*: deprived   272 *blasts*: blighting gusts *many-headed beast*: opinion, Hydra-like *world*   277 *bewraies*: reveals   278 *warie walking*: as against honest confidence   281 *vse thy tallent*: sophistical allusion to the Parable of the Talents (Matt. 25: 14–30)   *warrant*: permit, justification   282 *detract*: quibbling on 'disparage'   285 *closely*: in secret

The mightie who can with such sinnes dispence,
In steed of shame doe honors great bestow:
A worthie author doth redeeme th' offence,   290
And makes the scarelet sinne as white as snow.
The Maiestie that doth descend so low,
    Is not defilde, but pure remaines therein:
    And being sacred, sanctifies the sin.

What, doost thou stand on thys, that he is olde,   295
Thy beauty hath the more to worke vppon:
Thy pleasures want shal be supply'd with gold,
Cold age dotes most when the heate of youth is gone:
Enticing words preuaile with such a one,
    Alluring shewes most deepe impression strikes,   300
    For age is prone to credite what it likes.

Heere interupt she leaues me in a doubt,
When loe began the combat in my blood:
Seeing my youth inuirond round about,
The ground vncertaine where my reasons stood;   305
Small my defence to make my party good,
    Against such powers which were so surely layde,
    To ouerthrow a poore vnskilful mayde.

Treason was in my bones my selfe conspyring,
To sell my selfe to lust, my soule to sinne: 310
Pure-blushing shame was euen in retiring,
Leauing the sacred hold it glory'd in.
Honor lay prostrate for my flesh to win,
    When cleaner thoughts my weakenes can vpbray
    Against my selfe, and shame did force me say.   315

---

288 *can with such sinnes dispence*: do not need to bother referring their behaviour to such moral criteria as chastity   292 *so low*: into *sinne*, and with reminders of social condescension 294 *being sacred*: as anointed rulers, hedged with divinity   296 *more to worke vppon*: greater challenge   297 *want*: lack   302 *interupt*: having   broken   off   her   discourse   304 *inuirond*: surrounded (the following lines develop an imagery of siege)   305 *ground*: bases of argument (with a quibble on the *ground* bravely *stood* by soldiers)   307 *powers*: developing the military image   *layde*: tactically distributed   309 *my selfe conspyring*: plotting with me 311–12 *euen in retiring,* | *Leauing the sacred hold*: in the very act of drawing back from the virtuous struggle (of 304–8, while *hold* extends in meaning through 'that which is kept' to 'stronghold')   314 *can vpbray*: did upbraid, began to rebuke

Ah *Rosamond*, what doth thy flesh prepare,
Destruction to thy dayes, death to thy fame:
Wilt thou betray that honor held with care,
T' intombe with blacke reproch a spotted name,
Leauing thy blush the collours of thy shame.   320
   Opening thy feete to sinne, thy soule to lust,
   Gracelesse to lay thy glorie in the dust.

Nay first let th' earth gape wide to swallow thee,
And shut thee vp in bosome with her dead:
Ere Serpent tempt thee taste forbidden tree,   325
Or feele the warmth of an vnlawfull bed:
Suffring thy selfe by lust to be misled;
   So to disgrace thy selfe and grieue thine heires,
   That *Cliffords* race should scorne thee one of theyrs.

Neuer wish longer to inioy the ayre,   330
Then that thou breath'st the breath of chastitie:
Longer then thou preseru'st thy soule as faire
As is thy face, free from impuritie:
Thy face that makes th' admired in euery eye:
   Where natures care such rarities inroule,   335
   Which vs'd amisse, may serue to damne thy soule.

But what? he is my King and may constraine me,
Whether I yeelde or not I liue defamed:
The world will thinke authority did gaine me,
I shal be iudg'd hys loue, and so be shamed: 340
We see the fayre condemn'd, that neuer gamed.
   And if I yeeld, tis honorable shame,
   If not, I liue disgrac'd, yet thought the same.

What way is left thee then vnhappy mayde,
Whereby thy spotlesse foote may wander out   345
Thys dreadfull danger, which thou seest is layd,
Wherein thy shame doth compasse thee about?

---

321 *Opening thy feete*: with a sexual purpose   325 *Serpent tempt thee*: see Gen. 3
329 *That Cliffords race . . . one of theyrs*: Rosamond, proud of descent (cf. 78–9), was, as Drayton tells us in 'The Argument' to his *Epistle*, '*the daughter of the Lord* Walter Clyfford'   335 *rarities inroule*: precious features register   341 *gamed*: sported (with hints of profit, gambled and prostituted for)   345 *wander out*: windingly find a way out of

Thy simple yeeres cannot resolue this doubt.
   Thy youth can neuer guide thy foote so euen,
   But in despight some scandall will be giuen.   350

Thus stood I ballanc'd equallie precize,
Till my fraile flesh did weigh me downe to sinne:
Till world and pleasure made me partialize,
And glittering pompe my vanitie did winne;
When to excuse my fault my lusts beginne,   355
   And impious thoughts alledg'd this wanton clause,
   That though I sinn'd, my sinne had honest cause.

So well the golden balles cast downe before me,
Could entertaine my course, hinder my way:
Whereat my rechlesse youth stooping to store me,   360
Lost me the gole, the glory, and the day.
Pleasure had set my wel-skoold thoughts to play,
   And bade me vse the vertue of mine eyes,
   For sweetly it fits the fayre to wantonise.

Thus wrought to sinne, soone was I traind from Court,   365
To a solitarie Grange there to attend
The time the King should thether make resort,
Where he loues long-desired work should end.
Thether he daily messages doth send,
   With costly iewels orators of loue: 370
   Which (ah too well men know) doe women moue.

The day before the night of my defeature,
He greets me with a Casket richly wrought:
So rare, that arte did seeme to striue with nature,
T' expresse the cunning work-mans curious thought;   375

348 *simple yeeres*: inexperienced youth   349 *euen*: steadily   350 *in despight*: both 'for all that' and 'spitefully'   351 *equallie precize*: absolutely equal (with a specious hint of moral exactness)   353 *partialize*: favour one side of what had been *equallie precize*   356 *alledg'd this wanton clause*: urged in mitigation this licentious proviso   358–61 *So well the golden balles . . . and the day*: swift-footed Atalanta, who would only marry the suitor who outran her, was overcome by Hippomenes because she stopped to pick up the golden apples (here Henry's wealth and favour) he dropped as lures during their race   363 *vertue*: property, ability (to seduce, as against 'good conduct')   365 *traind*: conducted (suggestions of 'decoyed, manipulated')   372 *defeature*: both 'defeat' and 'disfigurement (by ill fame)'   375 *curious*: elaborate, sophisticated

The mistery whereof I prying sought,
   And found engrauen on the lidde aboue,
   Amymone how she with *Neptune* stroue.

Amymone old *Danaus* fayrest daughter,
As she was fetching water all alone   380
At *Lerna*: whereas *Neptune* came and caught her,
From whom she striu'd and strugled to be gone,
Beating the ayre with cryes and pittious mone.
   But all in vaine, with him sh' is forc'd to goe:
   Tis shame that men should vse poore maydens so.   385

There might I see described how she lay,
At those proude feete, not satisfied with prayer:
Wailing her heauie hap, cursing the day,
In act so pittious to expresse dispaire:
And by how much more greeu'd, so much more fayre;   390
   Her teares vpon her cheekes poore carefull gerle,
   Did seeme against the sunne cristall and perle.

Whose pure cleere streames, which loe so faire appeares,
Wrought hotter flames, O myracle of loue,
That kindles fire in water, heate in teares,   395
And makes neglected beautie mightier proue:
Teaching afflicted eyes affects to moue;
   To shew that nothing ill becomes the fayre,
   But crueltie, that yeeldes vnto no prayer.

This hauing viewd and therewith something moued,   400
Figured I found within the other squares
Transformed *Io, Ioues* deerely loued,
In her affliction how she strangely fares,

376 *mistery*: secret, cryptic message   378 *Amymone . . . with Neptune stroue*: standard classical
texts (e.g. Apollodorus and Servius) have *Amymone* accord with the sea-god's desires, rather than be
forced; Rosamond, it would seem, originally misconstrued or now rationalizes the *mistery*
381 *Lerna*: marshes near Argolis   386 *described*: pictured   389 *act*: the *pittious* tableaux
of 387–8, 391–2   390 *greeu'd*: grievously sorrowful, hurtfully offended   394 *flames*: of
passion in *Neptune*   395 *water*: *Neptune* as sea-god   397 *affects*: passions (in
Neptune)   398 *ill becomes*: sits ill upon, appears uncomely in relation to; the phrase opens out
at *But*, to describe not just what is particular to *the fayre* (even whose weeping *becomes* her) but her
context (in which the *crueltie* of 399 does *ill* suit, demeans, *the fayre*)   400 *therewith something
moued*: having been somewhat moved by it   402–6 *Transformed Io . . . spyes*: changed into a

Strangelie distress'd, (O beautie borne to cares)
   Turn'd to a Heiffer, kept with iealous eyes,   405
   Alwaies in danger of her hatefull spyes.

These presidents presented to my view,
Wherein the presage of my fall was showne,
Might haue fore-warn'd me well what would ensue,
And others harmes haue made me shunne mine owne;   410
But fate is not preuented though fore-knowne.
   For that must hap decreed by heauenly powers,
   Who worke our fall, yet make the fault still ours.

Witnes the world, wherein is nothing rifer,
Then miseries vnkend before they come: 415
Who can the characters of chaunce discipher,
Written in clowdes of our concealed dome?
Which though perhaps haue beene reueald to some,
   Yet that so doubtfull as successe did proue them,
   That men must know they haue the heauens aboue them.   420

I sawe the sinne wherein my foote was entring,
I sawe how that dishonour did attend it,
I sawe the shame whereon my flesh was ventring,
Yet had I not the powre for to defende it;
So weake is sence when error hath condemn'd it: 425
   We see what's good, and thereto we consent vs;
   But yet we choose the worst, and soone repent vs.

And now I come to tell the worst of ilnes,
Now drawes the date of mine affliction neere:
Now when the darke had wrapt vp all in stilnes,   430
And dreadfull blacke, had dispossess'd the cleere:
Com'd was the night, mother of sleepe and feare,
   Who with her sable mantle friendly couers,
   The sweet-stolne sports, of ioyfull meeting Louers.

heifer by *Ioue*, her lover, *Io* was given by the suspicious Juno to hundred-eyed Argus for guard (*Metamorphoses*, 1. 588–667); if Rosamond is shown by the example of *Amymone* how futile it is to resist the King's love, the fate of *Io*—spied on and later (at the queen of heaven's behest) pursued by a stinging gadfly—anticipates what will happen to her after the seduction (see 568–609)   415 *vnkend*: not known   416 *characters*: signs   418 *some*: astrologers, augurers   419 *so doubtfull . . . proue them*: events worked out so uncertainly related to the prediction   420 *the heauens aboue them*: making divine decisions about life, regardless of human foretelling   426 *consent*: agree that it is *good*   428 *ilnes*: that which is bad 431 *cleere*: brightness (of day)

When loe I ioyde my Louer not my Loue,   435
And felt the hand of lust most vndesired:
Enforc'd th' vnprooued bitter sweete to proue,
Which yeeldes no mutuall pleasure when tis hired.
Loue's not constrain'd, nor yet of due required,
   Iudge they who are vnfortunately wed,   440
   What tis to come vnto a loathed bed.

But soone his age receiu'd his short contenting,
And sleepe seald vp his languishing desires:
When he turnes to his rest, I to repenting,
Into my selfe my waking thought retires: 445
My nakednes had prou'd my sences liers.
   Now opned were mine eyes to looke therein,
   For first we taste the fruite, then see our sin.

Now did I find my selfe vnparadis'd,
From those pure fieldes of my so cleane beginning: 450
Now I perceiu'd how ill I was aduis'd,
My flesh gan loathe the new-felt touch of sinning:
Shame leaues vs by degrees, not at first winning.
   For nature checks a new offence with lothing:
   But vse of sinne doth make it seeme as nothing.   455

And vse of sinne did worke in me a boldnes,
And loue in him, incorporates such zeale:
That iealosie increas'd with ages coldnes,
Fearing to loose the ioy of all his weale.
Or doubting time his stealth might els reueale,   460
   H' is driuen to deuise some subtile way,
   How he might safeliest keepe so rich a pray.

A stately Pallace he foorthwith did buylde,
Whose intricate innumerable wayes,
With such confused errors so beguil'd   465
Th' vnguided entrers with vncertaine strayes,

---

437 *Enforc'd*: I was forced (a self-exculpating hint of violence)   *vnprooued*: untried   *proue*: endure   439 *not constrain'd*: won't be forced   *of due required*: obligatory, paid as a necessary debt   442–3 *his age ... desires*: sex quickly tired the old king, and he dozed off   443 *languishing*: drooping, fading   448–9 *first we taste ... vnparadis'd*: another allusion to Gen. 3   450 *those pure fieldes*: Edenic images continue, characterizing the *Country home* of 87 (cf. 534) and abstractly implying realms of purity   451 *aduis'd*: by the *Matrone* and in my action   453 *at first winning*: when we are first won to sinful love (cf. 311–12)   455 *vse*: habitual practice   457 *zeale*: eager possessiveness   465 *errors*: wanderings   466 *strayes*: straying paths

And doubtfull turnings kept them in delayes,
    With bootlesse labor leading them about,
    Able to finde no way, nor in, nor out.

Within the closed bosome of which frame,   470
    That seru'd a Center to that goodly round:
    Were lodgings, with a garden to the same,
    With sweetest flowers that eu'r adorn'd the ground.
    And all the pleasures that delight hath found,
        To entertaine the sence of wanton eyes,   475
        Fuell of loue, from whence lusts flames arise.

Heere I inclos'd from all the world a sunder,
    The Minotaure of shame kept for disgrace:
    The monster of fortune, and the worlds wonder,
    Liu'd cloystred in so desolate a case: 480
    None but the King might come into the place,
        With certaine maides that did attend my neede,
        And he himselfe came guided by a threed.

O Iealousie, daughter of enuy and loue
    Most wayward issue of a gentle Syer;   485
    Fostred with feares, thy Fathers ioyes t' improue,
    Myrth-marring Monster, borne a subtile lyer;
    Hatefull vnto thy selfe, flying thine owne desier:
        Feeding vpon suspect that dooth renue thee,
        Happie were Louers if they neuer knewe thee.   490

---

467 *doubtfull*: baffling   471 *seru'd a Center to*: acted as central point for   473 *that eu'r*:
which always (unless *sweetest* is genuinely absolute, as 474 encourages)   474 *all the pleasures*:
indecorous garden ornaments (marble Cupids, sporting satyrs, and the like) implied, as in
Drayton's *Rosamond*, 139–46   478 *Minotaure*: half man and half bull, kept in the labyrinth by
Minos until slain by Theseus (*Metamorphoses*, 8. 152–76); Rosamond, in the *stately Pallace*, is
similarly trapped (and doomed to die), and a *monster* by virtue of the unnatural *shame* which the
King and she have brought upon her   *kept for disgrace*: locked away on account of (to avoid)
scandal; the *Minotaure*, bestial offspring of Minos' wife Pasiphae and a bull, was *kept* in the labyrinth
'removere pudorem' says Ovid (8. 157); hints of merely deferred scandal ('held to my *disgrace*', note
worlds wonder, 479) and '*kept* for graceless purposes' (evoking that 17th-cent. and modern idiom
'*kept* woman')   480 *in so desolate a case*: in such lonely and hopeless circumstances   483 *guided by a threed*: as Theseus, using the clue of *threed* provided by Ariadne,
traced his way in and out of the labyrinth; see 478 and nn.   486 *t' improue*: sharpening *loue* by
preventing the intrusion of rivals   487 *a subtile lyer*: because *Iealousie* makes the innocent
deeds of loved ones look guilty, while using fibs of its own to test fidelity   488 *flying thine owne
desier*: repelled by mistrust from the desired object (desire's very force provoking the flight)
489 *suspect*: suspicion

Thou hast a thousand gates thou enterest by,
Conducting trembling passions to our hart:
Hundred eyed *Argos*, euer waking Spye,
Pale hagge, infernall fury, pleasures smart,
Enuious Obseruer, prying in euery part;   495
   Suspicious, fearefull, gazing still about thee,
   O would to God that loue could be without thee.

Thou didst depriue (through false suggesting feare)
Him of content, and me of libertie:
The onely good that women holde so deare,   500
And turnst my freedome to captiuitie,
First made a Prisoner, ere an enemy:
   Enioynd the raunsome of my bodies shame,
   Which though I paide could not redeeme the same.

What greater torment euer could haue beene,   505
Then to inforce the fayre to liue retired?
For what is Beautie if it be not seene,
Or what is't to be seene vnlesse admired?
And though admyred, vnlesse in loue desired?
   Neuer were cheekes of Roses, locks of Amber,   510
   Ordayn'd to liue imprisond in a Chamber.

Nature created Beautie for the view,
Like as the fire for heate, the Sunne for light:
The Faire doe holde this priuiledge as due,
By auncient Charter, to liue most in sight,   515
And she that is debarr'd it, hath not right.
   In vaine our friends in this vse their dehorting,
   For Beautie will be where is most resorting.

Witnes the fayrest streetes that Thames doth visit,
The wondrous concourse of the glittering Faire: 520
For what rare woman deckt with Beautie is it,
   That thither couets not to make repaire.

492 *trembling passions*: of fear   493 *Hundred eyed Argos*: see 402–6 and n.   494 *pleasures smart*: punisher of pleasure   498 *false suggesting*: wrongly prompting, evil-tempting   502 *ere an enemy*: before I became a foe (since *Iealousie* did, in some sense, make her his antagonist)   503 *of*: consisting of   504 *redeeme the same*: release my body   510 *locks of Amber*: the golden hair esteemed in 16th-cent. women   514–15 *priuiledge … By auncient Charter*: as at 160 and explicitly 254, the image is of rights recorded   515 *most in sight*: publicly   516 *debarr'd it*: deprived of high profile and libertie   *hath not right*: is wronged   517 *vse their dehorting*: dissuade   518 *resorting*: visiting and congregating   519 *fayrest … Thames doth visit*: most beautiful districts of London

The solitary Country may not stay her,
    Heere is the center of all beauties best,
    Excepting *Delia*, left to adorne the West.   525

Heere doth the curious with iudiciall eyes,
Contemplate beauty gloriously attired:
And heerein all our cheefest glory lyes,
To liue where we are prais'd and most desired.
O how we ioy to see our selues admired,   530
    Whilst niggardly our fauours we discouer,
    We loue to be belou'd, yet scorne the Louer.

Yet would to God my foote had neuer moued
From Countrey safety, from the fields of rest:
To know the danger to be highly loued,   535
And lyue in pompe to braue among the best.
Happy for me, better had I beene blest,
    If I vnluckely had neuer strayde:
    But liu'd at home a happy Country mayde.

Whose vnaffected innocencie thinks   540
No guilefull fraude, as doth the Courtly liuer:
She's deckt with trueth, the Riuer where she drinks
Doth serue her for her glasse, her counsell giuer:
She loues sincerely, and is loued euer.
    Her days are peace, and so she ends her breath,   545
    True life that knowes not what's to die till death.

So should I neuer haue beene registred,
In the blacke booke of the vnfortunate:
Nor had my name enrold with Maydes misled,
Which bought theyr pleasures at so hie a rate.   550
Nor had I taught through my vnhappy fate,
    This lesson which my selfe learnt with expence,
    How most it hurts that most delights the sence.

525 *Delia, left to adorne the West*: see headnote   526 *the curious*: sophisticated and enquiring person   *iudiciall*: judicious   531 *niggardly our fauours we discouer*: we reveal our beauties hardly at all (masks glimpsed from *fauours* as 'faces')   535 *to be highly loued*: of being loved (and strongly) by someone in high office   536 *best*: most noble in the kingdom 538 *strayde*: from *home* into error   540 *Whose*: she whose   *vnaffected*: unswayable, without affectations   542–3 *the Riuer . . . her glasse*: no insidious wines and pride-nurturing mirrors for her   544 *sincerely*: without falsification, in purity   *euer*: constantly   547 *So should I*: had I lived in this way I should

Shame followes sinne, disgrace is duly giuen,
Impietie will out, neuer so closely doone: 555
No walles can hide vs from the eyes of heauen,
For shame must end what wickednesse begun:
Forth breakes reproch when we least thinke thereon.
   And thys is euer propper vnto Courts:
   That nothing can be doone but Fame reports.   560

Fame doth explore what lyes most secrete hidden,
Entring the closet of the Pallace dweller:
Abroade reuealing what is most forbidden,
Of trueth and falshood both an equall teller:
Tis not a guarde can serue for to expell her,   565
   The sword of iustice cannot cutte her wings,
   Nor stop her mouth from vtt'ring secrete things.

And this our stealth she could not long conceale,
From her whom such a forfeit most concerned:
The wronged Queene, who could so closely deale,   570
That she the whole of all our practise learned,
And watcht a time when least it was discerned,
   In absence of the King, to wreake her wrong,
   With such reuenge as she desired long.

The Laberinth she entred by that threed   575
That seru'd a conduct to my absent Lord:
Left there by chaunce, reseru'd for such a deede,
Where she surpriz'd me whom she so abhord.
Enrag'd with madnes, scarce she speakes a word,
   But flyes with eger fury to my face,   580
   Offring me most vnwomanly disgrace.

Looke how a Tygresse that hath lost her whelpe,
Runs fearcely raging through the woods astray:
And seeing her selfe depriu'd of hope or helpe,
Furiously assaults what's in her way,   585

---

559 *euer propper vnto*: always in the nature of   562 *closet*: inner chamber   563 *Abroade*: to the world at large   565 *Tis not a*: there is no   566 *sword . . . wings*: standard iconography of *iustice* and *Fame*   568 *she*: Fame   569 *forfeit*: misdeed   570 *so closely deale*: handle matters so secretly   571 *practise*: behaviour, plotting   573 *wreake*: vindicate   576 *seru'd a conduct*: offered guidance   577 *reseru'd*: allotted   580 *to my face*: to confront me (perhaps with *eger*, which can mean 'sharp', nails lashing out)   581 *Offring me*: threatening me with   *disgrace*: while the Queen loses ethical poise and beauty, Rosamond's *grace* is threatened by violence

To satisfie her wrath, not for a pray:
  So fell she on me in outragious wise,
  As could Disdaine and Iealousie deuise.

And after all her vile reproches vsed,
She forc'd me take the poyson she had brought: 590
To end the lyfe that had her so abused,
And free her feares, and ease her iealous thought.
No crueltie her wrath would leaue vnwrought,
  No spightfull act that to reuenge is common:
  For no beast fearcer then a iealous woman.   595

Those hands that beauties ministers had bin,
Must now gyue death, that me adorn'd of late:
That mouth that newly gaue consent to sin,
Must now receiue destruction in there-at.
That body which my lusts did violate,   600
  Must sacrifice it selfe t' appease the wrong,
  So short is pleasure, glory lasts not long.

The poyson soone disperc'd through all my vaines,
Had dispossess'd my liuing sences quite:
When naught respecting death, the last of paines,   605
Plac'd his pale collours, th' ensigne of his might,
Vpon hys new-got spoyle before his right;
  Thence chac'd my soule, setting my day ere noone,
  When I least thought my ioyes could end so soone.

And as conuaid t' vntimely funerals,   610
My scarce colde corse not suffred longer stay:
Behold the King (by chance) returning, falls
T' incounter with the same vpon the way,
As he repaird to see his deerest ioy.
  Not thinking such a meeting could haue beene,   615
  To see his loue, and seeing beene vnseene.

587 *wise*: way, fashion   594 *is common*: generally belongs   597 *adorn'd*: as themselves
and in dressing Rosamond   601 *appease the wrong*: atone for my sin   604 *dispossess'd . . .
sences quite*: evicted the living action of my senses   605 *naught respecting*: remorseless
606 *pale collours*: the near-whites of a pallid cheek, as a flag ('drum and colours', cf.
ensigne)   607 *before his right*: prematurely   608 *noone*: middle age   612 *falls*: happens   614 *repaird*: made his way

Iudge those whom chaunce depriues of sweetest treasure,
What tis to lose a thing we hold so deare:
The best delight, wherein our soule takes pleasure,
The sweet of life, that penetrates so neare.   620
What passions feeles that hart, inforc'd to beare
 The deepe impression of so strange a sight?
 Tongue, pen, nor art, can neuer shew aright.

Amaz'd he standes, nor voyce nor body steares,
Words had no passage, teares no issue found: 625
For sorrow shut vp words, wrath kept in teares,
Confus'd affects each other doe confounde:
Oppress'd with griefe his passions had no bounde:
 Striuing to tell his woes, wordes would not come;
 For light cares speake, when mightie griefes are dombe.   630

At length extremitie breakes out a way,
Through which th' imprisoned voice with teares attended,
Wayles out a sound that sorrowes doe bewray:
With armes a crosse and eyes to heauen bended,
Vapouring out sighes that to the skyes ascended.   635
 Sighes, the poore ease calamitie affords,
 Which serue for speech when sorrow wanteth words.

O heauens (quoth he) why doe myne eyes behold,
The hatefull rayes of this vnhappy sonne?
Why haue I light to see my sinnes controld,   640
With blood of mine owne shame thus vildly donne?
How can my sight endure to looke thereon?
 Why doth not blacke eternall darknes hide,
 That from myne eyes my hart cannot abide?

What saw my life, wherein my soule might ioy?   645
What had my dayes, whom troubles still afflicted?
But onely this, to counterpoize annoy,
This ioy, this hope, which death hath interdicted:

620 *penetrates so neare*: touches us so deeply 623 *art*: skill in composition 624 *steares*: stirs 634–5 *With armes a crosse . . . ascended*: folded arms and upturned eyes were, like deep sighs, conventional signs of love-grief 634 *bended*: directed 639 *vnhappy*: bringing misfortune 640 *light*: that of sight rather than the *sonne* 640–1 *my sinnes controld . . . donne*: Rosamond enshrines the King's deeds of *shame*, and the *blood* of that blush-suffusing *shame* has by its shedding (or at least death) 'curbed, correctively summed' his *sinnes* 648 *interdicted*: forbidden

This sweete, whose losse hath all distresse afflicted.
   This that did season all my sowre of life,   650
   Vext still at home with broyles, abroade in strife.

Vext styll at home with broyles, abrode in strife,
Dissention in my blood, iarres in my bed:
Distrust at boord, suspecting still my life,
Spending the night in horror, dayes in dred;   655
Such life hath tyrants, and thys lyfe I led.
   These myseries goe mask'd in glittering showes,
   Which wisemen see, the vulgar little knowes.

Thus as these passions doe him ouer-whelme,
He drawes him neere my bodie to behold it: 660
And as the Vine maried vnto the Elme
With strict imbraces, so doth he infold it;
And as he in hys carefull armes doth hold it,
   Viewing the face that euen death commends,
   On sencelesse lips, millions of kysses spends.   665

Pittifull mouth (quoth he) that liuing gauest
The sweetest comfort that my soule could wish:
O be it lawfull now, that dead thou hauest,
Thys sorrowing farewell of a dying kisse.
And you fayre eyes, containers of my blisse,   670
   Motiues of loue, borne to be matched neuer:
   Entomb'd in your sweet circles sleepe for euer.

Ah how me thinks I see death dallying seekes,
To entertaine it selfe in loues sweet place:
Decayed Roses of discoloured cheekes,   675
Doe yet retaine deere notes of former grace:

---

649 *all distresse afflicted*: brought every unhappiness to me   651 *broyles*: conflicts
653 *Dissention in my blood*: quarrels within the family (bringing, doubtless, 'agitation in my veins')
iarres in my bed: marital quarrels   654 *boord*: table (where poisoning was possible)   *suspecting still*: constantly in fear for   658 *Which*: a thing which   661 *Vine maried vnto the Elme*: wrapped around it, usually imaging female embraces of the male   662 *strict*: close
664 *euen death commends*: looks attractive even in death (with a trace of death's 'compliments' developed in the next stanza but one)   668 *lawfull now*: as the kisses were not during Rosamond's life   669 *dying*: because of 680 ff.   671 *Motiues*: prompters
675 *discoloured*: pale, tainted   676 *deere notes*: precious signs

And ougly death sits faire within her face;
  Sweet remnants resting of vermilion red,
  That death it selfe, doubts whether she be dead.

Wonder of beautie, oh receiue these plaints,   680
The obsequies, the last that I shall make thee:
For loe my soule that now already faints,
(That lou'd thee lyuing, dead will not forsake thee,)
Hastens her speedy course to ouer-take thee.
  Ile meete my death, and free my selfe thereby,   685
  For ah what can he doe that cannot die?

Yet ere I die, thus much my soule doth vow,
Reuenge shall sweeten death with ease of minde:
And I will cause posterity shall know,
How faire thou wert aboue all women kind.   690
And after ages monuments shall find,
  Shewing thy beauties title not thy name,
  Rose of the world that sweetned so the same.

This said, though more desirous yet to say,
(For sorrow is vnwilling to giue ouer)   695
He doth represse what griefe would els bewray,
Least that too much his passions might discouer:
And yet respect scarce bridles such a Louer.
  So farre transported that he knowes not whether,
  For loue and Maiestie dwell ill together.   700

Then were my funerals not long deferred,
But doone with all the rites pompe could deuise:
At *Godstow*, where my body was interred,
And richly tomb'd in honorable wise.
Where yet as now scarce any note descries   705
  Vnto these times, the memory of me,
  Marble and Brasse so little lasting be.

677 *sits*: looks   678 *resting*: remaining   686 *what can he doe ... die?*: the man who
cannot die must be unable to do anything   691 *after ages*: later times   692–3 *thy beauties
title ... of the world*: displaying the word *Rosamond*, *monuments* will give her quality as well as *name*
because of its etymology as *Rose of the world* (*rosa* plus *mundus*); her *Rose* properties *sweetned* the
world; for less attractive word-play see Drayton's *Rosamond*, 129–30 and n.   698 *respect*:
caution   699 *whether*: where to   705 *yet as now*: even so as of now   *descries*: picks out,
discloses

For those walles which the credulous deuout,
And apt-beleeuing ignorant did found,
With willing zeale that neuer call'd in doubt,   710
That time theyr works should euer so confound,
Lye like confused heapes as vnder-ground.
　　And what their ignorance esteem'd so holy,
　　The wiser ages doe account as folly.

And were it not thy fauourable lynes,   715
Reedified the wracke of my decayes,
And that thy accents willingly assignes,
Some farther date, and giue me longer daies,
Fewe in this age had knowne my beauties praise.
　　But thus renewd my fame redeemes some time,   720
　　Till other ages shall neglect thy rime.

Then when confusion in her course shall bring,
Sad desolation on the times to come:
When myrth-lesse Thames shall haue no Swan to sing,
All Musique silent, and the Muses dombe.   725
And yet euen then it must be known to some,
　　That once they florisht, though not cherisht so,
　　And Thames had Swannes as well as euer Po.

But heere an end, I may no longer stay thee,
I must returne t' attend at *Stigian* flood: 730
Yet ere I goe, thys one word more I pray thee,
Tell *Delia* now her sigh may doe me good,
And will her note the frailtie of our blood.
　　And if I passe vnto those happy banks,
　　Then she must haue her praise, thy pen her thanks. 735

708–9 *walles which the credulous ... did found*: the Benedictine nunnery at *Godstow*, founded in 1133, was granted at the Dissolution (1539) to Dr Owen, the King's physician; he maintained only part of it, as a dwelling, and sections of the fabric decayed   709 *apt-beleeuing*: ready of faith   712 *as vnder-ground*: grassed over   714 *wiser ages*: since the Reformation   715 *fauourable*: towards me, so 'able to win favour for me' 716 *Reedified ... my decayes*: rebuilt the wreck of my reputation (and mortal beauty)   717 *that*: (ellipsis supplied by *were it not*)   717–18 *assignes, | Some farther date*: grants my repute a point of expiration further off   718 *longer daies*: a lengthier span   719 *praise*: quality, fame   722 *in her course*: in her turn, in her wake   724 *Swan*: metaphor of a poet 727 *though not cherisht so*: though they (*Musique* and *the Muses*) were not valued as befitted their flourishing   728 *Thames had Swannes as well as euer Po*: comparing Elizabethan poets to Florentine masters, such as Dante and Petrarch   730 *Stigian flood*: River Styx (see 12 n. and 13)   732 *her sigh may doe me good*: see 8–14   733 *will her*: urge her to 734 *those happy banks* (of *sweet Elisean rest*, 9)

So vanisht shee, and left me to returne,
To prosecute the tenor of my woes:
Eternall matter for my Muse to mourne;
But ah the worlde hath heard too much of those,
My youth such errors must no more disclose.   740
   Ile hide the rest, and greeue for what hath beene,
   Who made me knowne, must make me liue vnseene.

736–7 *returne . . . my woes*: go back to working out and applying (in the sonnets to *Delia*) the drift, essential stuff, of my griefs   739 *those*: the *woes* recorded in the sonnet-sequence preceding the complaint

7

Michael Drayton, from Englands Heroicall Epistles *(1597)*

LETTER-WRITING, hardly considered an art today, was cultivated as such by
Elizabethans. Treatises like Angel Day's *English Secretorie* (1586) advised on
rhetorical tactics. Style was shaped by Horace, Cicero, and that Ovid
'whose imitator', as Drayton declared in the preface to *Englands Heroicall
Epistles*, 'I partly professe to be'. Like the late paired *Heroides*, Drayton's
letters come in twos. The poet (1563–1631) is resourceful in meshing and
diversifying his exchanges, and, though the texts printed below stand up on
their own, a dimension is taken from Rosamond and Jane Shore when
Henry II's reply and Edward IV's advances are cut away. Drayton's book
resembles Tudor Ovids in another respect: it has notes (printed at the end
of each piece). This commentary helped Drayton distance himself from the
poetic machinery of *de casibus* complaint, which had, by 1597, begun to
creak. In the fifth satire of *Virgidemiarum, Six Bookes,* published that year,
Joseph Hall (for instance) mocked the 'dreerie fates' and 'branded whining
ghost' of the *Myrroure* tradition. Ovidian technique had other advantages.
When he dedicated Rosamond's letter to Lucy, Countess of Bedford,
Drayton nicely caught the involvedness which his 'written' idiom could
express: 'much confidence, no certainty, wordes begetting teares, teares
confounding matter, large complaints in little papers'. The style of *Jane
Shore* (dedicated to Sir Thomas Mounson) could hardly be more different.
Trenchant, keenly imaginative, and aware of the misogyny stacked against
her, Mistress Shore comes across as an attractive adulteress. It is hard to
believe that early readers would have maintained the unforgiving view
advanced in Drayton's Notes. In subject-matter the two poems are as
strikingly diverse. *Rosamond* explores the artifice of courtly pastoral; *Jane
Shore*, dense in social reference, is close to City Comedy. Yet the texts have
in common an air of creative inevitability. Drayton was an assiduous reviser.
By the time they appeared in *Poems* (1619), most of his works from the
1590s had been rewritten. *Englands Heroicall Epistles*, however, were largely
unchanged. Later readers recognized the quality of the texts; while most of
Drayton fell out of favour, his verse letters were admired through the
seventeenth century.

THE EPISTLE OF ROSAMOND TO KING HENRIE THE SECOND

If yet thine eyes (great *Henry*) may endure
These tainted lynes, drawne with a hand impure,
Which faine would blush, but feare keeps blushes back,
And therefore suted in dispayring blacke,
This in loues name, ô that these lypps might craue,   5
But that sweete name (vile I) prophaned haue;
Punish my fault, or pittie mine estate,
Reade it for loue, if not for loue, for hate.
If with my shame thine eyes thou faine would'st feede,
Heere let them surfeit, on my shame to reede;   10
This scribled paper which I send to thee,
If noted rightly, dooth resemble mee:
As this pure ground, whereon these letters stand,
So pure was I, ere stayned by thy hand;
Ere I was blotted with this foule offence,   15
So cleere and spotlesse was mine innocence:
Now like these marks, which taint this hatefull scroule,
Such the black sinnes, which spotte my leprous soule.
O *Henry* why, by losse thus shouldst thou winne?
To get by conquest? to enrich with sinne?   20
Why on my name this slaunder doost thou bring,
To make my fault renowned by a King?
Fame neuer stoopes to things but meane and poore,
The more our greatnes, makes our fault the more.
Lights on the ground, themselues doe lessen farre,   25
But in the ayre, each small sparke seemes a starre.
Why on a womans frailetie wouldst thou lay
This subtile plot, mine honour to betray?
Or thy vnlawfull pleasure should'st thou buy
With vile expence of kinglie maiestie?   30

4 *suted*: clothed (and 'matched to', since *blacke* garb about the *hand* befits the *lynes*' content)
7 *estate*: circumstance   12 *noted*: understood   13 *ground*: prepared material on which a
picture or inscription is drawn (here epistolary paper)   21 *slaunder*: opprobrium (not invariably, in 16th-cent. usage, false)   22 *renowned by*: notorious by virtue of your being
23 *but meane*: merely humble   24 *The more . . . fault the more*: the greater we are in the world,
the more our *fault* is amplified   25 *farre*: very much   27 *lay*: devise, apply (since *plot* can
mean 'charted design')

'Twas not my minde consented to this ill,
Then had I beene transported by my will,
For what my body was enforst to doe,
(Heauen knowes) my soule did not consent vnto;
For through mine eyes, had shee her liking seene,   35
Such as my loue, such had my louer beene.
True loue is simple, like his mother Truth,
Kindlie affection, youth to loue with youth;
No sharper corsiue to our blooming yeares,
Then the cold badge of winter-blasted haires.   40
Thy kinglie power makes to withstand thy foes,
But canst not keepe backe age, with time it growes;
Though honour our ambitious sexe doth please,
Yet in that honour, age a foule disease.
Nature hath her free course in all, and then,   45
Age is alike in Kings, and other men,
Which all the world will to my shame impute
That I my selfe did basely prostitute;
And say, that gold was fuell to the fire,
Gray haires in youth not kindling greene desire.   50
O no; that wicked woman wrought by thee,
My temptor was to that forbidden tree;
That subtile serpent, that seducing deuill,
Which bad mee taste the fruite of good and euill:
That *Circe,* by whose magicke I was charm'd,   55
And to this monstrous shape am thus transform'd;
That viperous hagge, the foe to her owne kind,
That wicked spirit, vnto the weaker minde:
Our frailties plague, our natures onely curse,
Hells deep'st damnation, the worst euills worse.   60
But *Henry,* how canst thou affect me thus,
T' whom thy remembrance now is odious?

35 *her liking*: what she liked (with a hint of resemblance, developed by 36)   36 *my loue*: what my desire patterned   37 *his mother*: usually Venus   38 *Kindlie*: of the same sort, natural 39 *corsiue*: caustic   40 *winter-blasted*: blighted by the winter of age (life was often correlated with the seasons), whitened as though by frost   41 *makes*: works   49 *the fire*: of *desire* in me   50 *greene*: youthful (and, in wooden *fuell*, hard to ignite)   51 *that wicked woman*: Daniel's *seeming Matrone*, at *Complaint*, 211 ff.   52–4 *My temptor . . . fruite of good and euill*: as in Daniel's *Complaint*, 325 and 448–9, adducing Gen. 3   55 *charm'd*: the power of Homer's *Circe* to transform men to beasts was often moralized as an allegory of sensual corruption 56 *monstrous*: disfigured with sin, but cf. 87–8 and its source in Daniel's *Complaint*, 477–83 57 *hagge*: fiendish woman (cf. *spirit*), ugly old female   *kind*: gender   59 *curse*: blight 60 *worst euills worse*: utmost wrong evil can do   61 *affect*: feel affection for   62 *T' whom thy remembrance*: the recollection of whom, to you

My haplesse name, with *Henries* name I found
Cut in the glasse with *Henries* Diamond:
That glasse from thence faine would I take away,   65
But then I feare the ayre would me betray;
Then doe I striue to wash it out with teares,
But then the same more euident appeares.
Then doe I couer it with my guiltie hand,
Which that names witnes doth against mee stand: 70
Once did I sinne, which memory doth cherrish,
Once I offended, but I euer perrish.
What griefe can be, but time dooth make it lesse?
But infamy tyme neuer can suppresse.
Some-times to passe the tedious irkesome howres,   75
I clymbe the top of Woodstocks mounting towers,
Where in a Turret secretly I lye
To viewe from farre such as doe trauaile by,
Whether (mee thinks) all cast theyr eyes at mee,
As through the stones my shame did make them see,   80
And with such hate the harmles walls doe view,
As vnto death theyr eyes would mee pursue.
The married women curse my hatefull life,
Which wrong a lawfull bed, a Queene, a wife;
The maydens wish I buried quicke may die,   85
The lothsome staine to their virginitie.
Well knew'st thou what a monster I would bee,
When thou didst builde this Labyrinth for mee,
Whose strange *Meanders* turning euery way,
Be like the course wherein my youth did stray: 90
Onely a Clue to guide mee out and in,
But yet still walke I, circuler in sinne.

63 *haplesse*: unfortunate   64 *glasse*: window   66 *betray*: to observation (otherwise reduced by cloudy window-glass), more generally to chills and sickness   70 *Which that names witnes . . . stand*: the inscribed window (*it* of the previous line) set up as evidence against Rosamond (like a *witnes* at the *stand* in court); context suggests *Rosamond* as the *name* which distresses, but in his reply Henry exploits the ambiguity of there being (as 63–4 shows) two names in question 71 *Once*: with one person   72 *perrish*: with theological overtones, 'am damned' 76 *mounting*: soaring   79 *Whether*: whither   85–6 *The maydens . . . virginite*: on live (*quicke*) burial as punishment for sexual irregularity see the Notes to Drayton's *Shores Wife*, 47–50   87–8 *what a monster . . . this Labyrinth*: as in Daniel's *Complaint*, 477–83, Rosamond is likened to the Minotaur; see Drayton's Notes below   89 *strange Meanders turning*: in Ovid's description of the Labyrinth (*Metamorphoses*, 8. 162–8) the same comparison is made; see Drayton's Notes below   91 *Clue*: of thread, such as guided Theseus *out and in* of the Labyrinth 92 *circuler*: round and round, completely (like a closed geometric figure); the latter became common in 17th-cent. English, then obsolete

As in the Tarras heere this other day
My maide and I did passe the time away,
Mongst manie pictures which we passed by,   95
The silly girle at length hapt to espie
Chast *Lucrece* picture, and desires to know
What shee should be herselfe that murdred so?
Why girle (quoth I) this is that Romaine dame:
Not able then to tell the rest for shame,   100
My tongue doth mine owne guiltines betray;
With that I send the pratling girle away,
Least when my lisping guiltie tongue should hault,
My lookes should be the Index to my fault.
As that life blood which from the hart is sent,   105
In beauties fielde pitching his Crimson Tent,
In louely sanguine sutes the Lilly cheeke,
Whilst it but for a resting place dooth seeke;
And changing often-times with sweet delight,
Conuerts the white to red, the red to white.   110
The louely blush, the palenes dooth distaine,
The palenes makes the blush more faire againe:
Thus in my breast a thousand thoughts I carry,
Which in my passion diuersly doe varry.
When as the sunne hales towards the westerne shade,   115
And the trees shadowes three times greater made,
Foorth goe I to a little Current neere,
Which like a wanton trayle creepes heere and there,
Where with mine angle casting in my baite,
The little fishes (dreading the deceit)   120
With fearefull nibbling flie th' inticing gin,
By nature taught what danger lyes therein.
Things reasonlesse thus warnd by nature bee,
Yet I deuourd the baite was layd for mee;
Thinking thereon, and breaking into grones,   125
The bubling spring which trypps vppon the stones

93 *Tarras*: terrace   96 *silly*: naïve   104 *lookes*: appearance (a hint of wild-eyed glancing)   *Index to*: indicator of (an *Index* finger was commonly printed in margins, against significant matter, in 16th-cent. books)   106 *beauties fielde*: the face, imaged heraldically (*fielde* as the background of an escutcheon) and as the place where a power is encamped for battle (cf. *Tent*)   107 *sanguine*: colour of blood, frequent in heraldic usage   *sutes*: clothes
111 *distaine*: tint with another colour, dye, stain   112 *more faire againe*: whiter in colour once more (and 'still more beautiful')   113 *in my breast*: the heart was regarded as a seat of *thoughts*   115 *hales*: is drawn, hastens   117 *Current*: stream   118 *wanton trayle*: luxuriant tendril (which actively *creepes*), lavishly ornamental tracing, seductive train of robe   120 *dreading the deceit*: fearing that the bait deceives   121 *gin*: snaring trick, trapping-engine

Chides mee away, least sitting but too nie,
I should pollute that natiue puritie.
Rose of the World, so dooth import my name,
Shame of the worlde, my life hath made the same;   130
And to th' vnchast thys name shall giuen bee,
Of *Rosamond*, deriu'd from sinne and mee.
The *Clyffords* take from mee that name of theirs,
Famous for vertue many hundred yeeres.
They blot my birth with hatefull bastardie,   135
That I sprang not from their Nobilitie;
They my alliance vtterly refuse,
Nor will a strumpet shall their name abuse.
Heere in the Garden, wrought by curious hands,
Naked *Diana* in the fountaine standes,   140
With all her Nimphs got round about to hide her,
As when *Acteon* had by chaunce espyde her:
This sacred image I no sooner view'd,
But as that metamorphosd man pursu'd
By his owne hounds: so by my thoughts am I,   145
Which chase mee still, which way so ere I flie.
Touching the grasse, the honny-dropping dew,
Which falls in teares before my limber shue,
Vpon my foote consumes in weeping still,
As it would say, Why went'st thou vnto ill?   150
Thus to no place in safetie can I goe
But euery thing doth giue mee cause of woe.
In that faire Casket of such wondrous cost
Thou sent'st the night before mine honour lost,
Amimone was wrought, a harmelesse maide,   155
By *Neptune* that adulterous God betrayd;
Shee prostrate at his feete begging with prayers,
Wringing her hands, her eyes swolne vp with teares:

129–30 *Rose of the World … Shame of the worlde*: see Drayton's Notes below, which show him meditating Daniel's *Complaint*, 687–93, 701–14, and rendering Rosamond's epitaph in the chronicles: 'Rosa mundi sed non rosa munda' ('Rose of the world but not a pure rose') 137 *alliance*: often used of blood relations   139 *curious*: skilled, fastidious   142 *As when Acteon*: see *Metamorphoses*, 3. 155–252, where *Acteon* is transformed into a stag and *pursu'd* | *By his owne hounds* (144–5) after seeing *Diana* bathing   147 *honny-dropping dew*: sweet sticky substance deposited by aphids but believed in this period to fall from heaven (e.g. at evening: see 115–17); often confused with *dew*, nectar, sweet saps exuded by plants   148 *limber*: lithe and nimble   149 *consumes in weeping still*: the *dew* of 147 loses drop-like delicacy and disperses itself in a steady drench of tears (on Rosamond's *shue*)   155 *Amimone*: see Daniel's *Complaint*, 378–99, and nn.   *wrought*: worked (upon it)

This was not the entrapping baite of men,
But by thy vertue gentlie warning then;   160
To shew to mee for what intent it came,
Least I therein should euer keepe my shame.
And in this Casket (ill I see it now)
Was *Ioues*-loue *I-o* turnd into a Cowe.
Yet was shee kept with *Argus* hundred eyes,   165
So wakefull still be *Iunos* iealousies;
By this I well might haue fore-warned beene,
T' haue cleerd my selfe to thy suspecting Queene,
Who with more hundred eyes attendeth mee
Then had poore *Argus* single eyes to see.   170
In this thou rightlie imitatest *Ioue*,
Into a beast thou hast transformd thy loue.
Nay worser farre; (degenerate from kinde)
A monster, both in body and in minde.
The waxen Taper which I burne by night,   175
With his dull vapory dimnes mocks my sight;
As though the dampe which hinders his cleere flame,
Came from my breath, in that night of my shame,
When it did burne as darknesse vglie eye
When shot the starre of my virginitie.   180
And if a starre but by the glasse appeare,
I straight intreate it not to looke in heere;
I am already hatefull to the light,
It is enough, betray mee not to night.
Then sith my shame so much belongs to thee,   185
Rid mee of that, by onelie murdring mee;
And let it iustly to my charge be layd
Thy roiall person I would haue betrayd:

---

160 *gentlie*: honourably   162 *Least I therein . . . my shame*: in case I, in the absence of this explicit evidence (the *Casket*) of *intent*, should avoid shame (by pleading ignorance)   163 *ill*: an ill omen   164–70 *Ioues-loue I-o . . . eyes to see*: compare Daniel's *Complaint*, 402–6, and nn. 168 *cleerd*: confessed   169–70 *more hundred eyes . . . to see*: for every one of *Argus'* hundred eyes the Queen had a hundred spying upon Rosamond; *Argus* makes a *poore* job of guarding *I-o* because Mercury lulls him to sleep with music, before—*poore Argus* in another sense—decapitating him (*Metamorphoses*, 1. 682–721)   173 *kinde*: what is natural   174 *A monster*: the Minotaur, half man and half bull, inherited from Daniel's *Complaint* and 87–8, perhaps informs Rosamond's identification with *Io*, as a *Cowe*   176 *mocks my sight*: by making *sight* seem possible yet thwarting it, by teasing the *sight* with delusions   177 *dampe*: noxious vapour 180 *shot the starre*: a portentous and suitably fleeting equivalent   181 *by the glasse*: through the window   184 *betray*: reveal   185 *sith*: since   188 *I would haue betrayd*: Rosamond invites a trumped-up *charge* (though *iustly*, sustained by grievance and *would*'s forward-leaning ambivalence, registers)

Thou shalt not neede by circumstance t'accuse mee,
If I denie it, let the heauens refuse mee.   190
My lifes a blemish which dooth cloude thy name,
Take it away, and cleere shall shine thy fame.
Yeeld to my sute, if euer pitty moou'd thee,
In this shewe mercie, as I euer lou'd thee.

NOTES OF THE CHRONICLE HISTORIE

Well knew'st thou what a monster I would bee,
When thou didst builde this Labyrinth for mee.

In the *Cretean* Labyrinth a monster was inclosed, called a *Minotaur,* the history whereof is well knowne, but the Labyrinth was framed by *Dædalus,* with so many intricate waies, that being entred, one could either hardly or never return, being in maner of a maze, saue that it was larger, the waies being walld in on euery side, out of the which *Theseus* by *Ariadnes* help (lending him a clue of thred) escaped. Some report that it was a house, hauing one halfe beneath the ground, another aboue, the chamber doores therein so deceitfully enwrapped, and made to open so many sundry wayes, that it was held a matter almost imposs-ible to returne.

Some haue held it to haue been an Allegorie of mans life; true it is, that the comparison will hold, for what liker to a Labyrinth then the maze of life? But it is affirmed by antiquitie that there was indeede such a building, though *Dædalus* beeing a name applied to the workmans excellencie, make it suspected; for *Dædalus* is nothing els but ingenious, or artificiall. Heereupon it is vsed among the auncient Poets for any thing curiously wrought.

Rosamonds Labyrinth, whose ruins together with her well being paued with square stone in the bottom, and also her towre from which the Labyrinth did run, (are yet remaining,) was altogether vnder ground, being vaults arched and waled with brick and stone, almost inextricably wound one within another, by which if at any time her lodging were layd about by the Queene, she might easily auoyde perrill

(line numbers: 5, 10, 15, 20, 25)

---

189 *by circumstance*: by invoking circumstantial evidence (damaging to the King himself)
190 *refuse mee*: deny me salvation   193 *sute*: request

NOTES. 1–2 *Well knew'st . . . for mee*: 87–8   20–8 *Rosamonds Labyrinth . . . situated*: few records survive of the magnificent medieval palace, which included a circular chapel, great cloister, and enclosed gardens west of the residential quarters; though the complex was developed by Henry VII, by the time Princess Elizabeth was imprisoned there (in 1554) only the gatehouse was undecayed enough for security; further damaged in the Civil War, the ruins were demolished *c.*1710   25 *layd about*: besieged imminent, and if neede be, by secrete issues take the ayre abroad, many furlongs round about Wodstocke in Oxfordshire, wherein it was situated. Thus much for *Rosamonds* Labyrinth.

Whose strange Meanders *turning euery way.*

Mæander is a riuer in *Lycia*, a Prouince of *Natolia* or *Asia minor*, famous   30
for the sinuositie and often turning thereof, rising from certaine hills in *Mæonia*, heereupon are intricate turnings by a transumptiue and Metonimicall kind of speech, called *Mæanders*, for this riuer did so strangely path it selfe, that the foote seemed to touch the head.

Rose of the World, *so dooth import my name,*   35
Shame of the worlde, *my life hath made the same.*

It might be reported, how at *Godstow* where this Rose of the world was sumptuously interred, a certaine Bishop in the visitation of his diocese, caused the monument which had been erected to her honour, vtterly to be demolished, but be that seuere chastisement of *Rosamond* then dead,   40
at this time also ouerpassed, least she should seeme to be the *Shame of the world.*

THE EPISTLE OF SHORES WIFE TO KING EDWARD THE FOURTH

As the weake chyld, that from the Mothers wing,
Is taught the Lutes delicious fingering,
At euery strings soft touch, is mou'd with feare,
Noting his Maisters curious listning eare;
Whose trembling hand, at euery straine bewrayes,   5
In what doubt hee, his new set lesson playes;

26 *issues*: exits, routes leading away   29 *Whose strange . . . way*: 89   32–3 *transumptiue and Metonimicall*: metaphorical and substitutive (roughly interchangeable terms, drawn from classical rhetoric)   34 *path*: find a course for   35–6 *Rose of the World . . . the same*: 129–30   38 *a certaine Bishop*: St Hugh of Lincoln, in 1191, according to Stow's *Annales*   *visitation*: pastoral visiting and inspection

1 *from the Mothers wing*: away from maternal comfort, newly fledged   3 *At euery strings soft touch*: every time he (the *weake chyld*) tentatively touches a string   4 *curious*: attentive, skilful, fastidious   5 *straine*: musical notes or phrase   6 *new set lesson playes*: plays the piece of music he has recently been required to learn

As this poore chylde, so sit I to indite,
At euery word still quaking as I write.
Would I had led an humble Shepheards life,
Nor knowne the name of *Shores* admired wife,   10
And liu'd with them in Country fields that range,
Nor seene the golden Cheape, nor glittering Change,
To stand a Comet gaz'd at in the skyes,
Subiect to all tongues, obiect to all eyes.
Oft haue I heard my beauty praisd of many,   15
But neuer yet so much admir'd of any;
A Princes Eagle-eye to finde out that,
Which vulgar sights doe sildome wonder at,
Makes mee to thinke affection flatters sight,
Or in the obiect some-thing exquisite.   20
To housed beauty, sildome stoopes report,
Fame must attend on that which liues in Court.
What swanne of great *Apollos* brood doth sing,
To vulgar loue, in courtly Sonetting?
O what immortall Poets sugred pen,   25
Attends the glory of a Cittizen?
Oft haue I wondred what should blinde your eye,
Or what so farre seduced Maiestie,
That hauing choyce of beauties so diuine,
Amongst the most to choose this least of mine?   30
More glorious sunnes adorne faire Londons pride,
Then all rich Englands continent beside;
Who takes in hand to make account of this,
May number Rumneys flowers, or Isis fish;
Who doth frequent our Temples, walks, and streets,   35
Noting the sundry beauties that hee meets,
Thinks not that Nature left the wide world poore,
And made thys place the Chequer of her store?

7 *indite*: compose   12 *golden Cheape*: the goldsmiths' district, Cheapside, quibbling (as often in 16th-cent. literature) on 'low price, pennywise' (which had developed from *Cheape* as 'place of trade, of bargains')   *glittering Change*: even more than *Cheape*, implies activity ('exchange, buying and selling', with *glittering* coins) as well as place, and various commercial sites in London might be implied   16 *so much*: as by you   17 *Eagle-eye*: keen and lofty   18 *vulgar sights*: the eyes of common people   19 *affection flatters*: love pleasingly deceives   23 *swanne of great Apollos brood*: singer nurtured by the lyric god, true poet   24 *vulgar loue*: socially humble beloved   31 *sunnes*: at which an *Eagle-eye* can traditionally gaze without harm   *pride*: magnificence   32 *continent beside*: spread of land in addition, total (that which is contained) beyond London   33 *takes ... account of*: sets out to calculate   34 *May number*: might as well attempt to count   *Rumney's flowers, or Isis fish*: see Drayton's Notes below   36 *sundry beauties*: various beautiful women   38 *Chequer of her store*: exchequer of her abundance

As heauen and earth were lately fallne at iarrs,
And growne to vying wonders, dropping starrs.   40
That if but some one beautie should incite,
Some sacred Muse, some rauisht spirit to write,
Heere might he fetch such true *Promethian* fire,
As after ages should his lynes admire;
Gathering the honny from the choysest flowers,   45
Scorning the wither'd weedes in Countrie bowers.
Heere in thys Garden (onely) springs the Rose,
In euery common hedge the Bramble growes,
Nor are we so turn'd Neapolitan,
That might incite some foule-mouth'd *Mantuan*,   50
To all the world to lay out our defects,
And haue iust cause to rayle vpon our sex;
To pranck old wrinkels vp in new attire,
To alter natures course, proue tyme a lyer,
Abusing fate, and heauens iust doome reuerse,   55
On beauties graue to set a Crimson hearse;
With a deceitfull foyle to lay a ground,
To make a glasse to seeme a Diamond.
Nor cannot without hazard of our name,
In fashion follow the Venetian Dame,   60
Nor the fantastick French to imitate,
Attir'd halfe Spanish, halfe Italionate;
Nor wast, nor curle, body nor brow adorne,
That is in Florence, or in Genoa borne.
But with vaine boasts how witlesse fond am I,   65
Thus to draw on mine owne indignity?
And what though married when I was but young,
Before I knew what dyd to loue belong;

39 *As*: as if   *at iarrs*: into conflict   40 *growne to vying ... starrs*: and proceeded (as the quarrel heightened) into competing with marvels, casting meteors about   42 *rauisht spirit*: rapt creative intellect   43 *true Promethian fire*: that authentic divine *fire*, here of inspiration, which Prometheus stole from heaven   44 *after*: subsequent   45 *flowers*: of beauty, in London   49 *Neapolitan*: painted and courtesanish   50 *That might incite ... Mantuan*: see Drayton's Notes below, and annotation   53 *To pranck old wrinkels vp in new attire*: that it is our custom fashionably to doll up elderly bodies (synecdochic *wrinkels* preparing for a complaint against cosmetics)   54 *proue tyme a lyer*: show time (which declares the *old* elderly) to be wrong; with a quibble on the commonplace of *tyme* the revealer, truth-teller   55 *doome*: fate, judgement   56 *On beauties graue ... Crimson hearse*: rouge (instead of mourning colours) laid on the cheek where beauty has been buried   57 *foyle*: metal film against which a stone was set to advantage   *ground*: background layer on which the stone was mounted   59 *hazard of our name*: risking our reputation   64 *That is ... borne*: in the style fashionable in Florence or Genoa   65 *witlesse fond*: idiotically naïve   66 *mine owne indignity*: both 'the shame laid upon me' and 'my indignation'

Yet he which now's possessed of the roome,
Cropt beauties flower when it was in the bloome,   70
And goes away enriched with the store,
Whilst others gleane, where he had reapt before,
And he dares sweare that I am true and iust,
And shall I then deceiue his honest trust?
Or what strange hope should make you to assaile,   75
Where strongest battery neuer could preuaile?
Belike you thinke that I repulsd the rest,
To leaue a King the conquest of my brest,
Or haue thus long preseru'd my selfe from all,
A Monarch now should glory in my fall.   80
Yet rather let mee die the vilest death,
Then lyue to draw such sinne-polluted breath;
But our kinde harts, mens teares cannot abide,
And we least angry oft, when most we chyde;
Too well know men what our creation made vs,   85
And nature too well taught them to inuade vs.
They know but too well, how, when, what, and where,
To write, to speake, to sue, and to forbeare,
By signes, by sighes, by motions, and by teares,
When vowes should serue, when othes, when smiles, when praiers,   90
What one delight our humors most doth moue,
Onely in that you make vs nourish loue.
If any naturall blemish blot our face,
You doe protest it giues our beautie grace;
And what attire we most are vsd to weare,   95
That (of all other) excellent'st you sweare;
And if we walke, or sit, or stand, or lye,
It must resemble some one Dietie;
And what you know we take delight to heare,
That are you euer sounding in our eare;   100
And yet so shamelesse when you tempt vs thus,
To lay the fault on beauty, and on vs:

---

69 *roome*: place assigned (to her husband and master)   71 *store*: harvest, plenty, matter to be
hoarded   73 *dares sweare*: stock phrase, implying ready confidence (troubled here by the
presumption of *dares*)   74 *honest trust*: undertones of 'dull-witted trustingness'
75–6 *assaile . . . neuer could preuaile*: Shore's wife in her virtue is (as commonly in such passages) a
fortified city, Edward a besieger attacking where force has not (and *neuer could*) succeed
85 *what our creation made vs*: how fraile we are by nature   89 *motions*: promptings
90 *serue*: be effective, please (as a lover is 'servant' of his mistress)   91 *What one*: which-
ever   *humors*: temperaments, whims   98 *one Dietie*: particular goddess

Romes wanton *Ouid* did those rules impart;
O that your nature should be help'd by Art.
Who would haue thought, a King that cares to raigne,   105
Inforc'd by loue, so Poet-like should faine?
To say that Beautie, Times sterne rage to shun,
In my cheekes (Lillies) hid her from the sun;
And when she meant to triumph in her May,
Made that her East, and heere shee broke her day,   110
And swear'st that Sommer still is in my sight,
And but where I am, all the world is night:
And that the fayr'st, ere since the world began,
To me, a sunne-burnt, base Egyptian;
But yet I know more then I meane to tell,   115
(Oh would to God you knew it not too well.)
That women oft theyr most admirers raise,
Though publiquely not flattering theyr owne praise.
Our churlish husbands, which our youth enioyd,
Who with our dainties haue their stomacks cloyd,   120
Doe lothe our smooth hand with theyr lips to feele,
T' enrich our fauours, by our beds to kneele;
At our commaund to waite, to send, to goe,
As euery howre our amorous seruants doe;
Which makes a stolne kisse often wee bestow,   125
In earnest of a greater good wee owe;
When hee all day torments vs with a frowne,
Yet sports with *Venus* in a bedde of Downe;
Whose rude imbracement, but too ill beseemes,
Her span-broade wast, her white and daintie limmes;   130
And yet still preaching abstinence of meate,
When he himselfe, of euery dish will eate.

103–4 *Romes wanton Ouid . . . by Art*: alluding to *Ars amatoria*, echoed (e.g. 2. 295–306, 641–6) by Jane Shore and her correspondent   105 *cares*: is assiduous   106 *faine*: both 'wish to be' and 'feign, deceive with *Art*'   108 *hid her from the sun*: to avoid the browning thought ugly in 16th-cent. women   109 *triumph in her May*: go gloriously in her springtime of life (with a hint of May Day rites, when the young were up early, dressed festively, and looking for love) 110 *East*: where dawn of *day* is *broke*   111 *still is in my sight*: is always wherever I look, around me (because 'in my eyes')   114 *To me*: in comparison with me   *Egyptian*: gypsy 117 *theyr most admirers raise*: give preferment to those who most *praise* them   118 *flattering*: closely attending to   119 *churlish*: base, inconsiderate   121 *Doe lothe*: are disinclined 122 *T' enrich our fauours*: give us jewels (perhaps of praise) to adorn our features   125 *makes*: brings it about that   127–8 *hee all day . . . bedde of Downe*: not (as at 132) an accusation of infidelity but of ungrateful frowning at a wife by day while enjoying her (in luxurious comfort) by night   129 *rude*: rough, ignorant   *but too ill beseemes*: is only too ill suited to 130 *span-broade*: of hand's-breadth slenderness   131 *abstinence of meate*: comparisons between Lenten diet and sexual strictness were often made   132 *of euery dish*: all kinds of food (and from every plate)

Blame you our husbands then, if they denie
Our publique walking, our loose libertie,
If with exception still they vs debarre,   135
The circuite of the publique Theater;
To heare the smooth-tongu'd Poets Syren vaine,
Sporting in his lasciuious Comick scene:
Or the young wanton wits, when they applaude
The slie perswasions of some subtile Baude;   140
Or passionate Tragedian in his rage,
Acting a loue-sicke passion on the stage;
When though abroad restraining vs to rome,
They very hardly keepe vs safe at home,
And oft are touch'd with feare, and inward griefe,   145
Knowing rich prizes soonest tempt a theefe.
What sports haue we, whereon our minds to set?
Our dogge, our Parrat, or our Marmuzet;
Or once a weeke to walke into the field;
Small is the pleasure that these toyes doe yeeld.   150
But to this griefe, a medicine you apply,
To cure restraint with that sweet libertie;
And soueraigntie; (ô that bewitching thing,)
Yet made more great, by promise of a King:
And more, that honour which doth most intice   155
The holiest Nunne, and shee that's nere so nice.
Thus still wee striue, yet ouer-come at length,
For men want mercy, and poore women strength:
Yet graunt, that we, could meaner men resist
When Kings once come, they conquer as they list.   160
Thou art the cause *Shore* pleaseth not my sight;
That his embraces giue me no delight;

135 *with exception*: by particular forbidding   136 *circuite of*: Elizabethan *publique* playhouses
tended to be round   137 *Syren vaine*: vein of seductive song   142 *passion*: intense set
speech, emotional scene   143 *When . . . to rome*: even when they prevent us wandering away
from home   144 *very hardly*: only with great difficulty (undertones of severity), scarcely
147 *sports*: recreations   148 *Marmuzet*: used to describe any kind of small monkey in the 16th
cent.   149 *into the field*: the green places in London, or country beyond the city limits
150 *toyes*: trifles   152 *cure restraint*: correct my being locked away (hints of unleashed excess,
libertie in a wanton sense)   153 *soueraigntie*: queen-like sway (over a lover, until 154 raises the
political stakes   154 *more great*: the *soueraigntie* is more greatly valued, but involves a greater
power too   156 *nere so nice*: the epitome of fastidiousness   157 *ouer-come*: i.e. 'are
overcome'

Thou art the cause, I to my selfe am strange.
Thy comming, is my full, thy set, my change.
Long Winter nights be minuts, if thou heare,   165
Short minutes if thou absent be a yeare.
And thus by strength thou art become my fate,
And mak'st me loue, euen in the midst of hate.

NOTES OF THE CHRONICLE HISTORIE

Would I had led an humble Shepheards life,
Nor knowne the name of Shores admired wife.

Two or three poems written by sundry men, haue magnified this
womans beauty: whom that ornament of England and Londons more   5
particuler glory, Sir *Thomas Moore* very highly hath praysed for her
beauty, she beeing aliue in his time, though being poore and aged. Her
stature was meane, her haire of a darke yellow, her face round and full,
her eye gray, delicate harmony being betwixt each parts proportion, and
each proportions colour, her body fat, white, and smooth, her countenance cheerefull, and like to her condition. That picture which I haue   10
scene of hers, was such as she rose out of her bed in the morning,
hauing nothing on but a ritch Mantle cast vnder one arme ouer her
shoulder, and sitting in a chaire on which her naked arme did lye. What
her Fathers name was, or where shee was borne is not certainly
knowne: but *Shore* a young man of right good person, wealth, and   15
behauiour, abandoned her bed after the King had made her his Concubine. *Richard* the third causing her to doe open penance in Paules
Churchyard, commaunded that no man should releeue her, which the
tyrant did not so much for his hatred to sinne, but that by making his
Brothers life odious, he might couer his horrible treason the more   20
cunningly.

163 *to my selfe am strange*: am estranged from myself   164 *full*: fulfilment (as whole in
happiness as a *full* moon)   *thy set, my change*: your departure (like a setting sun) is my falling away
from fulfilment (as a moon, after being *full*, wanes)   168 *hate*: within marriage
    NOTES. 1–2 *Would I had led ... wife*: 9–10   3 *Two or three ... sundry men*: e.g. *Shores
Wife* by Thomas Churchyard (printed above, pp. 112–24), *Beawtie Dishonoured Written under the
Title of Shores Wife* by Anthony Chute (1593)   *magnified*: celebrated (with a hint of specious
enlargment)   *Sir Thomas Moore*: his account of Jane Shore can be found in his *History of King
Richard III*   7 *meane*: middling   8 *gray*: seems to have described bluish eyes in 16th-
cent. usage   9 *fat, white*: attractively plump and fair   9–10 *countenance*: bearing, mien
10 *like to her condition*: resembling (for a *countenance* can be feigned) her temperament   *That
picture*: now apparently lost   17–18 *Paules Churchyard*: outside St Paul's, already an important
London church

May number Rumneys flowers, or Isis fish.

Rumney is that famous Marsh in Kent, at whose side Rie an Hauen-
towne dooth stand. Heereof the excellent English Antiquarie Maister
Camden, and Maister *Lumbert* in his perambulation doe make mention;   25
and Marishes are commonly called those low grounds, which abut vpon
the Sea, and from the Latine word are so denominated. Isis heere is
vsed for Thamesis by a Senecdochicall kinde of speech, or by a poeticall liberty in vsing one for another, for it is sayd that Thamesis is
compounded of Tame and Isis, making when they are met, that   30
renowned water running by London, a Citty much more renowned then
that water: which being plentifull of fish, is the cause also why all things
else are plentifull therein. Moreouer I am perswaded that there is no
Riuer in the world beholds more stately buildings on eyther side cleane
through, then the Thames. Much is reported of the Graund Canale in   35
Venice, for that the Fronts on eyther side are so gorgeous.

That might incite some foule-mouth'd Mantuan.

Mantuan a pastorall Poet, in one of his Eglogs bitterly enueieth against
woman-kinde, some of the which by way of an Appendex, might be
heere inserted, seeing the fantastick and insolent humors of many of   40
that sexe deserue much sharper phisick, were it not that they are grown
wiser, then to amend, for such an idle Poets speech as *Mantuan*, yea, or
for *Euripides* himselfe, or *Senecas* inflexible Hippolitus.

The circuite of the publique Theater.

Ouid, a most fit Author for so dissolute a Sectarie, calls that place   45
Chastities shipwrack, for though *Shores* wife wantonly plead for liberty,
which is the true humor of a Curtizan, yet much more is the prayse of
modesty then of such liberty. Howbeit the Vestall Nuns had seats

22 *May number . . . fish*: 34   23–4 *Hauen-towne*: seaport   25 *Camden*: in *Britannia*,
1586   25 *Lumbert*: William Lambarde's *Perambulation* was published in 1576   27 *from
the Latine word*: in fact, its root is Germanic with late Latin offshoots   29–30 *Thamesis . . . of
Tame, and Isis*: a common but false Elizabethan derivation   34 *cleane*: all the way
37 *That might incite . . . Mantuan*: 50; the *Eclogues* of Baptista Mantuanus (1447–1516) were
standard reading in Elizabethan grammar schools   38 *one of his Eglogs*: number 4
41 *phisick*: medicine, correction   42 *wiser . . . amend, for*: too clever to reform on account of
42 *idle*: as they would call it   43 *for Euripides*: whose reputation for misogyny, far from
justified, goes back to Aristophanes' *Thesmophoriazusae*   43 *Senecas inflexible Hippolitus*: see
Phaedra, 559–79, 684–718   44 *The circuite of . . . Theater*: 136   45 *a most fit Author*:
because of his sensuality in e.g. the glanced-at *Ars amatoria so dissolute a Sectarie*: someone belonging to (and preaching for) such a decadent sect of women   46 *Chastities shipwrack*:
see *Ars amatoria*, 1. 100, 'Ille locus casti damna pudoris habet' ('to chastity that place is fatal')
48 *Howbeit*: for all that

assigned them in the Roman Theater, whereby it should appeare, it was
counted no impeachment to modestie, though they offending therein   50
were buried quicke: a sharpe lawe for them, who may say as *Shores* wife
dooth,

> *When though abroad restraining vs to rome,*
> *They very hardly keepe vs safe at home.*

50 *impeachment*: discredit   *therein*: in the matter of *modestie*   51 *quicke*: alive   53–4:
When though . . . at home: 143–4

8

William Shakespeare, A Louers Complaint *(1609)*

PROBABLY written *c.*1602–5, though conceivably an early poem revised in the mid-1600s, *A Louers Complaint* was published with Shakespeare's Sonnets in 1609. After Daniel's *Delia ... With the Complaint of Rosamond* (1592), it became conventional for plaints to be attached (often following other lyric matter) to sonnet-sequences. On occasion, as in Shakespeare's case, great care went into meshing the short poems with the long. That this anthology provides a generic context for reading *A Louers Complaint* should not deflect attention from the work's relations with the Sonnets (above, pp. 13, 32, 46 and n. 23, &c.). Like those fourteen-line poems, *A Louers Complaint* lost its readership during the seventeenth century. In general Shakespeare's non-dramatic works did not appeal to Augustan and pre-Romantic taste. When the Sonnets found a new audience, during the early nineteenth century, the grounds of their appeal were lyric and quasi-auto-biographical in ways which detached them from *A Louers Complaint*. Commentators ignored the poem, and editions of the Sonnets excluded it. This created a situation in which the work—stylistically perplexed, in any case—was exposed to the specious doubts of those scholars who, in the opening decades of the present century, scoured the Shakespeare corpus for irregularities and ascribed parts of it to his contemporaries. Chapman was often said to have written *A Louers Complaint*. Detailed work in the 1960s crushed that hypothesis, and returned the poem to the canon. But *A Louers Complaint* is still in need of readers.

A LOUERS COMPLAINT

From off a hill whose concaue wombe reworded,
A plaintfull story from a sistring vale
My spirrits t' attend this doble voyce accorded,
And downe I laid to list the sad tun'd tale,
Ere long espied a fickle maid full pale   5
Tearing of papers, breaking rings atwaine,
Storming her world with sorrowes wind and raine.

Vpon her head a plattid hiue of straw,
Which fortified her visage from the Sunne,
Whereon the thought might thinke sometime it saw   10
The carkas of a beauty spent and donne;
Time had not sithed all that youth begun,
Nor youth all quit, but spight of heauens fell rage,
Some beauty peept, through lettice of sear'd age.

Oft did she heaue her Napkin to her eyne,   15
Which on it had conceited charecters:
Laundring the silken figures in the brine,
That seasoned woe had pelleted in teares,
And often reading what contents it beares:
As often shriking vndistinguisht wo,   20
In clamours of all size both high and low.

Some-times her leueld eyes their carriage ride,
As they did battry to the spheres intend:
Sometime diuerted their poore balls are tide
To th' orbed earth; sometimes they do extend   25

---

1 *concaue wombe*: cave or other hollow in the hillside; see pp. 42 ff., 65–6, 74 ff.   *reworded*: echoed;
see pp. 44–5   2 *sistring*: chiefly because contiguous and similarly *concaue*   3 *attend*:
listen to, wait upon   *doble*: echoing (perhaps 'deceiving'); see pp. 35–6, 43–5   *accorded*: agreed
4 *sad tun'd*: though modulated speech can be a 'tune', this points up affinities with ballad and other
sung plaint   5 *fickle*: full of changes, agitated, false (in love or speech); see pp. 14 n. 5,
34–7, 44   8 *plattid hiue of straw*: hat of plaited straw resembling a beehive (commonly worn by
country girls)   10 *thought might thinke*: mind might imagine   12 *sithed*: alluding to
Time's 'scythe'   14 *lettice*: lattice-work   casement   or   screen   15 *heaue*: raise
16 *conceited charecters*: subtly articulate devices or mottos   18 *seasoned*: long harboured,
salty *pelleted*: made into pellets (like a 'meatball' (cf. *seasoned*), or 'gunstone, cannon-
ball')   20 *vndistinguisht*: blurredly confused, indiscriminate   22 *leueld charecters*
ride: bear themselves in such a way (quibbling on gun-*carriage*, cf. eye-*balls* as ammunition in 24)
23 *battry*: a hail of cannon-shot   *spheres*: planets in orbit

Their view right on, anon their gases lend
To euery place at once and no where fixt,
The mind and sight distractedly commixt.

Her haire nor loose nor ti'd in formall plat,
Proclaimd in her a carelesse hand of pride;   30
For some vntuck'd descended her sheu'd hat,
Hanging her pale and pined cheeke beside,
Some in her threeden fillet still did bide,
And trew to bondage would not breake from thence,
Though slackly braided in loose negligence.   35

A thousand fauours from a maund she drew,
Of amber, christall and of bedded Iet,
Which one by one she in a riuer threw,
Vpon whose weeping margent she was set,
Like vsery applying wet to wet,   40
Or Monarches hands that lets not bounty fall
Where want cries some, but where excesse begs all.

Of folded schedulls had she many a one,
Which she perusd, sighd, tore and gaue the flud,
Crackt many a ring of Posied gold and bone,   45
Bidding them find their Sepulchers in mud,
Found yet mo letters sadly pend in blood,
With sleided silke, feate and affectedly
Enswath'd and seald to curious secrecy.

These often bath'd she in her fluxiue eies,   50
And often kist, and often gaue to teare,
Cried O false blood thou register of lies,
What vnapproued witnes doost thou beare!

30 *carelesse hand of pride*: hand neglectful of (taking no *pride* in) appearance (though *pride* can register in neglect)   31 *sheu'd*: sheaf-like   33 *threeden fillet*: ribboned hairband   36 *maund*: basket: 37 *bedded*: i.e. 'in beads'   39 *weeping margent*: muddy edge (hinting 'brink lined with *weeping* willows')   *set*: fixed, sat, planted   40 *Like vsery*: which accumulates coin upon coin, as she adds *wet to wet*   42 *Where want ... all*: where poverty appeals for assistance while affluence insistently seeks to have everything   43 *schedulls*: written papers   45 *Posied*: engraved with mottoes   *bone*: ivory   48 *sleided*: separated into threads   *feate and affectedly*: adroitly and elaborately, with loving deftness   49 *Enswath'd and seald*: letters were often secured with sealing-wax and silken thread   *to curious secrecy*: into intricate concealment   50 *fluxiue*: flowing   51 *gaue to teare*: made to tear (then held back), sacrificed to tearing; generally emended to 'gan to teare'   53 *vnapproued*: not confirmed in practice, false

Inke would haue seem'd more blacke and damned heare!
This said in top of rage the lines she rents,   55
Big discontent, so breaking their contents.

A reuerend man that graz'd his cattell ny,
Sometime a blusterer that the ruffle knew
Of Court, of Cittie, and had let go by
The swiftest houres obserued as they flew,   60
Towards this afflicted fancy fastly drew:
And priuiledg'd by age desires to know
In breefe the grounds and motiues of her wo.

So slides he downe vppon his greyned bat;
And comely distant sits he by her side,   65
When hee againe desires her, being satte,
Her greeuance with his hearing to deuide:
If that from him there may be ought applied
Which may her suffering extasie asswage
Tis promist in the charitie of age.   70

Father she saies, though in mee you behold
The iniury of many a blasting houre,
Let it not tell your Iudgement I am old,
Not age, but sorrow, ouer me hath power;
I might as yet haue bene a spreading flower   75
Fresh to my selfe, if I had selfe applyed
Loue to my selfe, and to no Loue beside.

But wo is mee, too early I attended
A youthfull suit, it was to gaine my grace;
O one by natures outwards so commended,   80
That maidens eyes stucke ouer all his face,

54 *Inke would have seem'd ... heare*: the letters, *pend* with false passion in *blood*, would more appropriately have been written in hellish-black *Inke*   57 *reuerend*: grave, aged; for religious overtones see pp. 13, 39–41, 49 ff.   58 *Sometime*: formerly   *blusterer*: braggart, roisterer   *ruffle*: clamour and ostentation   60 *obserued*: noted with profit   61 *fastly*: both 'hastily' and 'close by'   63 *motiues*: see p. vi   64 *slides ... downe vppon*: smoothly eases himself down with the support of   *greyned bat*: forked staff   65 *comely distant*: at a decent distance   69 *extasie*: frenzy   71 *Father*: title of respect for any venerable man; on the link with *reuerend* at 57 see pp. 39, 49–50   72 *blasting*: blighting   75 *spreading*: opening its petals   79 *it was to gaine my grace*: the *suit* (or 'request') was that I should grant my approval (and so 'amorous favour')   80 *natures outwards*: good looks bestowed by Nature   81 *stucke ouer all*: attention was 'glued to' him

Loue lackt a dwelling and made him her place,
And when in his faire parts shee didde abide,
Shee was new lodg'd and newly Deified.

His browny locks did hang in crooked curles,   85
And euery light occasion of the wind
Vpon his lippes their silken parcels hurles:
Whats sweet to do, to do wil aptly find,
Each eye that saw him did inchaunt the minde:
For on his visage was in little drawne,   90
What largenesse thinkes in parradise was sawne.

Smal shew of man was yet vpon his chinne,
His phenix downe began but to appeare
Like vnshorne veluet, on that termlesse skin
Whose bare out-brag'd the web it seem'd to were.   95
Yet shewed his visage by that cost more deare,
And nice affections wauering stood in doubt
If best were as it was, or best without.

His qualities were beautious as his forme,
For maiden tongu'd he was and thereof free;   100
Yet if men mou'd him, was he such a storme
As oft twixt May and Aprill is to see,
When windes breath sweet, vnruly though they bee.
His rudenesse so with his authoriz'd youth,
Did liuery falsenesse in a pride of truth.   105

Wel could hee ride, and often men would say
That horse his mettell from his rider takes;
Proud of subiection, noble by the swaie,
What rounds, what bounds, what course, what stop he makes!

---

82 *Loue*: oddly, Venus   86 *light occasion*: gentle occurrence (with a hint of 'frivolous excuse')   88 *to do wil aptly find*: doing (and its agents) will readily find means to   90–1 *For on his visage . . . was sawne*: i.e. an observer's thinking enlarges his face's beauty into *What* that viewer *thinkes* (the verb works twice) must have been seen in Eden   93 *phenix downe*: his soft young beard compared to breast-feathers of the unique and marvellous phoenix   94 *termlesse*: beyond description (as well, perhaps, as 'untouched by *terms* of years')   95 *bare out-brag'd*: naked condition (around and under the *downe*) outboasted in beauty   *web*: woven stuff   96 *shewed*: appeared   *cost more deare*: silken floss more precious and lovable (with quibbles on *deare* as 'expensive' and *cost* as 'outlay')   97 *nice*: fastidiously attentive   100 *maiden tongu'd*: softly spoken, chaste in speech (lending paradox to *free*, 'eloquent' and 'licentious')   104–5 *His rudenesse . . . pride of truth*: the boyish roughness of 101–3, allowable in the young (and indicating youth), thus concealed *falsenesse* in a uniform of proud integrity   108 *swaie*: of the youth's government

And controuersie hence a question takes,   110
Whether the horse by him became his deed,
Or he his mannad'g, by th' wel doing Steed.

But quickly on this side the verdict went,
His reall habitude gaue life and grace
To appertainings and to ornament,   115
Accomplisht in him-selfe not in his case:
All ayds them-selues made fairer by their place,
Cam for addicions, yet their purpos'd trimme
Peec'd not his grace but were al grac'd by him.

So on the tip of his subduing tongue   120
All kinde of arguments and question deepe,
Al replication prompt, and reason strong
For his aduantage still did wake and sleep,
To make the weeper laugh, the laugher weepe:
He had the dialect and different skil,   125
Catching al passions in his craft of will,

That hee didde in the general bosome raigne
Of young, of old, and sexes both inchanted,
To dwel with him in thoughts, or to remaine
In personal duty, following where he haunted.   130
Consents bewitcht, ere he desire haue granted,
And dialogu'd for him what he would say,
Askt their own wils and made their wils obey.

Many there were that did his picture gette
To serue their eies, and in it put their mind,   135
Like fooles that in th' imagination set
The goodly obiects which abroad they find

---

110 *by him became his deed*: by virtue of the rider looked well in his acts; vague pronouns register a difficulty of judgement and (given the metamorphic hints of *became*) the problem of disentangling horse from skilled youth from *deed*   112 *mannad'g*: i.e. manage, 'display of equestrian skill'   114 *reall habitude*: actual possessed quality   116 *case*: appearance, situation, guise   118 *Cam for*: offered themselves as (*Cam* an old form of 'came')   *purpos'd trimme*: intended garnish   119 *Peec'd*: supplemented, patched and mended   120 *on the tip of*: at the ready   122 *Al replication*: every kind of reply   125 *dialect*: skill in argument (dialectic), apt idiom for persuasion   *different skil*: art of varying speech   126 *craft of will*: skilful realization (in and through *dialect*) of what he wants   127 *the general bosome*: everyone's hearts   130 *haunted*: frequented   131 *Consents bewitcht*: consenting women, charmed by the youth   *ere he desire*: even before he might request (amorous favours)   132 *dialogu'd*: thought out in dialogue   134 *his picture*: e.g. a portrait miniature   137 *abroad*: in the world at large

Of lands and mansions, theirs in thought assign'd,
And labouring in moe pleasures to bestow them,
Then the true gouty Land-lord which doth owe them. 140

So many haue that neuer toucht his hand
Sweetly suppos'd them mistresse of his heart:
My wofull selfe that did in freedome stand,
And was my owne fee simple (not in part)
What with his art in youth and youth in art 145
Threw my affections in his charmed power,
Reseru'd the stalke and gaue him al my flower.

Yet did I not as some my equals did
Demaund of him, nor being desired yeelded,
Finding my selfe in honour so forbidde, 150
With safest distance I mine honour sheelded,
Experience for me many bulwarkes builded
Of proofs new bleeding which remaind the foile
Of this false Iewell, and his amorous spoile.

But ah who euer shun'd by precedent, 155
The destin'd ill she must her selfe assay,
Or forc'd examples gainst her owne content
To put the by-past perrils in her way?
Counsaile may stop a while what will not stay:
For when we rage, aduise is often seene 160
By blunting vs to make our wits more keene.

---

139 *labouring ... bestow them*: these *fooles*, not possessing estates, administer them in imagination with more enjoyment (and attribute more pleasurable qualities to them) than the gout-ridden *Land-lord* who actually does own (old sense of *owe*) them 142 *them*: themselves 144 *my owne fee simple (not in part)*: in full possession of myself, like the owner of 'land held in perpetuity' 147 *al my flower*: cf. sexual 'defloration' 148 *my equals*: in age and station 149 *desired*: asked, erotically wanted 151 *distance*: in aloofness and, usage suggests, social inferiority 153 *proofs new bleeding*: fresh evidences of injury (with a hint of breached maiden-heads) *foile*: both 'duelling-sword' (for use in the fray of seduction) and 'dull metal ground' (base setting for a *Iewell*) 154 *spoile*: booty, plunder (while also connoting 'damage') 156 *assay*: try 157 *forc'd examples*: insisted upon *precedent*, urged (and made applicable) cautionary instances *content*: satisfaction 158 *by-past*: circumvented (because they affected other people) and 'in the past' 160 *rage*: are wanton 161 *By blunting*: even while it blunts *wits more keene*: faculties and senses sharper

Nor giues it satisfaction to our blood,
That wee must curbe it vppon others proofe,
To be forbod the sweets that seemes so good,
For feare of harmes that preach in our behoofe;   165
O appetite from iudgement stand aloofe!
The one a pallate hath that needs will taste,
Though reason weepe and cry it is thy last.

For further I could say this mans vntrue,
And knew the patternes of his foule beguiling,   170
Heard where his plants in others Orchards grew,
Saw how deceits were guilded in his smiling,
Knew vowes were euer brokers to defiling,
Thought Characters and words meerly but art,
And bastards of his foule adulterat heart.   175

And long vpon these termes I held my Citty,
Till thus hee gan besiege me: Gentle maid
Haue of my suffering youth some feeling pitty
And be not of my holy vowes affraid,
Thats to ye sworne to none was euer said,   180
For feasts of loue I haue bene call'd vnto
Till now did nere inuite nor neuer woo.

All my offences that abroad you see
Are errors of the blood none of the mind:
Loue made them not, with acture they may be,   185
Where neither Party is nor trew nor kind;
They sought their shame that so their shame did find,
And so much lesse of shame in me remaines,
By how much of me their reproch containes.

162 *blood*: as the seat of appetite   163 *proofe*: experience   165 *in our behoofe*: for our
good   168 *it is thy last*: it will be your last tasting, your ruin   169 *further I could . . .
vntrue*: I could (then as now) say more about the youth's falseness   170 *patternes of*: both
'examples of' and 'strategies by which'   171 *his plants*: the imagery of 175 reinforces the
suggestion of illegitimate offspring here   *Orchards*: gardens (places of pleasure, image of fruitful
wombs)   173 *brokers to defiling*: agents of dishonour   174 *Characters and words*: letters
and the words they make up, writing and speech   175 *bastards*: bred in immorality and likely
to deceive   *adulterat*: corrupt (and cuckolding the *others* of 171)   177 *gan*: did, began to
184 *errors*: strayings, faults   185 *acture*: acceptability in action   186 *Where neither Party
. . . nor kind*: the youth is reported as justifying his *offences* on the dubious grounds that those he
seduced were no more *trew* or *kind* ('natural and sincere, generous') than he   188–9 *so much
lesse . . . containes*: the more my *shame* is put into *their reproch* the *lesse* of it is left in me

Among the many that mine eyes haue seene, 190
Not one whose flame my hart so much as warmed,
Or my affection put to th' smallest teene,
Or any of my leisures euer Charmed,
Harme haue I done to them but nere was harmed,
Kept hearts in liueries, but mine owne was free, 195
And raignd commaunding in his monarchy.

Looke heare what tributes wounded fancies sent me,
Of palyd pearles and rubies red as blood:
Figuring that they their passions likewise lent me
Of greefe and blushes, aptly vnderstood 200
In bloodlesse white, and the encrimson'd mood,
Effects of terror and deare modesty,
Encampt in hearts but fighting outwardly.

And Lo behold these tallents of their heir,
With twisted mettle amorously empleacht 205
I haue receau'd from many a seuerall faire,
Their kind acceptance, wepingly beseecht,
With th' annexions of faire gems inricht,
And deepe brain'd sonnets that did amplifie
Each stones deare Nature, worth and quallity. 210

The Diamond? why twas beautifull and hard,
Whereto his inuis'd properties did tend,
The deepe greene Emrald in whose fresh regard,
Weake sights their sickly radience do amend.
The heauen hewd Saphir and the Opall blend 215
With obiects manyfold; each seuerall stone,
With wit well blazond smil'd or made some mone.

---

192 *teene*: trouble, sorrow   193 *leisures*: times of leisure   195 *in liueries*: dressed as my servants   197 *wounded fancies*: women *wounded* by love   202 *deare*: inwardly felt, precious   203 *but*: only   204 *tallents*: rich pieces (sent as *tributes*, and implying the senders' qualities)   205 *With twisted ... empleacht*: entwined with strands of gold or silver   206 *seueral*: different, distinct   208 *th' annexions*: the attachment, appendices (four syllables, unless emended to 'th' annexations')   209 *amplifie*: hold forth about   210 *deare Nature*: innate quality, preciousness   212 *his inuis'd*: its hidden   213–14 *in whose ... amend*: it was thought that looking at an *Emerald* (and catching its *regard*) refreshed the feeble eyebeams radiated by *Weake sights*   215 *heauen hewd*: sky-blue   215–16 *blend ... manyfold*: mixed with an eye-catching variety of colours and forms (or 'of mixed colour, and in addition to these stones other *objects*')   217 *blazond*: glossed, adorned with devices (in the *sonnets*)

Lo all these trophies of affections hot,
Of pensiu'd and subdew'd desires the tender,
Nature hath chargd me that I hoord them not,   220
But yeeld them vp where I my selfe must render:
That is to you my origin and ender:
For these of force must your oblations be,
Since I their Aulter, you enpatrone me.

Oh then aduance (of yours) that phraseles hand,   225
Whose white weighes downe the airy scale of praise,
Take all these similies to your owne command,
Hallowed with sighes that burning lunges did raise:
What me your minister for you obaies
Workes vnder you, and to your audit comes   230
Their distract parcells, in combined summes.

Lo this deuice was sent me from a Nun,
Or Sister sanctified of holiest note,
Which late her noble suit in court did shun,
Whose rarest hauings made the blossoms dote,   235
For she was sought by spirits of ritchest cote,
But kept cold distance, and did thence remoue,
To spend her liuing in eternall loue.

---

219 *pensiu'd*: thoughtful (tending to 'melancholy')   *tender*: offering   221 *my selfe must
render*: must make payment of my self   222 *my origin and ender*: start and finish of my
concerns, source of my life and death   223 *of force*: perforce   *oblations*: offerings
224 *I their Aulter . . . me*: I am the altar on which they are sacrificed and you are the patron saint or
goddess of me   225 *phraseles*: beyond description   226 *white . . . praise*: in a balance
between their whiteness and *praise* of them, the latter (light as air) lifts up (in the air), or else the
white lends ballast to a scale-pan which is otherwise (containing but *praise*) *airy* light
227 *similies*: likenesses figured by the *tributes* and *sonnets*   228 *burning*: with passion, and
'incendiary' if the *lungs* are seen as bellows   229–30 *What me . . . vnder you*: whatever obeys
me (your agent) on your behalf operates beneath your sway   230–1 *to your audit . . . summes*:
the scattered items (or bundles of such) comprised by *What* (once property of the discarded
mistresses) *comes* to the reckoning in aggregates of goods and value   232 *deuice*: emblematic
contrivance (especially heraldic)   233 *of holiest note*: noted for holiness   234 *suit in*:
attendance at (with a hint of appeal for favour)   *shun*: give up   235 *hauings*: endowments
blossoms: young men (flowers of good family)   236 *ritchest cote*: wealthiest extraction (*cote* as
'coat of arms')   238 *in eternall loue*: love of God rather than the secular

But oh my sweet what labour ist to leaue
The thing we haue not, mastring what not striues,   240
Playning the Place which did no forme receiue,
Playing patient sports in vnconstrained giues,
She that her fame so to her selfe contriues,
The scarres of battaile scapeth by the flight,
And makes her absence valiant, not her might.   245

Oh pardon me in that my boast is true,
The accident which brought me to her eie,
Vpon the moment did her force subdewe,
And now she would the caged cloister flie:
Religious loue put out religions eye: 250
Not to be tempted would she be emur'd,
And now to tempt all liberty procur'd.

How mightie then you are, Oh heare me tell,
The broken bosoms that to me belong,
Haue emptied all their fountaines in my well: 255
And mine I powre your Ocean all amonge:
I strong ore them and you ore me being strong,
Must for your victorie vs all congest,
As compound loue to phisick your cold brest.

My parts had powre to charme a sacred Nunne,   260
Who disciplin'd I dieted in grace,
Beleeu'd her eies, when they t' assaile begun,
All vowes and consecrations giuing place:

---

239 *what labour ist*: what kind of labour (if it deserves the name) is it   240 *not striues*: offers
no resistance   241 *Playning*: to erase an engraved or carved image, yet here there was no
forme figured   *the Place*: implying the heart   242 *Playing . . . vnconstrained giues*: pretending
to endure patiently fetters which have not been imposed against one's will   243 *her fame so to
her selfe contriues*: fixes up a reputation for herself in this self-orchestrated way (*to her selfe* also
implies an audience of one for the *fame*)   250 *Religious*: devoted (though far from spiritual)
251 *emur'd*: put behind walls (upon entering the *cloister*)   252 *tempt all*: attempt the utmost,
be ready for anything (by risking *all* the *tempt*ations of experience)   254 *broken bosoms*: the
heart-*broken* women cast off   257–8 *I strong . . . vs all congest*: that I master them while you
master me means that, on account of your being victorious, I and they (mixing with *your Ocean*) must
all come together   259 *compound*: composite (with a quibble on 'compounded of drugs in a
medicine' elicited by *phisick*)   *phisick*: treat with medicine   260 *parts*: properties and attri-
butes (bodily, intellectual, and accomplished)   261 *I dieted in*: ay, nurtured upon (directed in
a regimen of)   263 *giuing place*: making room, ousted

O most potentiall loue, vowe, bond, nor space
In thee hath neither sting, knot, nor confine   265
For thou art all and all things els are thine.

When thou impressest what are precepts worth
Of stale example? when thou wilt inflame,
How coldly those impediments stand forth
Of wealth, of filliall feare, lawe, kindred, fame,   270
Loues armes are peace, gainst rule, gainst sence, gainst shame
And sweetens in the suffring pangues it beares,
The *Alloes* of all forces, shockes and feares.

Now all these hearts that doe on mine depend,
Feeling it breake, with bleeding groanes they pine,   275
And supplicant their sighes to you extend
To leaue the battrie that you make gainst mine,
Lending soft audience, to my sweet designe,
And credent soule, to that strong bonded oth,
That shall preferre and vndertake my troth.   280

This said, his watrie eies he did dismount,
Whose sightes till then were leaueld on my face,
Each cheeke a riuer running from a fount,
With brynish currant downe-ward flowed apace:
Oh how the channell to the streame gaue grace!   285
Who glaz'd with Christall gate the glowing Roses,
That flame through water which their hew incloses.

Oh father, what a hell of witch-craft lies,
In the small orb of one perticular teare?
But with the invndation of the eies: 290
What rocky heart to water will not weare?

---

264 *potentiall*: powerful   266 *thou art all . . . thine*: you are everything, and if there is anything
not comprised by you then you own and govern it anyway   267 *impressest*: conscript for battle,
incise or print with a design   271 *are peace*: overcome so quickly that there is no fight
273 *Alloes*: bitterness (juice of the aloe plant, used medicinally)   277 *battrie*: artillery assault
278 *Lending soft audience*: granting a hearing   280 *preferre and vndertake*: recommend and
sponsor, advance and put into action   281–2 *eies he did dismount . . . face*: the *eies* like guns out
of action were 'removed from their mountings', their *sightes* (both 'gun-sights' and 'pupils', that part
which sees) turned aside from being 'aimed' at the maiden's visage (cf. 22–3 and 309)
286 *Who glaz'd . . . glowing Roses*: which *streame* sheened under a transparent barrier (of its going)
the youth's *glowing* cheeks; alludes to the kind of jewel or miniature in crystal highly valued in the
period   291 *to water*: under its flow and dissolving into it

What brest so cold that is not warmed heare,
O cleft effect, cold modesty hot wrath:
Both fire from hence, and chill extincture hath.

For loe his passion but an art of craft,   295
Euen there resolu'd my reason into teares,
There my white stole of chastity I daft,
Shooke off my sober gardes, and ciuill feares,
Appeare to him as he to me appeares,
All melting, though our drops this diffrence bore,   300
His poison'd me, and mine did him restore.

In him a plenitude of subtle matter,
Applied to Cautills, all straing formes receiues,
Of burning blushes, or of weeping water,
Or sounding palenesse: and he takes and leaues,   305
In eithers aptnesse as it best deceiues:
To blush at speeches ranck, to weepe at woes
Or to turne white and sound at tragick showes;

That not a heart which in his leuell came,
Could scape the haile of his all hurting ayme,   310
Shewing faire Nature is both kinde and tame:
And vaild in them did winne whom he would maime.
Against the thing he sought, he would exclaime,
When he most burnt in hart-wisht luxurie,
He preacht pure maide, and praisd cold chastitie.   315

Thus meerely with the garment of a grace,
The naked and concealed feind he couerd,
That th' vnexperient gaue the tempter place,
Which like a Cherubin aboue them houerd.
Who young and simple would not be so louerd?   320
Aye me I fell, and yet do question make,
What I should doe againe for such a sake.

---

294 *extincture*: extinction   295 *passion*: display of feeling   296 *resolu'd*: dissolved, reduced   297 *daft*: doffed   298 *ciuill*: socially decorous   300 *drops*: used of jewels as well as tears, resembling jewels (often *drops* in this period), but also liquid drugs anticipating *poison'd ... restore*   302 *subtle matter*: craft (and the stuff it devises with) 303 *Cautills*: tricks   305 *sounding*: swooning   307 *ranck*: coarse   309 *leuell*: aim, range   314 *luxurie*: lust   315 *pure maide*: like a virginal girl, purity itself 318 *vnexperient*: someone (or more) without experience   319 *houerd*: ostensibly protective   321 *question make*: ask myself, raise it as a problem   322 *againe*: if the option of falling came up once more

O that infected moysture of his eye,
O that false fire which in his cheeke so glowd:
O that forc'd thunder from his heart did flye,   325
O that sad breath his spungie lungs bestowed,
O all that borrowed motion seeming owed,
Would yet againe betray the fore-betrayed,
And new peruert a reconciled Maide.

323 *infected*: contagiously corrupt   327 *owed*: owned   328 *fore-*: already (and perhaps then in advance)   329 *reconciled*: truly repentant (above, pp. 49–51), brought back to virtue, at peace with her situation and self

9

Psalms and Lamentations

HUNDREDS of editions of the Psalms were published during the sixteenth and seventeenth centuries—mostly reprints of the Sternhold–Hopkins paraphrase (1556/62), used in public worship. Objections to this clumsy version were common. 'Shall our Church, unto our Spouse and King | More hoarse, more harsh than any other, sing?', asked Donne in his 'Upon the Translation of the Psalmes by Sir Philip Sydney, and the Countesse of Pembroke his Sister'. Encouraged by Clément Marot and Théodore de Bèzea (Beza), whose virtuosic Psalter was completed by 1562, Philip and Mary Sidney (also known as Mary Herbert after her marriage to the Earl of Pembroke) set about producing a version of similar beauty and variety. It is from their collection that 137 is edited. Love plaints impinge on the French Psalms because Marot employed the metre and melodies of secular song. This was meant to do more than take the Devil's best tunes. As Donne's sermons insistently remind us, the Psalms are verses of love; they can woo a congregation, seduce it into faith. Certainly 137 has the shape of erotic complaint: it sets the Jewish people, like an abandoned woman, on a river-bank under willows, speaking of loss, rising to anger. This psalm expresses the misery of captive Israel after the destruction of Jerusalem and the First Temple. Lamentations is now thought to refer to the same event, in 587 BC, and its imprecation against Edom (4: 21–2) has been taken to mask hostility to Babylon. Post-Reformation commentators were unsure, though, how far 137 and Lamentations involved the same sorrow; most followed Calvin in hearing both prophecy and mourning in the voice of Jeremiah, Jerusalem. The Book of Psalms is an anthology, and Lamentations more a gathering than a narrative. Even so, because of the formal integrity of the latter (based on acrostics and balanced chapter-lengths) there are drawbacks in printing a section out of context. Psalm 137 is edited from Trinity College, Cambridge, MS R.3.16. This gives the first forty-three psalms (essentially Sir Philip's) revised by his sister, plus versions of 44–150 (Mary Sidney's work) apparently incorporating changes made during the 1590s. For chapter 1 of Lamentations the King James Bible (1611) is used. The existence of original annotation is indicated by asterisks, but the notes themselves are cued by verse-numbers.

MARY SIDNEY, COUNTESS OF PEMBROKE

PSALM 137. *SUPER FLUMINA*

Nigh seated where the Riuer flowes
   That watreth Babells thankfull plaine
Which then our teares in pearled rowes
   Did help to water with theire raine,
The thought of Sion bredd such woes   5
   That though our Harpes wee did retaine
      Yet vseles, and vntouched there
      On Willowes onely hang'd they were.

Now whiles our Harpes were hanged so
   The men (whose Captiues then wee laie,)   10
Did on our griefes insulting growe,
   And more to grieue us thus did saie:
You that of Musique make such showe,
   Come sing vs now a Sion laie.
      O no! wee haue nor voice, nor hand,   15
      For such a song in such a land.

Though farr I lie (sweete Sion hill)
   In forraigne Soile exil'd from thee:
Yet let my hand forgett his skill
   If euer thou forgotten be;   20
And let my tongue fast glued still
   Vnto my roofe lie Mute in mee
      If thy neglect within mee spring,
      Or ought I doe, but Salem sing.

But thou O Lord shalt not forgett   25
   To quitt the paines of Edoms race:
Who causelessly, yet hottly sett
   Thy holy Citty to deface

1 *where the Riuer flowes*: Babylon (the *Babell* of 2) was built beside the Euphrates on the fertile Mesopotamian plain (in part of what is now Iraq)   10 *men*: the Babylonians   22 *my roofe*: roof of my mouth   23 *thy neglect*: neglect of thee   24 *Salem*: Jerusalem 26 *quitt the paines of Edoms race*: avenge the pains caused by the descendants of Edom; whether the Edomites (inhabitants of an area south of Israel) participated in the destruction of Jerusalem in 587 BC remains uncertain, and the verse is often taken to be a coded allusion to the Babylonians 27–8 *sett . . . to deface*: set about defacing

> Did thus the bloodie Victors whett
>   What tyme they entred first the place,   30
>   Downe, downe with it at any hand
>   Make all flatt plaine, let nothing stand.
>
> And Babylon that didst vs waste,
>   They self shalt one daie wasted be
> Yea happie he, who what thou hast   35
>   Vnto vs don shall doe to thee:
> Like bitternes shall make thee taste
>   Like woefull obiects cause thee see
>   Yea happie who thy litle ones
>   Shall take, and dash against the stones.   40

THE LAMENTATIONS OF IEREMIAH
CHAPTER I

1. The miserable estate of Ierusalem by reason of her sinne,
12 Shee complaineth of her griefe,   18 and confesseth Gods
iudgement to be righteous.

1 How doeth the citie sit solitarie that was full of people? how is she become as a widow? Shee that was great among the nations, and princesse among the prouinces, how is she become tributarie?

2 Shee *weepeth sore in the *night, and her teares are on her cheekes: among all her louers she hath none to comfort her, all her friends haue dealt treacherously with her, they are become her enemies.

3 Iudah is gone into captiuitie, because of affliction, and *because of great seruitude: she dwelleth among the heathen, she findeth no rest: all her persecutors ouertook her betweene the straits.

4 The wayes of Zion do mourne, because none come to the solemne feasts: all her gates are desolate: her priests sigh: her virgins are afflicted, and she is in bitternesse.

---

29 *whett*: make themselves keen for attack   30 *What tyme*: when   31–2 *Downe, downe . . . nothing stand*: this is imagined as spoken by the *Victors* in their onslaught

---

Marginal notes, 1611
1 Ier[emiah] 13.17   2 Iob 7.3   3 *Heb[rew] for the greatnesse of seruitude*

5 Her aduersaries *are the chiefe, her enemies prosper: for the LORD hath afflicted her; for the multitude of her transgressions, her *children are gone into captiuitie before the enemie.

6 And from the daughter of Zion all her beautie is departed: her princes are become like Harts that find no pasture, and they are gone without strength before the pursuer.

7 Ierusalem remembred in the dayes of her affliction, and of her miseries, all her *pleasant things that she had in the dayes of old, when her people fell into the hand of the enemie, and none did helpe her, the aduersaries saw her, and did mocke at her Sabbaths.

8 Ierusalem hath grieuously sinned, therefore she *is remoued: all that honoured her, despise her, because they haue seene her nakednesse: yea, shee sigheth and turneth backward.

9 Her filthinesse is in her skirts, she remembreth not her last end, therfore she came downe wonderfully: shee had no comforter: O Lord, behold my affliction: for the enemie hath magnified himselfe.

10 The aduersarie hath spread out his hand vpon all her *pleasant things: for she hath seene that the heathen entred into her Sanctuarie, whom thou didst command that *they should not enter into thy congregation.

11 All her people sigh, they seek bread, they haue giuen their pleasant things for meate to *relieue the soule: see, O Lord, and consider: for I am become vile.

12 ¶*Is it nothing to you, all ye that *passe by? behold and see, if there be any sorow like vnto my sorowe, which is done vnto me, wherewith the LORD hath afflicted me, in the day of his fierce anger.

13 From aboue hath he sent fire into my bones, and it preuaileth against them: he hath spread a net for my feete, he hath turned me backe: he hath made me desolate, and faint all the day.

14 The yoke of my transgressions is bound by his hand: they are wreathed, and come vp vpon my necke: he hath made my strength to fall, the Lord hath deliuered me into their hands, from whom I am not able to rise vp.

15 The Lord hath troden vnder foot all my mightie men in the midst of me: he hath called an assembly against mee, to crush my yong men. The Lord hath troden *the virgine, the daughter of Iudah, as in a wine presse.

---

5 Deut[eronomy] 28.13   Ier[emiah] 52.28   7 *Or, desireable*   8 *Heb* [rew] *is become a* *remouing or wandering*   10 *Or, desireable*   Deu[teronomy] 23.3   11 *Or, to make the* *soule to come againe*   12 *Or, it is nothing*   *Heb*[rew] *passe by the way*   15 *Or, the* *winepresse of the virgine, &c.*

16 For these things I weepe, *mine eye, mine eye runneth downe with water, because the comforter that should *relieue my soule is farre from me: my children are desolate, because the enemy preuailed.

17 Zion spreadeth forth her hands, and there is none to comfort her: the LORD hath commanded concerning Iacob, that his aduersaries should bee round about him: Ierusalem is as a menstruous woman among them.

18 ¶The LORD is *righteous, for I haue rebelled against his *commandement: heare, I pray you, all people, and behold my sorow: my virgins and my yong men are gone into captiuitie.

19 I called for my louers, but they deceiued me: my priests and mine elders gaue vp the ghost in the citie, while they sought their meat to relieue their soules.

20 Behold, O LORD: for I am in distresse: my *bowels are troubled: mine heart is turned within mee, for I haue grieuously rebelled: abroad the sword bereaueth, at home there is as death.

21 They haue heard that I sigh, there is none to comfort me: all mine enemies haue heard of my trouble, they are glad that thou hast done it: thou wilt bring the day that thou hast *called, and they shall be like vnto me.

22 Let all their wickednes come before thee: and doe vnto them, as thou hast done vnto me for all my transgressions: for my sighes are many, and my heart is faint.

---

16 Ier[emiah] 13.17 and 14.17. chap. 2.18   *Heb[rew] bring backe*   18 Dan[iel] 9.7
Heb[rew] mouth   20 Isa[iah] 16.11. [Ieremiah] 48.36   21 *Or, proclaimed*

10

After Shakespeare

THIS section begins with an extract from *The Maides Tragedy* (1619). Written by John Fletcher (1579–1625) and Francis Beaumont (1584–1616) — probably in 1610–11 — it is one of the most powerful examples of the courtly drama produced by Shakespeare's company, the King's Men, during his later years. The passage given here, attributable to Fletcher, comes from the second scene of Act II, where Aspatia, rejected by Amintor (who has been persuaded by the King to marry the royal mistress, Evadne), invokes the Ariadne of *Heroides*, 10, to further her laments. The second piece is by Lady Mary Wroth (1586/7–1651/3) — a Sidney (niece of Sir Philip and his sister, the Countess of Pembroke). Lauded in the Jacobean period by Ben Jonson, George Wither, and others, she is too little read today. In this lyric from her prose romance, *The Countesse of Mountgomeries Urania* (1621), the shepherdess Urania walks about the island of 'Pantalaria', deploring her isolation. The letter of 'A Forsaken Lady . . . ', published in 1649 by Richard Lovelace (1618–57/8), makes a rather different contribution to the subgenre. At a time when epistolary plaint was usually Ovidian in contour, it moves from Petrarchan anguish ('the flames I burne in, Oh!') to a 'bright reason' which transcends abjection. Lovelace's persona fiercely writes her way into taking the moral high ground from her 'False Servant'. In 'The Nymph Complaining . . . ', by contrast, Andrew Marvell (1621–78) creates a speaker whose reluctance to press as far as blame — never mind beyond it — wins a disconcerting, lucent pathos (above, pp. 66–7). The section also includes 'Ariadne Deserted by Theseus . . . ' by William Cartwright. A product of Westminster School and Christ Church, member of Jonson's 'tribe of Ben', Cartwright left four plays and a series of court-orientated poems which promise more than his short life (1611–43) could fulfil. The ode-like poem given here, for musical declamation, is formally innovative but commonplace in subject. From Thomas Underdowne's *Theseus and Ariadne* (1566), beyond William Bowles's *Complaint of Ariadna* (in the Dryden *Sylvae*, 1685), authors of every sort were drawn to the theme. Many, like Bowles, took their material from the digression in Catullus, 64, where '*The Poet in the* Epithalamium *of* Peleus *and* Thetis, *describes the Genial Bed, on which was wrought the Story of* Theseus *and* Ariadna'. Others, resembling Fletcher's Aspatia, were more conscious of *Heroides*, 10. Cartwright mingles both sources in his text, set to music by Henry Lawes. The score was published in the latter's *Ayres and Dialogues* (1653), though it is now most easily found in *British Library Manuscripts*, pt. III. *Add. MS. 53723 (Henry Lawes's Autograph)*, ed. Elise Bickford Jorgens (New York, 1986). Admired by Pepys, the work was also praised by Milton: the first printing of his sonnet 'To Mr. H. Lawes, on his Aires', in *Choice Psalmes* (1648), keys 'Priest of *Phoebus* Quire | That tun'st their happiest lines in Hymn, or Story' to the gloss 'The story of Ariadne set by him to Music.'

JOHN FLETCHER

'Show me the peece of needle worke you wrought'

From *The Maides Tragedy*

[*Aspatia, Antiphila, Olimpias*]

[ASPATIA.] Show me the peece of needle worke you wrought.
ANTIPHILA. Of *Ariadne* Madame?
ASPATIA.   Yes that peece:
   This should be *Theseus*, has a cousening face,
   You ment him for a man.
ANTIPHILA.   He was so Madame.
ASPATIA. Why then tis well enough, neuer looke black;   5
   You haue a full winde, and a false heart *Theseus*;
   Does not the story say, his Keele was split,
   Or his masts spent, or some kind rock or other
   Met with his vessell?
ANTIPHILA.   Not as I remember.
ASPATIA. It should ha' been so. Could the Gods know this,   10
   And none of all their number raise a storme?
   But they are all as ill. This false smile was exprest well,
   Iust such another caught me. You shall not goe so;
   Antiphila, in this place worke a quick-sand,
   And ouer it a shallow smiling water,   15
   And his ship plowing it, and then a feare,
   Doe that feare brauely wench.

---

3 *cousening*: deceiving   6 *You haue a full winde . . . Theseus*: the *worke* depicts that part of the *story* where Theseus (after being helped through the labyrinth by Ariadne's thread, and sailing with her from Crete) abandons his mistress on the island of Naxos

OLIMPIAS.   Twill wrong the storie.
ASPATIA. Twill make the story, wrong'd by wanton Poets,
    Liue long and be beleeu'd. But wheres the Lady?
ANTIPHILA. There Madame.   20
ASPATIA. Fie, you haue mist it there *Antiphila*,
    You are much mistaken wench:
    These colours are not dull and pale enough,
    To show a soule so full of miserie
    As this poore Ladies was. Doe it by me,   25
    Doe it againe, by me the lost *Aspatia*,
    And you will find all true but the wilde Iland.
    Suppose I stand vpon the Sea breach now
    Mine armes thus, and mine haire blowne with the wind,
    Wilde as the place she was in; let all about me   30
    Be hearers of my story; doe my face,
    If thou hadst euer feeling of a sorrow,
    Thus, thus, *Antiphila*; make me looke good girle
    Like sorrowes monument, and the trees about me
    Let them be dry and leauelesse; let the rocks   35
    Groane with continuall surges, and behind me
    Make all a desolation: see, see wenches,
    A miserable life of this poore picture.
OLIMPIAS. Deare Madame.
ASPATIA.   I haue done, sit downe, and let vs
    Vpon that point fixe all our eyes, that point there;   40
    Make a dumbe silence till you feele a sudden sadnesse
    Giue vs new soules.

LADY MARY WROTH

'Vnseene, vnknowne, I here alone complaine'

From *The Countesse of Mountgomeries Urania*

Vnseene, vnknowne, I here alone complaine
    To Rocks, to Hills, to Meadowes, and to Springs,
Which can no helpe returne to ease my paine,
    But back my sorrowes the sad Eccho brings.

27 *the wilde Iland*: windswept Naxos   27 *Sea breach*: breakwater, mole   38 *life*: living
illustration (of what the *picture* imitates)

Thus still encreasing are my woes to me,
   Doubly resounded by that monefull voice,
Which seemes to second me in miserie,
   And answere giues like friend of mine owne choice.
Thus onely she doth my companion proue,
   The others silently doe offer ease:
But those that grieue, a grieuing note doe loue;
   Pleasures to dying eies bring but disease:
And such am I, who daily ending liue,
Wayling a state which can no comfort giue.

RICHARD LOVELACE

A FORSAKEN LADY TO HER FALSE SERVANT THAT IS DISDAINED BY HIS NEW MISTRIS

Were it that you so shun me 'cause you wish
(Cruel'st) a fellow in your wretchednesse,
Or that you take some small ease in your owne
Torments, to heare another sadly groane,
I were most happy in my paines, to be
So truly blest, to be so curst by thee:
But Oh! my cries to that doe rather adde,
Of which too much already thou hast had,
And thou art gladly sad to heare my moane;
Yet sadly hearst me with derision.

   Thou most unjust, that really dost know,
And feelst thy selfe the flames I burne in, Oh!
How can you beg to be set loose from that
Consuming stake, you binde another at?

---

12 *disease*: discomfort, ill ease   13 *ending*: expiring

---

2 *fellow*: companion   5 *most happy*: i.e. to be of use to you   14 *Consuming stake*: the *stake* to which those burnt alive (for heresy, which often images deception in love) were tied

Uncharitablest both wayes, to denie   15
That pity me, for which your selfe must dye,
To love not her loves you, yet know the paine
What 'tis to love, and not be lov'd againe.

Flye on, flye on swift Racer, untill she
Whom thou of all ador'st shall learne of thee,   20
The pace t' outfly thee, and shall teach thee groan,
What terrour 'tis t' outgo, and be outgon.

Not yet looke back, nor yet, must we
Run then like spoakes in wheeles eternally
And never overtake? Be dragg'd on still   25
By the weake Cordage of your untwin'd will,
Round without hope of rest? No, I will turne
And with my goodnes boldly meete your scorne;
My goodnesse which Heav'n pardon, and that fate
Made you hate love, and fall in love with hate.   30

But I am chang'd! bright reason that did give
My soule a noble quicknes, made me live
One breath yet longer, and to will, and see,
Hath reacht me pow'r to scorne as well as thee:
That thou which proudly tramplest on my grave,   35
Thy selfe mightst fall, conquer'd my double slave,
That thou mightst sinking in thy triumphs moan,
And I triumph in my destruction.

Hayle holy cold! chaste temper hayle! the fire
Rav'd o're my purer thoughts I feele t' expire,   40
And I am candied Ice; yee pow'rs! If e're
I shall be forc't unto my Sepulcher;
Or violently hurl'd into my Urne,
Oh make me choose rather to freeze, then burne.

23–5 *Not yet looke back . . . overtake?*: the *Servant's* pursuit of his new love (19–22) now seems to involve the speaker, racing along behind; *spoakes in wheeles* suggests charioteering, and perhaps (see 27–8 and n.) a course round which to career   25–7 *dragg'd on . . . hope of rest*: unravelled twine and dragging *Cordage* modulate the chariot imagery into hints of a spinning-wheel and machine of torture   27–8 *No, I will turne . . . scorne*: if a racing-course metaphor persists, the *turne* brings her to face those whom she pursues; it is a word generally used of retaliation and betrayal given positive implications ('*turne* to a life of *goodnes*, *turne* the other cheek to your wrong') 32 *quicknes*: vitality   34 *reacht*: granted   36 *my double slave*: overwhelmed once by love of me and now (she intends) by *scorne*   41 *candied*: crystallized

WILLIAM CARTWRIGHT

ARIADNE DESERTED BY THESEUS, AS SHE SITS UPON A ROCK IN THE ISLAND NAXOS, THUS COMPLAINS

Theseus! O *Theseus* heark! but yet in vain
    Alas deserted I Complain,
It was some neighbouring Rock, more soft than he,
    Whose hollow Bowels pittied me,
And beating back that false, and Cruell Name,   5
    Did Comfort and revenge my flame.
    Then Faithless whither wilt thou fly?
    Stone dare not harbour Cruelty.

Tell me you Gods who e'r you are,
Why, O why made you him so fair?   10
    And tell me, Wretch, why thou
    Mad'st not thy self more true?
Beauty from him may Copies take,
And more Majestique Heroes make,
    And falshood learn a Wile,   15
    From him too, to beguile.
      Restore my Clew
      'Tis here most due,
For 'tis a Labyrinth of more subtile Art,
To have so fair a Face, so foul a Heart.   20

The Ravenous Vulture tear his Breast,
The rowling Stone disturb his rest,
    Let him next feel
    Ixion's Wheel,
And add one Fable more   25
    To cursing Poets store;
And then—yet rather let him live, and twine
His Woof of daies, with some thred stoln from mine;

---

5 *beating back*: returning it (with anger) as an echo   17 *my Clew*: the thread by which Theseus was guided in and out of the *Labyrinth*   21–2 *Ravenous Vulture . . . rowling Stone*: mythical punishments of Prometheus and Sisyphus (cf. *Ixion*)   27–8 *twine* | *His Woof of daies* (usually accomplished with *thred* spun by the Fates)

But if you'l torture him, how e'r,
Torture my Heart, you'l find him there.   30

    Till my Eyes drank up his,
       And his drank mine,
    I ne'r thought Souls might kiss,
       And Spirits joyn:
       Pictures till then   35
    Took me as much as Men,
       Nature and Art
    Moving alike my heart,
But his fair Visage made me find
       Pleasures and Fears,   40
       Hopes, Sighs, and Tears,
As severall seasons of the Mind.
    Should thine Eye, *Venus*, on his dwell,
    Thou wouldst invite him to thy Shell,
    And Caught by that live Jet   45
    Venture the second Net,
And after all thy dangers, faithless he,
Shouldst thou but slumber, would forsake ev'n thee.

    The Streames so Court the yeelding Banks,
And gliding thence ne'r pay their thanks;   50
    The Winds so wooe the Flow'rs,
    Whisp'ring among fresh Bow'rs,
   And having rob'd them of their smels,
   Fly thence perfum'd to other Cels.
This is familiar Hate to Smile and Kill,   55
Though nothing please thee yet my Ruine will.
    Death hover, hover o'r me then,
      Waves let your Christall Womb
      Be both my Fate, and Tomb,
    I'l sooner trust the Sea, than Men.   60

    Yet for revenge to Heaven I'l call
    And breath one Curse before I fall,

---

44 *thy Shell*: in some accounts *Venus* was borne from the sea on such a vehicle   45 *that live*
Jet: his eyes like dark jewels   46 *second Net*: the first, cast by Vulcan, caught *Venus* in adultery
with Mars   54 *Cels*: flowers (with their enclosing petals); *Fly* also makes the *Winds* resemble
bees seeking the *Cels* of their honeycomb

Proud of two Conquests *Minotaure*, and Me,
That by my Faith, This by thy Perjury,
Mayst thou forget to Wing thy Ships with White,   65
That the Black Sayl may to the longing sight
Of thy Gray Father, tell thy Fate, and He
Bequeath the Sea his Name, falling like me:
Nature and Love thus brand thee, whiles I dye
'Cause thou forsak'st, *Ægeus* 'cause thou drawest nigh.   70

   And yee O Nymphs below who sit,
    In whose swift Flouds his Vows he writ;
Snatch a sharp Diamond from the richer Mines,
And in some Mirrour grave these sadder Lines,
      Which let some God Convey   75
      To him, that so he may
    In that both read at once, and see
    Those Looks that Caus'd my destiny.
In *Thetis* Arms I *Ariadne* sleep,
Drown'd first by my own Tears, then in the deep;   80
Twice banished, First by Love, and then by Hate,
The life that I preserv'd became my Fate;
Who leaving all, was by him left alone,
That from a Monster freed himself prov'd one.

   Thus then I—But look! O mine Eyes   85
     Be now true Spies,
     Yonder, yonder,
     Comes my Dear,
     Now my wonder,
     Once my fear,   90
    See Satyrs dance along
    In a confused Throng,
    Whiles Horns and Pipes rude noise
    Do mad their lusty Joyes,

65–8 *Mayst thou forget . . . his Name*: Theseus promised his father, *Ægeus*, that he would show white sails on his return from Crete if victorious; in his haste, he kept the ship's black rig, and his father leapt to his death in the Ægean   69 *Nature and Love thus brand thee*: may you be marked as guilty for what you do to your nearest and dearest as well as how you behave in love   71 *O Nymphs below*: Nereids, daughters of the sea-god   79 *Thetis*: one of the Nereids 85–102 *But look! . . . Theseus, or some God*: Cartwright draws on Catullus (see headnote) for this conclusion, though Ariadne's touching confusion of Bacchus with Theseus is his own 94 *mad*: madden

Roses his forehead Crown, 95
And that recrowns the Flow'rs,
Where he walks up and down
He makes the desarts Bow'rs,
The Ivy, and the Grape
Hide, not adorn his Shape. 100
And Green Leaves Cloath his waving Rod,
'Tis either *Theseus*, or some God.

ANDREW MARVELL

THE NYMPH COMPLAINING FOR THE DEATH OF HER FAUN

The wanton Troopers riding by
Have shot my Faun and it will dye.
Ungentle men! They cannot thrive
To kill thee. Thou neer didst alive
Them any harm: alas nor cou'd 5
Thy death yet do them any good.
I'me sure I never wisht them ill;
Nor do I for all this; nor will:
But, if my simple Pray'rs may yet
Prevail with Heaven to forget 10
Thy murder, I will Joyn my Tears
Rather then fail. But, O my fears!
It cannot dye so. Heavens King
Keeps register of every thing:
And nothing may we use in vain. 15
Ev'n Beasts must be with justice slain;
Else Men are made their *Deodands*.
Though they should wash their guilty hands

1 *Troopers*: cavalry soldiers (a new word in mid-17th-cent. English)   4 *To kill thee*: as a result of killing thee   11 *Joyn my Tears*: to the *Pray'rs*   17 *Deodands*: in English Law until the 19th cent. objects which, having been the immediate cause of a person's death, were sacrificed to God as expiatory offerings   18–19 *wash their guilty hands . . . which doth part*: as in ancient purification rites, the killers might seek to expunge their blood-guilt in the *life-blood* that flows out of (*parts* | *From*) the faun

In this warm life-blood, which doth part
From thine, and wound me to the Heart,   20
Yet could they not be clean: their Stain
Is dy'd in such a Purple Grain.
There is not such another in
The World, to offer for their Sin.
    Unconstant *Sylvio*, when yet   25
I had not found him counterfeit,
One morning (I remember well)
Ty'd in this silver Chain and Bell,
Gave it to me: nay and I know
What he said then; I'me sure I do.   30
Said He, look how your Huntsman here
Hath taught a Faun to hunt his *Dear*.
But *Sylvio* soon had me beguil'd.
This waxed tame; while he grew wild,
And quite regardless of my Smart,   35
Left me his Faun, but took his Heart.
    Thenceforth I set my self to play
My solitary time away,
With this: and very well content,
Could so mine idle Life have spent.   40
For it was full of sport; and light
Of foot, and heart; and did invite,
Me to its game: it seem'd to bless
Its self in me. How could I less
Than love it? O I cannot be   45
Unkind, t' a Beast that loveth me.
    Had it liv'd long, I do not know
Whether it too might have done so
As *Sylvio* did: his Gifts might be
Perhaps as false or more than he.   50
But I am sure, for ought that I
Could in so short a time espie,
Thy Love was far more better then
The love of false and cruel men.
    With sweetest milk, and sugar, first   55
I it at mine own fingers nurst.
And as it grew, so every day
It wax'd more white and sweet than they.

---

22 *in such a Purple Grain*: so indelibly scarlet; *in . . . Grain* was often used of reddish colours, *Purple* retains in 17th-cent. poetry its earlier crimson tint

It had so sweet a Breath! And oft
I blusht to see its foot more soft,   60
And white, (shall I say then my hand?)
NAY any Ladies of the Land.
  It is a wond'rous thing, how fleet
'Twas on those little silver feet.
With what a pretty skipping grace,   65
It oft would challenge me the Race:
And when 't had left me far away,
'Twould stay, and run again, and stay.
For it was nimbler much than Hindes;
And trod, as on the four Winds.   70
  I have a Garden of my own,
But so with Roses over grown,
And Lillies, that you would it guess
To be a little Wilderness.
And all the Spring time of the year   75
It onely loved to be there.
Among the beds of Lillyes, I
Have sought it oft, where it should lye;
Yet could not, till it self would rise,
Find it, although before mine Eyes.   80
For, in the flaxen Lillies shade,
It like a bank of Lillies laid.
Upon the Roses it would feed,
Until its Lips ev'n seem'd to bleed:
And then to me 'twould boldly trip,   85
And print those Roses on my Lip.
But all its chief delight was still
On Roses thus its self to fill:
And its pure virgin Limbs to fold
In whitest sheets of Lillies cold.   90
Had it liv'd long, it would have been
Lillies without, Roses within.
  O help! O help! I see it faint:
And dye as calmely as a Saint.
See how it weeps. The Tears do come   95
Sad, slowly dropping like a Gumme.
So weeps the wounded Balsome: so
The holy Frankincense doth flow.

97 *the wounded Balsome*: resinous tree (several varieties in this family, flourishing in Asia and North Africa) which, incised, yields balm   98 *holy Frankincense*: another aromatic resin drawn from trees (usually of the genus *Boswellia*), used for burning as incense

The brotherless *Heliades*
Melt in such Amber Tears as these.   100
   I in a golden Vial will
Keep these two crystal Tears; and fill
It till it do o'reflow with mine;
Then place it in *Diana's* Shrine.
   Now my sweet Faun is vanish'd to   105
Whether the Swans and Turtles go
In fair *Elizium* to endure,
With milk-white Lambs, and Ermins pure.
O do not run too fast: for I
Will but bespeak thy Grave, and dye.   110
   First my unhappy Statue shall
Be cut in Marble; and withal,
Let it be weeping too: but there
Th' Engraver sure his Art may spare;
For I so truly thee bemoane,   115
That I shall weep though I be Stone:
Until my Tears, still dropping, wear
My breast, themselves engraving there.
There at my feet shalt thou be laid,
Of purest Alabaster made: 120
For I would have thine Image be
White as I can, though not as Thee.

99 *Heliades*: daughters of the sun-god and Clymene who, mourning their brother Phaethon, are changed into poplars; when their mother strips bark and twigs, they drip blood, while their *Tears* harden into *Amber*: see e.g. *Metamorphoses*, 2. 340–66   110 *bespeak*: make arrangements for, order

Roger L'Estrange, Translator, Five Love-Letters from a Nun to a Cavalier *(1678)*

THE authorship of these stylish texts is uncertain. When first published as *Les Lettres portugaises* (1669), they were presented as translations from an actual correspondence. Early rumours identified the addressee as Noël Bouton, Chevalier de Chamilly. Insecure testimony claimed that the nun was one Mariana Alcoforada. Most scholars now believe that the letters were composed in French (not taken from Portuguese) by Gabriel-Joseph de la Vergne de Guilleragues. *Les Lettres* made their way so quickly into several languages that it would indeed be appropriate if they were written to be read as translations. Though their English renderer Roger L'Estrange (1616–1704) maintains the claim that private affairs are recorded in them, he also knows that they belong to a genre. In a note 'To the Reader' he calls *Les Lettres* 'one of the most Artificial Pieces perhaps of the Kind, that is anywhere Extant'. It is not hard to find traits in the epistles which relate them to earlier complaints (some are listed above, pp. 68–9). To read no further than the first letter, however—with its distressed unfocusing of pronouns, quicksilver deployment of question and exclamation, and alertly straggling farewell ('I cannot quitt this Paper yet . . . Mad fool that I am, to talk at this Rate . . . ')—is to find a rhetorical extravagance within the rush of informal prose scarcely matched in previous texts. Psychologically, too, the *Five Love-Letters* are absorbing. Mariane explores her predicament in a spiralling obsessive movement (enabled by her prose medium) which returns to such motifs as the cavalier's betraying eyes, her desire to serve, revenge, suicide, but which matures through anger to scorn. At the start of *Novas cartas portuguesas* (1972) the feminist authors write: 'We have also agreed that what is of interest is not so much the object of our passion, which is a mere pretext, but passion itself.' This distinction is in the texts they start from; writing bears in upon Mariane an awareness that her love 'does not at all depend upon your Manner of treating me' but has a rationale of its own. All the other plaints in this anthology explore a given predicament. The nun's epistles go further, in that they register the effect of reading the cavalier's replies. Complaint becomes a process, and we are left to infer motives, shifting and interactive, left textually blank by the nun. One measure of the potency of these gaps is their prompting the publication of *the Cavalier's Answers* in some editions of the *Five Love-Letters*. That the supposed replies offer an apologia for the lover, imputing self-deception and hysteria to Mariane, suggests that, while her critique of the cavalier's masculine egotism is, by most twentieth-century standards, mild, it had enough edge and impact to disconcert at least some early readers.

FIVE LOVE-LETTERS FROM A NUN TO A CAVALIER

Done out of French into English

The First Letter

Oh my Inconsiderate, Improvident, and most unfortunate Love; and those Treacherous Hopes that have betray'd both Thee, and Me! The Passion that I design'd for the Blessing of my Life, is become the Torment of it: A Torment, as prodigious as the Cruelty of his Absence that causes it. Bless mee! But must this Absence last for ever? This Hellish   5
Absence, that Sorrow it self wants words to express? Am I then never to see those Eyes again, that have so often exchang'd Love with Mine, and Charm'd my very soul with Extacy, and Delight? Those Eyes that were ten thousand worlds to mee, and all that I desir'd; the only comfortable Light of Mine, which, since I understood the Resolution of your Insup-   10
portable Departure, have Serv'd mee but to weep withall, and to lament the sad Approach of my Inevitable fate. And yet in this Extremity I cannot, me-thinks, but have some Tenderness, even for the Misfortunes that are of your Creating. My Life was vow'd to you the first time I saw you: and since you would not accept of it as a Present, I am   15
Content to make it a sacrifice. A Thousand times a day I send my Sighs to hunt you out: and what Return for all my Passionate Disquiets, but the good Counsel of my Cross fortune? that whispers me at every turn; Ah wretched *Mariane*! why do'st thou flatter, and Consume thy self in the vain pursuit of a Creature never to be Recover'd? Hee's gone, hee's   20
gone; Irrevocably gone; h'as past the seas to fly thee. Hee's now in *France*; dissolv'd in pleasures; and thinks no more of thee, or what thou suffer'st for his false sake, then if he had never known any such woman. But hold: Y'ave more of Honour in you then to do so ill a thing; and so have I, then to believe it, especially of a Person that I'm so much con-   25

cern'd to justify. *Forget me?* 'Tis Impossible. My Case is bad enough at best, without the Aggravation of vain suppositions. No, no: The Care and Pains you took to make me think you lov'd me, and then the Joyes that That Care gave Me, must never be forgotten: and Should I love you less this Moment, then when I lov'd you most, (in Confidence that you lov'd me so too) I were Ungratefull. 'Tis an Unnatural, and a strange thing methinks, that the Remembrance of those blessed hours should be now so terrible to me; and that those delights that were so ravishing in the Enjoyment, should become so bitter in the Reflection. Your last Letter gave me such a Passion of the heart, as if it would have forc'd its way thorough my Breast, and follow'd you. It laid me three hours sensless: I wish it had been *dead*; for I had dy'd of Love. But I reviv'd: and to what End? only to die again, and lose that Life for you, which you your Self did not think worth the saving. Beside that there's no Rest for me, while you're Away, but in the grave. This fit was fol- low'd with other Ill Accidents which I shall never be without, till I see you. In the mean while, I bear them yet without repining, because they came from you. But with your Leave: Is this the Recompense that you intend me? Is this your way of treating those that love you? Yet 'tis no Matter, for (do what you will) I am resolv'd to be firm to you to my last gasp; and never to see the Eyes of any other Mortal. And I dare assure you that it will not be the worse for you neither, if you never set your heart upon any other woman: for certainly a Passion under the degree of mine, will never content you: You may find more Beauty perhaps elsewhere (tho' the time was when you found no fault with mine) but you shall never meet with so true a heart; and all the rest is nothing.

Let me entreat you not to stuff your Letters with things Unprofitable, and Impertinent to our Affair: and you may save your self the trouble too of desiring me to THINK of you. Why 'tis Impossible for me to forget you: and I must not forget the hope you gave me neither, of your Return, and of spending some part of your time here with us in *Port- ugal*. Alas! And why not your whole Life rather? If I could but find any way to deliver my self from this unlucky Cloyster, I should hardly stand gaping here for the performance of your Promise: but in defiance of all opposition, put my self upon the March, Search you out, follow you, and love you throughout the whole world. It is not that I please my self with this Project as a thing feasible; or that I would so much as entertain any hope of Comfort; (tho' in the very delusion I might find pleasure) but as it is my Lot to be miserable, I will be only sensible of that which is my Doom. And yet after all this, I cannot deny but upon this Opportun- ity of writing to you which my Brother has given me, I was surpriz'd with some faint Glimmerings of Delight, that yielded me a temporary

Respite to the horrour of my despair. Tell me I conjure you; what was it that made you so sollicitous to entangle me, when you knew you were to leave me? And why so bloudily bent to make me Unhappy? why could   70
you not let me alone at quiet in my Cloyster as you found me? Did I ever do you any Injury?

But I must ask your Pardon; for I lay nothing to your Charge. I am not in condition to meditate a Revenge: and I can only complain of the Rigour of my Perverse fortune. When she has parted our Bodies, she   75
has done her worst, and left us nothing more to fear: Our hearts are Inseparable; for those whom Love has United are never to be divided. As you tender my soul let me hear often from you. I have a Right methinks to the Knowledg both of your Heart, and of your fortune; and to your Care to inform me of it too. But *what ever you do, be sure to come;*   80
and above all things in the world, to let me see you. Adieu. And yet I cannot quitt this Paper yet. Oh that I could but convey my self in the Place on't! Mad fool that I am, to talk at this Rate of a thing that I my self know to be Impossible! *Adieu.* For I can go no farther. *Adieu.* Do but Love me for ever, and I care not what I endure.   85

The Second Letter

There is so great a difference betwixt the Love I write, and That which I feel, that if you measure the One by the Other, I have undone my self. Oh how happy were I if you could but judg of my Passion by the violence of your own! But That I perceive is not to be the Rule betwixt you, and me. Give me leave however to tell you with an honest freedom,   5
that tho' you cannot love me, you do very ill yet to treat me at this Barbarous Rate: It puts me out of my Wits to see my self forgotten; and it is as little for your Credit perhaps, as it is for my Quiet. Or if I may not say that you are Unjust, it is yet the most Reasonable thing in the World to let me tell you that I am Miserable: I foresaw what it would   10
come to, upon the very Instant of your Resolution to leave me. Weak Woman that I was! to expect, (after this) that you should have more Honour, and Integrity then other Men, because I had unquestionably deserv'd it from you, by a transcendent degree of Affection above the Love of Other Women. No, no; Your Levity, and Aversion have over-   15
rul'd your Gratitude, and Justice; you are my Enemy by Inclination: whereas only the Kindness of your Disposition can Oblige me. Nay your Love it self, if it were barely grounded upon my Loving of you, could never make me happy. But so far am I even from that Pretence, that in six Moneths I have not receiv'd one sillable from you; Which I   20

78 *tender*: value   19 *that Pretence*: being able to claim that

must impute to the blind fondness of my own Passion, for I should
otherwise have foreseen that my Comforts were to be but Temporary,
and my Love Everlasting. For Why should I think that you would ever
content your self to spend your Whole Life in *Portugal*; and relinquish
your Country, and your fortune, only to think of me? Alas! my sorrows   25
are Inconsolable, and the very Remembrance of my past Enjoyments
makes up a great part of my present pain. But must all my hopes be
blasted then, and fruitless? Why may not I yet live to see you again
within these Walls, and with all those Transports of Extacy, and
Satisfaction, as heretofore? But how I fool my self! for I find now that   30
the Passion, which on my side, took up all the faculties of my soul, and
Body, was only excited on your part by some loose Pleasures, and that
they were to live and die together. It should have been my Business,
even in the Nick of those Critical, and Blessed Minutes, to have
Reasoned my self into the Moderation of so Charming, and deadly an   35
Excess; and to have told my self before-hand, the fate which I now
suffer. But my Thoughts were too much taken up with You to consider
my self; So that I was not in Condition to attend the Care of my Repose,
or to bethink my self of what might poison it, and disappoint me in the
full Emprovement of the most Ardent Instances of your Affection. I was   40
too much pleas'd with you, to think of parting with you, and yet you may
remember that I have told you now and then by fits, that you would be
the Ruin of me. But those Phancies were soon dispers'd; and I was glad
to yield them up too; and to give up my self to the Enchantments of your
false Oaths, and Protestations. I see very well the Remedy of all my   45
Misfortunes, and that I should quickly be at Ease if I could leave Loving
you. But Alas! That were a Remedy worse then the disease. No, no: I'le
rather endure any thing then forget you. Nor could I if I would. 'Tis a
thing that did never so much as enter into my Thought. But is not your
Condition now the worse of the two? Is it not better to endure what I   50
now suffer, then to enjoy Your faint satisfactions among your French
Mistresses? I am so far from Envying your Indifference, that I Pitty it. I
defie you to forget me absolutely: and I am deceiv'd if I have not taken
such a Course with you, that you shall never be perfectly happy without
me. Nay perhaps I am at this Instant the less miserable of the two; in   55
regard that I am the more employ'd. They have lately made me door-
keeper here in this Convent. All the people that talk to me think me
mad; for I answer them I know not what; And certainly the rest of the
Convent must be as mad as I, they would never else have thought me
Capable of any Trust. How do I envy the good Fortune of poor *Eman-*   60
uel, and *Francisco*! Why cannot I be with you perpetually as they are? tho

40 *Emprovement*: experiencing

in your Livery too? I should follow you as Close without dispute, and serve you at least as faithfully; for there is nothing in this World that I so much desire as to see you; But however, let me entreat you to think of me; and I shall Content my self with a bare place in your Memory. And yet I cannot tell neither, whether I should or no: for I know very well that when I saw you every day I should hardly have satisfy'd my self within these Bounds. But you have taught me since, that whatsoever you will have me do, I must do. In the *Interim*, I do not at all repent of my Passion for you; Nay, I am well enough satisfi'd that you have seduc'd me; and your Absence it self tho' never so rigorous, and perhaps Eternal, does not at all lessen the vigour of my Love: which I will avow to the Whole world, for I make no secret on't. I have done many things irregularly 'tis true; and against the Common Rules of good Manners: and not without taking some Glory in them neither, because they were done for your sake. My honour, and Religion are brought only to serve the Turn of my Love, and to carry me on to my lives end, in the Passionate Continuance of the Affection I have begun. I do not write this, to draw a Letter from you; wherefore never force your self for the Matter: for I will receive nothing at your hands; no not so much as any Mark of your Affection, unless it comes of its own accord, and in a Manner, whether you Will or No. If it may give you any satisfaction, to save your self the trouble of Writing, it shall give me some likewise, to excuse the Unkindness of it; for I am wonderfully enclin'd to pass over all your faults. A *French* Officer, that had the Charity this morning to hold me at least three hours in a discourse of you, tells me that *France* has made a Peace. If it be so; Why cannot you bestow a visit upon me, and take me away with you? But 'tis more then I deserve, and it must be as you please; for my Love does not at all depend upon your Manner of treating me. Since you went away I have not had one Minutes Health, nor any sort of Pleasure, but in the Accents of your Name, which I call upon a Thousand times a day. Some of my Companions that understand the deplorable Ruin you have brought upon me, are so good as to entertain me many times concerning you. I keep as Close to my Chamber as is possible; which is the dearer to me even for the many Visits you have made me there. Your Picture I have perpetually before me, and I Love it more then my hearts bloud. The very Counterfeit gives me some Comfort: But oh the Horrours too! When I consider that the Original, for ought I know, is lost for ever. But why should it be possible, even to be possible, that I may never see you more? Have you forsaken me then for ever? It turns my Brain to think on't. Poor *Mariane*! But my Spirits fail me, and I shall scarce out-live this Letter?—Mercy—Farwel, Farwel.

The Third Letter

What shall become of me? Or what will you advise me to do? How strangely am I disappointed, in all my Expectations! Where are the Letters from you? the Long and Kind Letters that I look'd for by every Post? To keep me alive in the hopes of Seeing you again; and in the Confidence of your faith, and Justice; to settle me in some tolerable state of Repose, without being abandon'd to any insupportable Extream? I had once cast my Thoughts upon some Idle Projects of endeavouring my own Cure, in Case I could but once assure my self that I was totally forgotten. The distance you were at; Certain Impulses of Devotion; the fear of utterly destroying the Remainder of my Imperfect health, by so many restless Nights, and Cares; the Improbability of your Return; The Coldness of your Passion, and the Formality of your last *Adieu's*; Your Weak, and frivolous pretences for your departure: These, with a thousand other Considerations, (of more weight, then profit) did all concurre to encourage me in my design, if I should find it necessary; In fine; having only my single self to encounter I could not doubt of the success, nor could it enter into my Apprehension what I feel at this day. Alas! how wretched is my Condition, that am not allow'd so much as to divide these sorrows with you, of which you your self are the Cause? You are the Offender, and I am to bear the Punishment of your Crime. It strikes me to the very heart, for fear you, that are now so Insensible of my Torments, were never much affected with our mutual delights. Yes, yes; 'Tis now a Clear Case that your whole Address to me was only an Artificial disguise. You betray'd me as often as you told me, how over-joy'd you were that you had got me alone: and your Passions, and Transports were only the Effects of my own Importunities. Yours was a deliberate design to fool me; your business was to make a Conquest, not a friend; and to triumph over my Heart, without ever engaging or hazzarding your own. Are not you very Unhappy now, and (at least) Ill-natur'd, if not ill-bred, only to make this wretched use of so Superlative a friendship? Who would have thought it possible that such a Love as mine, should not have made you happy? 'Tis for your sake alone if I am troubl'd for the Infinite delights that you have lost, and might as easily have enjoy'd, had you but thought them worth the while. Ah! If you did but understand them aright, you would find a great difference betwixt the Pleasure of Obliging me, and that of Abusing me; and betwixt the Charming felicities of Loving violently, and of being so belov'd. I do not know either what I am, or what I do, or what I would be at. I am torn to pieces by a Thousand contrary Motions, and in a Condition deplorable beyond imagination. I love you to death, and

5
10
15
20
25
30
35
40

so tenderly too that I dare hardly wish your heart in the same condition with mine. I should destroy my self, or die with Grief, could I believe your nights and Thoughts, as restless as I find Mine; your Life as Anxious and disturb'd; your Eyes still flowing and all things and people Odious to you. Alas! I am hardly able to bear up under my own Mis-   45 fortunes; how should I then Support the Weight of yours; which would be a Thousand times more grievous to me? And yet all this While I cannot bring my self to advise you, not to Think of me. And to deal freely with you, there is not any thing in *France* that you take pleasure in, or that comes near your heart, but I'm most furiously jealous of it. I do   50 not know what 'tis I write for. Perhaps you'l pitty me; but what good will that pitty do me? I'le none on't. Oh how I hate my self when I consider what I have forfeited to oblige you! I have blasted my Reputation; I have lost my Parents; I have expos'd my self to the Lawes of my Country against Persons of my Profession; and finally, to your Ingratitude, the   55 worst of my Misfortunes. But why do I pretend to a Remorse, when at this Instant, I should be glad with all my Soul, if I had run ten thousand greater hazzards for your dear Sake? and for the danger of my Life and Honour; the very thought on't is a kind of doleful Pleasure to me, and all's no more then the delivery of whats your own, and what I hold most   60 Pretious, into your Disposition; And I do not know how all these risques could have been better Imploy'd. Upon the Whole matter, every thing displeases me, my Love, my Misfortune; and alas! I cannot perswade my self that I am well us'd even by You. And yet I Live, (false as I am) and take as much pains to preserve my life, as to lose it. Why do   65 I not die of shame then, and shew you the despair of my Heart, as well as of my Letters? If I had lov'd you so much as I have told you a thousand times I did, I had been in my Grave long ere this. But I have deluded you, and the Cause of Complaint is now on your side. Alas! why did you not tell me of it? Did I not see you go away? Am I not out of   70 all hopes of ever seeing you again? And am I yet alive? I have betray'd you, and I beg your pardon. But do not grant it though; Treat me as severely as you will: Tell me that my Passion is Weak, and Irresolute. Make your self yet harder to be pleas'd. Write me word that you would have me die for you. Do it, I conjure you; and assist me in the Work of   75 surmounting the Infirmity of my Sex; and that I may put an end to all my fruitless deliberations, by an effectual despair. A Tragical Conclu- sion would undoubtedly bring me often into your thoughts, and make my Memory dear to you. And who knows how you might be Affected, with the Bravery of so Glorious a death? A death Incomparably to be   80 preferr'd before the Life that you have left me. Farwel then; and *I wish I had never seen the Eyes of you*. But my heart Contradicts my Pen; for I feel, in the very moment that I write it, that I would rather chuse to Love you in any state of Misery, then agree to the bare Supposition that I had never Seen you. Wherefore since you do not think fit, to mend my fortune, I shall chearfully submit to the worst on't. *Adieu*; but first promise me, that if I die of grief, you will have some Tenderness for my Ashes: Or at least that the Generosity of my Passion shall put you out of Love with all other things. This Consolation shall satisfie me, that if you must never be mine, I may be secur'd that you shall never be Anothers. You cannot be so Inhumane sure, as to make a mean use of my most Affectionate despairs, and to recommend your self to any other Woman, by shewing the Power you have had upon me. Once more, *Adieu*. My Letters are long, and I fear troublesom; but I hope you'l forgive them, and dispense with the fooleries of a Sot of your own making. *Adieu*. Me-thinks I run over and over too often with the story of my most deplorable Condition: Give me leave now to thank you from the Bottom of my heart for the Miseries you have brought upon me, and to detest the Tranquillity I liv'd in before I knew you. My Passion is greater every Moment than other. *Adieu*. Oh what a World of things have I to tell you!

The Fourth Letter

Your Lieutenant tells me that you were forc'd by foul Weather to put in upon the Coast of *Algarve*. I am afraid the Sea does not agree with you; and my Fears for your Misfortunes make me almost to forget my own. Can you imagin your Lieutenant to be more concern'd in what befals you, than I am? If not, How comes he to be so well inform'd, and not one sillable to me? If you could never find the means of writing to me since you went, I am very Unhappy; but I am more so, if you could have written, and would not. But what should a body expect from so much Ingratitude, and Injustice? And yet it would break my heart, if heaven should punish you upon any account of mine. For I had much rather   10 gratifie my Kindness, than my Revenge. There can be nothing clearer, than that you neither Love me, nor Care what becomes of me; and yet am I so foolish, as to follow the Dictate of a blind, and besotted Passion, in oposition to the Counsels of a demonstrative Reason. This Coldness of yours, when you and I were first acquainted, would have sav'd me   15 many a sorrowful Thought. But where's the Woman, that in my Place, would have done otherwise than I did? Who would ever have question'd the Truth of so pressing and Artificial an Importunity? We cannot easily bring our selves to suspect the Faith of those we Love. I know very well,

18 *Artificial*: conducted with great artifice

that a slender Excuse will serve your Turn; and I'le be so kind as to save
you even the Labour of That too, by telling you, that I can never consent to conclude you guilty, but in order to the infinite Pleasure I shall
take to acquit you, in perswading my self that you are Innocent. It was
the Assiduity of your Conversation that refin'd me; your Passion that
inflam'd me; Your good Humour that Charm'd me; your Oaths, and   25
Vows that confirm'd me; but 'twas my own precipitate Inclination that
seduc'd me; and what's the Issue of these fair, and promising Beginnings, but Sighs, Tears, Disquiets, nay, and the worst of Deaths too,
without either Hope, or Remedy. The Delights of my Love, I must
confess, have been strangely surprizing; but follow'd with Miseries not   30
to be express'd; (as whatever comes from you works upon me in
Extreams). If I had either obstinately oppos'd your Address; or done
any thing to put you out of humour, or make you jealous, with a design
to draw you on: If I had gon any crafty, artificial wayes to work with you;
or but so much as check'd my early, and my growing Inclinations to   35
comply with you, (tho' it would have been to no purpose at all) you
might have had some Colour then to make use of your Power, and deal
with me accordingly. But so far was I from opposing your Passion, that I
prevented it; for I had a kindness for your Person, before you ever told
me any thing of your Love; and you had no sooner declar'd it, but with   40
all the joy imaginable I receiv'd it, and gave my self up wholly to that
Inclination. You had at that time your Eyes in your Head, tho' I was
Blind. Why would you let me go on then to make my self the miserable
Creature which now I am? Why would you train me on to all those
Extravagances which to a person of your Indifference must needs have   45
been very Importune? You knew well enough that you were not to be
always in *Portugal*; Why must I then be singl'd out from all the rest, to
be made thus Unfortunate? In this Country without dispute you might
have found out handsomer Women than my self, that would have serv'd
your turn every jot as well, (to your course purpose) and that would have   50
been true to you as far as they could have seen you, without breaking
their hearts for you, when you were gon: and such as you might have
forsaken at last, without either Falsness, or Cruelty: Do you call this the
Tenderness of a Lover, or the Persecution of a Tyrant? And 'tis but
destroying of your own neither. You are just as easie, I find, to believe ill   55
of me, as I have always been to think better of you than you have
deserv'd. Had you but lov'd me half so well as I do you, you would
never have parted with me upon so easie Terms. I should have master'd
greater Difficulties, and never have upbraided you with the Obligation
neither. Your Reasons, 'tis true, were very feeble, but if they had been   60
the strongest imaginable, it had been all one to me: for nothing but

death it self could ever have torn me from you. Your Return into *France* was nothing in the World but a Pretext of your own contriving. *There was a Vessel* (you said) *that was thither bound.* And why could not you let that Vessel take her Course? *Your Relations sent for you away.* You are no stranger sure to the Persecution, that for your sake, I have suffer'd from mine. *Your Honour* (forsooth) *engag'd you to forsake me.* Why did you not think of that scruple, when you deluded me to the loss of mine? *Well! but you must go back to serve your Prince.* His Majesty, I presume, would have excus'd you in that point; for I cannot learn that he has any need of your Service. But, Alas! I should have been too happy, if you and I might have liv'd, and dy'd together. This only Comfort I have in the bitterness of our deadly separation, that I was never false to you; and that for the whole World I would not have my Conscience tainted with so black a Crime. But can you then, that know the Integrity of my Soul, and the Tenderness that I have for you; can you (I say) find in your heart to abandon me for ever, and expose me to the Terrours that attend my wretched Condition? Never so much as to think of me again, but only when you are to sacrifice me to a new Passion. My Love, you see, has distracted me; and yet I make no complaint at all of the violence of it: for I am so wonted to Persecutions, that I have discover'd a kind of pleasure in them, which I would not live without, and which I enjoy, while I love you, in the middle of a thousand afflictions. The most grievous part of my Calamity, is the hatred, and disgust that you have given me for all other things: My Friends, my Kindred, the Convent it self is grown intollerable to me; and whatsoever I am oblig'd either to see, or to do, is become odious. I am grown so jealous of my Passion, that methinks all my Actions, and all my Dutys ought to have some regard to you. Nay, every moment that is not employ'd upon your service, my Conscience checks me for it, either as misbestow'd, or cast away. My Heart is full of Love, and Hatred; and, Alas! what should I do without it? should I survive this restlessness of thought, to lead a Life of more tranquility, and ease, such an Emptiness, and such an Insensibility could never consist. Every Creature takes Notice how strangely I am chang'd in my Humour, my Manners, and in my Person. My Mother takes me to task about it: One while she speaks me fair, and then she chides me, and asks me what I ail. I do not well know what answers I have made her; but I Phancy that I have told her all. The most severe, even of the Religious themselves, take pity of me, and bear with my Condition. The whole World is touch'd with my Misfortunes; your single self excepted, as wholy unconcern'd: Either you are not pleas'd to write at all; or else your Letters are so cold; so stuff'd with Repetitions; the Paper not half full, and your Constraint so grosly disguis'd, that one may see with half an Eye the pain you are in till they are over. *Dona Brites* would not let me be quiet the other day, till she had got me out of my Chamber, on to the Balcon that looks (you know) toward *Mertola*: she did it to oblige me, and I follow'd her: But the very sight of the Place struck me with so terrible an Impression, that it set me a Crying the whole day after. Upon this, she took me back again, and I threw my self upon my Bed, where I pass'd a thousand Reflections upon the despairs of my Recovery. I am the worse I find for that which people do to relieve me; and the Remedies they offer me do but serve to aggravate my Miseries. Many a time have I seen you pass by from this Balcon; (and the sight pleas'd me but too well) and there was I that fatal day, when I first found my self strook with this unhappy Passion. Methought you look'd as if you had a mind to oblige me, even before you knew me; and your Eye was more upon me than the rest of the Company. And when you made a stop, I fool'd my self to think that it was meant to me too, that I might take a fuller view of you, and see how every thing became you. Upon giving your Horse the spur (I remember) my heart was at my mouth for fear of an untoward leap you put him upon. In fine; I could not but secretly concern my self in all your Actions; and as you were no longer indifferent to me, so I took several things to my self also from you; and as done in my favour. I need not tell you the sequel of Matters (not that I care who knows it) nor would I willingly write the whole Story, lest I should make you thought more culpable (if possible) than in Effect (perhaps) you are. Beside that it might furnish your Vanity with subject of reproach, by shewing that all my Labours, and Endeavours to make sure of you, could not yet keep you from forsaking me. But what a fool am I, in thinking to work more upon your Ingratitude, with Letters, and Invectives, than ever I could with my Infinite Love, and the liberty that attended it! No, no: I am too sure of my ill Fortune, and you are too unjust to make me doubt of it; and since I find my self deserted, what mischief is there in Nature which I am not to fear? But are your Charms only to work upon me? Why may not other Women look upon you with my Eyes? I should be well enough content perhaps to find more of my Sex (in some degree) of my Opinion; and that all the Ladyes of *France* had an esteem for you, provided that none of them either doted upon you, or pleas'd you: This is a most ridiculous, and an impossible Proposition. But there's no danger (I may speak it upon sad Experience) of your troubling your head long with any one thing; and you will forget me easily enough, without the help of being forc'd to't by a new Passion. So infinitely do I love you, that (since I am to lose you) I could e'en wish that you had had some fairer colour for't.

115 *strook*: struck

It is true, that it would have made me more miserable; but you should 145
have had less to answer for then. You'l stay in *France*, I perceive, in
perfect Freedom, and perhaps not much to your Satisfaction; The
Incommodities of a long Voyage; some Punctilioes of good Manners;
and the fear of not returning Love for Love, may perchance keep you
there. Oh, you may safely trust me in this Case: Let me but only see you 150
now and then, and know that we are both of us in the same Country, it
shall content me. But why do I flatter my self? Who knows but that the
Rigour and Severity of some other Woman may come to prevail upon
you more than all my Favours? tho' I cannot believe you yet to be a
Person that will be wrought upon by ill usage. 155
    Before you come to engage in any powerful Passion, let me entreat
you to bethink your self of the Excess of my Sorrows; the Uncertainty of
my Purposes; the Distraction of my Thoughts; the Extravagance of my
Letters; the Trusts I have repos'd in you; my Despairs, my Wishes, and
my Jealousies. Alas! I am affraid that you are about to make your self 160
unfortunate. Take warning, I beg of you, by my Example, and make
some Use to your self of the Miseries that I endure for you. I remember
you told me in Confidence, (and in great Earnest too) some five, or six
Months ago, that you had once a Passion for a *French* Lady. If she be
any Obstacle to your Return, deal frankly with me, and put me out of 165
my Pain. It will be a kind of Mercy to me, if the faint hope which yet
Supports me, must never take effect, even to lose my Life, and that
together. Pray'e send me her picture, and Some of her Letters, and
write me all she says. I shall find Something there undoubtedly that will
make me either better, or worse. In the Condition that I am, I cannot 170
long continue; and any Change whatsoever must be to my Advantage. I
should take it kindly if you would send me your Brothers, and your
Sisters pictures too. Whatsoever is dear to you must be so to me; and I
am a very faithful Servant to any thing that is related to you: and it
cannot be otherwise: for you have left me no power at all to dispose of 175
my self. Sometimes me-thinks I could Submit even to attend upon the
Woman that you Love. So low am I brought by your Scorns, and ill
Usage, that I dare not so much as say to my self, *Methinks I might be
allow'd to be jealous, without displeasing you.* Nay, I chide my self as the
most mistaken Creature in the World to blame you: and I am many 180
times convinc'd that I ought not to importune you as I do, with those
passages, and thoughts which you are pleas'd to disown.
    The Officer that waits for this Letter grows a little Impatient: I had
once resolv'd to keep it clear from any possibility of giving you Offence.
But it is broken out into Extravagances, and 'tis time to put an end to't. 185
But Alas! I have not the heart to give it over. When I write to you, me-

thinks I speak to you: and our Letters bring us nearer together. The first shall be neither So long, nor So troublesome. But you may venture to open it, and read it upon the assurance that I now give you. I am not to entertain you, I know, with a Passion that displeases you, and you shall hear no more on't. It is now a year within a few days, that I have deliver'd my self wholly up to you, without any Reserve. Your Love I took to be both Warm, and Sincere: And I could never have thought you would have been so weary of my favours, as to take a Voyage of five hundred leagues; and run the Hazzards of Rocks, and Pirates, only to avoid them. This is a Treatment that certainly I never deserv'd at any mans hands. You can call to mind my Shame, my Confusion, and my Disorders. But you have forgotten the Obligations you had to Love me even in despite of your Aversion. The Officer calls upon me now the fourth time for my Letter. He will go away without it, he Says; and presses me, as if he were running away from another Mistress. Farwell. You had not half the difficulty to leave me (tho' perhaps for ever) which I have, only to part with this Letter. But *Adieu*. There are a thousand tender names that I could call you now. But I dare not deliver my self up to the freedom of Writing my thoughts. You are a thousand times dearer to me than my Life, and a thousand times more than I imagine too. Never was any thing So barbarous, and so much belov'd. I must needs tell you once again, that *you do not write to me*. But I am now going to begin afresh, and *the Officer will be gone*. Well, and what matters it? Let him go. 'Tis not so much for your sake that I write, as my own; for my Business is only to divert, and entertain my self: Beside that the very Length of this Letter will make you afraid on't: And you'le never read it thorough neither. What Have I done to draw all these Miseries upon me? And why should you of all others be the poisoner of my peace, and blast the Comfort of my Life? Why was I not born in some other Country? forgive me, and farwell. See but to what a Miserable point I am reduc'd, when I dare not so much as intreat you to Love me. *Adieu*.

The Fifth Letter

You will find, I hope, by the different Ayre and stile of this Letter, from all my former, that I have chang'd my Thoughts too; and you are to take this for an Eternal farwell; for I am now at length perfectly convinc'd, that since I have Irrecoverably lost your Love, I can no longer justify my own. Whatsoever I had of Yours shall be sent you by the first Opportunity: There shall be no more writing in the Case; No, not so much as your Name upon the Pacquett. *Dona Brites* is a Person whom I can trust as my own soul, and whom I have entrusted (as you know very well),

Unfortunate Wretch that I am! in Confidences of another Quality
betwixt you and me. I have left it to her Care to see your Picture and 10
your Bracelets dispatch'd away to you, (those once beloved Pledges of
your Kindness) and only in due time to assure me that you have receiv'd
them. Would you believe me now, if I should swear to you, that within
these five days, I have been at least fifty times upon the very point of
Burning the One, and of Tearing the Other into a Million of Pieces? 15
But, You have found me too easy a fool, to think me Capable of so
Generous an Indignation. If I could but vex you a little in the story of
my Misfortunes; it would be some sort of Abatement me-thinks to the
Cruelty of them. Those Bawbles (I must confess, both to Your shame,
and Mine) went nearer my heart than I am willing to tell you, and when 20
it came to the Pinch of parting with them, I found it the hardest thing in
the World to go thorough with it: So Mortal a Tenderness had I for any
thing of Yours, even at that Instant when you your self seem'd to me the
most Indifferent thing in Nature: But there's no resisting the force of
Necessity and Reason. This Resolution has cost me Many, and Many a 25
Tear; A thousand, and a thousand Agonies, and Distractions, more
than you can imagine; and more, Undoubtedly, than you shall ever hear
of from me. *Dona Brites* (I say) has them in Charge; upon Condition,
never to name them to Me again; No, not so much as to give me a sight
of them, though I should beg for't upon my Knees; but, in fine, to 30
hasten them away, without one Syllable to Me of their Going.

If it had not been for this Trial to get the Mastery of my Passion, I
should never have understood the force of it; and if I could have foreseen the Pains, and the hazzards of the Encounter, I am afraid that I
should never have ventur'd upon the Attempt: for I am verily 35
perswaded that I could much better have Supported your Ingratitude it
self, though never so foul, and Odious than the Deadly, Deadly
Thought of this Irrevocable Separation. And it is not your Person
neither that is so dear to me, but the Dignity of my unalterable Affection. My soul is strangely divided; Your falseness makes me abhor you, 40
and yet at the same time my Love, my Obstinate, and Invincible Love,
will not consent to part with you.

What a Blessing were it to me now, if I were but endu'd with the
Common Quality of other Women, and only Proud enough to despise
you? Alas! Your Contempt I have born already: Nay, had it been your 45
Hatred, or the most Raging Jealousie; All this, compar'd with your
Indifference, had been a Mercy to me. By the Impertinent Professions,
and the most Ridiculous Civilities of your Last Letter, I find that all
mine are Come to your hand; and that you have read them over too: but
as unconcern'd, as if you forsooth had no Interest at all in the Matter. 50

Sot that I am, to lie thus at the Mercy of an Insensible, and Ungrateful Creature; and to be as much afflicted now at the Certainty of the Arrival of those Papers, as I was before, for fear of their Miscarriage! What have I to do with your telling me the *TRUTH OF THINGS*? Who desir'd to know it? Or the *SINCERITY* you talk of; a thing you never   55 practis'd toward me, but to my Mischief. Why could you not let me alone in my Ignorance? Who bad you Write? Miserable Woman that I am! Me-thinks after so much pains taken already to delude me to my Ruin, you might have streyn'd one point more, in this Extremity, to deceive me to my Advantage, without pretending to excuse your self.   60 'Tis too late to tell you that I have cast away many a Tender Thought upon the Worst of Men; the most Oblig'd, and the most Unthankful. Let it suffice that I know you now as well as if I were in the heart of you. The only favour that I have now to desire from you, after so many done for you, is This: (and I hope you will not refuse it me) Write no more to   65 me; and remember that I have conjur'd you never to do it. Do all that is Possible for you to do, (if ever you had any Love for me) to make me absolutely forget you. For Alas! I dare not trust my self in any sort of Correspondence with you. The least hint in the World of any kind Reflection upon the reading of this Letter, would perchance expose me   70 to a Relapse; and then the taking of me at my Word, on the other side, would most certainly transport me into an Extravagance of Choler, and Despair. So that in my Opinion it will be your best course not to meddle at all with Me, or my Affairs: for which way so ever you go to work, it must inevitably bring a great disorder upon both. I have no Curiosity to   75 know the success of this Letter: Me-thinks the Sorrows you have brought upon me already, might abundantly content you (even if your Design were never so malicious) without disturbing me in my Prepara-tions for my future Peace. Do but leave me in my Uncertainty, and I will not yet despair, in time, of arriving at some degree of Quiet. This I dare   80 promise you, that I shall never hate you; for I am too great an Enemy to Violent Resolutions ever to go about it. Who knows but I may yet live to find a truer friend than I have lost? But Alas! What signifies any mans Love to me, if I cannot Love him? Why should his Passion work more upon my heart, than mine could upon Yours? I have found by sad   85 Experience, that the first Motions of Love, which we are more properly said to Feel, than to Understand, are never to be forgotten: That our souls are perpetually Intent upon the Idol which we our selves have made: That the first Wounds, and the first Images are never to be cur'd, or defac'd: That all the Passions that pretend to succour us either by   90 Diversion, or Satisfaction, are but so many vain Promises of bringing us to our Wits again, which, if once lost, are never to be recover'd: And that all the Pleasures that we pursue, (many times without any desire of finding them) amount to no more, than to convince us, that nothing is so dear to us as the Remembrance of our Sorrows. Why must you pitch upon Mee, for the subject of an Imperfect, and Tormenting Inclination; which I can neither Relinquish with Temper, nor Preserve with Honour? The dismal Consequences of an Impetuous Love, which is not Mutual? And why is it that by a Conspiracy of Blind Affection, and Inexorable fate, we are still condemn'd to Love where we are Despis'd, and to hate where we are Belov'd?

But what if I could flatter my self with the Hope of diverting my Miseries by any other Engagement? I am so sensible of my own Condition, that I should make a very great scruple of Using any other Mortal as you have treated me. and though I am not Conscious of my Obligation to spare you, yet if it were in my Power to take my Revenge upon you, by changing you for any other, (a thing very Unlikely) I could never agree to the gratifying of my Passion that way.

I am now telling my self in your behalf, that it is not reasonable to expect, that the simplicity of a Religious should confine the Inclinations of a Cavalier. And yet methinks, if a body might be allow'd to reason upon the Actions of Love, a man should rather fix upon a Mistress in a Convent than any where else. For they have nothing there to hinder them from being perpetually Intent upon their Passion: Whereas in the World, there are a thousand fooleries, and Amusements, that either take up their Thoughts intirely, or at least divert them. And what Pleasure is it (or rather how great a Torment, if a body be not Stupid) for a man to see the Woman that he loves, in a Continual Hurry of Delights; taken up with Ceremony, and Visits; no discourses but of Balls, Dresses, Walks &c. Which must needs expose him every hour to fresh jealousies? Who can secure himself that Women are not better Satisfied with these Entertainments than they ought to be? even to the Disgusting of their own Husbands? How can any man pretend to Love, who without examining Particulars, contentedly believes what's told him, and looks upon his Mistress under all these Circumstances with Confidence, and Quiet? It is not that I am now Arguing my self into a Title to your Kindness, for this is not a way to do my business: especially after the Trial of a much more probable Method, and to as little purpose. No, no: I know my Destiny too Well, and there's no struling with it. My Whole Life is to be miserable. It was so, when I saw you every day; When we were together, for fear of your Infidelity; and at a distance, because I could not endure you out of my sight: My heart ak'd every time you came into the Convent; and my very life was at stake

95–6 *pitch upon Mee*: select me (implying some casualness)

when you were in the Army: It put me out of all Patience to consider
that neither my Person, nor Condition were Worthy of you: I was afraid   135
that your Pretensions to me might turn to your Damage: I could not
Love you enough me thought: I liv'd in dayly Apprehension of some
Mischief or other from my Parents: So that upon the Whole Matter, my
Case was not much better at that time then it is at present. Nay had you
but given me the least Proof of your Affection since you left *Portugal*, I   140
should most certainly have made my Escape, and follow'd you in a
disguise. And what would have become of me then, after the loss of my
honour, and my friends to see my self abandon'd in *France*? What a
Confusion should I have been in? What a plunge should I have been at?
What an Infamy should I have brought upon my family, which I do   145
assure you, since I left loving of you, is very dear to me. Take Notice I
pray'e, that in Cold thoughts I am very Sensible that I might have been
much more Miserable than I am; and that once in my Life I have talk'd
Reason to you: but whether my Moderation pleases you, or not; and
what Opinion soever you entertain of me, I beseech you keep it to your   150
self. I have desir'd you already, and I do now re-conjure you, never to
Write to me again.

Methinks you should sometimes reflect upon the Injuries you have
done me; and upon your Ingratitude to the most Generous Obligations
in Nature. I have Lov'd you to the degree of Madness; and to the   155
Contempt of all other things, and Mortals. You have not dealt with me
like a Man of honour. Nothing but a Natural Aversion could have kept
you even from adoring me. Never was any Woman bewitch'd upon So
easy terms. What did you ever do that might entitle you to my favour?
What did you ever Lose, or but so much as hazzard for my Sake? Have   160
you not entertain'd your self with a thousand other delights? No, not so
much as a Sett at Tennis, or a Hunting-Match, that you would ever
forbear upon any Accompt of Mine. Were you not still the first that
went to the Army, and the last that came back again? Were you ever the
more Careful of Your Person there, because I begg'd it of you, as the   165
greatest Blessing of my Soul? Did you ever so much as offer at the
Establishment of your fortune in *Portugal*? A place where you were so
much esteem'd. But one single Letter of your Brothers hurry'd you
away, without so much as a moments time to consider of it: and I am
certainly inform'd too, that you were never in better humour in your   170
Whole Life, than upon that Voyage. You your self cannot deny, but that
I have reason to hate you above all men Living; and yet, in Effect, I may
thank my Self; for I have drawn all these Calamities upon my own head.
I dealt too openly, and plainly with you at first: I gave you my heart too
soon. It is not Love alone that begets Love; there must be Skill, and   175

Address; for it is Artifice, and not Passion, that creates Affection. Your
first design was to make me Love you, and there was not any thing in
the World which you would not then have done, to compass that End:
Nay rather than fail, I am perswaded you would have lov'd Me too, if
you had judg'd it necessary. But you found out easier ways to do your   180
Business, and so thought it better to let the Love alone. Perfidious
Man! Can you ever think to carry off this Affront, without being call'd
to an Accompt for't? If ever you Set foot in *Portugal* again; I do declare it
to you, that I'le deliver you up to the Revenge of my Parents. It is a long
time that I have now liv'd in a kind of Licentious Idolatry, And the   185
Conscience of it strikes me with horrour, and an Insupportable
Remorse; I am Confounded with Shame of What I have done for your
Sake; and I have no longer (alas!) the Passion that kept the foulness of it
from my Sight. Shall this tormented heart of Mine never find ease? Ah
barbarous Man! When shall I see the End of this Oppression? And yet   190
after all this I cannot find in my heart to wish you any Sort of harm; Nay
in my Conscience I could be yet well enough content to see you happy;
which as the Case stands, is utterly Impossible.

Within a While, you may yet perhaps receive another Letter from me,
to shew you that I have outliv'd all your Outrages, and Philosophiz'd my   195
self into a state of Repose. Oh what a Pleasure will it be to me, when I
shall be able to tell you of your Ingratitude, and Treacheries, without
being any longer concern'd at them my Self! When I shall be able to
discourse of you with Scorn; When I shall have forgotten all my Griefs,
and Pleasures, and not so much as think of your Self, but when I have a   200
mind to't.

That you have had the better of me, 'tis true; for I have Lov'd you to
the very Loss of my Reason: But it is no less true that you have not
much cause to be proud on't. Alas I was young, and Credulous:
Cloyster'd up from a Child; and only Wonted to a rude, and disagree-   205
able sort of People. I never knew what belong'd to fine Words, and
Flatteries, till (most unfortunately) I came acquainted with you: And all
the Charmes, and Beauties you so often told me of, I only looked upon
as the Obliging Mistakes of your Civility, and Bounty. You had a good
Character in the World; I heard every body Speak well of you: and to all   210
this, you made it your Business to engage me; but you have now (I thank
you for't) brought me to my self again, and not without great need of
your Assistance. Your two last Letters I am resolv'd to keep, and to read
them over oftener than ever I did any of the former, for fear of a
Relapse. You may well afford them, I am sure, at the Price that they   215
have cost me. Oh how happy might I have been, if you would but have

215 *well afford*: easily spare, profitably sell

given me Leave to Love you for ever! I know very well that betwixt my Indignation, and your Infidelity, my present thoughts are in great Disorder. But remember what I tell you: I am not yet out of hope of a more peaceable Condition, which I will either Compass, or take some other 220 Course with my self; which I presume, you will be well enough content to hear of. But I will never have any thing more to do with you. I am a fool for saying the Same things over, and over again so often. I must leave you, and not so much as think of you. Now do I begin to Phansie that I shall not write to you again for all This; for what Necessity is 225 there that I must be telling of you at every turn how my Pulse beats?

Restoration Ovids

APHRA BEHN's paraphrase of *Heroides*, 5, was published in *Ovid's Epistles, Translated by Several Hands*, ed. John Dryden (1680). Confessedly without Latin, the poet (1640–89) was vulnerable to mockery—and received it in *A Satyr on Modern Translators* (1684), perhaps by Prior. But the freedom of Behn's adaptation was calculated. Her plastic, often impetuous rhymed couplets brilliantly rework an Ovid whose 'Verse' (as Dryden puts it) 'runs upon Carpet ground'. She frequently permits herself rhyming triplets (conventionally indicated by braces in the right margin), and studs her text with pithy saws (marked by inverted commas at the start of verse-lines). In larger effects, likewise, Behn follows her own bent. The added material on rival wooers of Paris and Oenone (25–41), like the comparison between court and country life (in the tradition of vernacular complaint) at 233 ff., socializes a relationship which, in Ovid, is private. Repeatedly she returns to gifts, tokens, charms (38–9, 209, 288–92). Behn is more concerned than Ovid with the physiological effects of love (40–51) and dread (113–20). Ostentatiously free in the last ninety or so lines, she sacrifices Cassandra's prophecy of Paris' infidelity, Oenone's account of the swift satyrs who pursue her, and the description of her skill as a gatherer of herbs. Not content to descant on *Heroides*, 5, Behn admits material from elsewhere in Ovid's collection. The formidable passage on Oenone's statue-like grief, her wind-tossed hair, and echoing voice is taken from Ariadne's self-description at *Heroides*, 10. 17–58 (adapted by Fletcher's Aspatia; above, pp. 228–9). Another *tour de force*, at 181–91 (cf. 162–71), depicts the groves of love in terms which derive from, yet finely modulate, the Sappho of *Heroides*, 15. 135–56. Like many women poets in this period, Aphra Behn had the name 'Sappho' applied to her. This mixed praise with abuse. For Sappho reached the Renaissance not only as a major writer, but as a wanton who, even when not representing lesbianism (as in Donne's 'Sapho to Philaenus'), was thought of as licentious. So sharp was the disparity between these images that two classical Sapphos were sometimes postulated; so urgent was the need to debase female authorship that the split was not generally accepted. In large measure Sappho's reputation for indulgence derived from *Heroides*, 15. This epistle, set in Sappho's later life, shows the poet succumbing to love for a man, Phaon. There is a mixture of delicious eroticism and humiliating abasement in the letter, which reads like the product of creative envy in its male author. Yet if the 'Sappho to Phaon' of *Heroides* is to some extent a travesty, how much more so is the text reprinted below. More forceful than telling, it carries to parodic extremes the kind of physiological emphases laid by Behn. The text is reproduced from a collection by Matthew Stevenson (*fl.* 1654–85), *Wits Paraphras'd: Or, Paraphrase upon Paraphrase. In a Burlesque on the Several Late Translations of Ovids Epistles* (1680)—a title which shows what a hostage to satire had been given by the looseness (in some sense) of Behn's 'Paraphrase', and a date which advertises what an instant success *Ovid's Epistles* had none the less been.

APHRA BEHN

A PARAPHRASE ON OENONE TO PARIS

The Argument

Hecuba *being with Child of* Paris, *dreamt she was delivered of a Firebrand;* Priam *consulting the Prophets, was answer'd the Child shou'd be the Cause of the Destruction of* Troy, *wherefore* Priam *commanded it should be deliver'd to wild Beasts as soon as born; but* Hecuba *conveys it secretly to Mount* Ida, *there to be foster'd by the Shepherds, where he falls in love with the Nymph* Oenone, *but at length being known and own'd, he sayls into* 5
Greece, *and carries* Helen *to* Troy, *which* Oenone *hearing, writes him this Epistle.*

To thee, dear *Paris*, Lord of my Desires,
Once tender Partner of my softest Fires;
To thee I write, mine, whilst a Shepherds Swain,
But now a Prince, that Title you disdain.
Oh fatal Pomp, that cou'd so soon divide   5
What Love, and all our Vows so firmly ty'd!
What God our Loves industrious to prevent,
Curst thee with power, and ruin'd my Content?
Greatness which does at best but ill agree
With Love, such Distance sets 'twixt Thee and Me.   10
Whilst thou a Prince, and I a Shepherdess,
My raging Passion can have no redress.
Wou'd God, when first I saw thee, thou hadst been
This Great, this Cruel, Celebrated thing,
That without hope I might have gaz'd and bow'd,   15

And mixt my Adoration with the Crowd;
Unwounded then I had escap'd those Eyes,
Those lovely Authors of my Miseries.
Not that less Charms their fatal pow'r had drest,
But Fear and Awe my Love had then supprest: 20
My unambitious Heart no Flame had known,
But what Devotion pays to Gods alone.
I might have wonder'd, and have wisht that He,
Whom Heaven shou'd make me love, might look like Thee.
More in a silly Nymph had been a sin,   25
This had the height of my Presumption been.
But thou a Flock didst feed on *Ida*'s Plain,
And hadst no Title, but *The lovely Swain*.
A Title! which more Virgin Hearts has won,
Then that of being own'd King *Priam*'s Son.   30
Whilst me a harmless Neighbouring Cottager
You saw, and did above the rest prefer.
You saw! and at first sight you lov'd me too,
Nor cou'd I hide the wounds receiv'd from you.
Me all the Village Herdsmen strove to gain,   ⎤   35
For me the Shepherds sigh'd and su'd in vain,   ⎬
Thou hadst my heart, and they my cold disdain.   ⎦
Not all their Offerings, Garlands, and first born
Of their lov'd Ewes, cou'd bribe my Native scorn.
My Love, like hidden Treasure long conceal'd,   40
Cou'd only where 'twas destin'd, be reveal'd.
And yet how long my Maiden blushes strove
Not to betray the easie newborn Love.
But at thy sight the kindling Fire wou'd rise,
And I, unskil'd, declare it at my Eyes.   45
But oh the Joy! the mighty Extasy
Possest thy Soul at this Discovery.
Speechless, and panting at my feet you lay,
And short-breath'd Sighs told what you cou'd not say.
A thousand times my hand with Kisses prest,   50
And look'd such Darts, as none cou'd e're resist.
Silent we gaz'd, and as my Eyes met thine,
New Joy fill'd theirs, new Love and shame fill'd mine!
You saw the Fears my kind disorder shows,
And broke your Silence with a thousand Vows!   55
Heavens, how you swore! by ev'ry Pow'r Divine
You wou'd be ever true! be ever mine:

Each God, a sacred witness you invoke,
And wish'd their Curse when e're these Vows you broke.
Quick to my Heart the perjur'd Accents ran,   60
Which I took in, believ'd, and was undone.
'Vows are Loves poyson'd Arrows, and the heart
So wounded, rarely finds a Cure in Art.
At least this heart which Fate has destin'd yours, ⎫
This heart unpractic'd in Loves mystick pow'rs,   ⎬   65
For I am soft, and young as *April* Flowers.   ⎭
   Now uncontroul'd we meet, uncheck't improve
Each happier Minute in new Joys of Love!
Soft were our hours! and lavishly the Day
We gave intirely up to Love, and Play.   70
Oft to the cooling Groves, our Flocks we led,   ⎫
And seated on some shaded, flowry Bed,   ⎬
Watch'd the united Wantons as they fed.   ⎭
And all the Day my list'ning Soul I hung,   ⎫
Upon the charming Musick of thy Tongue,   ⎬   75
And never thought the blessed hours too long.   ⎭
No Swain, no God like thee cou'd ever move,   ⎫
Or had so soft an Art in whispering Love,   ⎬
No wonder that thou wert Ally'd to *Jove*.   ⎭
And when you pip'd, or sung, or danc'd, or spoke,   80
The God appear'd in every Grace, and Look.
Pride of the Swains, and Glory of the Shades,
The Grief, and Joy of all the Love-sick Maids.
Thus whilst all hearts you rul'd without Controul,
I reign'd the absolute Monarch of your Soul.   85
   Each *Beach* my Name yet bears, carv'd out by thee,
Paris, and his *Oenone* fill each Tree;
And as they grow, the Letters larger spread,
Grow still! a witness of my Wrongs when dead!
   Close by a silent silver Brook there grows ⎫   90
A Poplar, under whose dear gloomy Boughs   ⎬
A thousand times we have exchang'd our Vows!   ⎭
Oh may'st thou grow! to an endless date of Years!
Who on thy Bark this fatal Record bears;
When Paris *to* Oenone *proves untrue,*   95
Back Xanthus *Streams shall to their Fountains flow.*

79 *Ally'd to Jove*: a largely fanciful explanation of Paris' success in wooing (at which *Jove* excelled)
and, in 81, of his beauty; in some accounts Paris' line went back to Dardanus, son of
Jove   82 *Shades*: under sheltering trees

Turn! turn! your Tide, back to your Fountains run!
The perjur'd Swain from all his Faith is gone!
　　Curst be that day, may Fate point out the hour,
As Ominous in his black Kalender;   100
When *Venus, Pallas,* and the Wife of *Jove*
Descended to thee in the Mirtle Grove,
In shining Chariots drawn by winged Clouds:
Naked they came, no Veil their Beauty shrouds;
But every Charm, and Grace expos'd to view,   105
Left Heav'n to be survey'd, and judg'd by you.
To bribe thy voice, *Juno* wou'd Crowns bestow,
Pallas more gratefully wou'd dress thy Brow
With Wreaths of Wit! *Venus* propos'd the choice
Of all the fairest *Greeks*! and had thy Voice.   110
Crowns, and more glorious Wreaths thou didst despise,
And promis'd Beauty more than Empire prize!
This when you told, Gods! what a killing fear ⎫
Did over all my shivering Limbs appear?   ⎬
And I presag'd some ominous Change was near! ⎭   115
The Blushes left my Cheeks, from every part
The Blood ran swift to guard my fainting heart.
You in my Eys the glimmering Light perceiv'd ⎫
Of parting Life, and on my pale Lips breath'd ⎬
Such Vows, as all my Terrors undeceiv'd.   ⎭   120
But soon the envying Gods disturb'd our Joys,
Declare thee Great! and all my Bliss destroys!
　　And now the Fleet is Anchor'd in the Bay
That must to *Troy* the glorious Youth convey.
Heavens! how you look'd! and what a Godlike Grace   125
At their first Homage beautify'd your Face!
Yet this no Wonder, or Amazement brought,
You still a Monarch were in Soul, and thought!
Nor cou'd I tell which most the Sight augments,
Your Joys of Pow'r, or parting Discontents.   130
You kist the Tears which down my Cheeks did glide,
And mingled yours with the soft falling Tide,
And 'twixt your Sighs a thousand times you said
Cease my Oenone! *Cease my charming Maid!*
If Paris *lives his Native* Troy *to see,*   135
My lovely Nymph, thou shalt a Princess be!

120 *undeceiv'd*: allayed by proving unfounded　　129 *augments*: gratifyingly heightens

But my Prophetick Fear no Faith allows,
My breaking Heart resisted all thy Vows.
Ah must we part, I cry'd! *those killing words*
No further Language to my Grief affords.   140
Trembling, I fell upon thy panting Breast ⎤
Which was with equal Love, and Grief opprest, ⎬
Whilst sighs and looks, all dying spoke the rest, ⎦
About thy Neck my feeble Arms I cast,
Not *Vines*, nor *Ivy* circle *Elms* so fast.   145
To stay, what dear Excuses didst thou frame,
And fanciedst Tempests when the Seas were calm?
How oft the Winds contrary feign'd to be,
When they alas were only so to me!
How oft new Vows of lasting Faith you swore,   150
And 'twixt your Kisses all the old run o're?
 But now the wisely Grave, who Love despise,
(Themselves past hope) do busily advise,
Whisper Renown, and Glory in thy Ear,
Language which Lovers fright, and Swains ne're hear.   155
For *Troy* they cry! these Shepherds Weeds lay down,
Change Crooks for Scepters! Garlands for a Crown!
'But sure that Crown does far less easie sit,
'Than Wreaths of Flow'rs, less innocent and sweet.
'Nor can thy Beds of State so grateful be,   160
'As those of Moss, and new fall'n Leaves with me!
 Now tow'rds the *Beach* we go, and all the way
The Groves, the Fern, dark Woods, and Springs survey;
That were so often conscious to the Rites
Of sacred Love, in our dear stol'n Delights.   165
With Eyes all languishing, each place you view,
And sighing cry, *Adieu, dear Shades, Adieu!*
Then 'twas thy Soul e'en doubted which to do,
Refuse a Crown, or those dear Shades forgoe!
Glory and Love! the great dispute persu'd,   170
But the false Idol soon the God subdu'd.
 And now on Board you go, and all the Sails
Are loosned, to receive the flying Gales;
Whilst I half dead on the forsaken Strand, ⎤
Beheld thee sighing on the Deck to stand, ⎬   175
Wafting a thousand Kisses from thy Hand. ⎦

164 *conscious to*: privy to, aware of

And whilst I cou'd the lessening Vessel see,
I gaz'd, and sent a thousand Sighs to thee!
And all the Sea-born *Neriads* implore
Quick to return thee to our Rustick shore.   180
  Now like a Ghost I glide through ev'ry Grove,
Silent, and sad as Death, about I rove,
And visit all our Treasuries of Love!
This Shade th' account of thousand Joys does hide,
As many more this murmuring Rivers side,   185
Where the dear Grass, as sacred, does retain
The print, where thee and I so oft have lain.
Upon this Oak thy Pipe, and Garland's plac'd,
That *Sycamore* is with thy Sheephook grac'd.
Here feed thy Flocks, once lov'd though now thy scorn;   190
Like me forsaken, and like me forlorn!
  A Rock there is, from whence I cou'd survey
From far the blewish Shore, and distant Sea,
Whose hanging top with toyl I climb each day,
With greedy View the prospect I run o're,   195
To see what wish't for Ships approach our shore.
One day all hopeless on its point I stood,
And saw a Vessel bounding o're the Flood,
And as it nearer drew, I cou'd discern
Rich Purple Sayls, Silk Cords, and Golden Stern;   200
Upon the Deck a Canopy was spread
Of Antique work in Gold and Silver made,
Which mixt with Sun-beams dazling Light display'd.
But oh! beneath this glorious Scene of State
(Curst be the sight) a fatal Beauty sate.   205
And fondly you were on her Bosome laid,
Whilst with your perjur'd Lips her Fingers plaid;
Wantonly curl'd and dally'd with that hair,
Of which, as sacred Charms, I Bracelets wear.
Oh! hadst thou seen me then in that mad state,   210
So ruin'd, so design'd for Death and Fate,
Fix't on a Rock, whose horrid Precipice
In hollow Murmurs wars with Angry Seas;
Whilst the bleak Winds aloft my Garments bear,
Ruffling my careless and dishevel'd hair,   215
I look't like the sad Statue of Despair.

179 *Neriads*: the old sea-god Nereus had, according to myth, fifty or a hundred daughters (usually 'Nereids') who sported among the waves

With out-stretch'd voice I cry'd, and all around
The Rocks and Hills my dire complaints resound.
I rend my Garments, tear my flattering Face,
Whose false deluding Charms my Ruin was.   220
Mad as the Seas in Storms, I breath Despair,
Or Winds let loose in unresisting Air.
Raging and Frantick through the Woods I fly,
And *Paris!* lovely, faithless, *Paris*, cry.
But when the Ecchos sound thy Name again,   225
I change to new variety of Pain.
For that dear Name such tenderness inspires,
And turns all Passion to Loves softer Fires:
With tears I fall to kind Complaints again,
So Tempests are allay'd by Show'rs of Rain.   230
   Say, lovely Youth, why wou'dst thou thus betray
My easie Faith, and lead my heart astray?
I might some humble Shepherds Choice have been,
Had I that Tongue ne're heard, those Eyes ne're seen.
And in some homely Cott, in low Repose,   235
Liv'd undisturb'd with broken Vows and Oaths:
All day by shaded Springs my Flocks have kept,
And in some honest Arms at Night have slept.
Then unupbraided with my wrongs thou'dst been
Safe in the Joys of the fair Grecian Queen: 240
What Stars do rule the Great? no sooner you
Became a Prince, but you were Perjur'd too.
Are Crowns and Falshoods then consistant things?
And must they all be faithless who are Kings?
The Gods be prais'd that I was humbly born,   245
Even tho' it renders me my *Paris* scorn.
And I had rather this way wretched prove,
Than be a Queen and faithless in my Love.
Not my fair Rival wou'd I wish to be,
To come prophan'd by others Joys to thee.   250
A spotless Maid into thy Arms I brought,
Untouch't in Fame, ev'n Innocent in thought;
Whilst she with Love has treated many a Guest,
And brings thee but the leavings of a Feast:
With *Theseus* from her Country made Escape,   255
Whilst she miscall'd the willing Flight, a Rape.

255–6 *With Theseus . . . a Rape*: according to Plutarch and others, Helen was abducted when a child
by Theseus and rescued by her brothers, the Dioscuri

So now from *Atreus* Son, with thee is fled,
And still the Rape hides the Adult'rous Deed.
And is it thus Great Ladies keep intire
That Vertue they so boast, and you admire?   260
Is this a Trick of Courts, can Ravishment
Serve for a poor Evasion of Consent?
Hard shift to save that Honour priz'd so high,
Whilst the mean Fraud's the greater Infamy.
How much more happy are we Rural Maids,   265
Who know no other Palaces than Shades?
Who want no Titles to enslave the Croud,
Least they shou'd babble all our Crimes aloud;
No Arts our good to show, our Ills to hide,
Nor know to cover faults of Love with Pride.   270
I lov'd, and all Loves Dictates did persue,
And never thought it cou'd be Sin with you.
To Gods, and Men, I did my Love proclaim
For one soft hour with thee, my charming Swain,
Wou'd Recompence an Age to come of Shame,   275
Cou'd it as well but satisfie my Fame.
But oh! those tender hours are fled and lost,
And I no more of Fame, or Thee can boast!
'Twas thou wert Honour, Glory, all to me: ⎫
Till Swains had learn'd the Vice of Perjury,   ⎬   280
No yielding Maids were charg'd with Infamy.   ⎭
'Tis false and broken Vows make Love a Sin,
Hadst thou been true, We innocent had been.
But thou less faith than *Autumn* leaves do'st show,
Which ev'ry Blast bears from their native Bough.   285
Less Weight, less Constancy, in thee is born
Than in the slender mildew'd Ears of Corn.
    Oft when you Garlands wove to deck my hair, ⎫
Where mystick Pinks, and Dazies mingled were,   ⎬
You swore 'twas fitter Diadems to bear: ⎭   290
And when with eager Kisses prest my hand,
Have said, *How well a Sceptre 'twou'd command!*
And if I danc't upon the Flow'ry Green,   ⎫
With charming, wishing Eyes, survey my Miene,   ⎬
And cry! the Gods design'd thee for a Queen!   ⎭   295
Why then for *Helen* dost thou me forsake?
Can a poor empty Name such difference make?

257 *Atreus Son*: Menelaus, husband of Helen

Besides, if Love can be a Sin thine's one,
Since *Helen* does to *Menelaus* belong.
Be Just, restore her back, She's none of thine,   300
And, charming *Paris*, thou art only mine.
'Tis no Ambitious Flame that makes me sue
To be again belov'd, and blest with you;
No vain desire of being Ally'd t' a King,
Love is the only Dowry I can bring,   305
And tender Love is all I ask again;
Whilst on her dang'rous Smiles fierce War must wait
With Fire and Vengeance at your Palace gate,
Rouze your soft Slumbers with their rough Alarms,
And rudely snatch you from her faithless Arms: 310
Turn then fair Fugitive, e're 'tis too late,
E're thy mistaken Love procures thy Fate;
E're a wrong'd Husband does thy Death design,
And pierce that dear, that faithless Heart of thine.

MATTHEW STEVENSON

SAPHO TO PHAON

The Argument

The Poetess Sapho *being forsaken by her Lover* Phaon (*who was gone from* Lesbos *to* Sicily)
and resolved in Despair to drown her self, writes this Letter to him before she dies.

While *Phaon* to the Hot-house hies,
With no less Fire poor *Sapho* fries.
I burn, I burn with Nodes and Poxes,
Like Fields of Corn with brand-tail'd Foxes.
My Bag-pipes can no longer please,   5
Nor can I get one minutes ease;
Grunting all day I sit alone,
And all my old dear Cronies shun.
The *Lesbian* Sparks must claim no part,
Where thou hast stung me to the heart.   10

1 *Hot-house*: bagnio, brothel   3 *Nodes*: gouty swellings, bone-cramping tumours
4 *Like Fields . . . Foxes*: see Judg. 15: 4–5 (where Samson ties 'firebrands' to three hundred paired
foxes and sends them into the Philistines' 'standing corn')   9 *Sparks*: fashionable young
wits

Ah wretch! how cou'dst thou be so cruel,
In my hot bloud to raise a fuel!
When Youth and Beauty did you stay,
Then play the Rogue, and run away?
If nought oblige but equal pelf,   15
Go, keep your favours to your self.
    Yet, silly as I am, I knew
The time, (which I shall ever rue;)
A time for all your mighty looks,
When I was something in your books: 20
A thousand Tales of fustion-stuff;
For I remember well enough
How close about my Neck you hung,
When I began a Bawdy Song.
You thought me chief amongst the Misses,   25
And often stopt my mouth with Kisses,
Whose melting touch my heart did stab,
In Earnest of a coming Job.
You us'd a thousand wanton tricks,
And play'd the Devil on two sticks.   30
We to the business stifly stood,
And did as long as doing's good;
Nor cou'd we for our lives give o're,
'Till we were fit to do no more.
    Beware, *Sicilian* Wenches; he   35
Will coaks you all as well as me.
If you'll take notice of his Shams,
He'll tell you a thousand lying Flams:
'Tis such another flattering Villain,
He'll cheat you all, were you a million.   40
My Hair hangs down about my Knees,
And falls as fast as Leaves from Trees.
Of all ill luck I am the Pattern;
You'd swear I'm grown a very Slattern.
For whom shou'd I go fine and gawdy?   45
Why without him I am no body;
And I ne'er lov'd to trick or trim
My self for any one but him.

21 *fustion-stuff*: inflated nonsense (from 'fustian', a coarse cloth)   28 *In Earnest of a coming Job*: his kisses induced a sense of impending orgasm   30 *play'd the Devil on two sticks*: dallied nimbly with me (alluding to a game in which an hourglass-shaped piece of wood was twirled around a string run between *two sticks* held in the hands)   38 *Flams*: falsehoods, fanciful stories

Oh! if I cou'd but once more see
That subtile piece of Letchery;   50
'Tis not thy Love I ask, not thine,
So thou wilt but accept of mine:
But to sneak off when none did hold thee
Without Farewel, I needs must scold thee.
You might have said, you ill-bred Bumkin,   55
God b'w'ye, Kiss my Arse, or something:
You might have ta'n your leave at least,
And not have gone off like a Beast:
For hadst thou but the least word spoken,
I had gi'n thee something for a Token;   60
Tho' naught behinde was left by thee,
But Shankers, Shame, and Infamie.
    My Friends can witness what a quarter
And din I made at thy Departure.
When of thy baseness I was told,   65
I was ready e'en to die with cold;
Speechless, one word I cou'd not utter,
Onely what in my Cups I mutter:
And tho they brought good store of Alè-in,
I cou'd not speak one word for railing.   70
At last, my passion finding vent,
In a Distraction out I went,
And like a Bedlam run about
The streets, in hope to smell thee out.
Exposing all I had to see,   75
E'en all that *Jove* had sent to me;
Without respect to Modestie,
Forgetting Shame, and all but thee;
So ill does Shame and Love agree.
    For thee alone my Rest I want;   80
I cannot sleep for dreaming on't:
Which made the Night more welcome to me
Than any Day since you went from me.
Yet little did I dream you went:
For who'd dream of a Parliament?   85
Or you wou'd leave me here a widow,
To feed my fancy with your shadow?

---

62 *Shankers*: venereal ulcers, chancres   63 *quarter*: calling for mercy   73 *Bedlam*: mad
person   85 *Parliament*: debate, falling out

Yet spight of absence, I make shift
To help my self at a dead lift.
Wrapt in thy arms the stroaks I number,   90
And do enjoy thee in a slumber.
Thy Words I hear, thy Kisses feel,
With all the Joys I blush to tell.
    But when I wake, and miss thee there,
How I begin to curse and swear!   95
Then to divert my present pain,
Take t' other Nap, and to't again.
    Soon as I rise mad as a Hawk
To see my self so plaguy bawk't,
I run to Bawdy-house and Stoves,   100
The Scenes of our unhappy Loves.
Then like a drunken Bitch I ramble,
And rail alone at every Shamble.
Then do I cast my Eyes about
Upon the little bawdy Vault,   105
Whose mossie floor, and roof of stone,
Pleas'd better than a Bed of Down.
But when I spy'd the grassie Bed
Retains the print our bodies made,
On thy dear side I squat me down,   110
And with a Flood the place I drown,
For to refresh the wither'd Trees,
Since thou art gone, with Virgin-Lees.
    No Birds frequent the Valleys now,
But the vile Screetch-Owl, or the Crow;   115
Who onely mourn for scarcitie
Of Carrion, as I long for thee.
    Oh, *Phaon*, didst thou know my pain,
Thou wou'd, thou wou'dst come back again.
With the Disease I got from you,   120
My Eyes have got the Running too:
My constant Tears the Paper stain;
My hand can scarce direct my Pen.
Or cou'dst thou see a little further,
How I my self intend to murther: 125

89 *at a dead lift*: in a hopeless situation (as when straining to *lift* a *dead* weight)   100 *Stoves*: sweating-rooms, stews, whore-houses   113 *Virgin-Lees*: her piss and associated effluvia (including menstrual blood, often called *Lees* in the period) might as well be virginal for all the signs of sexual intercourse they now show

Didst thou but spy the fatal Loop,
Sure thou wou'd strive to cut the Rope.
   Peace, *Sapho*, cease thy idle gabble;
Thou may'st as well appease the Rabble:
Thou may (since thou art left behind)   130
As well go piss against the wind.
Cease, fool, and since thou art forsook,
What you have lost you may go look.
   No more thy hopeless Love attend,
   But hang thy self, and there's an end.   135

133 *you may go look*: i.e. you'll have a long wait for it

13

Later Lyrics and Satires

AMONG the numerous petitions and plaints fictively attributed to women after the Restoration, *The Maids Complaint against the Batchelors* (1675) stands out. Other pamphlets, pandering to male stereotypes of 'female' language, offer to entertain the reader with aimless and empty prose. This *Complaint*, by contrast, is crisp, varied, and attentive to contemporary speech (several of its usages supplement or predate entries in the *Oxford English Dictionary*). Though patently male-authored, and less cutting about men than it thinks, the pamphlet also has the weaknesses of both sexes in its sights. It is followed by three lyrics by women. Ventriloquized text is attributed to 'Ephelia' in her *Female Poems* of 1679 (above, p. 38); but the song printed below not only stands among the unchallenged parts of her collection but is of structural interest in relation to gender in framed plaint (above, pp. 11–17, 38–9). Aphra Behn's 'The Reflection', published in 1684, has a muted ease which—even while it seems to limit the author—is poignantly apt for its theme. 'The Complaint', an early work by Jane Barker (1652–*c*.1717), shows that, however constraining the kind might be for women writers (above, pp. 80–2), it could express grievance with abrasive cogency. The section ends with a pair of parodies. John Gay (1685–1732) wrote his burlesque in the wake of controversy about Ambrose Philips's pastorals. Based on the first half of Virgil's eighth *Eclogue*, it also echoes (at 67–74, 75–88, 115–20) 1 and 2. Gay's notes help his readers identify sources. His Latin is glossed here from H. R. Fairclough's translation in the Loeb *Virgil*, rev. edn. (London, 1935). The text was accompanied in 1714 by the engraving which faces it. 'A Sorrowful Lamentation for the Loss of a Man and No Man' also reflects artistic quarrels, this time at the opera-house. Its occasion is the departure from England of the Italian castrato, Francesco Bernardi, known as Senesino (*fl.* 1707–40, died *c*.1759). After he had starred in a number of Handel roles in London, the singer's relations with the opera establishment declined, and he went abroad following the break-up of the Academy in 1728. The feminine persona of the ballad (published in 1729) prefers him to Faustina Bordoni and Francesca Cuzzoni, the sopranos whose competitive peformances led Gay to burlesque them as Polly and Lucy in *The Beggar's Opera*. The author of this piece, Henry Carey (*c*.1687–1743), is known today for the words and music of one ballad, 'Sally in our Alley'. But his witty-pathetical poems (such as

'The Marriage of Bacchus being Part of the Story of Theseus and Ariadne Imitated from Ovid'), his parodic tragedy, farce, and burlesque opera won him an extensive eighteenth-century audience.

THE MAIDS COMPLAINT AGAINST THE BATCHELORS: OR, AN EASTER-OFFERING FOR YOUNG MEN AND APPRENTICES

Passionately setting forth The Unkindness of Men, with their Slighting the good Old way of Matrimony, and forcing several Thousands of Ripe and Willing Virgins to Spin out Miserable Lives on Earth for want of Husbands, and lead Apes in Hell after their Death

Though Grave People tell us that *Modesty* is the best Ornament of our Sex, and endeavour to silence us with an old musty Proverb, That *Maids should be seen and not heard*; yet we find our selves at present obliged to dispense with these Formalities, and under a necessity of publishing our *Just Complaints* as loud as the Press can speak them: The   5
insufferable Carriage of you, *Barbarous Batchelers*! hath reduced us to this Extremity: Too long, Alas! *too long* have we endured your Cruelties, and born, beyond all Patience, your Neglects and Ill-usage: How often have we *Sighed* in private, and made *Vows* to Heaven in *Vain* for the *Blessing* of Husbands? The silent Language of our *Blushes* has suffi-   10
ciently spoke our Passion; and you might (had you not been *Insensible*) have read our desires plainly Legible in our *Languishing Eyes*: As soon as we Arrived at the Long-wisht for *Teens*, what *Arts* have we not used to engage your rambling Affections? How have we made it our Business to spruce up and finifie our selves that we might appear to the best   15
Advantage? Witness our perpetual *Washings, Combings, Curlings, Pow-derings* and a thousand Chargeable Devices of the *Tailer*, and the *Tire-woman*, our studied Behaviour, various *Dresses*, affected Postures, tempting *Smiles*, and *Amorous Glances* whereby we even darted our very *Souls* at you, were all but so many modest *Invitations* for you to *fall on*;   20

TITLE *Easter-Offering*: the timeliness of the pamphlet (a seasonal gift) is enlivened by a quibbling glance at the church collection for ministers taken each Easter Sunday   SUBTITLE *lead Apes in Hell*: supposed fate of spinsters in the next world   15 *finifie*: adorn, make fine 17–18 *Tire-woman*: dressmaker (selling 'attire')

yet (*Cowards* that you are) you seem still to *decline* the Encounter, and view us with no more *Passion*, than if we were only Ivory *Statues*, or so many handsome *Pictures*. Can you think we were at all this trouble for nothing; or imagine that we would ever have *Trimm'd* up these *Tenements* of our Bodies so Curiously, but with an intent to *Lett them*? must you not confess your selves *Inhumane*, and more Uncharitable than Beasts and Savages to suffer so many plump *Virgins* to Languish and Pine away with the *Green-Sickness*, when it lies solely in your Power to Relieve them? 25

Perhaps you may Alledge in your own Defence, That you have been ready on all Occasions to offer your *Assistance*, but Alas! it was by *such* a Method of Cure as was worse than the Disease; Palliating the *White Feaver* with the more grievous Plague of a *Timpany*. 30

We know well enough, *Young-Men*! what you would be at; you are willing enough to *Break Bulk*, but not *Pay Custome*; and would *Board* us without Priviledge from the *Parson*; which, neither our *Honour*, nor *Interest* can admit: such Slippry *Blades* are not to be trusted without being Tyed to the good *Behaviour* with the Enchanted Cable of a *For Better for Worse*. Our Prudent Mothers, from sad Experience, have often read us Lectures against that Folly of hazarding the stock of our *honesty* in the leaky bottom of your Insignificant *promises*: Come, come, we remember what you have formerly told us, that an Amorous *Perjury* is but a necessary *failing*; and that *Jupiter* puts the *Vows* of Lovers in a *bottomless* Bag, never to rise up in Judgement against them: and therefore, though we would gladly be *Trading* in an honest civil way, yet we conceive the times somwhat hard, and have no inclination to try Peoples Charity with a *Fatherless* Bantling at our Backs; and therefore resolve with the Song. 35 40 45

> ——*Or Marry or else forsake us,*
> *For having fill'd our Belly's and your desires,*
> *You'l be burn'd before you will take us.* 50

But the plain truth is, to our unspeakable grief we find you such *Heathen* Libertines, that the Divine and most *comfortable* Institution of *Matrimony*, is grown odious, or at least contemptible to most of you: As if the *Common* afforded sweeter Pasture than the *Inclosure*, or durty 55

24–5 *Tenements*: properties for leasehold, letting   28 *Green-Sickness*: chlorosis, which gives a green tint to the complexion; mostly affecting young women, it was reckoned to be cured by marriage   32–3 *White Feaver*: an anaemic condition (cf. *Green-Sickness*), more often called 'white jaundice'   33 *Timpany*: morbid swelling, tumour (though here a pregnancy) 35 *Break Bulk*: start unloading cargo (which flaws its integrity, as in the *Break*ing of a maidenhead) *Custome*: duty payable on valuable imports   38–9 *For Better for Worse*: quoting the marriage vows   41 *bottom*: ship's hold *Insignificant*: meaningless   47 *Bantling*: bastard 51 *burn'd*: in hell

Puddle-water that every one lies *dabling* in, were to be preferred before
a private Spring: A *Miss*, a *Miss*, is the only thing; and there is scarce a
Prentice of sixteen, but puts the *Chouse* upon his Master to help maintain
some small piece of *Harlotry* abroad: you count *Fornication* but a *Venial
Trifle*, and yet think honest Marriage an unpardonable sin. A Whore is   60
become a necessary *Appurtenance*, and to keep her *nobly* part of the
Character of a *Gentleman*; whilst to love a Mans own *Wife* is voted worse
than *Cuckoldry*, and an Infallible mark of a Sot and a Fop. *Brisk* and
Aiery is the Word (in plain *English*, *Rompish* and *Impudent*) and to be
honest, or modest, you count *Ill-breeding* in a Woman. There is scarce   65
any of you that Court *Beauty* seriously, and *Vertue* none at all: your
pretences of making *Love* to us, are only, either baits to *debauch* us, or
designs to get our *Money*: If ever you venture to Marry us, we do but
purchase contempt and slavery for term of Life; and *sell* our selves at the
Price of our Portions: Not to say of our *Health* and *Lives* too, though 'tis 70
most seriously true, that your Bodies are generaly as *filthy* as your Souls,
and fuller of Diseases than an *Hospitall*. We will not tell you of your
dissimulations and perfideousness, nor yet of your flatteries and breach
of *Vows*, since you glory in all these, as your choicest accomplishments;
and we cannot be so impertinent as to be angry with you: for sure in   75
your present *Reprobate-state* you are worthy none of your passions but
Horn. Hence forwards therefore, when you *whine* and *fawn* on us, we
will only be so kind as to *Laugh* at you. 'Twill be rare diversion to see
you like *Monkies* acting your passionate Amours with a thousand *ridiculous* Grimaces; repeating shreds of *Plays* instead of Natural wit, which   80
you are strangers to: and *hiring* Poets to write most passionate Letters of
dull nonsense to us. To observe what little silly tricks you use to *Charm* us
with variety of *gay Cloths*, till you have either made the *Confiding Taylor* a
Bankrupt, or he has got you in *Limbo* for your entrusted bravery; and
then at last having wasted both your *Estates* and *Bodies*: How you either   85
are trappan'd into the dreadful Marriage *Noose* by a Common
Strumpet, under pretence of a *Fortune*, or doat in good earnest on some
greasie Kitchin-wench, or at best are glad meerly for a wretched Lively-
hood, to Wed some ugly deformed most *abominable* old Widdow of
fourscore, who frights you out of your little wits in the day-time by her   90

57 *Miss*: a newfangled title in this period for a young, unmarried woman, strongly associated with
the debased sense of 'mistress', concubine   58 *puts the Chouse upon*: cheats   63–4 *Brisk
and Aiery*: pert and delicate, wanton and fanciful   64 *Rompish*: vulgarly sportive
76–7 *worthy . . . but Horn*: deserve only to be married and betrayed, cuckolded   83 *Confiding*:
trusting   84 *Limbo*: either 'confinement, debtors' prison' or 'pawn'   86 *trappan'd*:
snared, beguiled

Meager *looks*; and in the Night with her everlasting *Cough* and nasty
Rheumes.

One of these *Chances* is certainly your Fate; and therefore be advised
in time: leave off these silly extravagant *Rambles* attended with nothing
but *shame* and Infamy, and List your selves amongst honest drudging   95
good *Common wealths-men*, who take care both for the *necessities* of the
time present, and the *Interests* of Posterity, so as to People the World in
the next Age with the *Labours* of a lawful Bed, and not a *spurious* Issue:
Then shall you find that the embraces of a *modest* Wifc arc not only
more *cheap* and *wholesome*, but much more *pleasant* than the treacherous   100
Dalliances of a wanton *Miss*, though never so *sprightly* or well skill'd in
all the modes of *Petulancy*: and that the Feaverish heats of never-
satisfied *Lust* are no more to be compared to the comfortable and constant warmth of a well-grounded *Love*, than *Bristoll* stones are to real
Diamonds.   105

And in this hope, that you will lay these considerations to heart, and
for the future behave your selves more *kindly*, and prevent us from the
necessity of running into *Nunneries*, or *leading Apes* in Hell (both which
are so *contrary* to our inclinations that we dread nothing more) we com-
mit you to the Counsel of your *Pillows*, and rest if you please,   110

Given at our general Assembly   *Your very* ready *and*
   in *Fancies* Theatre, this   *most affectionate*
   Easter-Eve.   *Servants.*

'EPHELIA'

SONG

I

Beneath a spreading Willows shade,
Ephelia, a harmless Maide,
Sate rifling Natures store
Of every Sweet, with which she made
A Garland for her *Strephons* Head   5
As Gay as ever Shepherd wore.

92 *Rheumes*: bleary, dampish ailments   102 *Petulancy*: forwardness, immodesty
104 *Bristoll stones*: false gems made from a transparent rock crystal found in the Clifton limestone
near Bristol

2

She seem'd to know no other Care,
But wether Pinks, or Roses there,
Or Lillys look'd most sweet,
Scarce thinking on her Faithless Swain,   10
Who Ranging on the neighb'ring Plain,
A wanton Shepherdess did meet.

3

But by Mischance, he led her near
Th' Unlucky, Fatal Willow, where
His kind *Ephelia* sate;   15
He told the Kindness that she show'd,
Boasted the Favours she bestow'd,
And glory'd that he was ingrate.

4

The Angry Nymph, did rudely tare
Her Garland first, and then her Hair,   20
To hear her Self abus'd:
Oh Love! (she said) is it the Fate
Of all that Love, to meet with Hate,
And be like me, unkindly us'd?

APHRA BEHN

THE REFLECTION: A SONG

I

Poor Lost *Serena*, to Bemoan
      The Rigor of her Fate,
High'd to a Rivers-side alone,
      Upon whose Brinks she sat.
Her Eyes, as if they would have spar'd,   5
      The Language of her Tongue,
In Silent Tears a while declar'd
      The Sense of all her wrong.

II

But they alas too feeble were,
   Her Grief was swoln too high   10
To be Exprest in Sighs and Tears;
   She must or speak or dye.
And thus at last she did complain,
   Is this the Faith, said she,
Which thou allowest me, *Cruel Swain*,   15
   For that I gave to thee?

III

Heaven knows with how much Innocence
   I did my Soul Incline
To thy Soft Charmes of Eloquence,
   And gave thee what was mine.   20
I had not one Reserve in Store,
   But at thy Feet I lay'd
Those Arms that Conquer'd heretofore,
   Tho' now thy Trophies made.

IV

Thy Eyes in Silence told their Tale   25
   Of Love in such a way,
That 'twas as easie to Prevail,
   As after to Betray.
And when you spoke my Listning Soul,
   Was on the Flattery Hung: 30
And I was lost without Controul,
   Such Musick grac'd thy Tongue.

V

Alas how long in vain you strove
   My coldness to divert!
How long besieg'd it round with Love,   35
   Before you won the Heart.
What Arts you us'd, what Presents made,
   What Songs, what Letters writ:
And left no Charm that cou'd invade,
   Or with your Eyes or Wit.   40

VI

Till by such Obligations Prest,
　　By such dear Perjuries won:
I heedlesly Resign'd the rest,
　　And quickly was undone.
For as my Kindling Flames increase, 45
　　Yours glimmeringly decay:
The Rifled Joys no more can Please,
　　That once oblig'd your Stay.

VII

Witness ye Springs, ye Meads and Groves,
　　Who oft were conscious made 50
To all our Hours and Vows of Love;
　　Witness how I'm Betray'd.
Trees drop your Leaves, be Gay no more,
　　Ye Rivers waste and drye:
Whilst on your Melancholy Shore, 55
　　I lay me down and dye.

JANE BARKER

THE COMPLAINT

I

How oft, ah wretch, hast thou profusely swore
　　Me, as the Gods thou did'st adore;
　　And that my Words shou'd be to thee,
　　As of Divine Authority:
　　In this my Power exceeded theirs, 5
To me thou ne'er did'st wander in thy *Prayers*.

II

And oft thou prayest, bathed in thy Tears,
　　Drop'd from the clouds of loving fears;
　　And on my Hand thy *Faith* confess,
　　And after that beg for redress; 10
　　Whilst on the Altar of my *lip*,
For Sacrifice, let no occasion slip.

III

But now thou'rt grown prophane *Atheistical*,
  Not chang'd thy Faith, but cast off all:
  So *Sacrilegious* too thou art,   15
  Thou'rt not content to rob in part,
  To bear my Rites (thy Vows) away;
But by thy cruelty thou do'st assay
To bring the beauteous *Fabrick* to decay.

the Dumps.   Lud. Du Guernier inv. et Sculp.

6. 'The Dumps', from John Gay, 'Wednesday', in *The Shepherd's Week* (1714)

JOHN GAY

WEDNESDAY: OR, THE *DUMPS

From *The Shepherd's Week*

Sparabella

The Wailings of a Maiden I recite,
A Maiden fair, that *Sparabella* hight.
Such Strains ne'er warble in the Linnets Throat,
Nor the gay Goldfinch chaunts so sweet a Note,
No Mag-pye chatter'd, nor the painted Jay,   5
No Ox was heard to low, nor Ass to bray.
No rusling Breezes play'd the Leaves among,
While thus her Madrigal the Damsel sung.

A while, O *D——y*, lend an Ear or twain,
Nor, though in homely Guise, my Verse disdain;   10
Whether thou seek'st new Kingdoms in the Sun,
Whether thy Muse does at *New-Market* run,

---

* Dumps, *or* Dumbs, *made use of to express a Fit of the* Sullens. *Some have pretended that it is derived from* Dumops *A King of* Egypt, *that built a Pyramid and dy'd of Melancholy. So* Mopes *after the same Manner is thought to have come from* Merops, *another* Egyptian *King that dy'd of the same Distemper; but our* English *Antiquaries have conjectured that* Dumps, *which is, a grievous Heaviness of Spirits, comes from the Word* Dumplin, *the heaviest kind of Pudding that is eaten in this Country, much used in* Norfolk, *and other Counties of* England.
Line   5. *Immemor Herbarum quos est mirata juvenca*
                Certantes quorum stupefactæ carmine Lynces;
                Et mutata suos requierunt flumina cursus. Virg.
            9. *Tu mihi seu magni superas jam saxa Timavi,*
                Sive oram Illyrici legis æquoris——
    11. *An Opera written by this Author, called the* World in the Sun, *or the* Kingdom of Birds; *he is also famous for his Song on the* New-market Horse Race, *and several others that are sung by the* British *Swains.*

Sparabella: from 'sparable', a small iron nail worn in country people's shoes (with a quibble on the upper-class name 'Arabella')   5 n. *Immemor Herbarum . . . cursus. Virg.*: At whose rivalry the heifer marvelled and forgot to graze, at whose song lynxes stood spell-bound, and rivers were changed and stayed their course (*Eclogues*, 8. 2–4)   9 *D——y*: Tom D'Urfey (1653–1723), popular song-writer and performer   9 n. *Tu mihi . . . æquoris*: But thou, my friend, whether even now thou are passing the crags of great Timavrus, or skirting the coast of the Illyrian main (*Eclogues*, 8. 6–7)   11 *Kingdoms in the Sun*: D'Urfey's comic fantasy *Wonders in the Sun: Or, the Kingdom of the Birds* (see Gay's n.) was performed in 1706, to music by various composers   12 *at New-Market run*: his 'The Horse-Race; A Song Made and Sung to the King at Newmarket'

Or does with Gossips at a Feast regale,
And heighten her Conceits with Sack and Ale,
Or else at Wakes with *Joan* and *Hodge* rejoice,   15
Where *D——y*'s Lyricks swell in every Voice;
Yet suffer me, thou Bard of wond'rous Meed,
Amid thy Bays to weave this rural Weed.

    Now the sun drove adown the western Road,
And Oxen laid at rest forget the Goad,   20
The Clown fatigu'd trudg'd homeward with his Spade,
Across the Meadows stretch'd the lengthen'd Shade;
When *Sparabella* pensive and forlorn,
Alike with yearning Love and Labour worn,
Lean'd on her Rake, and strait with doleful Guise   25
Did this sad Plaint in moanful Notes devise.

    Come Night as dark as Pitch, surround my Head,
From *Sparabella Bumkinet* is fled;
The Ribbon that his val'rous Cudgel won,
Last *Sunday* happier *Clumsilis* put on.   30
Sure, if he'd Eyes (*but Love, they say, has none*)
I whilome by that Ribbon had been known.
Ah, Well-a-day! I'm shent with baneful Smart,
For with the Ribbon he bestow'd his Heart.
    My Plaint, ye Lasses, with this Burthen aid,   35
'Tis hard so true a Damsel dies a Maid.

    Shall heavy *Clumsilis* with me compare?
View this, ye Lovers, and like me despair.

Line
  17. Meed, *an old Word for* Fame *or* Renown.
        18. ————*Hanc sine tempora circum*
            Inter Victrices ederam tibi serpere lauros.
      25. *Incumbens tereti Damon sic cæpit Olivæ.*
  33. Shent, *an old Word Signifying* Hurt *or* harmed.
        37. *Mopso Nisa datur. quid non speremus Amantes?* Virg.

13 *with Gossips at a Feast*: probably alludes to D'Urfey's song 'Gillian of Croyden'
15 *Joan and Hodge*: standard, rustic names (perhaps recalling their appearance in D'Urfey's song
'The Country Sheep-Shearing')   18 n. *Hanc . . . lauros*: grant that about thy brows this ivy
may creep among the victor's laurels (*Eclogues*, 8. 12–13)   25 n. *Incumbens . . . Olivæ*: leaning
on his shapely olive-staff, Damon thus began (*Eclogues*, 8. 16)   29 *won*: in rustic combats
35 *Burthen*: refrain (with useful undertones of weightiness)   37 n. *Mopso Nisa . . . Amantes?*
Virg.: To Mopsus is Nysa given! For what may we lovers not look? (*Eclogues*, 8. 26)

Her blubber'd Lip by smutty Pipes is worn,
And in her Breath Tobacco Whiffs are born;   40
The cleanly Cheese-press she could never turn,
Her awkward Fist did ne'er employ the Churn;
If e'er she brew'd, the Drink wou'd strait grow sour,
Before it ever felt the Thunder's Pow'r:
No Huswifry the dowdy Creature knew;   45
To sum up all, her Tongue confess'd the Shrew.
  My Plaint, ye Lasses, with this Burthen aid,
'Tis hard so true a Damsel dies a Maid.

I've often seen my Visage in yon Lake,
Nor are my Features of the homeliest Make.   50
Though *Clumsilis* may boast a whiter Dye,
Yet the black Sloe turns in my rolling Eye;
And fairest Blossoms drop with ev'ry Blast,
But the brown Beauty will like Hollies last.
Her wan Complexion's like the wither'd Leek,   55
While *Katherine* Pears adorn my ruddy Cheek.
Yet she, alas! the witless Lout hath won,
And by her Gain, poor *Sparabell's* undone!
Let Hares and Hounds in coupling Straps unite,
The clocking Hen make Friendship with the Kite,   60
Let the Fox simply wear the Nuptial Noose,
And join in Wedlock with the wadling Goose;
For Love hath brought a stranger thing to pass,
The fairest Shepherd weds the foulest Lass.
  My Plaint, ye Lasses, with this Burthen aid,   65
'Tis hard so true a Damsel dies a Maid.

Line   49. *Nec sum adeo informis, nuper me in Littore vidi.*   Virg.
        53. *Alba ligustra cadunt, vaccinia nigra leguntur.*   Virg.
        59. *Jungentur jam Gryphes equis; ævoque sequenti*
            Cum canibus timidi venient ad pocula Damæ.   Virg.

44 *Thunder's Pow'r*: to *sour* the beer, as atmospheric changes can   49 n. *Nec sum adeo . . . vidi.*
Virg.: Nor am I so unsightly; on the shore the other day I looked at myself (*Eclogues*, 2. 25)
53 n. *Alba ligustra . . . leguntur. Virg.*: The white privets fall, the dark hyacinths are culled (*Eclogues*,
2. 18)   56 *Katherine Pears*: which ripen red, darkening towards brown   59 *coupling*
Straps: used to link horses in pairs   59 n. *Jungentur . . . Damæ. Virg.*: Griffins now shall mate
with mares, and, in the age to come, the timid deer shall come with hounds to drink (*Eclogues*, 8.
27–8)

Sooner shall Cats disport in Waters clear,
And speckled Mackrels graze the Meadows fair,
Sooner shall scriech Owls bask in Sunny Day,
And the slow Ass on Trees, like Squirrels, play,   70
Sooner shall Snails on insect Pinions rove,
Than I forget my Shepherd's wonted Love!
 My Plaint, ye Lasses, with this Burthen aid,
 'Tis hard so true a Damsel dies a Maid.

Ah! didst thou know what Proffers I withstood,   75
When late I met the *Squire* in yonder Wood!
To me he sped, regardless of his Game,
Whilst all my Cheek was glowing red with Shame;
My Lip he kiss'd, and prais'd my healthful Look,
Then from his Purse of Silk a *Guinea* took,   80
Into my Hand he forc'd the tempting Gold,
While I with modest struggling broke his Hold.
He swore that *Dick* in Liv'ry strip'd with Lace,
Should wed me soon to keep me from Disgrace;
But I nor Footman priz'd nor golden Fee,   85
For what is Lace or Gold compar'd to thee?
 My Plaint, ye Lasses, with this Burthen aid,
 'Tis hard so true a Damsel dies a Maid.

Now plain I ken whence *Love* his Rise begun
Sure he was born some bloody *Butcher's* Son,   90

Line   67. *Ante leves ergo pascentur in æthere Cervi*
     Et freta destituent nudos in littore Pisces——
     Quam nostro illius labatur pectore vultus. Virg.

 89. To ken. *Scire.* Chaucero, *to Ken; and* Kende *notus. A. S.* cunnan. *Goth.* Kunnan.
Germanis Kennen. *Danis* Kiende. *Islandis* Kunna. *Belgis* Kennen. *This Word is of general
use, but not very common, though not unknown to the Vulgar.* Ken *for* prospicere *is well known
and used* to discover by the Eye. *Ray. F. R. S.*

   Nunc scio quid sit Amor, &c.
   Crudelis mater magis an puer improbus ille?
   Improbus ille puer, crudelis tu quoque mater. Virg.

67 n. *Ante leves . . . vultus. Virg.*: Sooner, then, shall the nimble stag graze the air, and the seas leave
their fish bare on the strand —— than that look of his shall fade from my heart (*Eclogues*, 1. 59–60,
63) 71 *Pinions*: wings 89 n. *To ken. . . . Ray. F.R.S.*: quoted from 'Glossarium Nor-
thanhymbricum' in the second edition of John Ray, *A Collection of English Words not Generally Used*,
2nd edn. (1691) *Nunc scio . . . mater. Virg.*: Now I know what Love is, &c. Was the mother more
cruel, or that boy more heartless? Heartless was he; cruel, too, wast thou, O mother! (*Eclogues*, 8. 43,
49–50)

Bred up in Shambles, where our Younglings slain,
Erst taught him Mischief and to sport with Pain.
The *Father* only silly Sheep annoys,
The *Son*, the sillier Shepherdess destroys.
Does *Son* or *Father* greater Mischief do? 95
The *Sire* is cruel, so the *Son* is too.
   My Plaint, ye Lasses, with this Burthen aid,
'Tis hard so true a Damsel dies a Maid.

   Farewel, ye Woods, ye Meads, ye Streams that flow;
A sudden Death shall rid me of my Woe. 100
This Penknife keen my Windpipe shall divide.—
What, shall I fall as squeaking Pigs have dy'd!
No—To some Tree this Carcass I'll suspend.—
But worrying Curs find such untimely End!
I'll speed me to the Pond, where the high Stool 105
On the long Plank hangs o'er the muddy Pool,
That Stool, the dread of ev'ry scolding Quean.—
Yet, sure a Lover should not dye so mean!
There plac'd aloft, I'll rave and rail by Fits,
Though all the Parish say I've lost my Wits; 110
And thence, if Courage holds, my self I'll throw,
And quench my Passion in the Lake below.
   Ye Lasses, cease your Burthen, cease to moan,
And, by my Case forewarn'd, go mind your own.

   The Sun was set; the Night came on a-pace, 115
And falling Dews bewet around the Place,
The Bat takes airy Rounds on leathern Wings,
And the hoarse Owl his woeful Dirges sings;
The prudent Maiden deems it now too late,
And 'till to Morrow comes, defers her Fate. 120

Line   99.————————— *vivite Sylvæ,*
            Præceps aerii specula de montis in undas
            Deferar.   Virg.

99 n. *vivite Sylvæ . . . Deferar. Virg.*: Farewell, ye woods! Headlong from some towering mountain-way I will plunge into the waves (*Eclogues*, 8. 58–60)   105 *high Stool*: the cucking-stool (or 'ducking-stool') used for dousing scolds in a pond   107 *scolding Queans*: shrewish husseys, bitching women

HENRY CAREY

A SORROWFUL LAMENTATION FOR THE LOSS OF A MAN AND NO MAN

In the Simple Stile

As Musing I rang'd in the Meads all alone,
A beautiful Creature was making her Moan;
Oh! the Tears they did trickle so fast from her Eyes,
That she pierc'd both the Air, and my Heart with her Cries.

I gently requested the Cause of her Moan,   5
She told me her lov'd SENESINO was flown;
And in that sad posture she'd ever remain,
Unless the dear Creature would come back again.

Why, who is this Mortal so cruel, said I,
That draws such a Stream from so lovely an Eye?   10
He must be a base and a false hearted Man:
This fann'd but her Sorrows, and thus she began:

'Tis neither for Man or for Woman, said she,
That thus in lamenting I water the Lee;
But 'tis for a Singer so charming and sweet,   15
Whose Musick, alas! I shall never forget.

Perhaps 'tis some *Linnet* or *Blackbird* said I,
Perhaps 'tis your Sky *Lark* has ta'en to the Sky;
Come dry up your Tears, and abandon your Grief;
Another I'll get but I'll give you Relief.   20

No *Linnet*, no *Blackbird*, no *Sky-Lark*, said she,
But one who is better by far than all Three;
My Dear SENESINO, for whom thus I Cry,
Is sweeter than all the wing'd Songsters that fly.

Perhaps, pretty Creature! your *Parrot* is flown;   25
Your *Monkey*, or *Lap-Dog* occasion your Moan?
To all my Surmises she answer'd me *noh*,
And sob'd out eternally SE-NE-SI-NOH!

For Heaven's Sake, dear Creature! your Sorrows unfold,
To ease you, I'll spare nor for Silver or Gold: 30
But still she reply'd, ah! alas 'tis in vain,
Nor Silver nor Gold can recall him again.

A Curse upon Silver, a Curse upon Gold!
That could not my dear SENESINO with-hold;
'Twas Gold that first tempted him over the Main,   35
'Tis Gold has transported him thither again.

Adieu to FAUSTINA, CUZZONI likewise,
Whom Parties of Courtiers extol to the Skies;
Adieu to the Op'ra, adieu to the Ball!
My Darling is gone; and a Fig for them all.   40

14

Alexander Pope, Eloisa to Abelard *(1717)*

READERS as different as Johnson and Byron concurred in praising this poem. Imitations and replies (more than a dozen of the latter, up to and including Landor) flowed from the press. In periodical verse and, later, the Gothic novel, Eloisa's pen can be traced. The influence which Pope (1688–1744) exerted could be so general because of his range. Elegy, rhapsody, dream-vision, prayer: the heterogeneity of complaint at its most impressive since Spenser. Pope's main exemplar was Ovid. Among his earlier poems is a translation of 'Sapho to Phaon'. 'Come! . . . Come *Abelard*!' rings through the central section; the verse is fraught with that desire for mutuality which writing tries to satisfy in *Heroides*. Yet Eloisa overcomes desire, or redirects it, and the tonalities of *contemptus mundi* (which often register in medieval plaint) emerge. That Eloisa's plight was famous made Pope's task easier and more difficult. Where an epistolary poet like Drayton, dealing with some relatively obscure corner of English history, had to find ways of narrating events through a heroine which would convey necessary information to the actual reader without seeming redundant for the implied one, Pope could narrow the gap between Abelard and his own audience. This freed complaint for the dilating work of grievous argument. Pope's chief means of conveying what remained to be told (and which was mostly known to the reader) was to translate narrative into insistence: 'Thou know'st . . .', 'Canst thou forget . . .'. That Abelard, cruelly castrated, might not wish to remember gladder times makes Eloisa's eloquent pressure—sustained through verse paragraphs punctuated as much for the voice as the eye—convincing. Such was Pope's success that the poem was scarcely revised for later printings. Perhaps inevitably, changes clustered (at 103 and 259–60) around the castration itself. Though an engraving from the second edition is reproduced above (p. 81), the 1717 text is preferred here, not least for its greater directness at these points.

ELOISA TO ABELARD

The Argument

Abelard *and* Eloisa *flourish'd in the twelfth Century; they were two of the most distinguish'd persons of their age in learning and beauty, but for nothing more famous than for their unfortunate passion. After a long course of Calamities, they retired each to a several Convent, and consecrated the remainder of their days to religion. It was many years after this separation, that a letter of* Abelard's *to a Friend which contain'd* 5 *the history of his misfortunes, fell into the hands of* Eloisa. *This awakening all her tenderness, occasion'd those celebrated letters (out of which the following is partly extracted) which give so lively a picture of the struggles of grace and nature, virtue and passion.*

In these deep solitudes and awfull cells,
Where heav'nly-pensive, contemplation dwells,
And ever-musing melancholy reigns;
What means this tumult in a Vestal's veins?
Why rove my thoughts beyond this last retreat? 5
Why feels my heart its long-forgotten heat?
Yet, yet I love!—From *Abelard* it came,
And *Eloisa* yet must kiss the name.
    Dear fatal name! rest ever unreveal'd,
Nor pass these lips in holy silence seal'd. 10
I Iide it, my heart, within that close disguise,
Where, mix'd with God's, his lov'd Idea lies.
Oh write it not, my hand—The name appears
Already written—wash it out, my tears!
In vain lost *Eloisa* weeps and prays, 15
Her heart still dictates, and her hand obeys.
    Relentless walls! whose darksom round contains
Repentant sighs, and voluntary pains:
Ye rugged rocks! which holy knees have worn;
Ye grots and caverns shagg'd with horrid thorn! 20
Shrines! where their vigils pale-ey'd virgins keep,
And pitying saints, whose statues learn to weep!

ARGUMENT *several*: separate   4 *a Vestal's veins*: cf. the virgins who tended the shrine of Vesta in classical Rome   10 *holy silence seal'd*: by convent vows   12 *Idea*: mental image (of Abelard, overtones of Platonic absoluteness)   16 *dictates*: both 'commands' and 'utters to be written'   18 *pains*: as at 104 implies 'penance, punishment' as well as 'suffering' 20 *horrid*: bristling

Tho' cold like you, unmov'd, and silent grown,
I have not yet forgot my self to stone.
Heav'n claims me all in vain, while he has part,   25
Still rebel nature holds out half my heart;
Nor pray'rs nor fasts its stubborn pulse restrain,
Nor tears, for ages, taught to flow in vain.
    Soon as thy letters trembling I unclose,
That well-known name awakens all my woes.   30
Oh name for ever sad! for ever dear!
Still breath'd in sighs, still usher'd with a tear.
I tremble too where-e'er my own I find,
Some dire misfortune follows close behind.
Line after line my gushing eyes o'erflow,   35
Led thro' a sad variety of woe:
Now warm in love, now with'ring in thy bloom,
Lost in a convent's solitary gloom!
There stern religion quench'd th' unwilling flame,
There dy'd the best of passions, Love and Fame.   40
    Yet write, oh write me all, that I may join
Griefs to thy griefs, and eccho sighs to thine.
Nor foes nor fortune take this pow'r away.
And is my *Abelard* less kind than they?
Tears still are mine, and those I need not spare,   45
Love but demands what else were shed in pray'r;
No happier task these faded eyes pursue,
To read and weep is all they now can do.
    Then share thy pain, allow that sad relief;
Ah more than share it! give me all thy grief.   50
Heav'n first taught letters for some wretch's aid,
Some banish'd lover, or some captive maid;
They live, they speak, they breathe what love inspires,
Warm from the soul, and faithful to its fires,
The virgin's wish without her fears impart,   55
Excuse the blush, and pour out all the heart,
Speed the soft intercourse from soul to soul,
And waft a sigh from *Indus* to the *Pole*.
    Thou know'st how guiltless first I met thy flame,
When Love approach'd me under Friendship's name;   60

40 *Fame*: Eloisa was renowned as a scholar before entering the nunnery (cf. 'The Argument')
51 *letters*: the use of writing, characters

My fancy form'd thee of Angelick kind,
Some emanation of th' all-beauteous Mind.
Those smiling eyes, attemp'ring ev'ry ray,
Shone sweetly lambent with celestial day:
Guiltless I gaz'd; heav'n listen'd while you sung;   65
And truths *divine came mended from that tongue.
From lips like those what precept fail'd to move?
Too soon they taught me 'twas no sin to love.
Back thro' the paths of pleasing sense I ran,
Nor wish'd an Angel whom I lov'd a Man.   70
Dim and remote the joys of saints I see,
Nor envy them, that heav'n I lose for thee.
   How oft', when press'd to marriage, have I said,
Curse on all laws but those which love has made?
Love, free as air, at sight of human ties,   75
Spreads his light wings, and in a moment flies.
Let wealth, let honour, wait the wedded dame,
August her deed, and sacred be her fame;
Before true passion all those views remove,
Fame, wealth, and honour! what are you to Love?   80
The jealous God, when we profane his fires,
Those restless passions in revenge inspires;
And bids them make mistaken mortals groan,
Who seek in love for ought but love alone.
Should at my feet the world's great master fall,   85
Himself, his throne, his world, I'd scorn 'em all:
Not *Cæsar*'s empress wou'd I deign to prove;
No, make me mistress to the man I love;
If there be yet another name more free,
More fond than mistress, make me that to thee!   90
Oh happy state! when souls each other draw,
When love is liberty, and nature, law:
All then is full, possessing, and possest,
No craving Void left aking in the breast:
Ev'n thought meets thought ere from the lips it part,   95
And each warm wish springs mutual from the heart.
This sure is bliss (if bliss on earth there be)
And once the lot of *Abelard* and me.

       * *He was her Preceptor in Philosophy and Divinity.*

63 *attemp'ring*: subduing, making mild   66 *mended*: improved; Abelard added lustre even to
divine love   79 *views   remove*: considerations dissolve, prospects move   elsewhere
81 *jealous God*: i.e. Cupid

Alas how chang'd! what sudden horrors rise!
A naked Lover bound and bleeding lies!   100
Where, where was *Eloise*? her voice, her hand,
Her ponyard, had oppos'd the dire command.
Barbarian stay! that bloody hand restrain;
The crime was common, common be the pain.
I can no more; by shame, by rage supprest,   105
Let tears, and burning blushes speak the rest.
    Canst thou forget that sad, that solemn day,
When victims at yon' altar's foot we lay?
Canst thou forget what tears that moment fell,
When, warm in youth, I bade the world farewell?   110
As with cold lips I kiss'd the sacred veil,
The shrines all trembled, and the lamps grew pale:
Heav'n scarce believ'd the conquest it survey'd,
And Saints with wonder heard the vows I made.
Yet then, to those dread altars as I drew,   115
Not on the Cross my eyes were fix'd, but you;
Not grace, or zeal, love only was my call,
And if I lose thy love, I lose my all.
Come! with thy looks, thy words, relieve my woe;
Those still at least are left thee to bestow.   120
Still on that breast enamour'd let me lie,
Still drink delicious poison from thy eye,
Pant on thy lip, and to thy heart be prest;
Give all thou canst—and let me dream the rest.
Ah no! instruct me other joys to prize,   125
With other beauties charm my partial eyes,
Full in my view set all the bright abode,
And make my soul quit *Abelard* for God.
    Ah think at least thy flock deserve thy care,
Plants of thy hand, and children of thy pray'r.   130
From the false world in early youth they fled,
By thee to mountains, wilds, and deserts led.
You *rais'd these hallow'd walls; the desert smil'd,
And Paradise was open'd in the Wild.

*He founded the Monastery.

107–8 *Canst thou ... we lay*: the scene is Eloisa's profession (Abelard's vows were secured elsewhere), *lay* implying passivity rather than their posture   127 *all the bright abode*: i.e. heaven   132 *mountains, wilds, and deserts*: stark lodging of hermits

No weeping orphan saw his father's stores   135
Our shrines irradiate, or emblaze the floors;
No silver saints, by dying misers giv'n,
Here brib'd the rage of ill-requited heav'n:
But such plain roofs as piety could raise,
And only vocal with the Maker's praise.   140
In these lone walls (their day's eternal bound)
These moss-grown domes with spiry turrets crown'd,
Where awful arches make a noon-day night,
And the dim windows shed a solemn light;
Thy eyes diffus'd a reconciling ray,   145
And gleams of glory brighten'd all the day.
But now no face divine contentment wears,
'Tis all blank sadness, or continual tears.
See how the force of others' pray'rs I try,
(Oh pious fraud of am'rous charity!)   150
But why should I on others' pray'rs depend?
Come thou, my father, brother, husband, friend!
Ah let thy handmaid, sister, daughter move,
And, all those tender names in one, thy love!
The darksom pines that o'er yon' rocks reclin'd   155
Wave high, and murmur to the hollow wind,
The wandring streams that shine between the hills,
The grots that eccho to the tinkling rills,
The dying gales that pant upon the trees,
The lakes that quiver to the curling breeze;   160
No more these scenes my meditation aid,
Or lull to rest the visionary maid:
But o'er the twilight groves, and dusky caves,
Long-sounding isles, and intermingled graves,
Black Melancholy sits, and round her throws   165
A death-like silence, and a dread repose:
Her gloomy presence saddens all the scene,
Shades ev'ry flow'r, and darkens ev'ry green,
Deepens the murmur of the falling floods,
And breathes a browner horror on the woods.   170

136 *irradiate*: splendidly illuminate (as by stained glass)   *emblaze*: adorn with (the benefactor's) heraldic devices   137 *silver saints*: i.e. statues   142 *domes*: buildings   145 *reconciling*: with theological overtones, guiding a return to God   149 *others' pray'rs*: those of what 129 calls *thy flock*   150 *am'rous charity*: the desire to have Abelard come offered as concern for the convent's best interests, erotic love (*amor*) conceived as *caritas*   159 *gales*: breaths of wind   160 *curling*: ripple-making   164 *isles*: aisles

Yet here for ever, ever must I stay;
Sad proof how well a lover can obey!
Death, only death, can break the lasting chain;
And here ev'n then, shall my cold dust remain,
Here all its frailties, all its flames resign,   175
And wait, till 'tis no sin to mix with thine.
　　Ah wretch! believ'd the spouse of God in vain,
Confess'd within the slave of love and man.
Assist me heav'n! but whence arose that pray'r?
Sprung it from piety, or from despair?   180
Ev'n here, where frozen chastity retires,
Love finds an altar for forbidden fires.
I ought to grieve, but cannot what I ought;
I mourn the lover, not lament the fault;
I view my crime, but kindle at the view,   185
Repent old pleasures, and sollicit new:
Now turn'd to heav'n, I weep my past offence,
Now think of thee, and curse my innocence.
Of all affliction taught a lover yet,
'Tis sure the hardest science to forget!   190
How shall I lose the sin, yet keep the sense,
And love th' offender, yet detest th' offence?
How the dear object from the crime remove,
Or how distinguish penitence from love?
Unequal task! a passion to resign,   195
For hearts so touch'd, so pierc'd, so lost as mine.
Ere such a soul regains its peaceful state,
How often must it love, how often hate!
How often, hope, despair, resent, regret,
Conceal, disdain—do all things but forget.   200
But let heav'n seize it, all at once 'tis fir'd,
Not touch'd, but rapt; not waken'd, but inspir'd!
Oh come! oh teach me nature to subdue,
Renounce my love, my life, my self—and you.
Fill my fond heart with God alone, for he   205
Alone can rival, can succeed to thee.
　　How happy is the blameless Vestal's lot!
The world forgetting, by the world forgot.
Eternal sun-shine of the spotless mind!
Each pray'r accepted, and each wish resign'd;   210

177 *spouse of God*: i.e. the nun in Eloisa

Labour and rest, that equal periods keep;
'Obedient slumbers that can wake and weep';
Desires compos'd, affections ever even,
Tears that delight, and sighs that waft to heaven.
Grace shine around her with serenest beams,   215
And whisp'ring Angels prompt her golden dreams.
For her the Spouse prepares the bridal ring,
For her white virgins *Hymenæals* sing;
For her th' unfading rose of *Eden* blooms,
And wings of Seraphs shed divine perfumes;   220
To sounds of heav'nly harps, she dies away,
And melts in visions of eternal day.
  Far other dreams my erring soul employ,
Far other raptures, of unholy joy:
When at the close of each sad, sorrowing day,   225
Fancy restores what vengeance snatch'd away,
Then conscience sleeps, and leaving nature free,
All my loose soul unbounded springs to thee.
O curst, dear horrors of all-conscious night!
How glowing guilt exalts the keen delight!   230
Provoking Dæmons all restraint remove,
And stir within me ev'ry source of love.
I hear thee, view thee, gaze o'er all thy charms,
And round thy phantom glue my clasping arms.
I wake—no more I hear, no more I view,   235
The phantom flies me, as unkind as you.
I call aloud; it hears not what I say;
I stretch my empty arms; it glides away:
To dream once more I close my willing eyes;
Ye soft illusions, dear deceits, arise!   240
Alas no more!—methinks we wandring go
Thro' dreary wastes, and weep each other's woe;
Where round some mould'ring tow'r pale ivy creeps,
And low-brow'd rocks hang nodding o'er the deeps.
Sudden you mount! you becken from the skies;   245
Clouds interpose, waves roar, and winds arise.
I shriek, start up, the same sad prospect find,
And wake to all the griefs I left behind.

---

212 *'Obedient slumbers ... weep'*: 'Taken from Crashaw', Pope noted in the edition of 1751;
'Description of a Religious House', line 16   217 *the Spouse*: Christ   219 *rose of Eden*:
flowers in general (the *rose* is un-scriptural), as described by e.g. *Paradise Lost*, 4   229 *all-
conscious*: keenly responsive, privy to all thoughts

For thee the fates, severely kind, ordain
A cool suspense from pleasure and from pain;   250
Thy life a long, dead calm of fix'd repose;
No pulse that riots, and no blood that glows.
Still as the sea, ere winds were taught to blow,
Or moving spirit bade the waters flow;
Soft as the slumbers of a saint forgiv'n,   255
And mild as opening gleams of promis'd heav'n.
    Come *Abelard*! for what hast thou to dread?
The torch of *Venus* burns not for the dead;
Cut from the root my perish'd joys I see,
And love's warm tyde for ever stopt in thee.   260
Nature stands check'd; Religion disapproves;
Ev'n thou art cold—yet *Eloisa* loves.
Ah hopeless, lasting flames! like those that burn
To light the dead, and warm th' unfruitful urn.
    What scenes appear where-e'er I turn my view,   265
The dear Ideas, where I fly, pursue,
Rise in the grove, before the altar rise,
Stain all my soul, and wanton in my eyes!
I waste the Matin lamp in sighs for thee,
Thy image steals between my God and me,   270
Thy voice I seem in ev'ry hymn to hear,
With ev'ry bead I drop too soft a tear.
When from the Censer clouds of fragrance roll,
And swelling organs lift the rising soul;
One thought of thee puts all the pomp to flight,   275
Priests, Tapers, Temples, swim before my sight:
In seas of flame my plunging soul is drown'd,
While Altars blaze, and Angels tremble round.
    While prostrate here in humble grief I lie,
Kind, virtuous drops just gath'ring in my eye,   280
While praying, trembling, in the dust I roll,
And dawning grace is opening on my soul:
Come, if thou dar'st, all charming as thou art!
Oppose thy self to heav'n; dispute my heart;
Come, with one glance of those deluding eyes,   285
Blot out each bright Idea of the skies.

259–60 *Cut from the root . . . stopt in thee*: deleted in editions subsequent to 1720   263–4 *lasting flames . . . urn*: some classical tombs were perpetually lit in this way   269 *Matin lamp*: for those up early to pray   272 *ev'ry bead*: of the rosary   284 *dispute*: debate for possession of

Take back that grace, those sorrows, and those tears,
Take back my fruitless penitence and pray'rs,
Snatch me, just mounting, from the blest abode,
Assist the Fiends and tear me from my God!   290
    No, fly me, fly me! far as Pole from Pole;
Rise *Alps* between us! and whole oceans roll!
Ah come not, write not, think not once of me,
Nor share one pang of all I felt for thee.
Thy oaths I quit, thy memory resign,   295
Forget, renounce me, hate whate'er was mine.
Fair eyes, and tempting looks (which yet I view!)
Long lov'd, ador'd ideas! all adieu!
O grace serene! oh virtue heav'nly fair!
Divine oblivion of low-thoughted care!   300
Fresh blooming hope, gay daughter of the sky!
And faith, our early immortality!
Enter each mild, each amicable guest;
Receive, and wrap me in eternal rest!
    See in her Cell sad *Eloisa* spread,   305
Propt on some tomb, a neighbour of the dead!
In each low wind methinks a Spirit calls,
And more than Echoes talk along the walls.
Here, as I watch'd the dying lamps around,
From yonder shrine I heard a hollow sound.   310
Come, sister come! (it said, or seem'd to say)
Thy place is here, sad sister come away!
Once like thy self, I trembled, wept, and pray'd,
Love's victim then, tho' now a sainted maid:
But all is calm in this eternal sleep;   315
Here grief forgets to groan, and love to weep,
Ev'n superstition loses ev'ry fear:
For God, not man, absolves our frailties here.
    I come, ye ghosts! prepare your roseate bow'rs,
Celestial palms, and ever blooming flow'rs.   320
Thither, where sinners may have rest, I go,
Where flames refin'd in breasts seraphic glow.
Thou, *Abelard*! the last sad office pay,
And smooth my passage to the realms of day:
See my lips tremble, and my eye-balls roll,   325
Suck my last breath, and catch my flying soul!

295 *quit*: release you of   300 *low-thoughted care*: melancholy sorrow   323 *last sad office*:
i.e. rites for the dying

Ah no—in sacred vestments may'st thou stand,
The hallow'd taper trembling in thy hand,
Present the Cross before my lifted eye,
Teach me at once, and learn of me to die. 330
Ah then, thy once-lov'd *Eloisa* see!
It will be then no crime to gaze on me.
See from my cheek the transient roses fly!
See the last sparkle languish in my eye!
Till ev'ry motion, pulse, and breath, be o'er; 335
And ev'n my *Abelard* belov'd no more.
O death all-eloquent! you only prove
What dust we doat on, when 'tis man we love.
　　Then too, when fate shall thy fair frame destroy,
(That cause of all my guilt, and all my joy) 340
In trance extatic may thy pangs be drown'd,
Bright clouds descend, and Angels watch thee round,
From opening skies may streaming glories shine,
And Saints embrace thee with a love like mine.
　　May *one kind grave unite each hapless name, 345
And graft my love immortal on thy fame.
Then, ages hence, when all my woes are o'er,
When this rebellious heart shall beat no more;
If ever chance two wandring lovers brings
To *Paraclete*'s white walls, and silver springs, 350
O'er the pale marble shall they join their heads,
And drink the falling tears each other sheds,
Then sadly say, with mutual pity mov'd,
Oh may we never love as these have lov'd!
From the full quire when loud *Hosanna*'s rise, 355
And swell the pomp of dreadful sacrifice,
Amid that scene, if some relenting eye
Glance on the stone where our cold reliques lie,
Devotion's self shall steal a thought from heav'n,
One human tear shall drop, and be forgiv'n. 360
And sure if fate some future Bard shall join
In sad similitude of griefs to mine,

---

* Abelard *and* Eloisa *were interr'd in the same grave, or in monuments adjoining, in the* Monastery *of the* Paraclete*: He died in the year* 1142*, she in* 1163.

345 *name*: used (as in Scripture) for person, and doubtless of tomb inscription　　356 *dreadful sacrifice*: formal description of the Eucharist　　361 *some future Bard*: for the allusion to Pope see above, pp. 79–80

Condemn'd whole years in absence to deplore,
And image charms he must behold no more,
Such if there be, who loves so long, so well; 365
Let him our sad, our tender story tell;
The well-sung woes shall sooth my pensive ghost;
He best can paint 'em, who shall feel 'em most.

363 *deplore*: lament

Textual Notes

In the collations which follow, rejected words and punctuation marks from the copy-texts used in this anthology appear to the right of square brackets. Adopted readings, shown on the left, derive from errata lists (Churchyard, Drayton), alternative early manuscript and printed sources, and emendations suggested by various scholars. Each collation is preceded by the page-number on which the text begins above. Except in the case of Chaucer's *Of Quene Annelida and False Arcite*, no attempt has been made to show rejected readings where the copy-text has been followed.

88. 'Als i me rode þis endre dai'. From Lincoln's Inn MS Hale 135, fo. 137ᵛ; c.1300. The manuscript is difficult, not all readings secure.
    4 Als i me rode þis endre dai] þis endre dai als i me rode   5 pleyinge] *obscure in MS*   8 clingge,] clingges   25 ȝiif] þiif

89. 'Y louede a child of þis cuntre'. From Gonville and Caius College, Cambridge, MS 383/603, p. 210; 14th cent.
    The tune is given at the start. 'Biyd on biere y telle yt, to none oþur y ne dai.'

89. 'Þis enþer day I mete a clerke'. From St John's College, Cambridge, MS S 54, fos. 2ᵛ–3ʳ, 14th cent.
    6 layne] leue   7 A, dere god, qwat I am fayn, &c.] *not in MS*   9 now telle a] now a   skyll] kyll   10 siccurly] sicculy   11 mayn] may[ ] *cropped in MS*   16 qwat xal I sayn] qd ar I xal say   21 pleyn] pley

90. Canticus Amoris. From Bodleian Library MS Douce 322, fos. 8ᵛ–9ᵛ; late 14th cent. The text differs significantly in some other manuscripts.
    14 Through] Though   15 me] we   31 Sewe] shewe   50 thys] hys   62 þou ... me ... soo] I ... the ... loo   75 man] aman   90 þus] þys

93. 'A Balade, Sayde by a Gentilwomman Whiche Loued a Man of Gret Estate'. From Trinity College, Cambridge, MS R.3.20, pp. 152–4; early 15th cent. By John Lydgate.
    18 chyldheede] chyldhoode   44 shal, I] I shal

95. 'What so men seyn'. From Cambridge University Library MS Ff.1.6 (the Findern manuscript), fo. 56ʳ; late 15th cent.?

96. 'My woofull hert thus clad in payn'. From Cambridge University Library MS Ff.1.6 (the Findern manuscript), fo. 69ᵛ; late 15th cent.?
    1 thus] this   15 I loue hym and no moo] *substituted for* My Joy ffor well or w[oo], *which is deleted*

99. Of Quene Annelida and False Arcite. From *The Workes of Geffray Chaucer*, ed. William Thynne (1532), Eeee3ᵛ–5ᵛ.
The more interesting variants between Thynne and the received text—using the version derived from manuscript by Vincent J. DiMarco in *The Riverside Chaucer*, 3rd edn., gen. ed. Larry D. Benson (Boston, 1987)—are listed below. Unless stated, Thynne (*T*) is to the left of brackets and the canonical text (*R*) to the right. Where *T* has been emended from *R*, differing accidentals in DiMarco's text ('u' for 'v' etc.) are not given.

    TITLE OF QUENE ANNELIDA] The Compleynt of feire Anelida   1 O thou] Thou   3 temples] temple   5 the] thy   8 my] *R: not in T*   12 which al] which that al   13 And] As   16 with] *R:* hath *T*   17 Crisa] Cirsa *T:* Cirrea *R*   21a *Cithice*] *R: Cithie T*   21b *Prelia laurigero subeunte*] *R: Presea laurigero suburente T*   24 The]

With   25 ycome] he come   31 token] tokenyng   35 horse and on] hors,
on   41 of beautie] of the beaute   42 of grace] of alle grace   47 for] *R: not in
T*   53 Grece, and euerich] Grece, everich   54 speares rested] speres, ne rested
58 Ipomedon, and Partynope] Ipomedon, Parthonope   63 care] fare   68 dwel]
wonnen   73 than the] then is the   78 yer olde] yer of elde   84 her might] her
ne myghte   85 knight eke] knyght [Arcite] eke   86 therto withal] therwithal
91 trusteth] trusted   92 loueth] loved   98 not suche crafte men] not to men such
craft   109 than it] then that hit   112 him, did] hym hit dyde   115 shewed him]
shewed hit him   119 herte] heste   125 al was] al this nas   128 thought] *R:
though T*   132 For so] So   136 whan she] when that she   138 priuely
dothe she] prevely she   143 for] of   150 Lamek] *R:* Lameth *T*   163 or] and
166 shal] sholde   168 her] *R: not in T*   169 wayleth, and swouneth] waileth, swowneth
174 Ne none] Non   182 whether] wher   183 This] His   185 dred it] dredeth
189 lust] *R: not in T*   192 leste he] lest that he   193 meate or syp] fee or shipe
194 lande, and nowe] londe, now   197 women] *R:* woman *T*   198 hede] her   and
false Arcyte] and Arcite   199 him, her dere herte] him 'dere herte'   203 they . . .
they] he . . . he   209 with] of   SUBTITLE Annelyda to] Anelida the quene upon
211 thyrled] thirleth   214 to] in   215 waped] awhaped   216 Sens] Sith
nought] not for   217 trewe] trewest   236 him yet alway] him alwey
237 whom to] whom me   238 shulde] shal   241 Nowe] Nay   neuer be founde]
never founde   243 shaped so] shapen hit so   250 Your] And your   251 On]
Upon   253 there neyther] ther now nother   254 vouchsafe] vouchen sauf
263 wote, of] wot, out of   263-4 quyte | But] *no stanza break*   264 I was so
playne Arcyte] I, Arcite, shewed yow   265 In al my workes moche and lyte] Al that men
wolde to me write   268 in] on   269 Alas, ye retche] And of me rekke   274 aye]
Nay!   277 god thou] God, wel thou   278 turne] come   280 whyle I] while
that I   287 on] upon   289 vnfayned] *R:* on fayned *T*   293 wayle] wake
294 weyue] *R:* uoyde *T*   299 shulde] shal   301 mercy and gyltlesse] merci,
gilteles   302 lyfe I] lyf that I   304 if I vnto] if that I to   307 might] oghte
310 maken stedfast] make yow be stidfast   311 trouthe the souerayne] trouthe sover-
eyn   313 She] Who loueth, shal] loveth, she shal   316 renne] fleen   318 I
aught sayd out of the way] I seyd oght amys, I preye   324-5 auenture | For] *no stanza
break*   325 worlde there nys no] world nis   326 Walkyng] Wakynge   328 For]
And   331 Efte to profre a newe] To profren eft and newe   333 y drie] *R:* ydrie *T*
334 That] And   suche] thilke   347 wol synge in] shal singen   348 the destenye
and] my destinee or   357 may plainly] shal after   here.] *R:* here. | ¶ Explicit. *T*

112. **Shores Wife.** From the expanded edition of William Baldwin *et al.*, *A Myrrour for Magistrates*
(1563), Z1ᵛ–8ᵛ. By Thomas Churchyard.
The discursive title given by Baldwin on Z1ᵛ is 'Howe Shores wife, Edwarde the fowerthes
concubine, was by king Richarde despoyled of all her goodes, and forced to do open penance.'
Lines 36, 85, 155, 169, 218, 225, 330, 344, 365, and 372 are not indented in *1563*.
   In *Churchyards Challenge* (1593) four stanzas on Jane Shore's beauty are added after 70; there are
three on the harmony of love after 168; Mistress Shore's assistance to the needy is developed in
three stanzas after 182; nine stanzas on the subject of falling from high estate are inserted after 287;
Richard III's accession is regretted after 336; and there is an additional stanza on the world's
neglect of favourites out of office after 371.
   28 whele.] ~?   30 that crept is] *'Faultes escaped'*: that is crept is   66 of earth,] *'Faultes
escaped'*: of the earth   70 ayer.] ~͵   95 downe,] ~.   104 fond,] ~.
133 fyt.] ~,   140 streight.] streight͵   155 greate,] ~.   158 meade,] ~.
229 vnpure,] ~:   252 Who trustes] *'Faultes escaped'*: Whot rustes   322 feete.] ~,
329 came.] ~,   349 sake,] ~.   352 warning] *'Faultes escaped'*: warrant   357 to
dore.] to ~,   360 had] bad   379 faund on me before,] *'Faultes escaped'*: fawnd on
before

126. **'Complaint of the Absence of her Louer Being vpon the Sea'.** From Richard Tottel's anthology, *Songes and Sonettes, Written by the Ryght Honorable Lorde Henry Haward late Earle of Surrey, and Other* (1557), B4^r–v. By the Earl of Surrey.

127. **'The Complaint of a Woman Rauished, and also Mortally Wounded'.** From the second edition of Tottel, *Songes and Sonettes* (1557), Dd3^r.

    6 th' outragious] thoutragious

128. **A Louing Lady Being Wounded in the Spring Time, and Now Galded Eftsones with the Remembrance of the Spring, Doth Therfore Thus Bewayle.** From George Gascoigne, *A Hundreth Sundrie Flowres Bounde vp in One Small Poesie* (1573), 315–17.

    2 Dan] Dame

130. **'Oenones Complaint'.** From George Peele, *The Araygnement of Paris* (1584), C3^r.

    1 Melpomene] Melponie

130. **'A Poeme of a Mayde Forsaken'.** From *The Arbor of Amorous Deuises. Wherein, Young Gentlemen may Reade Many Plesant Fancies, and Fine Deuises*, compiled by Nicholas Breton (1597), A4^v–B1^r. Perhaps by Richard Edwards.

    21 Clarke,] ~.   23 a parte:] aparte.   24 strange and worthy] sttange and wotthy   32 ground.] ground. | *Finis.*

131. **'An Excellent Pastorall Dittie'.** From *Englands Helicon* (1600), I3^v–4^r. By Anthony Munday.

    12 teares] feares   36 more.] more. | *FINIS. Shep. Tonie.*

133. **'The Nimph Seluagia her Song'.** From *Englands Helicon* (1600), S3^r. By Bartholomew Young.

    20 weepe.] weepe. | *FINIS. Bar. Yong.*

135. **'Round, around about a wood as I walkt'.** From the second, enlarged edition of Thomas Morley, *Madrigals To Fovre Voices . . . The First Booke* (1600), D2^r.

    1 around] a round

135. **The Diseased Maiden Louer.** From the Pepys Collection, Magdalene College, Cambridge. Black-letter (here given as roman, with roman in italic); early 17th cent.

    SUBTITLE excellent] exeellent   8 a sigh and heauie] a heauie   27 Which] With   54 breake.] breake. | FINIS. | *Printed at London for I. Wright.*   108 minde.] minde. | FINIS. | *Printed at London for Iohn Wright.*

140. **The Ruines of Time.** From Edmund Spenser, *Complaints: Containing Sundrie Small Poemes of the Worlds Vanitie* (1591), B1^r–D4^v.

    84 Princesse.] ~,   101 abide] abie   154 more.] ~,   175 endure.] ~,   259 giue.] ~,   330 wretched] wetched   363 couetize] couertize   413 giuc?] ~.   414 *Mausolus*] *Mansolus*   436 *Meliboe*] *Melibœ*   497 praid.] ~,   511 worke,] might] ~,~   551 which] with   574 worlds] words   588 spide.] ~?   603 Lee] *Lee*   671 exceedingly] exceedtngly   686 desire.] desire. | FINIS.

165. **The Complaint of Rosamond.** From Samuel Daniel, *Delia: Contayning Certayne Sonnets. With the Complaint of Rosamond* (1592), H3^r–M4^v.

After 98, editions from 1601 add a stanza on the vulnerability of women to seduction; editions from 1594 add, after 595, three stanzas of denunciation by the Queen; twenty stanzas of self-examination and distress, prompted by the Queen's assault, follow 602 in editions from 1594.

    11 The euer] Th' euer   blest.] ~,   12 rest,] ~.   25 *Shores*] Shores   30 Whilome] *Whilome*   43 deygne] deynge   55 best,] ~.   58 finde,] ~:   104 tyrannize,] ~.   107 desire,] ~:   129 woman] women   167 chastity] chastitiy   173 But] Bnt   212 bad,] ~:   220 The one] Th' one   237–8] The error . . . thee.] *not indented*   257 weale;] ~,   258 choyce,] ~:   311 was euen in] was in   366 attend] ~:   368 long-desired work] long desired-work   376 sought,] ~.   397 afflicted eyes affects] afflicted affects   401 squares] ~:   408 showne,] ~:   424 had I not] had I had not   441 to come] to co come   475 To entertaine] T' entertaine   481 place,] ~.

519 Witnes] Witnest   520 wondrous] wonrdous   521 woman] women   536 best.]
~,   537 blest,] ~;   542 She's] Sh's   570 Queene] Qneene   deale,] ~:
605 naught respecting death,] naught respecting, death   606 th' ensigne] the'nsigne
623 aright] a right   631 a way] away   635 *Vapouring*] Vauporing   709 found,]
~:   716 decayes,] ~:   720 my fame] by fame,   738 mourne;] ~,
742 vnseene.] vnseene. | FINIS.

192. From Englands Heroicall Epistles (1597), fos. 1ʳ–4ᵛ, 57ᵛ–60ᵛ. By Michael Drayton.
Since *Shores Wife* by Churchyard and Daniel's *Complaint of Rosamond* provide introductory contexts,
'The Argument' which prefaces *Rosamond to King Henrie* in 1597 has—like that before Edward IV's
epistle to Jane Shore—been omitted. The accidentals of verses cited in Drayton's Notes have been
silently harmonized with his text.

The Epistle of Rosamond to King Henrie the Second
31 'Twas] T'was   101 tongue] tougue   115 shade] slade   N O T E S. 13 mans
life;] ~ ~,   23 vaults] vanltes   28 *Rosamonds*] Rosamands   29 *turning*] turned

The Epistle of Shores Wife to King Edward the Fourth
TITLE WIFE TO] wife, to   47 springs] *'Faultes escaped'*: spings   N O T E S. 54 home.]
home. | FINIS.

209. A Louers Complaint. From *Shake-speares Sonnets Neuer before Imprinted* (1609), K1ᵛ–L2ᵛ.
TITLE COMPLAINT.] complaint. | *BY* | WILLIAM SHAKE-SPEARE.   6 papers,] papers
atwaine] a twain   7 sorrowes] ~,   11 donne;] ~,   24 tide] ~,   25 extend]
~,   26 lend] ~,   28 commixt] commxit   37 amber,] ~,   41 fall] ~,
42 some,] ~;   59 Court,] ~,   72 houre,] ~;   78 attended] atttended
79 suit,] ~,   87 hurles:] ~,   107 takes;] takes   109 course,] ~, makes!]
~,   118 Cam] Can   126 will,] ~.   130 haunted.] ~,   131 Consents]
Consent's   142 of] os   173 vowes ~,   182 woo] vovv   186 kind;] ~,
189 containes.] ~,   228 Hallowed] Hollowed   239 leaue] ~,   241 Playning]
Playing   242 vnconstrained] vnconstraind   251 emur'd] enur'd   252 procur'd]
procure   260 Nunne] Sunne   270 wealth,] ~,   kindred,] ~,   284 apace] a
pace   293 O] Or   299 appeares,] ~:   308 showes;] ~.   312 maime.] ~,
319 houerd.] ~,   320 louerd?] ~.   329 Maide.] Maide. | FINIS.

223. 'Psalm 137. Super flumina'. From Trinity College, Cambridge, MS R.3.16, pp. 280–2. By
Mary Sidney, Countess of Pembroke.
32 flatt plaine] platt plais

224. 'The Lamentations of Ieremiah, Chapter 1'. From *The Holy Bible, Conteyning the Old
Testament, and the New: Newly Translated out of the Originall Tongues* (1611), Xxx5ᵛ–6ʳ.

228. 'Show me the peece of needle worke you wrought'. From Francis Beaumont and John
Fletcher, *The Maides Tragedy* (1619), E1ʳ⁻ᵛ. By Fletcher.
2 peece:] ~,   5 black;] ~,   6 Theseus;] ~,   9 vessell?] vessel.   10 ha']
ha   so. Could] so, could   11 storme?] ~,   12 ill. This] ill, this   13 me. You]
me, you   so;] ~,   15 And ouer it a shallow smiling water,] *line repeated*
19 beleeu'd. But] beleeu'd, but   19 Lady?] ~.   21 *Antiphila*] Antipila   25 was.
Doe] was, doe   27 Iland.] ~,   28 Sea breach] Sea, breach   30 in;] ~,
31 hearers] teares   story;] ~,   33 *Antiphila*;] ~,   34 monument] mount
35 leauelesse;] ~,   36 continuall] contiunall   37 desolation:] ~,

229. 'Vnseene, vnknowne, I here alone complaine'. From Lady Mary Wroth, *The Countesse of
Mountgomeries Urania* (1621), 2.

230. 'A Forsaken Lady to her False Servant that is Disdained by his New Mistris'. From
Richard Lovelace, *Lucasta: Epodes, Odes, Sonnets, Songs, &c. To Which is Added Aramantha, A
Pastorall* (1649), 29–31.
2 Cruel'st] Cruels't   12 And feelst] *indented*   17 you,] ~,

232. **'Ariadne Deserted by Theseus, as She Sits Upon a Rock in the Island Naxos, Thus Complains'.** From William Cartwright, *Comedies, Tragi-Comedies, with other Poems* (1651), 238–42.
    64 thy] my   71 yee] yet   85 Thus] That

235. **'The Nymph Complaining for the Death of her Faun'.** From Andrew Marvell, *Miscellaneous Poems* (1681), 14–17.

239. **Five Love-Letters from a Nun to a Cavalier.** Translated from *Les Lettres portugaises* (1669) by Roger L'Estrange (1678).
    2.74 true; and against] true; and and against   2.81 Affection, unless] *comma from catchword*
    3.2 disappointed] dissapointed   5.8–9 well), Unfortunate] well) Unfortunate
    5.184 a long] along   5.226 beats?] beats? | THE END.

260. **'A Paraphrase on Oenone to Paris'.** From *Ovid's Epistles, Translated by Several Hands*, ed. John Dryden (1680), 97–116. By Aphra Behn.
    TITLE TO PARIS] TO PARIS. By |M^{rs.}| *A. BEHN.*   ARGUMENT *Firebrand;*] ~,
    13 been] ~.   14 thing,] ~.   72 Bed,] ~;   173 Gales;] ~.   189 grac'd]
    grac't   202 made,] ~.   224 *Paris,*] ~;   225 again,] ~.   233 I] It
    252 thought;] ~.   268 aloud;] ~.   306 again;] ~.   313 does] dos

268. **'Sapho to Phaon'.** From Matthew Stevenson, *The Wits Paraphras'd: Or, Paraphrase upon Paraphrase. In a Burlesque on the Several Late Translations of Ovids Epistles* (1680), 1–8.

274. **The Maids Complaint against the Batchelors: Or, an Easter-Offering for Young Men and Apprentices. Passionately setting forth The Unkindness of Men, with their Slighting the good Old way of Matrimony, and forcing several Thousands of Ripe and Willing Virgins to Spin out Miserable Lives on Earth for want of Husbands, and lead Apes in Hell after their Death** (1675).
    TITLE *Main text headed by an alternative:* The Maids Complaint against the Batchelors: OR, The Longing Virgins Lamentation.   31 all Occasions] alll Occasions   39 *Worse.*] ~.
    44 Judgement against them:] Judgemənt against them,:   63 Sot and a] Sot aud a
    83 *Charm* us] *Charm* ns   113 *Servants.*] Servants. | FINIS.

277. **'Song'.** From *Female Poems on Several Occasions: Written by Ephelia* (1679), 34–5.

278. **'The Reflection: A Song'.** From Aphra Behn, *Poems upon Several Occasions: With A Voyage to the Island of Love* (1684), 83–5.

280. **'The Complaint'.** From *Poetical Recreations* (1688), *Part I: Occasionally Written by Mrs. Jane Barker*, 78–9.

283. **'Wednesday: Or, the Dumps'.** From John Gay, *The Shepherd's Week: In Six Pastorals* (1714), the Ferd. Burleigh edn., 21–8.
    6 No] Nor   89 n. *notus.*] ~.   cunnan.] ~.   Kennen.] ~,   *F. R. S.*] *F. R.S.*

288. **'A Sorrowful Lamentation for the Loss of a Man and No Man'.** From Henry Carey, *Poems on Several Occasions ... The Third Edition, much enlarged* (1729), 62–5.

291. **Eloisa to Abelard.** From *The Works of Mr. Alexander Pope* (1717), 389–408.
    51 wretch's] wretches   95 ere] e'er   141 day's] days   149 others'] others
    151 others'] others   189 all] ~,   207 lot!] ~?   212 weep';] ~.;
    214 heaven] heav'n   253 ere] e'er   282 soul:] ~.   306 on] in

Index of Titles and First Lines